The Raymond Williams Reader

BLACKWELL READERS

In a number of disciplines, across a number of decades, and in a number of languages, writers and texts have emerged which require the attention of students and scholars around the world. United only by a concern with radical ideas, Blackwell Readers collect and introduce the works of pre-eminent theorists. Often translating works for the first time (Levinas, Irigaray, Lyotard, Blanchot, Kristeva), or presenting material previously inaccessible (C.L.R. James, Fanon, Elias), each volume in the series introduces and represents work which is now fundamental to study in the humanities and social sciences.

The Lyotard Reader
Edited by Andrew Benjamin

The Irigaray Reader
Edited by Margaret Whitford

The Kristeva Reader
Edited by Toril Moi

The Levinas Reader
Edited by Sean Hand

The C.L.R. James Reader
Edited by Anna Grimshaw

The Wittgenstein Reader
Edited by Anthony Kenny

The Blanchot Reader
Edited by Michael Holland

The Lukács Reader
Edited by Arpad Kardakay

The Cavell Reader
Edited by Stephen Mulhall

The Guattari Reader
Edited by Garry Genosko

The Bataille Reader
Edited by Fred Botting and Scott Wilson

The Eagleton Reader
Edited by Stephen Regan

The Castoriadis Reader
Edited by David Ames Curtis

The Goffman Reader
Edited by Charles Lemert and Ann Branaman

The Frege Reader
Edited by Michael Beaney

The Virilio Reader
Edited by James Der Derian

The Hegel Reader
Edited by Stephen Houlgate

The Norbert Elias Reader
Edited by Johan Goudsblom and Stephen Mennell

The Angela Y. Davis Reader
Edited by Joy James

The Stanley Fish Reader
Edited by H. Aram Veeser

The Žižek Reader
Edited by Elizabeth Wright and Edmond Wright

The Talcott Parsons Reader
Edited by Bryan S. Turner

The Certeau Reader
Edited by Graham Ward

The Adorno Reader
Edited by Brian O'Connor

The Jameson Reader
Edited by Michael Hardt and Kathi Weeks

The Bauman Reader
Edited by Peter Beilharz

The Raymond Williams Reader
Edited by John Higgins

The Raymond Williams Reader

Edited by
John Higgins

BLACKWELL
Publishers

First published 2001

2 4 6 8 10 9 7 5 3 1

Blackwell Publishers Ltd
108 Cowley Road
Oxford OX4 1JF
UK

Blackwell Publishers Inc.
350 Main Street
Malden, Massachusetts 02148
USA

British Library Cataloguing in Publication Data

A CIP catalogue record for this book is available from the British Library.

Library of Congress Cataloging-in-Publication Data

Williams, Raymond.
    The Raymond Williams reader / edited by John Higgins.
        p. cm.—(Blackwell readers)
    Includes index.
    ISBN 0–631–21310–4 (hdbk. : alk. paper)—ISBN 0–631–21311–2 (pbk. : alk. paper)
    I. Higgins, John, 1954– II. Title   III. Series

PR6073.I4329 A6 2001
828′.91409—dc21
                                                                                00–057903

Typeset in on 10.5 on 12.5pt Bembo
by Kolam Information Services Private Ltd, Pondicherry, India

Printed in Great Britain by MPG Books Ltd, Bodmin, Cornwall

This book is printed on acid-free paper

Contents

Part III   Theory and Representation (1972–80)   149

Part IV   Cultural Materialism in Action (1980–88)   219

the poor
said handbag
are lucky to be alive
contributing nothing
to profit

Tom Raworth, *West Wind* (1984)

Preface

While the primary aim of this *Reader* is to introduce new students to the work of the British cultural critic, Raymond Williams (1921–88), the intention is also to give existing readers a chance to see that work differently by seeing it historically. Described by Terry Eagleton as 'the single most important critic of postwar Britain' (Eagleton 1984: 108), a reading of Williams's work still provides significant intellectual and theoretical challenges for anyone interested in either the history of literary and cultural studies or the practice of critical and oppositional thinking.

I have divided the *Reader* into four Parts and these offer a more or less chronological selection of Williams's academic and theoretical writing.[1] This arrangement is intended to give the reader a sense of both the dynamic development and sustaining continuity of Williams's thinking, and so avoid some of the errors present in received ideas and appropriations of his work. It may come as a surprise to see the very first deployment of the concept of 'structure of feeling' present as early as 1954, and how that is already articulated with the partial rejection of Marxist cultural theory; to find, in **Individuals and Societies**, that the critique of psychoanalytic theories of the subject was firmly in place by the time of writing *The Long Revolution* (1961), anticipating by more than a decade the 1970s debates around theory examined in *Marxism and Literature* (1977a); or to see the ways in which the politics of representation so vividly active in the assault on the New Conformists in the late 1980s were already present in the careful deconstruction of the idea of the masses in *Culture and Society* (1958). Throughout I have tried to achieve a balance between his central and best known writings and relatively neglected but still powerful work.

For anyone surveying Williams's work today, what is striking is its sheer intellectual and political energy, and the extraordinary scope and reach of its interests. No one better fits Edward Said's vivid description of the intellectual as someone who represents 'an individual vocation, an energy, a stubborn force engaging as a committed and recognizable voice in language and society' (Said 1993: 55). Williams was a committed and recognizable presence in many different fields of endeavour and achievement: as scholarly and fictional writer, he was the author of some twenty-four books of academic and political writing, plus a dozen or so novels and plays; as cultural and political activist, he played a founding role in the *New Left Review* in 1959, the May Day Manifesto group of 1968, and in the Socialist Society in 1982. In the 1960s, he was an active member of both the Campaign for Nuclear Disarmament and the Vietnam Solidarity Campaign and was elected the Chair of the National Convention of the Left in 1969. Between 1976 and 1978, he acted as a vociferously critical member of the Arts Council and, from the early 1980s, contributed to the burgeoning movement of critical ecology. Throughout, he maintained a regular commentary on cultural and political issues in a wide range of essays and reviews: in Scott Wilson's words, Raymond Williams was 'perhaps the only British academic ever to have fulfilled the role of the intellectual' (Wilson 1995: 252).[2] This sustained record of public activism conjoined with academic and creative writing suggests only perhaps Jean-Paul Sartre as a comparable figure in twentieth century thought. And, like Sartre, Williams was above all a critical intellectual. The key to his work is its fundamentally oppositional nature: 'If you look at the implied relationship of nearly all the books I have written, I have been arguing with what I take to be official English culture' (Williams 1979: 316).

This argument with official culture made up the work of a lifetime. It began for Williams with his opposition to, and finally rejection of, two perfectly available political and academic positions. These were the orthodox party line of Marxist literary and cultural theory, familiar to Williams through the work of figures such as Alick West and Christopher Caudwell; and the increasingly apolitical tenets of the now confidently professionalized discipline of English studies. The defining problem for the young Williams, as a student of English at Trinity College, Cambridge, was that he could neither accept the apolitical stance of most literary critical scholarship, nor endorse the dogmas of orthodox Marxist analysis. Caught between the rock of professional scholarship and the hard place of Stalinist literary orthodoxy, he was forced to invent a new space for an independent yet committed cultural and literary criticism.[3]

Williams had gone up to Cambridge to study English in the autumn of 1939, and he completed the first part of the English Tripos before being called up to military service in July 1941. After two years of training, he took part in the

Normandy offensive of 1944, as a lieutenant commanding a small unit of four tanks, and continued as such until the end of the war in 1945. Then, as a former student, he was given accelerated demobilization, and returned to Cambridge in October 1945 to complete his degree in June 1946. In September of the same year, he turned down the offer of a three-year senior research scholarship at Trinity College, and went to work as a staff tutor for Oxford University's Tutorial Classes Committee. For the next fifteen years, Williams worked in adult education alongside figures such as E.P. Thompson, Richard Hoggart and Christopher Hill.

Williams was characteristically active on many fronts in this formative period (1946–61). He was instrumental in founding two short-lived but influential journals, *Politics and Letters* (1947–48) and *The Critic* (1947), in which he and his fellow editors, Wolf Mankowitz and Henry Collins, sought to reconcile Leavisite literary criticism with committed Marxist social analysis; he contributed to the existing debates within adult education through articles in *The Highway* and *Adult Education*, and wrote an introductory textbook based on his courses, *Reading and Criticism* (1950), for Thomas Hodgkins's adult education series, *Man in Society*.[4] In this same period, he also completed three significant studies of naturalism and the drama: *Drama from Ibsen to Eliot* (1952), *Drama in Performance* (1954) and, with Michael Orrom, *Preface to Film* (1954).

At the same time, Williams was working towards the trilogy of studies which were to make him the leading figure of Britain's New Left. Though *Culture and Society 1780–1950* (1958), *The Long Revolution* (1961) and *Communications* (1962a) are often seen as the starting point of his intellectual career, they are best considered as the culmination of more than a decade's work in adult education, and as the partial solution to the problems he had set himself as a frustrated undergraduate student. With their publication in the late 1950s and early 1960s, Williams was greeted as the leading representative of New Left thinking, 'our best man', in Edward Thompson's telling phrase (Thompson 1961: 22). Part 1 of the *Reader*, 'Culture Wars', examines the dynamics of Williams's work in this formative period, in which he forged a concept of culture with which to resist both the elitism inherent in English studies and the reductionism of Marxist cultural theory.

Though *Culture and Society* enjoyed wide acclaim, it was probably William's earlier writings on the history of drama which led to the offer of a lectureship in drama at Cambridge in the spring of 1961. Tired of the increasingly hopeless battles in adult education around the shift from working-class to middle-class provision, he accepted the offer and joined Jesus College and the English Faculty in the autumn. He was to remain in the Faculty until his retirement in the summer of 1983, and retained his rooms and some teaching duties at Jesus College up until his death in 1988.

We can distinguish three main phases of his work while in Cambridge, and these correspond to Parts 2–4 of the *Reader*. First, there was the period of active opposition to Cambridge English which began with his arrival in 1961 and culminated in the publication of his *chef-d'oeuvre, The Country and the City*, in 1973; second, the decade of work on theory, and particularly on questions of Marxist and literary theory in the 1970s; and finally, the interrupted work of the 1980s, which focused mainly on what Williams saw as a 'new conformism', one which found concrete political expression in Thatcherism, but also came through in the broader currents of social and cultural analysis.

For many, it is the works of the first Cambridge phase which constitute the centre of Williams's achievement as an oppositional literary critic. With *Modern Tragedy* (1966), *The English Novel from Dickens to Lawrence* (1970) and especially *The Country and the City* (1973), he issued a powerful counter to the methodological and political norms of Cambridge English. This phase is represented by the essays selected for Part 2 of the *Reader*, 'Countering the Canon'. Part 3, 'Theory and Representation', examines the work which followed from the 'excitement of contact with more new Marxist work' he described in *Marxism and Literature* (1977a: 4), and which also came through in the essays gathered together as *Problems in Materialism and Culture* (1980), and was further elaborated in the often-neglected study, *Culture* (1981). The same period saw the publication of Williams's seminal study *Television: Technology and Cultural Form* in 1974.

Williams died suddenly and unexpectedly, at the age of 66, on January 26 1988. At that point, he was still working to complete a collection of essays, tentatively entitled *The Politics of Modernism* and his long novel, *People of the Black Country* (see Williams 1989a, 1989e, and 1990). His work in this final period was largely directed against what he came to call the 'New Conformism', and to locate the new mode of 'nomad capitalism' (Williams's anticipatory term for what is now commonly referred to as globalization) historically, in the terms of its deep connections to previous modes of capitalist exploitation. The new conformism turned out to be a selective reading and appropriation of many of the key constituent elements of modernism. Modernism therefore occupies a central position in most of the final writings, including the social, political and cultural analyses which made up *Towards 2000* (1983a) and in the key essays of *Writing in Society* (1984) and *The Politics of Modernism: Against the New Conformism* (which appeared posthumously in 1989 alongside three other useful collections: *Resources of Hope, What I Came to Say*, and *Raymond Williams on Television*).

On his death, a first wave of assessments celebrated Williams's achievements as 'the last of the great European male revolutionary socialist intellectuals' (West 1995: xi); 'a moral and intellectual touchstone' (Juliet Mitchell cited in Higgins 1989); and as 'father-figure to thousands' (Parrinder 1988). A second wave of more recent criticism has tended to concentrate on the limitations of his work, often seeing the difference of his theoretical vocabulary as a failing, and turning his relative lack of interest in questions of race, gender and postcolonialism into an opportunity for new topics of research and analysis.[5] The guiding principle behind the selections and structure of this *Reader* is that now is the moment for a new generation of readers to read and assess Williams's work historically and theoretically, and without particular bias or favour. It offers a starting point for the cultural materialist analysis of Williams's own work.

Notes

1   At the expense, it must be said, of his directly political writings and his fictional and dramatic work. For the political writings, see especially Williams et al. 1968, Williams 1983a, 1989b. For the fictional and dramatic writing, see the relevant entries in O'Connor's bibliography (O'Connor 1989).

2   For these and other details, see Inglis 1995, though this is a flawed work, whose usefulness and reliability are impaired at times by a powerful sense of *ressentiment*. This biography is best read alongside the extraordinarily detailed series of discussions between Williams and the *New Left Review, Politics and Letters* (Williams 1979).

3   I trace this whole line of argument more fully in Higgins 1999.

4   For detailed accounts of Williams's work in adult education, and an excellent selection of his writings from this period, see McIlroy and Westwood 1993; and, more generally, Inglis 1995, especially Ch. 6 'Workers' Education in the Garden of England'.

5   In reality, the temporality is not quite so strict nor the content so simple. 'First-wave' analyses might include O'Connor 1989, Blackburn 1989, Pinkney 1989, Morgan and Prestun 1993 and Eldridge and Eldridge 1994, and 'second-wave' analyses many of the essays in Dworkin and Roman 1993a, Inglis 1995, Prendergast 1995 and Wallace et al. 1997. See also Gorak 1988, Milner 1993, Dworkin 1997, Higgins 1999 and Mulhern 2000 for attempts at achieving more historically and theoretically balanced assessments of Williams's overall significance.

Acknowledgments

I would like in particular to acknowledge the stimulus provided by my fellow panellists at the 'Raymond Williams and Cultural Studies' session at the second *Crossroads in Cultural Studies* conference, held at Tampere University in Finland in 1998. Our session aroused an unusually passionate debate, and suggested there was a real need for a Raymond Williams reader. Though I am well aware they would each have constructed very different contents for a reader such as this, my thanks are due to Alvaro Pina, Mikko Lehtonen and, above all, Maria Elisa Cevasco for their varied inputs and advice. I am also glad to acknowledge here the financial support from the Human Sciences Research Council of South Africa and from the Bremner Travel Grants Committee of the University of Cape Town, which made possible my attendance at that conference.

Thanks are also due to Terry Eagleton and David Simpson for useful comments and conversations during visits to Cape Town; at Blackwell Publishers, to Andrew MacNeillie and Alison Dunnett for their unfailing encouragement and patience, and also to Blackwell's anonymous readers for their useful suggestions concerning the contents of the *Reader*. For invaluable encouragement, specific advice and moral support, many thanks are due to all the usual suspects, friends and family, and most particularly to Tony Morphet, Louise Green, and Mary Watson. Thanks also to Tom Raworth for permission to use some lines from his poem 'West Wind' from *Tottering State: New and Selected Poems 1963–1987* (London: Paladin, 1984) as an epigraph for this *Reader*.

Possibly my greatest debt is to Dominic for his clear-eyed view of the world, and I dedicate this book to him for future reading.

I would also like to record my gratitude to the staff of the libraries at the University of Cape Town and at Cambridge University for their ever courteous helpfulness.

The editor and publishers are grateful to the following for their kind permission:

'Culture is Ordinary' (1958) from *Conviction* (ed. Norman Mackenzie; Mac-Gibbon and Gee, London, 1958)

'Film and the Dramatic Tradition' (1954) from *Preface to Film* by Michael Orrom and Raymond Williams (Film Drama Ltd., London, 1954)

'The Masses' (1958) from *Culture and Society* (Chatto & Windus, London, 1958)

'Individuals and Societies' (1961) from *The Long Revolution* (Chatto & Windus, London, 1961)

'Tragedy and Revolution' (1966) from *Modern Tragedy* (Chatto & Windus, London, 1966)

'Literature and Rural Society' (1967) from *The Listener* 78, 16 November, 1967.

'Thomas Hardy and the English Novel' (1970) from *The English Novel from Dickens to Lawrence* (Chatto & Windus, 1970)

'Orwell' (1971) from *Orwell* (Fontana Modern Masters, London, Collins, 1971, republished in Flamingo, London, 1984)

'Lucien Goldmann and Marxism's Alternative Tradition' (1972) from *The Listener* 87, 23 March, 1972

'Base and Superstructure in Marxist Cultural Theory' (1973), revised text of a lecture given in Montreal, April 1973, *New Left Review* 82, pp. 3–16.

'Television and Representation' (1974) from *Television: Technology and Cultural Form* (Fontana, London, 1974)

'Language as Sociality' (1977) from *Marxism and Literature* (Oxford University Press, Oxford 1977)

'The Writer: Commitment and Alignment' (1980) *Marxism Today* June 1980.

'The Bloomsbury Fraction' (1980) in *Keynes and the Bloomsbury Group* (ed. D. Crabtree and A. P. Thirlwall) (Macmillan Press Ltd, London, 1980)

'Crisis in English Studies' (1981) Cambridge English Faculty lecture given 13 Feb 1981, *New Left Review* 129, 1981, pp. 51–66.

'Writing, Speech and the "Classical" ' (1984), lecture to the Classical Association, from *What I Came to Say* (ed. F. Mulhern) (Hutchinson Radius, London, 1984)

'Language and the Avant-Garde' (1986) from N. Fabb, D. Attridge, A. Durant and C. MacCabe (eds) *The Linguistics of Writing: Arguments Between Language and Literature* (Manchester University Press, Manchester, 1988)

Part I

Culture Wars (1954–61)

Part I: Introduction

The problem with understanding any truly influential body of work is that its very success is likely to blind future generations of readers to its actual significance. This, I think, is the problem with many of the current assessments of Raymond Williams. Williams did so much to transform the horizon of literary studies that it is now difficult to see the changes he helped to effect in what appears to us as a given intellectual and academic landscape.[1] For this reason I have chosen to transpose a phrase with significant contemporary resonance to describe the first major phase of his writing. While 'culture wars' is widely used as a term to describe the most recent disputes in literary theory around issues of postmodernism, pedagogy and the canon, it is relocated here to depict Williams's work in the 1950s.[2] The aim of this transposition is twofold: historically, it is to remind us of the decisive oppositional role that he played in the cultural politics – the culture wars – of his time; theoretically, it is to suggest there may be more continuities than we imagine in the key questions facing cultural critics today and a half century ago.

What was Williams's role in the culture wars of his time? Simply put, he was directly responsible for several decisive victories. Starting from a training in a literary studies which was heavily geared to aesthetic assessment, he worked to deepen the practice of textual analysis by historicizing it, and to broaden its scope by including diverse forms of cultural expression beyond the literary (film, television, media). In so doing, he opened the way for the new modes and objects of analysis associated with contemporary cultural studies. At the same time, his work challenged the dominant trends of existing Marxist analysis, in which culture was understood as the secondary effect of a determining economic base, and argued for the constitutive force of culture in social reproduction: his work pioneered an emphasis on the politics of representation in a still exemplary fashion. The essays selected here – **Culture is Ordinary**, **Film and the Dramatic Tradition**, **The Masses** and **Individuals and Societies** – are chosen both to recall the decisive interventions Williams made in the cultural politics of the 1950s, and also to indicate points of contact with our own continuing concerns as critics of culture and society.

More than any other single thinker, Williams worked to deconstruct the opposition between high and low culture that had been the structuring principle and helped to provide the *raison d'être* of English studies since the 1920s. The first essay – **Culture is Ordinary** – is the eloquent manifesto of Williams's new cultural politics. It was first published in Norman MacKenzie's *Conviction* in 1958 as one of a series of seminal statements by the leading figures of Britain's emerging New Left.[3] In it he expresses the rejection of the tenets of both the orthodox English studies and the orthodox Marxism that were his starting points as an intellectual and academic. 'I could not have begun this work if I had not learned from the Marxists and from Leavis' he noted; 'I cannot complete it unless I radically amend some of the ideas which they and others have left us' (**Culture is Ordinary**, p. 20). These amendments came together in the slogan 'culture is ordinary', used to challenge the 'apparent division of our culture into, on the one hand, a remote and self- gracious sophistication, on the other hand, a doped mass' (p. 24). While Williams took his central definition of culture as a 'whole way of life' from T.S. Eliot's influential *Notes Towards the Definition of Culture* ([1948] 1983), he decisively rejected Eliot's effective limitation of real culture to the fenced-off property of an intellectual aristocracy.[4]

One of the main casualties in this insistent division between elite and mass culture was the study and analysis of film. Williams was one of the first academic writers to both acknowledge the specific identity of film as a creative art, and to connect it to the broader history of dramatic and representational forms. For most literary critics, film belonged firmly to the category of low culture, and was therefore not worth studying. F.R. Leavis – doyen of English criticism – had gone so far as to suggest that film was even more of a threat to high culture than the tabloid press itself. 'Films have a much more potent influence', he wrote:

They provide now the main form of recreation in the civilized world, and they involve surrender, under conditions of hypnotic receptivity, to the cheapest emotional appeals, appeals all the more insidious because they are associated with a compellingly vivid illusion of actual life. It would be difficult to dispute that the result must be serious damage to the 'standard of living' . . .

(Leavis 1933: 20–1)

Similarly, for the Frankfurt School thinkers Theodor Adorno and Max Horkheimer, film was a part of the 'culture industry' and 'leaves no room for imagination or reflection on the part of the audience . . . sustained thought is out of the question' (Adorno and Horkheimer [1944] 1979: 124–5). Against such prevalent attitudes, Williams calmly maintained, in one of the many essays written during his period as a teacher in adult education, that film 'provides opportunities for criticism as a major educational discipline', and emphasized that 'the study of the cinema as an institution is an inevitable part of our sociology' (Williams 1953: 186). *Preface to Film* – from which we take the essay **Film and the Dramatic Tradition** – was co-authored by Williams with Michael Orrom and first published in 1954. It needs to be more widely recognized as one of the founding texts of contemporary cultural studies.

At the same time *Preface to Film* is notable for the ways in which it challenges the broader explanatory framework offered by Marxist cultural theory. Placing film firmly within the naturalist tradition as 'a particular kind of performance' (**Film and the Dramatic Tradition**, p. 25), Williams approached the problem of historical changes in dramatic convention through the concept of 'structure of feeling' rather than through the idea of economic base and cultural superstructure. While orthodox Marxism regarded all forms of artistic expression as the secondary effect of events and changes in the economic base, structure of feeling gave art a primary and constitutive force in social cohesion and social change. The central claim that 'it is in art, primarily, that the effect of the totality, the dominant structure of feeling, is expressed and embodied' (p. 33) was one of the first direct challenges from within the left to the orthodox currency of Marxist cultural theory, and helped to place the study of mass culture firmly on the agenda of New Left analysis. As Stuart Hall later acknowledged, the New Left 'took the first faltering steps of putting questions of cultural analysis and cultural politics at the centre of its politics' and no one argued their case 'more profoundly than Raymond Williams' (Hall 1989: 26, 27).

The Masses forms a significant part of the Conclusion to Williams's masterpiece, *Culture and Society*, and marks his prescient commitment to what we now call the politics of representation. In reality, the centre of this ambitious study is less the academic discovery of the 'culture and society tradition' which most commentators have focused upon; this is rather to be found in the contemporary political intervention the book sought to make.

The historical thesis was simple and direct: the 'new idea of culture' is the 'court of appeal in which real values are determined, usually in opposition to the "factitious" values thrown up by the market' (Williams 1958: 34); culture amounts to 'a criticism of what has been called the bourgeois idea of society' (1958: 328). He backed up his assertion with an impressively broad survey of thinkers from Edmund Burke and William Cobbett to Gissing and Shaw and through to Lawrence, Leavis and Orwell, and the existence of a culture and society tradition soon became a commonplace in literary and cultural history. But this historical argument was never intended to stand alone, as some purely academic case: it was always intended to support and sustain a sharp and contemporary political point. Along with other members of the New Left, Williams set out to challenge what appeared to be the increasing complacency of British political life in the postwar period, and the slow but steady erosion of the idea of participatory democracy in Britain. This was in danger of being replaced, he argued, by its 'submerged opposite': a class democracy in which 'democracy will merely describe the processes by which a ruling class conducts its business of ruling' (**The Masses**, p. 45).

Central to this tendency were the implications present in the representation of people as masses, and of masses as simply a 'new word for mob' (**The Masses**, p. 44). In a characteristic formulation, Williams argues that we 'have to return the meanings to experience' in order to resist the ideological dynamics at work in the usual deployment of the term in contemporary social thinking. In a brilliant reminder of the exclusionary dynamics of representation, he insists:

The masses are always the others, whom we don't know, and can't know. Yet now, in our kind of society, we see these others regularly, in their myriad variations; stand, physically, beside them. They are here, and we are here with them. And that we are with them is of course the whole point. To other people, we also are masses. Masses are other people.

(**The Masses**, p. 46)

'There are in fact no masses, there are only ways of seeing people as masses' (p. 00): with this pointed but simple statement, Williams issued a lasting challenge to all systems of representation in which the cohesion and identity of the self is predicated upon the denial of such qualities to others.

Though some readers of *Culture and Society* had been able largely to ignore the conclusion of the work and its political implications, and to focus instead on the finer detail of its history of the tradition, such a selective reading became more difficult with the publication of *The Long Revolution* in 1961. Here the combination of theoretical argument, historical contextualization, open political commentary and literary criticism present in the essays which made up *The Long Revolution* openly challenged existing academic categories and established disciplinary boundaries. Its central argument is that a third revolution has taken place alongside the industrial and democratic revolutions, one of equal importance and significance though the 'most difficult' to interpret. This is the cultural revolution, the revolution of literacy:

> We speak of a cultural revolution, and we must certainly see the aspiration to extend the active process of learning, with the skills of literacy and other advanced communication, to all people rather than to limited groups, as comparable in importance to the growth of democracy and the rise of scientific industry.
>
> (Williams 1961: 11)

With its chapters on creativity, the growth of standard English and the popular press, its social history of English writers and dramatic forms, and its prescient analysis of Britain in the 1960s, *The Long Revolution* was one of the first works to bring together the defining elements for a new cultural studies. Throughout, the emphasis is placed on the dynamics of representation, the ways in which when 'we examine actual relationships, we start from the descriptions we have learned' (1961: 89). In the extract we publish here, Williams examines the ways in which when 'we speak of "the individual" and of "society", we are using descriptions which embody particular interpretations of the experience to which they refer' (p. 65).

Writing in 1961, Williams displays to the full his curious knack for anticipating and prefiguring the key questions of much later theoretical debates, though of course from within the terms and limits of the conceptual vocabulary of his time. As he analyses the valencies of the term 'individual', he comments in particular on the ways in which certain versions of psychoanalysis 'are contained and limited by [the] theoretical separation of "the individual" and "society"' while others offer 'a highly significant emphasis on relationships' (**Individuals and Societies**, p. 70). Here there are significant points of contact with much more recent debate and analysis.

Williams welcomed the move, in much of the social psychology of the 1950s, away from 'the idea that the individual in some way *precedes* his society' (**Individuals and Societies**, p. 00); but he also stressed the need to resist the consequent tendency to overemphasize the fact of the individual's adaption to his or her social role. Against any purely passive notion of social adaption, he argued for the more active concept of 'individuation'. While individuation acknowledges how the 'self grows within a social process which radically influences it', it also emphasizes the ways in which 'the individual can help to change or modify the social process that has influenced and is influencing him' (**Individuals and Societies**, p. 74). It is surely arguable that the more recent adoption of the term 'subject', rather than 'individual', as the key word for our investigations of power and ideology deserves a similar interrogation. In his terms, 'subject' is always likely to imply a theoretically and politically damaging emphasis on passivity and subjection since its prior uses in linguistic and political theory all stressed the priority of system over subject. Not surprisingly, we shall see Williams returning to just this notion of 'individuation' in his discussion of system and subject in the later essay **Language as Sociality** (see Part 3 below pp. 108–207).

By the beginning of the 1960s, both Williams's champions and detractors admitted he occupied a central position in Britain's intellectual and academic life. 'Not to know about . . . *Culture and Society* is to brand oneself the intellectual equivalent of a square', as one advertisement for the book in the *New Left Review* put it. Similarly, while historian Edward Thompson could write some harsh criticisms of his work for some of its methodological and political failings (the lack of any full and proper contextualization of the texts discussed in *Culture and Society*; the idea of culture as a 'whole way of life' would be better replaced by the idea of culture as conflict), Thompson had no doubt that, in the context of the culture wars of the 1950s, Williams was the New Left's 'best man':

With a compromised tradition at his back, and with a broken vocabulary in his hands, he did the only thing that was left to him; he took over the vocabulary of his opponents, followed them into the heart of their own arguments, and fought them to a standstill in their own terms.

(Thompson 1961: 27)

'Our best man'. And today? Writing from his progressive position in the culture wars of our time, Charles Bernstein, doyen of American $L = A = N = G = U = A = G = E$ poetry, points out Williams's still relevant insistence that 'the common "intellectual and literary" tradition, like the common language, is a shared inheritance, with divergent and conflicting tendencies, and not a product of any single class or sector, *even if one wishes to lay claim to it*' (Bernstein 1984: 374).[5] While it may be the case, as Thompson hints, that Williams won the battle in the 1950s, there can be no doubt that, as Bernstein's reference shows, the struggle continues.

Notes

1   See, for example, the comment by the editors of *Views Beyond the Border Country*, whose contributors 'remain critical of [Williams's] failure to employ psychoanalysis, deconstruction, and other avant-garde approaches to theorize the relationship between colonial and post-colonial formations' (Dworkin and Roman 1993a: 13); Dworkin himself ('though he has been dead for only the last five [sic] years, he is already part of a different political age' (Dworkin 1993: 54)); or the British journal *New Formations*, who stress how Williams 'would doubtless have resisted the way that many of our articles draw on radical post-structuralism' (1988: 3). For discussion of these and other negative assessments, see Higgins 1995. For more positive assessments, see Milner 1993, Dworkin 1997, Higgins 1999, and Mulhern 2000.

2   See, for instance, Bloom 1987 and Graff 1992.

3   For useful discussions of the New Left, see Sinfield 1989 and Dworkin 1997.

4   See *Culture and Society* for Williams's critique of Eliot in this regard, and particularly his comment that Eliot argues 'we must retain social classes, and in particular a governing social class, with which the elite will overlap and constantly interact. This is Eliot's fundamentally conservative conclusion, for it is clear, when the abstractions are translated, that what he recommends is what now exists, socially. He is, of course, led necessarily to condemn the pressure for a classless society, and for a national educational system.' (1958: 241); and, more recently, John Xiros Cooper's comment, 'For Eliot, social class, not abstract intelligence, ought to constitute the horizon of inclusion for an elite' (Cooper 1995: 38).

5   For interesting discussions of the work of the L = A = N = G = U = A = G = E poets see Bernstein 1984, 1992, Perloff 1987 and Perelman 1996.

1

Culture is Ordinary

From Norman Mackenzie (ed.) (1958) Conviction. *London: MacGibbon and Kee*

The bus stop was outside the cathedral. I had been looking at the Mappa Mundi, with its rivers out of Paradise, and at the chained library, where a party of clergymen had got in easily, but where I had waited an hour and cajoled a verger before I even saw the chains. Now, across the street, a cinema advertised the *Six- Five Special* and a cartoon version of *Gulliver's Travels*. The bus arrived, with a driver and a conductress deeply absorbed in each other. We went out of the city, over the old bridge, and on through the orchards and the green meadows, and the fields red under the plough. Ahead were the Black Mountains, and we climbed among them, watching the steep fields end at the grey walls, beyond which the bracken and heather and whin had not yet been driven back. To the east, along the ridge, stood the line of grey Norman castles; to the west, the fortress wall of the mountains. Then, as we still climbed, the rock changed under us. Here, now, was limestone, and the line of the early iron workings along the scarp. The farming valleys, with their scattered white houses, fell away behind. Ahead of us were the narrower valleys: the steel-rolling mill, the gasworks, the grey terraces, the pitheads. The bus stopped, and the driver and conductress got out, still absorbed. They had done this journey so often, and seen all its stages. It is a journey, in fact, that in one form or another we have all made.

I was born and grew up halfway along that bus journey. Where I lived is still a farming valley, though the road through it is being widened and straightened, to carry the heavy lorries to the north. Not far away, my grandfather, and so back through the generations, worked as a farm labourer until he was turned out of his cottage and, in his fifties, became a roadman. His sons went at thirteen or fourteen on to the farms, his daughters into service. My father, his third son, left the farm at fifteen to be a boy porter on the railway, and later became a signalman, working in a box in this valley until he died. I went up the road to the village school, where a curtain divided the two classes – Second to eight or nine, First to fourteen. At eleven I went to the local grammar school, and later to Cambridge.

Culture is ordinary: that is where we must start. To grow up in that country was to see the shape of a culture, and its modes of change. I could stand on the mountains and look north to the farms and the cathedral, or south to the smoke and the flare of the blast furnace making a second sunset. To grow up in that family was to see the shaping of minds: the learning of new skills, the shifting of relationships, the emergence of different language and ideas. My grandfather, a big hard labourer, wept while he spoke, finely and excitedly, at the parish meeting, of being turned out of his cottage. My father, not long before he died, spoke quietly and happily of when he had started a trade- union branch and a Labour Party group in the village, and, without bitterness, of the 'kept men' of the new politics. I speak a different idiom, but I think of these same things.

Culture is ordinary: that is the first fact. Every human society has its own shape, its own purposes, its own meanings. Every human society expresses these, in institutions, and in arts and learning. The making of a society is the finding of common meanings and directions, and its growth is an active debate and amendment under the pressures of experience, contact, and discovery, writing themselves into the land. The growing society is there, yet it is also made and remade in every individual mind. The making of a mind is, first, the slow learning of shapes, purposes, and meanings, so that work, observation and communication are possible. Then, second, but equal in importance, is the testing of these in experience, the making of new observations, comparisons, and meanings. A culture has two aspects: the known meanings and directions, which its members are trained to; the new observations and meanings, which are offered and tested. These are the ordinary proceses of human societies and human minds, and we see through them the nature of a culture: that it is always both traditional and creative; that it is both the most ordinary common mean- ings and the finest individual meanings. We use the word culture in these two senses: to mean a whole way of life – the common meanings; to mean the arts and learning – the special processes of discovery and creative effort. Some writers reserve the word for one or other of these senses; I insist on both, and on the significance of their conjunction. The questions I ask about our culture are questions about our general and common purposes, yet also questions about deep personal meanings. Culture is ordinary, in every society and in every mind.

Now there are two senses of culture – two colours attached to it – that I know about but refuse to learn. The first I discovered at Cambridge, in a teashop. I was not, by the way, oppressed by Cambridge. I was not cast down by old buildings, for I had come from a country with twenty centuries of history written visibly into the earth: I liked walking through a Tudor court, but it did not make me feel raw. I was not amazed by the existence of a place of learning; I had always known the cathedral, and the bookcases I now sit to work at in Oxford are of the same design as those in the chained library. Nor was learning, in my family, some strange eccentricity; I was not, on a scholarship in Cambridge, a new kind of animal up a brand-new ladder. Learning was ordinary; we learned where we could. Always, from those scattered white houses, it had made sense to go out and become a scholar or a poet or a teacher. Yet few of us could be spared from the immediate work; a price had been set on this kind of learning, and it was more, much more, than we could individually pay. Now, when we could pay in common, it was a good, ordinary life.

I was not oppressed by the university, but the teashop, acting as if it were one of the older and more respectable departments, was a different matter. Here was culture, not in any sense I knew, but in a special sense: the outward and emphatically visible sign of a special kind of people, cultivated people. They were not, the great majority of them, particularly learned; they practised few arts; but they had it, and they showed you they had it. They are still there, I suppose, still showing it, though even they must be hearing rude noises from outside, from a few scholars and writers they call – how comforting a label is! – angry young men. As a matter of fact there is no need to be rude. It is simply that if that is culture, we don't want it; we have seen other people living.

But of course it is not culture, and those of my colleagues who, hating the teashop, make culture, on its account, a dirty word, are mistaken. If the people in the teashop go on insisting that culture is their trivial differences of behaviour, their trivial variations of speech habit, we cannot stop them, but we can ignore them. They are not that important, to take culture from where it belongs.

Yet, probably also disliking the teashop, there were writers I read then, who went into the same category in my mind. When I now read a book such as Clive Bell's *Civilisation*, I experience not so much disagreement as stupor. What kind of life can it be, I wonder, to produce this extraordinary fussiness, this extraordinary decision to call certain things culture and then separate them, as with a park wall, from ordinary people and ordinary work? At home we met and made music, listened to it, recited and listened to poems, valued fine language. I have heard better music and better poems since; there is the world to draw on. But I know, from the most ordinary experience, that the interest is there, the capacity is there. Of course, farther along that bus journey, the old social organization in which these things had their place has been broken. People have been driven and concentrated into new kinds of work, new kinds of relationship; work, by the way, which built the park walls, and the houses inside them, and which is now at last bringing, to the unanimous disgust of the teashop, clean and decent and furnished living to the people themselves. Culture is ordinary: through every change let us hold fast to that.

The other sense, or colour, that I refuse to learn, is very different. Only two English words rhyme with culture, and these, as it happens, are sepulture and vulture. We don't yet call museums or galleries or even universities culture-sepultures, but I hear a lot, lately, about culture-vultures (man must rhyme), and I hear also, in the same North Atlantic argot, of do-gooders and highbrows and superior prigs. Now I don't like the teashop, but I don't like this drinking-hole either. I know there are people who are humourless about the arts and learning, and I know there is a difference between goodness and sanctimony. But the growing implications of this spreading argot – the true cant of a new kind of rogue – I reject absolutely. For, honestly, how can anyone use a word like 'do-gooder' with this new, offbeat complacency? How can anyone wither himself to a state where he must use these new flip words for any attachment to learning or the arts? It is plain that what may have started as a feeling about hypocrisy, or about pretentiousness (in itself a two-edged word), is becoming a guilt-ridden tic at the mention of any serious standards whatever. And the word 'culture' has been heavily compromised by this conditioning: Goering reached for his gun; many reach for their chequebooks; a growing number, now, reach for the latest bit of argot.

'Good' has been drained of much of its meaning, in these circles, by the exclusion of its ethical content and emphasis on a purely technical standard; to do a good job is better than to be a do-gooder. But do we need reminding that any crook can, in his own terms, do a good job? The smooth reassurance of technical efficiency is no substitute for the whole positive human reference. Yet men who once made this reference, men who were or wanted to be writers or scholars, are now, with every appearance of satisfaction, advertising men, publicity boys, names in the strip newspapers. These men were given skills, given attachments, which are now in the service of the most brazen money-grabbing exploitation of the inexperience of ordinary people. And it is these men – this new, dangerous class – who have invented and disseminated the argot, in an attempt to influence ordinary people – who because they do real work have real standards in the fields they know – against real standards in the fields these men knew and have abandoned. The old cheapjack is still there in the market, with the country boys' half-crowns on his reputed packets of gold rings or watches. He thinks of his victims as a slow, ignorant crowd, but they live, and farm, while he coughts behind his portable stall. The new cheapjack is in offices with contemporary *décor*, using scraps of linguistics, psychology and sociology to influence what he thinks of as the mass mind. He too, however, will have to pick up and move on, and meanwhile we are not to be influenced by his argot; we can simply refuse to learn it. Culture is ordinary. An interest in learning or the arts is simple, pleasant and natural. A desire to know what is best, and to do what is good, is the whole positive nature of man. We are not to be scared from these things by noises. There are many versions of what is wrong with our culture. So far I have tried only to clear away the detritus which makes it difficult for us to think seriously about it at all. When I got to Cambridge I encountered two serious influences which have left a very deep impression on my mind. The first was Marxism, the second the teaching of Leavis. Through all subsequent disagreement I retain my respect for both.

The Marxists said many things, but those that mattered were three. First, they said that a culture must be finally interpreted in relation to its underlying system of production. I have argued this theoretically elsewhere – it is a more difficult idea than it looks – but I still accept its emphasis. Everything I had seen, growing up in that border country, had led me towards such an emphasis: a culture is a whole way of life, and the arts are part of a social organization which economic change clearly radically affects. I did not have to be taught dissatisfaction with the existing economic system, but the subsequent questions about our culture were, in these terms, vague. It was said that it was a class-dominated culture, deliberately restricting a common inheritance to a small class, while leaving the masses ignorant. The fact of restriction I accepted – it is still very obvious that only the *deserving* poor get much educational opportunity, and I was in no mood, as I walked about Cambridge, to feel glad that I had been thought deserving; I was no better and no worse than the people I came from. On the other hand, just because of this, I got angry at my friends' talk about the ignorant masses: one kind of Communist has always talked like this, and has got his answer, at Poznan and Budapest, as the imperialists, making the same assumption, were answered in India, in Indo-China, in Africa. There is an English bourgeois culture, with its powerful educational, literary and social institutions, in close contact with the actual centres of power. To say that most working people are excluded from these is self-evident, though the doors, under sustained pressure, are slowly opening. But to go on to say that working people are excluded from English culture is nonsense; they have their own growing institutions, and much of the strictly bourgeois culture they would in any case not want. A great part of the English way of life, and of its arts and learning, is not bourgeois in any discoverable sense. There are institutions, and common meanings, which are in no sense the sole product of the commercial middle class; and there are art and learning, a common English inheritance, produced by many kinds of men, including many who hated the very class and system which now take pride in consuming it. The bourgeoisie has given us much, including a narrow but real system of morality; that is at least better than its court predecessors. The leisure which the bourgeoisie attained has given us much of cultural value. But this is not to say that contemporary culture is bourgeois culture: a mistake that everyone, from Conservatives to Marxists, seems to make. There is a distinct working-class way of life, which I for one value – not only because I was bred in it, for I now, in certain respects, live differently. I think this way of life, with its emphases of neighbourhood, mutual obligation, and common betterment, as expressed in the great working-class political and industrial institutions, is in fact the best basis for any future English society. As for the arts and learning, they are in a real sense a national inheritance, which is, or should be, available to everyone. So when the Marxists say that we live in a dying culture, and that the masses are ignorant, I have to ask them, as I asked them then, where on earth they have lived. A dying culture, and ignorant masses, are not what I have known and see.

What I had got from the Marxists then, so far, was a relationship between culture and production, and the observation that education was restricted. The other things I rejected, as I rejected also their third point, that since culture and production are related, the advocacy of a different system of production is in some way a cultural directive, indicating not only a way of life but new arts and learning. I did some writing while I was, for eighteen months, a member of the Communist Party, and I found out in trivial ways what other writers, here and in Europe, have found out more gravely: the practical consequences of this kind of theoretical error. In this respect, I saw the future, and it didn't work. The Marxist interpretation of culture can never be accepted while it retains, as it need not retain, this directive element, this insistence that if you honestly want socialism you must write, think, learn in certain prescribed ways. A culture is common meanings, the product of a whole people, and offered individual meanings, the product of a man's whole committed personal and social experience. It is stupid and arrogant to suppose that any of these meanings can in any way be prescribed; they are made by living, made and remade, in ways we cannot know in advance. To try to jump the future, to pretend that in some way you *are* the future, is strictly insane. Prediction is another matter, an offered meaning, but the only thing we can say about culture in an England that has socialized its means of production is that all the channels of expression and communication should be cleared and open, so that the whole actual life, that we cannot know in advance, that we can know only in part even while it is being lived, may be brought to consciousness and meaning.

Leavis has never liked Marxists, which is in one way a pity, for they know more than he does about modern English society, and about its immediate history. He, on the other hand, knows more than any Marxist I have met about the real relations between art and experience. We have all learned from him in this, and we have also learned his version of what is wrong with English culture. The diagnosis is radical, and is rapidly becoming orthodox. There was an old, mainly agricultural England, with a traditional culture of great value. This has been replaced by a modern, organized, industrial state, whose characteristic institutions deliberately cheapen our natural human responses, making art and literature into desperate survivors and witnesses, while a new mechanized vulgarity sweeps into the centres of power. The only defence is in education, which will at least keep certain things alive, and which will also, at least in a minority, develop ways of thinking and feeling which are competent to understand what is happening and to maintain the finest individual values. I need not add how widespread this diagnosis has become, though little enough acknowledgement is still made to Leavis himself. For my own part, I was deeply impressed by it; deeply enough for my ultimate rejection of it to be a personal crisis lasting several years.

For, obviously, it seemed to fit a good deal of my experience. It did not tell me that my father and grandfather were ignorant wage-slaves; it did not tell me that the smart, busy, commercial culture (which I had come to as a stranger, so much so that for years I had violent headaches whenever I passed through London and saw underground advertisements and evening newspapers) was the thing I had to catch up with. I even made a fool of myself, or was made to think so, when after a lecture in which the usual point was made that 'neighbour' now does not mean what it did to Shakespeare, I said – imagine! – that to me it did. (When my father was dying, this year, one man came in and dug his garden; another loaded and delivered a lorry of sleepers for firewood; another came and chopped the sleepers into blocks; another – I don't know who, it was never said – left a sack of potatoes at the back door; a woman came in and took away a basket of washing.) But even this was explicable; I came from a bit of the old society, but my future was Surbiton (it took me years to find Surbiton, and have a good look at it, but it's served a good many as a symbol – without having lived there I couldn't say whether rightly). So there I was, and it all seemed to fit.

Yet not all. Once I got away, and thought about it, it didn't really fit properly. For one thing I knew this: at home we were glad of the Industrial Revolution, and of its consequent social and political changes. True, we lived in a very beautiful farming valley, and the valleys beyond the limestone we could all see were ugly. But there was one gift that was overriding, one gift which at any price we would take, the gift of power that is everything to men who have worked with their hands. It was slow in coming to us, in all its effects, but steam power, the petrol engine, electricity, these and their host of products in commodities and services, we took as quickly as we could get them, and were glad. I have seen all these things being used, and I have seen the things they replaced. I will not listen with patience to any acid listing of them – you know the sneer you can get into plumbing, baby Austins, aspirin, contraceptives, canned food. But I say to these Pharisees: dirty water, an earth bucket, a fourmile walk each way to work, headaches, broken women, hunger and monotony of diet. The working people, in town and country alike, will not listen (and I support them) to any account of our society which supposes that these things are not progress: not just mechanical, external progress either, but a real service of life. Moreover, in the new conditions, there was more real freedom to dispose of our lives, more real personal grasp where it mattered, more real say. Any account of our culture which explicitly or implicitly denies the value of an industrial society is really irrelevant; not in a million years would you make us give up this power.

So then the social basis of the case was unacceptable, but could one, trying to be a writer, a scholar, a teacher, ignore the indictment of the new cultural vulgarity? For the plumbing and the tractors and the medicines could one ignore the strip newspapers, the multiplying cheapjacks, the raucous triviality? As a matter of priorities, yes, if necessary; but was the cheapening of response really a consequence of the cheapening of power? It looks like it, I know, but is this really as much as one can say? I believe the central problem of our society, in the coming half-century, is the use of our new resources to make a good common culture; the means to a good, abundant economy we already under-stand. I think the good common culture can be made, but before we can be serious about this, we must rid ourselves of a legacy from our most useful critics – a legacy of two false equations, one false analogy, and one false proposition.

The false proposition is easily disposed of. It is a fact that the new power brought ugliness: the coal brought dirt, the factory brought overcrowding, communications brought a mess of wires. But the proposition that ugliness is a price we pay, or refuse to pay, for economic power need no longer be true. New sources of power, new methods of production, improved systems of transport and communication can, quite practically, make England clean and pleasant again, and with much more power, not less. Any new ugliness is the product of stupidity, indifference, or simply incoordination; these things will be easier to deal with than when power was necessarily noisy, dirty, and disfiguring.

The false equations are more difficult. One is the equation between popular education and the new commercial culture: the latter proceeding inevitably from the former. Let the masses in, it is said, and this is what you inevitably get. Now the question is obviously difficult, but I can't accept this equation, for two reasons. The first is a matter of faith: I don't believe that the ordinary people in fact resemble the normal description of the masses, low and trivial in taste and habit. I put it another way: that there are in fact no masses, but only ways of seeing people as masses. With the coming of industrialism, much of the old social organization broke down and it became a matter of difficult personal experience that we were constantly seeing people we did not know, and it was tempting to mass them, as 'the others', in our minds. Again, people were physically massed, in the industrial towns, and a new class structure (the names of our social classes, and the word 'class' itself in this sense, date only from the Industrial Revolution) was practically imposed. The improvement in communications, in particular the development of new forms of multiple transmission of news and entertainment, created unbridgeable divisions between transmitter and audience, which again led to the audience being interpreted as an unknown mass. Masses became a new word for mob: the others, the unknown, the unwashed, the crowd beyond one. As a way of knowing other people, this formula is obviously ridiculous, but, in the new conditions, it seemed an effective formula – the only one possible. Certainly it was the formula that was used by those whose money gave them access to the new communication techniques; the lowness of taste and habit, which human beings assign very easily to other human beings, was assumed, as a bridge. The new culture was built on this formula, and if I reject the formula, if I insist that this lowness is not inherent in ordinary people, you can brush my insistence aside, but I shall go on holding to it. A different formula, I know from experience, gets a radically different response.

My second reason is historical: I deny, and can prove my denial, that popular education and commercial culture are cause and effect. I have shown elsewhere that the myth of 1870 – the Education Act which is said to have produced, as its children grew up, a new cheap and nasty press – is indeed myth. There was more than enough literacy, long before 1870, to support a cheap press, and in fact there were cheap and really bad newspapers selling in great quantities before the 1870 Act was heard of. The bad new commercial culture came out of the social chaos of industrialism, and out of the success, in this chaos, of the 'masses' formula, not out of popular education. Northcliffe did few worse things than start this myth, for while the connection between bad culture and the social chaos of industrialism is significant, the connection between it and popular education is vicious. The Northcliffe Revolution, by the way, was a radical change in the financial structure of the press, basing it on a new kind of revenue – the new mass advertising of the 1890s – rather than the making of a cheap popular press, in which he had been widely and successfully preceded. But I tire of making these points. Everyone prefers to believe Northcliffe. Yet does nobody, even a Royal Commission, read the most ordinarily accessible newspaper history? When people do read the history, the false equation between popular education and commercial culture will disappear for ever. Popular education came out of the other camp, and has had quite opposite effects.

The second false equation is this: that the observable badness of so much widely distributed popular culture is a true guide to the state of mind and feeling, the essential quality of living of its consumers. Too many good men have said this for me to treat it lightly, but I still, on evidence, can't accept it. It is easy to assemble, from print and cinema and television, a terrifying and fantastic congress of cheap feelings and moronic arguments. It is easy to go on from this and assume this deeply degrading version of the actual lives of our contemporaries. Yet do we find this confirmed, when we meet people? This is where 'masses' comes in again, of course: the people *we* meet aren't vulgar, but God, think of Bootle and Surbiton and Aston! I haven't lived in any of those places; have you? But a few weeks ago I was in a house with a commercial traveller, a lorry driver, a bricklayer, a shopgirl, a fitter, a signalman, a nylon operative, a domestic help (perhaps, dear, she is your very own treasure). I hate describing people like this, for in fact they were my family and family friends. Now they read, they watch, this work we are talking about; some of them quite critically, others with a good deal of pleasure. Very well, I read different things, watch different entertainments, and I am quite sure why they are better. But could I sit down in that house and make this equation we are offered? Not, you understand, that shame was stopping me; I've learned, thank you, how to behave. But talking to my family, to my friends, talking, as we were, about our own lives, about people, about feelings, could I in fact find this lack of quality we are discussing? I'll be honest – I looked; my training has done that for me. I can only say that I found as much natural fineness of feeling, as much quick discrimination, as much clear grasp of ideas within the range of experience as I have found anywhere. I don't altogether understand this, though I am not really surprised. Clearly there is something in the psychology of print and image that none of us has yet quite grasped. For the equation looks sensible, yet when you test it, in experience – and there's nowhere else you can test it – it's wrong. I can understand the protection of critical and intelligent reading: my father, for instance, a satisfied reader of the *Daily Herald*, got simply from reading the company reports a clear idea, based on names, of the rapid development of combine and interlocking ownership in British industry, which I had had made easy for me in two or three academic essays; and he had gone on to set these facts against the opinions in a number of articles in the paper on industrial ownership. That I understand; that is simply intelligence, however partly trained. But there is still this other surprising fact: that people whose quality of personal living is high are apparently satisfied by a low quality of printed feeling and opinion. Many of them still live, it is true, in a

surprisingly enclosed personal world, much more so than mine, and some of
their personal observations are the finer for it. Perhaps this is enough to explain
it, but in any case, I submit, we need a new equation, to fit the observable facts.

Now the false analogy, that we must also reject. This is known, in discussions of culture, as a 'kind of Gresham's Law'. Just as bad money will drive out
good, so bad culture will drive out good, and this, it is said, has in fact been
happening. If you can't see, straight away, the defect of the analogy, your
answer, equally effective, will have to be historical. For in fact, of course, it has
not been happening. There is more, much more bad culture about; it is easier,
now, to distribute it, and there is more leisure to receive it. But test this in any
field you like, and see if this has been accompanied by a shrinking consumption
of things we can all agree to be good. The editions of good literature are very
much larger than they were; the listeners to good music are much more
numerous than they were; the number of people who look at good visual art
is larger than it has ever been. If bad newspapers drive out good newspapers, by
a kind of Gresham's Law, why is it that, allowing for the rise in population, *The
Times* sells nearly three times as many copies as in the days of its virtual
monopoly of the press, in 1850? It is the law I am questioning, not the
seriousness of the facts as a whole. Instead of a kind of Gresham's Law, keeping
people awake at nights with the now orthodox putropian nightmare, let us put
it another way, to fit the actual facts: we live in an expanding culture, and all
the elements in this culture are themselves expanding. If we start from this, we
can then ask real questions: about relative rates of expansion; about the social
and economic problems raised by these; about the social and economic
answers. I am working now on a book to follow my *Culture and Society*, trying
to interpret, historically and theoretically, the nature and conditions of an
expanding culture of our kind. I could not have begun this work if I had not
learned from the Marxists and from Leavis; I cannot complete it unless I
radically amend some of the ideas which they and others have left us.

I give myself three wishes, one for each of the swans I have just been watching
on the lake. I ask for things that are part of the ethos of our working-class
movement. I ask that we may be strong and human enough to realize them.
And I ask, naturally, in my own fields of interest.

I wish, first, that we should recognize that education is ordinary: that it is,
before everything else, the process of giving to the ordinary members of society
its full common meanings, and the skills that will enable them to amend these
meanings, in the light of their personal and common experience. If we start
from that, we can get rid of the remaining restrictions, and make the necessary
changes. I do not mean only money restrictions, though these, of course, are
ridiculous and must go. I mean also restrictions in the mind: the insistence, for

example, that there is a hard maximum number – a fraction of the population as a whole – capable of really profiting by a university education, or a grammar school education, or by any full course of liberal studies. We are told that this is not a question of what we might personally prefer, but of the hard cold facts of human intelligence, as shown by biology and psychology. But let us be frank about this: are biology and psychology different in the USA and USSR (each committed to expansion, and not to any class rigidities), where much larger numbers, much larger fractions, pass through comparable stages of education? Or were the English merely behind in the queue for intelligence? I believe, myself, that our educational system, with its golden fractions, is too like our social system – a top layer of leaders, a middle layer of supervisors, a large bottom layer of operatives – to be coincidence. I cannot accept that education is a training for jobs, or for making useful citizens (that is, fitting into this system). It is a society's confirmation of its common meanings, and of the human skills for their amendment. Jobs follow from this confirmation: the purpose, and then the working skill. We are moving into an economy where we shall need many more highly trained specialists. For this precise reason, I ask for a common education that will give our society its cohesion, and prevent it disintegrating into a series of specialist departments, the nation become a firm.

But I do not mean only the reorganization of entry into particular kinds of education, though I welcome and watch the experiments in this. I mean also the rethinking of content, which is even more important. I have the honour to work for an organization through which, quite practically, working men amended the English university curriculum. It is now as it was then: the defect is not what is in, but what is out. It will be a test of our cultural seriousness whether we can, in the coming generation, redesign our syllabuses to a point of full human relevance and control. I should like to see a group working on this, and offering its conclusions. For we need not fear change; oldness may or may not be relevant. I come from an old place; if a man tells me that his family came over with the Normans, I say 'Yes, how interesting; and are you liking it here?' Oldness is relative, and many 'immemorial' English traditions were invented, just like that, in the nineteenth century. What that vital century did for its own needs, we can do for ours; we can make, in our turn, a true twentieth-century syllabus. And by this I do not mean simply more technology; I mean a full liberal education for everyone in our society, and then full specialist training to earn our living in terms of what we want to make of our lives. Our specialisms will be finer if they have grown from a common culture, rather than being a distinction from it. And we must at all costs avoid the polarization of our culture, of which there are growing signs. High literacy is expanding, in direct relation to exceptional educational opportunities, and the gap between this and common literacy may widen, to the great damage of both, and with great consequent tension. We must emphasize not the ladder but the common highway, for every man's ignorance diminishes me, and every man's skill is a common gain of breath.

My second wish is complementary: for more and more active public provision for the arts and for adult learning. We now spend £20,000,000 annually on all our libraries, museums, galleries, orchestras, on the Arts Council, and on all forms of adult education. At the same time we spend £365,000,000 annually on advertising. When these figures are reversed, we can claim some sense of proportion and value. And until they are reversed, let there be no sermons from the Establishment about materialism: this is their way of life, let them look at it. (But there is no shame in them: for years, with their own children away at school, they have lectured working-class mothers on the virtues of family life; this is a similar case.)

I ask for increased provision on three conditions. It is not to be a disguised way of keeping up consumption, but a thing done for its own sake. A minister in the last Labour government said that we didn't want any geniuses in the film industry; he wanted, presumably, just to keep the turnstiles clicking. The short answer to this is that we don't want any Wardour Street thinkers in the leadership of the Labour Party. We want leaders of a society, not repair-workers on this kind of cultural economy.

The second condition is that while we must obviously preserve and extend the great national institutions, we must do something to reverse the concentration of this part of our culture. We should welcome, encourage and foster the tendencies to regional recreation that are showing themselves; for culture is ordinary, you should not have to go to London to find it.

The third condition is controversial. We should not seek to extend a ready-made culture to the benighted masses. We should accept, frankly, that if we extend our culture we shall change it: some that is offered will be rejected, other parts will be radically criticized. And this is as it should be, for our arts, now, are in no condition to go down to eternity unchallenged. There is much fine work; there is also shoddy work, and work based on values that will find no acceptance if they ever come out into the full light of England. To take our arts to new audiences is to be quite certain that in many respects those arts will be changed. I, for one, do not fear this. I would not expect the working people of England to support works which, after proper and patient preparation, they could not accept. The real growth will be slow and uneven, but state provision, frankly, should be a growth in this direction, and not a means of diverting public money to the preservation of a fixed and finished partial culture. At the same time, if we understand cultural growth, we shall know that it is a continual offering for common acceptance; that we should not, therefore, try to determine in advance what should be offered, but clear the channels and let all the offerings be made, taking care to give the difficult full space, the original full time, so that it is a real growth, and not just a wider confirmation of old rules.

Now, of course, we shall hear the old cry that things shouldn't be supported at a loss. Once again, this is a nation, not a firm. Parliament itself runs at a loss, because we need it, and if it would be better at a greater loss, I and others would willingly pay. But why, says Sir George Mammon, should *I* support a lot of doubtful artists? Why, says Mrs Mink, should I pay good money to educate, at *my* expense, a lot of irresponsible and ungrateful state scholars? The answer, dear sir, dear madam, is that *you* don't. On your own – learn your size – you could do practically nothing. We are talking about a method of common payment, for common services; we too shall be paying.

My third wish is in a related field: the field now dominated by the institutions of 'mass culture'. Often, it is the people at the head of these institutions who complain of running things at a loss. But the great popular newspapers, as newspapers, run at a loss. The independent television companies are planned to run at a loss. I don't mean temporary subsidies, but the whole basis of financing such institutions. The newspapers run at a heavy loss, which they make up with money from advertising – that is to say a particular use of part of the product of our common industry. To run at a loss, and then cover yourself with this kind of income, is of the essence of this kind of cultural institution, and this is entirely characteristic of our kind of capitalist society. The whole powerful array of mass cultural institutions has one keystone: money from advertising. Let them stop being complacent about other cultural institutions which run at a smaller loss, and meet it out of another part of the common product.

But what is it then that I wish? To pull out this keystone? No, not just like that. I point out merely that the organization of our present mass culture is so closely involved with the organization of capitalist society that the future of one cannot be considered except in terms of the future of the other. I think much of contemporary advertising is necessary only in terms of the kind of economy we now have: a stimulation of consumption in the direction of particular products and firms, often by irrelevant devices, rather than real advertising, which I and others want, the whole of this pseudo-advertising would be irrelevant. But then what? My wish is that we may solve the problems that would then arise, where necessary things like newspapers would be running at something like their real loss, without either pricing them out of ordinary means, or exposing them to the dangers of control and standardization (for we want a more free and more varied press, not one less so). It is going to be very difficult, but I do not believe we are so uninventive as to be left showing each other a pair of grim alternatives: either the continuance of this crazy peddling, in which news and opinion are inextricably involved with the shouts of the market, bringing in their train the new slavery and prostitution of the selling of personalities; or else a dull, monolithic, controlled system, in which news and opinion are in the gift of a ruling party. We should be thinking, now, about ways of paying for our common services which will guarantee proper freedom to those who actually provide the service, while protecting them and us against a domineering minority whether political or financial. I think there are ways, if we really believe in democracy.

But that is the final question: how many of us really believe in it? The capitalists don't; they are consolidating a power which can survive parliamentary changes. Many Labour planners don't; they interpret it as a society run by experts for an abstraction called the public interest. The people in the teashop don't; they are quite sure it is not going to be nice. And the others, the new dissenters? Nothing has done more to sour the democratic idea, among its natural supporters, and to drive them back into an angry self-exile, than the plain, overwhelming cultural issues: the apparent division of our culture into, on the one hand, a remote and self-gracious sophistication, on the other hand, a doped mass. So who then believes in democracy? The answer is really quite simple: the millions in England who still haven't got it, where they work and feel. There, as always, is the transforming energy, and the business of the socialist intellectual is what it always was: to attack the clamps on that energy – in industrial relations, public administration, education, for a start; and to work in his own field on ways in which that energy, as released, can be concentrated and fertile. The technical means are difficult enough, but the biggest difficulty is in accepting, deep in our minds, the values on which they depend: that the ordinary people should govern; that culture and education are ordinary; that there are no masses to save, to capture, or to direct, but rather this crowded people in the course of an extraordinarily rapid and confusing expansion of their lives. A writer's job is with individual meanings, and with making these meanings common. I find these meanings in the expansion, there along the journey where the necessary changes are writing themselves into the land, and where the language changes but the voice is the same.

2

Film and the Dramatic Tradition

From Raymond Williams and Michael Orrom (1954) Preface to Film. *London: Film Drama Ltd*

Film, in its main uses, is a particular medium within the general tradition of drama. Its essential novelty, as a dramatic medium, is that it offers different and, in certain respects, wholly new conditions of performance. Film is, in fact, from the standpoint of the general dramatic tradition, a particular kind of performance, which is also unique in the fact that the performance which it embodies is recorded and final. It is, that is to say, *a total performance*, which cannot be distinguished from the work that is being performed.

The greater part of the written theory and criticism of film, as well as a large part of actual film-making, has been severely limited in effectiveness because the relation of this new medium to the wide and general dramatic tradition has been neglected or even denied. Indeed, in the majority of books about film, the distinction of the film from all other arts is almost axiomatic. And we find, as a result, that terms like *stagey* and *literary* are, in this special vocabulary, modes of adverse criticism or rejection. But while it is obvious that film is a new and distinct medium, and while it is certain that anyone who is not fully aware of this will be unable to use the medium well, the distinction being made in the use of *stagey* and *literary* is not between film, on the one hand, and drama and literature on the other, but between the methods of film and the methods of a certain kind of play, or of the novel. Yet a particular kind of play is not the whole of drama, although in most periods most people tend to believe that the kind of play to which they are used is equivalent to drama as a whole. Nor is the novel the only literary form, although it is now so dominant that many people draw their ideas of what is *literary* from their experience of novel-reading. Thus, while it is necessary to distinguish the medium of film from the mediums of the average contemporary play or novel, it does not follow that the film has no relation, as an art, to drama; nor indeed, since in one important sense drama is a literary form, that the film has not an important relation to literature as a whole. To point out that the methods of *Citizen Kane* are different from the methods of *Candida* does not refute the general relation; it is really saying no more than that the dramatic methods of Ibsen are different from those of Shakespeare or Sophocles or the Nōh plays of Japan. Dramatic methods change, in the work of dramatic writers; and so also the conditions of performance of this work change. But all are changes within the dramatic tradition; and this is also the case with film, covering the changed conditions of performance, and the changed dramatic methods which these have made necessary.

The most emphatic insistence on the necessary conventions of the film medium is indeed perfectly compatible with a full recognition of the place it has in the general dramatic tradition. And the film has suffered because this recognition has not been widely made; for, because there was no such recognition, it did not mean that the tradition had no influence. It means, and for sixty years has meant, that the influence has been casual and indirect; so that those parts of the tradition which became influential were not the result of choices from the tradition as a whole, but rather the result of local and accidental contacts. The consequence is that while mediocre and irrelevant elements have had a definite effect, good and relevant elements have often been neglected. The film-maker who asserts that he is using his new medium without reference to the general tradition of drama and literature is plainly deceiving himself. In fact, the great majority of contemporary films are far too closely tied to the methods of the average contemporary play or novel (are often, indeed, merely inferior substitutes for them), while, beyond the range of these habits, a wide and fertile area of the dramatic tradition remains relatively unexplored. The major creative experiments in film still lie ahead of us; and we shall be the more strong and the more free to enter upon them if we can draw upon the general tradition of drama, and refuse to be bound by the limits of current habits and terms.

I shall discuss in this essay: first, the general nature of drama; second, the nature of dramatic conventions; third, the conventions, and the habits, of the drama and film of our own time; and fourth, the concept of *total performance*, which is the film's particular opportunity. [. . .]

Returning now to the main proposition that film, in its main uses, is a form of drama, in its wide traditional sense, we must note one particular objection, which arises from a technical property of film itself. It may be argued that in spite of all I have said earlier, the film is "not really" drama, because it is recorded on celluloid, "canned", and sent out to audiences who cannot then affect it. The audience, it is said, is a vital element in all drama, but in film it is only present when the performance has been finished. This denies the exercise of fruitful "participation" by the audience, which has always been recognized as valuable.

On formal grounds the point is, I think, altogether too marginal to deny the film's status as drama; but something needs to be said about it, under two heads: first, its effect upon the audience, and second, its effect on the performers. On the first point, the real issue is the effect of the conditions of watching film. It is an immensely powerful medium, and in the darkened auditorium the dominating screen, with its very large, moving figures, its very loud sound, its simultaneous appeal to eye and ear, can, it seems obvious, exercise a kind of "hypnotic" effect which very readily promotes phantasy and easy emotional indulgence. In the theatre, of course, once the auditorium had been darkened so that lighting effects could be gained, a similar condition has prevailed, but is perhaps less intense. The point is very important because there can be no doubt that it allows speculators to impose very crude emotions (which outside the cinema might be recognized and rejected), and also because it allows inferior artists to gain apparent effects by a process of powerful suggestion rather than of artistic expression. This is made easier when, as is now the case, audiences are disproportionately immature as individuals (as a breakdown of attendance figures into age-groups will show). I do not want to underestimate the problem, and I think in fact we do not yet really know enough about it to come to any definite conclusions.

But it is possible, I think, to see the issue as one in which a very powerful dramatic medium (containing the degree of creating illusion on which, technically, all art depends) has, for reasons that bear on the state of society as a whole, and not merely on the medium itself, been widely abused. There have, after all, been similar abuses of the novel, of the play, and of rhetoric. The argument points, I think, at this stage, to the maximum effort to promote films which are themselves emotionally disciplined. Whether the conditions of film-watching will finally hinder their communication can only be tested when this has, on a reasonable scale, been done.

The issue returns, in fact, in my view, to the film-maker; and here too, the fact that he must work without an audience is relevant. Can serious drama be made without a participating audience; or is the absence of an audience likely to promote, at worst, indulgence, at best, a very limited achievement? Certainly, there are moments in the theatre where an audience becomes, as it were, dramatically conscious, with an unforgettable richness of shared feeling. But, in fact, the effect of an audience on the *creation* of a work (a point which is often confused with its communication) has almost certainly been overstressed. The point has been further confused by the habits of naturalism, and by the disintegrated romantic drama behind it. A dramatist, traditionally, has created his work alone; aware of a potential audience, but not in direct contact with it. When it comes to performance, it is in fact perfectly possible for actors to conceive their vital relation to that work, and again, as with the dramatist, only potentially to an audience. Some actors will deny this; largely, I think, because they have been so often forced to come to performance with a work, which, for reasons which I shall come to discuss, is not yet complete; the final creation *takes place* – rather than *is communicated* – on the stage.

When the actor is being asked to do too much, he may in fact conceive a more vital relation with the audience than with the work. But, on the other hand – and here I am encouraged by the recent statements of many actors – where a satisfactory relation *to the work* can be conceived, a performance without an audience can be wholly satisfying and vital.[1] This happens in rehearsals, where it is not unusual for some best performances to be given; and the same condition is applicable to the making of a film, given the kind of integrity in its conception which this book is proposing. I think the greatest acting performance I have seen, on screen or stage, was that of Falconetti in Dreyer's *Jeanne d'Arc*; in any event, this would rank with great performances anywhere. And that depended, not on a relation to an audience, but on an acceptance of the discipline of the total emotion which Dreyer had conceived. This may be a special case, but there have been a number of other great performances in films, and there is, I think, enough general evidence to show that the inspiration to great performance can (as I would suggest it ideally should) arise from the actor's response to the whole emotion of the work. And if this is the case, the conditions of achievement in film are available, whatever local (and removable) disabilities may have been allowed to obscure the opportunity.

The point about the new kind of relation with an audience, which the technical property of film makes necessary, need not, then, be decisive. The relation of performers to audiences, and the audience's expectations, have varied widely in the whole dramatic tradition; the larger continuity overrides the particular variation of the cinema. And because the recognition of continuity is creatively important, I hold to the argument that film, in its main uses, is dramatic in terms of its elements of performance and imitation; and that it is capable of producing works in the categories of tragedy, comedy, farce, or in any of the new categories which the variations of dramatic history have produced. This is not of course to deny that film, as a particular dramatic medium, has its own conditions, and can employ, within them, a number of possible conventions . . . but it is first necessary, as a basis for that discussion, to consider the general problem of conventions, and of their relation to conditions of performance.

The ordinary dictionary senses of *convention* provide a useful starting point. Thus, *convention* is the act of coming together; an assembly; union; coalition, specially of representatives for some definite purpose; an agreement previous to a definitive treaty; a custom. *Conventional*, similarly, is: settled by stipulation or by tacit consent; as sanctioned and currently accepted by tacit agreement; agreeable to accepted standards; agreeable to contract. As one goes through these senses, and through those of the various derived words, one realizes an ambiguity which is important both because it indicates a possible source of confusion, which requires discussion, and because it indicates an important point of entry for an analysis of the place of conventions in drama.

The possible source of confusion is the fact that convention covers both *tacit consent* and *accepted standards*, and it is easy to see that the latter has often been understood as a set of formal rules. Thus, it is common in adverse comment to say that a work is just *conventional*; *a familiar routine; old stuff; the mixture as before.* We use the word in the same way in adverse comment on people and actions that we find dull, or narrow, or old-fashioned, or unoriginal, or unreceptive to new ideas. To explain the development of *conventional* as an adverse term in criticism would require an excursus that is not relevant here. Briefly, it is the result of the controversy that was part of what we usually call the Romantic Movement, in which the emphasis fell heavily on the right of the artist to disregard, where he saw fit, the rules that had been laid down by others for the practice of his art.[2] It is hardly likely that in this book, in which, so far as film is concerned, we are making a claim to discard certain rules and to invent others, we should fail to sympathize with this feeling, but it seems, nevertheless, unfortunate that *convention* and *conventional* should have been so heavily compromised in this way. An artist only leaves one convention to follow or create another; this, as will be argued, is the whole basis of his communication. But when *conventional* carries the implications of old-fashioned, or narrow, and further, when it is used, as it is now often used, as an easy, and adverse, contrast with *natural*, it is difficult to use the word at all without being misunderstood. Yet it is possible to think of the ambiguity as the means of an important insight; and it is this that will now be discussed.

Convention, as we have seen, covers *tacit agreement* as well as *accepted standards*. In the actual practice of drama, the convention, in any particular case, is simply the terms upon which author, performers and audience agree to meet, so that the performance may be carried on. *Agree to meet*, of course, is by no means always a formal or definite process; much more usually, in any art, the consent is largely customary, and often indeed it is virtually unconscious.

This can be seen most readily in the conventions of one's own period. In a naturalist play, for example, the convention is that the speech and action should as closely as possible appear to be those of everyday life; but few who watch such a play realize that this is a convention: to the majority it is merely "what a play is like", "the sort of thing a play tries to do". But, in fact, it is a very remarkable convention that actors should represent people behaving naturally, and usually privately, before a large audience, while all the time maintaining the illusion that, as characters, these persons are unaware of the audience's presence. The most desperate private confession, or the most dangerous conspiracy, can be played out on the stage, in full view and hearing of a thousand people; yet it will not occur to either actors or audience that this is in any way strange, because all, by the tacit consent of custom, have accepted this kind of procedure as a convention.

Not long ago, and perhaps still in some places, it was, however, thought very strange if a character spoke in soliloquy, whether this was thought of as "thinking aloud" or "directly addressing the audience". The complaint would be that this was "artificial", or "not true to life", or even "undramatic"; yet it is surely as natural, and as "true to life", when one is on a stage before a thousand people, to address them, as to pretend to carry on as if they were not there. As for the soliloquy being "undramatic", this is the kind of conditional statement, elevated into a "law", which we have already discussed; since it is well known that the soliloquy, in many periods, has been a normally accepted part of the dramatic procedure.

The various conventions which have been used in drama are too numerous to list. A two-day battle between considerable armies may be represented by the passage of a few soldiers in a few brief scenes, lasting perhaps no more than five minutes. The last hour of a man's life may be played out on a stage, with deliberate emphasis on the tension of waiting, and yet the dramatic "hour" may be no more than five or six minutes. A man may walk on to a bare stage, hung only by curtains, and from what he says we will agree that he is in Gloucestershire, or Illyria, or on a mythical island. He can be a Roman general, speaking to us in English blank verse from a wooden step that we take to be a rostrum in the Forum of Rome. He can be a ghost or a devil or a god, and yet drink, answer the telephone, or be wound off the stage by a crane. He can put on a grey cloak, and we will agree that he is invisible, though we continue to see him. He can speak to us, acknowledging his most private thoughts, and we will agree that while we hear him from the back of the gallery, he cannot be heard by a man a few feet away from him, or waiting in the wings. With the slightest of indications, we will accept that the events we watch are occurring four thousand years before Christ, or in the Middle Ages, or in a flat in Paris on the same night as we are in a theatre in Manchester. The men whom we see as inspector and criminal we recognize as having seen last week as criminal and inspector, or as butler and peer, but we do not challenge them. We accept; we agree; these are the conventions.

Since the use of conventions of this kind is inherent in the process of drama, it may at first seem surprising that when the basic convention, that of acted performance, has been accepted, there should be any difficulty in particular instances. Yet it is obvious that such difficulties are acute and recurrent. We will agree that the person on the stage is a spirit, and that, quite unaware of our intent presence, he is talking privately to his widow, in the year 1827; but if the widow attempts to address us in an aside, we shall be at once uneasy. We will agree that a murderer may hide behind a door (where we can still see him), and that he may look down, with an expression of agony, at his hands (which we at once agree are stained with innocent blood); but if he should come forward to the front of the stage, and in twenty lines of verse, or in recitative or song, or in dance, express (if more fully and more intensely) the same emotion, we at once, or many of us, feel uneasy, and are likely to say afterwards that it was "unreal". We may even, if we accept the phrases of the journeymen, conclude that the play was highbrow, or surrealist, or pretentious (an increasingly common word among those whose professional pretension is normality). And while we may be able to reject this kind of simplification, we shall not be able, merely by taking thought, to create an alternative convention.

This, indeed, is the central difficulty; for while I think it is true that the average audience is more open-minded than the average entrepreneur, so that the basis for change and development in convention always potentially exists, it is only academically true that a dramatist may use any convention that suits his material and intention. A convention, in the simplest sense, is only a method, a technical piece of machinery, which facilitates the performance. But methods change, and techniques change, and while, say, a chorus of dancers, or the cloak of invisibility, or a sung soliloquy, are known dramatic methods, they cannot be satisfactorily used unless, at the time of a performance, they are more than methods; unless, in fact, they are conventions. Dramatist, actors and audience must be able to agree that the particular method to be employed is acceptable; and, in the nature of the case, an important part of this agreement must usually *precede* the performance, so that what is to be done may be accepted without damaging friction.

Ultimately, however, we judge a convention, not by its abstract usefulness, and not by referring it to some ultimate criterion of probability, but rather by what it manages, in an actual work of art, to get done. If in fact it were not historically true that certain works have been able, by their own strength, to modify old conventions and to introduce new ones, we should have had no change at all, short of some absolutist decree. We accept, with a common and easy sentiment, such triumphs of the past. We read, sympathetically, the biographies of an Ibsen or a Stanislavsky. But the sympathy is merely sentimental unless it can be made active, and creative, at our own point in time.

Ibsen and Stanislavsky have won, as Æschylus won when he introduced the second actor, or Shakespeare when he transformed the Tragedy of Blood. Yet the history of art is not one of continual evolution into higher and better forms; there is debasement as well as refinement, and a novelty, even a transformation, may as well be bad as good. It would be absurd to imagine that our own contemporary segment from the great arc of dramatic possibility is, because the latest, necessarily the best. Yet, because of the nature of convention, because of the dependence of any dramatic method upon this particular type of agreement, it is not possible, in any age, to go very far from the segment which is that age's living tradition, or to begin from anywhere but within or on its borders.

Thus we have the necessity of tradition – convention as tacit consent – and at times the equal necessity of experiment, from the development of new modes of feeling, and from the perception of new or rediscovered technical means – convention as dramatic method. It is to the interplay of these two senses of convention that we must now turn.

If we think of a dramatic convention as a technical means in an acted performance, it is clear that there is no absolute reason why any means should not be employed, and judged by its dramatic result. But we have seen that, in practice, this absolute freedom of choice is not available: a dramatist must win the consent of his audience to any particular means that he wishes to employ, and while he may often be able to do this in the course of a work itself, by the power of the effect which the method makes possible, he cannot entirely rely on this, for even if the audience is sympathetic, too great a consciousness of the novelty or strangeness of the means may as effectively hamper the full communication of a play as would open hostility. It seems probable, when one looks back into the history of drama, that the effective changes took place when there was already a latent willingness to accept them, at least among certain groups in society, from whom the artist drew his support. But while it is possible to see this in retrospect, it could never have been easy, and is not easy now, to see such a situation with sufficient clarity in the flux of present experience. It may be possible, eventually, so to understand the relation of particular conventions to the life of the time in which they flourished, that a reasonable prediction of what is necessary in a present situation may be made and argued. I do not think any such understanding at present exists, but certain points seem to me to be sufficiently grounded to be put forward as a tentative argument.

In principle, it seems clear that the dramatic conventions of any given period are fundamentally related to the structure of feeling in that period. I use the phrase *structure of feeling* because it seems to me more accurate, in this context, than *ideas* or *general life*. All the products of a community in a given period are, we now commonly believe, essentially related, although in practice, and in detail, this is not always easy to see. In the study of a period, we may be able to reconstruct, with more or less accuracy, the material life, the general social organization, and, to a large extent, the dominant ideas. It is not necessary to discuss here which, if any, of these aspects is, in the whole complex, determining; an important institution like the drama will, in all probability, take its colour in varying degrees from them all. But while we may, in the study of a past period, separate out particular aspects of life, and treat them as if they were self-contained, it is obvious that this is only how they may be studied, not how they were experienced. We examine each element as a precipitate, but in the living experience of the time every element was in solution, an inseparable part of a complex whole. And it seems to be true, from the nature of art, that it is from such a totality that the artist draws; it is in art, primarily, that the effect of the totality, the dominant structure of feeling, is expressed and embodied. To relate a work of art to any part of that observed totality may, in varying degrees, be useful; but it is a common experience, in analysis, to realize that when one has measured the work against the separable parts, there yet remains some element for which there is no external counterpart. This element, I believe, is what I have named the *structure of feeling* of a period, and it is only realizable through experience of the work of art itself, as a whole.

Conventions – the means of expression which find tacit consent – are a vital part of this structure of feeling. As the structure changes, new means are perceived and realized, while old means come to appear empty and artificial. This could be shown, I believe, in the detailed study of a convention like the Greek chorus, which moved from dominance in the drama, through active equal participation, to the position of a mere observer and commentator, and finally, as its distance from the centre of action increased, into a mere interlude, and, finally, a hindrance. Or one might contrast the contained simplicity of pattern of an early miracle play, in which individual character is barely emphasized, with the wholly different and more complex pattern of an Elizabethan tragedy, in which individual character, in a particular sense, can be the primary stress. One can observe the conventions of a religious drama like the Greek, and contrast them with those of modern naturalism, and see the point of beginning of an analysis in the statements of the primary exponents of the latter. Ibsen, for example, writing:

The style ought to conform to the degree of ideality imparted to the whole present-
ment. My play is no tragedy in the ancient acceptation. My desire was to depict human
beings, and therefore I would not make them speak the language of the gods.[3]

Or Strindberg:

The naturalist has abolished guilt by abolishing God...Lady Julie is a modern character...The type is tragic, offering, as it does, the spectacle of a desperate fight with
nature; tragic, too, as a romantic inheritance now being dispersed by naturalism, whose
sole desire is happiness.[4]

Fundamental changes of feeling of this kind, changes in the whole conception
of a human being and of his relations with what is non-human, bring,
necessarily, changes of convention in their wake. It would be outside the
function of this essay to chart the detail of such changes, but it is right to
emphasize the degree of change, because we shall not understand the problem
of convention if we think of it as a matter of casual, and minor, technical
choice. All changes in the methods of an art like the drama are related,
essentially, to changes in man's radical structure of feeling. The recognition
of this truth must be our control in any immediate discussion. For it is never a
case of an artist selecting his technical means from the huge variety of the
historical record. If we understand the word *convention*, we realize that the
method must find its counterpart in the present structure of feeling, and be
agreed there. Only in this way can it be more than a device, and become a
convention.

   Convention, however, implies not only tacit consent but accepted standard,
and it is here, in the flux of the present, that the most serious difficulty arises.
For if it is true that the conventions of an art, in any period, correspond,
essentially, to the structure of feeling in that period, it is possible to argue that,
at any given time, the existing conventions are necessarily right, and that those
who criticize them, or seek to change them, are merely kicking against the
pricks. It is always important to bear this in mind, but to understand the matter
more closely we must look again at convention as an accepted standard.

   A new convention, like that of naturalism, for example, will become established because there are changes in the structure of feeling which demand
expression, and which the most creative artists will eventually realize in their
work. But by many these changes will be resisted, and bitterly attacked, in the
name of accepted standards. What is happening in a situation of this kind is the
result of the ways in which the structure of feeling is changing. Awareness of
such changes will, at first, be confined to a few minds only; and, among artists,
it may not be awareness in the sense of an intellectual understanding of such

change, but may express itself as an apparently purely personal originality. Soon, however, such work will begin to gain assent, and, as in the case of naturalism, attain the momentum of a movement. The new work will not only make explicit the changes in feeling, but will in itself promote and affect them. Resistance will continue, but in the normal course of events will slowly diminish. The new work will itself become the type. But while at first it was engaged in attacking "conventions" − that is to say, the methods which were supported by the former structure of feeling − it will, as it becomes established, be creating new "conventions", methods which come to be seen as valid and fruitful. It was attacking conventions as accepted standards, and, sometimes without consciously realizing that it was doing so, creating new conventions by tacit consent.

Now, in the case of any art, a convention, as a technical method, finds normally a material counterpart: in the case of drama, a certain type of theatre, a particular form of stage, particular methods of acting. These will become the accepted standards, but when changes occur, what was once an adequate method may become a hindrance; yet because it materially exists, it cannot be merely wished away. A dramatist may establish new conventions in his written play, but he is almost always likely to find that his play can only be performed in the theatre, on the stage, and with the methods of acting, which are the product of the conventions his play is attempting to replace.

A good example of what then occurs may be seen in the history of Chekhov's play *The Seagull*, which was a fiasco when produced by Karpov at the Alexandrinsky Theatre in 1896, according to the then conventional methods of production, but a triumph when, through the imaginative insight of Stanislavsky, new conventions of production were made available for the Moscow Art Theatre production in 1898. That a mere two years elapsed between the fiasco and the triumph indicates that this period was in fact the critical one for change; in less fortunate circumstances the interval might have been a generation.

When we examine the actual process of change of conventions, and in particular remember the fact that the old conventions will always have a solid and powerful material establishment, it will not seem surprising that even where the change can be seen, in retrospect, as inevitable, it was not established without considerable friction and even bitterness. In the changes of the past, however, we always have the reassurance of knowing how the battle finally went; we know whose is the victory, and we come down, naturally enough, on the side of the winning battalions. In the present, no such reassurance is available, and it is common to find that those who have taken the most vicarious pleasure form former victories are among the most bitter and complacent opponents of a newly proposed change. The battle has been won now;

why start all that fighting again? For that of course is the paradox of the situation: that the newly established methods become in their turn the "conventions", now no longer merely a hard-won consent, but the accepted standard, the truth which no reasonable person would doubt. [...]

The methods of dramatic naturalism, as employed by Chekhov and Stanislavsky, are, in the proper sense, conventions; that is to say, methods devised to realize a new way of feeling, to which sufficient assent was gained. We may now find these conventions unsatisfactory, but we will at least recognize them as authentic. The general dogma of naturalism, however, is in a very different case: we find it applied indiscriminately, in new plays, to orthodox religious drama, to melodramas of an essentially nineteenth-century type, to fantasies, and even (except for a few admirable survivors of an older tradition) to farce. We see, further, its methods being employed in new productions of older and very different forms of drama; any season of Shakespearean performances will provide adequate evidence.

If we are to think clearly about our own conventions, we must always bear in mind the three senses of naturalism which I have distinguished – a particular attitude to experience; a particular convention, as in Stanislavsky, of realizing "the inner, hidden psychological movement"; and, finally, that which we have just examined, which may properly be called the *naturalist habit*. These distinctions are particularly important when we are considering naturalism in film. It seems to me that there has been an important refinement of the art of film by the use of naturalism of the second (Stanislavsky) type. Its high point was the work of Pudovkin in the Russian cinema of the twenties. A film like *Mother* is an example of the rendering of an "inner, hidden psychological movement", by means which Pudovkin directly inherited from Stanislavsky, on whom, because of the greater flexibility of his medium, he may even be said to have improved. There have been other important works in this tradition, in France (*La Bête Humaine*), in Italy (*Bicycle Thieves*), in America (*Panic in the Streets*), and, of course, in England. I do not myself believe that this kind of film is finally satisfactory, and I think, incidentally, that the early Russian films of this kind have not, *in this mode*, been surpassed. But the tradition is serious and important, and it is perhaps understandable that to many film-makers it seems to be the vital method for new creative work.

My own view, for reasons that I shall explain, is that they are mistaken; but I do not want to appear to be denying the genuine seriousness of that kind of approach. It is from film-makers and critics who believe in this method that the important opposition to the crude "spectacular" film has come; and at a time when such crude and debasing works still occupy our cinemas, that kind of opposition is important. But I must insist on the distinction of this tradition from work of a very different kind, which at first sight closely resembles it. My essential point has already been made: that there is a vital difference between the film which is using naturalistic conventions to express an "inner, hidden psychological movement", and, on the other hand, the film in which a relatively crude, "routine" conception of experience is given *apparent* actuality by the convincing representation of *external* details. Any competent film-maker can, nowadays, reproduce such an external actuality – a house, a street, a general way of living, the appearance of a certain kind of person; but the test always is, in this essential distinction of types of naturalism which I am urging, whether the created actuality can be seen to have a necessary and genuinely revealing relation to the inner emotional movement; or whether, as I think is so in the majority of cases, we are offered what I would call a "false actuality", in which the convincingness of the external detail is operating as a substitute for a convincing actuality of considered and genuine feeling.

Obviously, in each particular case, a critical judgment would require detailed analysis and demonstration; and important distinctions might even have to be drawn within the same film. It is only, for example, in certain sequences of *La Bête Humaine*, or *Panic in the Streets*, that I find a genuine naturalism; many other sequences in them appear to me to be false, in the sense I have described. And I find the "actuality" of *The Third Man* or *Brief Encounter* almost wholly external. But I am concerned here, less to suggest certain particular judgments, than to establish what I believe to be a useful, and indeed, essential, principle. For unless we see that "naturalism" and "realism", where they are not related to and determined by a particular and convincing kind of feeling, are in themselves only varieties of "spectacle" pursued for its own sake, we shall not only confuse works that are good and bad, but, quite certainly, we shall fail to understand the true nature of our present difficulties.

Naturalism, as understood and practised by Stanislavsky, by Chekhov, or by Pudovkin, was always, in fact, a minority movement; confused, for the reasons I have indicated, with a larger, and apparently similar, movement, which lacked its serious determining principles. This ought to be recognized, but it is not a recognition on which we can rest. For, even when we have acknowledged its seriousness, we must, it seems to me, realize that the limitations of even the best naturalism have now become too apparent to be overlooked. [...]

All the experiments in the rejection of naturalism are, then, to be welcomed; but the decisive general advance can hardly be made until the separately promising methods have been taken into the whole form of a dramatic work, and given a unity there. What has been happening is that changes in feeling have forced the modification of particular methods, so that we see that new conventions are available; but because the pressure of the naturalist habit is still so formidable and so continuous there has been a tendency to try to absorb the new conventions, as interesting novelties, while retaining the old general assumptions. The new conventions are then merely a mitigation of naturalism, rather than a full alternative to it.

I have discussed all these points, as they relate to the drama as a whole, in the final chapter of *Drama in Performance*, where a more detailed demonstration was possible.[5] I have called the idea of writing for speech and movement and design, as parts of a controlled dramatic form, the idea of *total expression*. It is this idea, I believe, which naturalism, following on the previous disintegration of the romantic drama, has not allowed us to see. A play written from this idea of total expression contains, in its essential conception, the total performance which is necessary to communicate it in the theatre. That is to say, not only the speech, but also the movement and design, have been devised by the dramatist, in terms of his understanding of the appropriate conventions of actors and designers, so that the written play contains everything that is to be performed; the performance itself is the communication of this. It was towards this point, I think, that the drama had to work, once the dissatisfaction of dramatists with the "incomplete text" ("the words but a pale reflection", etc.) had become clear. Its establishment in practice is, I feel certain, inevitable, although the immediate difficulties are considerable. What I want now to indicate is the bearing of the idea on film, where the opportunities for its realization are marked.

The moving-picture camera itself is, I think, a most effective agent for the kind of controlled total effect which I have been urging. For any film is a total performance, not only in the sense that it is inseparable from the work being performed (as, essentially, in my view, the best drama has to be inseparable), but also in that every element in its performance is, or is capable of being, under the direct control of the original conception. To write adequately for film is, essentially, to write for speech, movement and design, as necessarily related parts of a whole; and the control of the pen over the total conception ought to become, directly, the control of the camera. I do not say that this cannot be done in the theatre – it is a question of methods of production, and of our understanding of the nature of performance. But, for a variety of reasons, the control is in some ways easier to conceive in film: the fact that a film is a finished performance – recorded and final – is perhaps the most important factor.

The majority tradition in the film, as in the theatre, has been the naturalist *habit*, with an understandably large emphasis on spectacle. The genuine use of a naturalist *convention* has, in a minority of films, been an important refining element in the tradition. In the rejection of naturalism, there has been a clear line of experiment, as fruitful, in some ways, as the corresponding movement in the theatre. There has never, of course, in this experimental work, been the same emphasis on language as in the general experiments – for example, the verse drama. Indeed, the outstanding failure of the film, as a whole form, has been its use of dramatic speech. For although, since the coming of sound, the majority of films have depended to an excessive degree on dialogue, which has allowed them to neglect significant movement and design, nearly all this dialogue, even in films which have been visually interesting, has been of the familiar naturalist kind – the tentative slur of approximation rather than the precise, patterned intensity of which dramatic speech is capable. Where it has not been this, it has been either sentimental rhetoric, or else mere spoken stage directions – things said to explain the situation and its development.

The kind of film which has most nearly realized the ideal of a wholly conceived drama, in which action, movement and design bear a continuous and necessary vital relationship, is the German expressionist film of the twenties. I believe this form was limited, as art, by the fact that its structure of feeling, which adequate conventions were found to express, was a very special case, which needed unusual psychological conditions in the audience for its full communication. As a principle, however, the integration of these films is notable. Yet it has always seemed to me significant that the most successful examples were in the *silent* film. For, if one looks at expressionist drama as a whole, one sees a very exciting new convention of movement and design, which has been achieved, however, at the cost of a radical neglect of speech. The words spoken in the normal expressionist play are (perhaps as a direct result of the theory; at least so some of its proponents argued) fragmentary, disjointed, typified – the cry, the exclamation, the slogan, rather than the full dramatic word. And of course that kind of use of words could be realized, without much loss, in the sub-titles of a silent film. There are certainly other reasons why there have been hardly any good expressionist films in sound, but it is clear that the use of sound, particularly for dramatic speech, would have presented the expressionists with very difficult problems, which might have ruined such conventional integration as they had achieved.

I have said that to write adequately for film is to write for speech, movement and design, but this point can be misunderstood if it is not considered in the context of the principle of integration to which I referred it. For example, it may have been remarked that when I was discussing the naturalist play and the novel I came to the point where a character, by the rules of probability, could say or do practically nothing, although that was the moment of crisis. The naturalist play, I argued, could not really get past such moments, whereas the novel evidently could: "words and pictures formed in her mind". The phrase, obviously, should have suggested the film, because of course it is clear that, at such a moment, the film would have a greater range than the play (it could, for example, associate certain images and scenes), and might even, by the use of a narrator's voice, equal the capacity of the novel in comment, analysis, description of submerged feeling, and so on. Except in fairly obvious descriptive ways, this latter method has barely been used; the former – associated images – has of course been used widely, but remains, essentially, the kind of separate action which Stanislavsky made famous.

Now I think the good naturalist film could be made much better, in many cases, by the use of such a narrative convention, aiming not merely at description but also at analysis and commentary. It is this faculty, I suppose, which has led some writers to call the film a kind of novel. Now the formal distinction is clear: the novel remains wholly verbal, the film, even with the narrative voice added, is performance and imitation – that is to say, drama. But this kind of distinction is less important than the point which arises when the convention of a narrating voice is considered in detail. The point will illustrate very well what I mean by integration. If such a "narration" is employed as a thing in itself, communicating matters which the acted performance can not, then, while it may be an important refinement of the naturalist film, it can hardly promote any dramatic integration. Used according to the principle of integration, such a voice would be *part of* the action; not a side-element. That is to say, it would follow and bear a necessary relation to the movement and design, which could then hardly be naturalist, for the movement and design would have to be expressing what the voice is also expressing, or else (as indeed often happens) they would be merely "accompanying visuals".

This example illustrates the general principle which I believe must govern the making of the dramatic film: the principle of integrated expression and performance, in which each of the elements being used – speech, music, movement, design – bears a controlled, necessary and direct relation, at the moment of expression, to any other that is being then used. All will bear towards a single end, which is the single conception, expressed through various directly interrelating means.

My final point is a general one, indicating the context of the present proposals. I have said that naturalism was a response to changes in the structure of feeling, which, in the event, it could not wholly express. The structure of feeling, as I have been calling it, lies deeply embedded in our lives; it cannot be merely extracted and summarized; it is perhaps only in art – and this is the importance of art – that it can be realized, and communicated, as a whole experience.

The apparent motive of the arguments in this book is technical; a response to difficulties in a particular medium, and a search for different conventions. A technical emphasis is, therefore, inevitable. But if what I have said about the full meaning of convention is accepted, the technical enquiry may be seen as the necessary form of the larger change: an enquiry into means of communicating that form of experience which is the origin of the problem, and the source of this kind of new approach. If the new conventions can be gained, it will be the communicated experience that finally matters, for us and for the audience. But the artist has not only to feel; he must, to the extent that he is an artist, find ways of realizing and communicating, wholly and definitively, the moving experience. Only when he has found such ways can the personal vision be confirmed in the public view.

Notes

1   Cf.: "A question that is put with not insignificant monotony to players who act for both stage and screen – it follows the monotonous and less significant question of, "Which do you prefer?" – is usually, "Don't you miss the audience?" My own answer is usually, "No: why should I? I do not miss the audience at rehearsals when the character is being created, and some of the most exciting moments of creative acting take place at rehearsals." I confess that is an evasive answer, for the simple, logical retort to it would be, "Surely you do not wish to go on rehearsing for ever?" My reply to this is an emphatic, "Certainly not". But it is a fallacy to believe . . . that the audience is ipso facto of assistance to the actor. It can betray him into seeking easy ways to please, repeating blandishments which he knows have been previously successful. It can force him to seek to dominate their mood, as he is frequently obliged to do, with force or tricks which are alien to the part he is playing. It can, in short, make him a flatterer or a fighting madman. "To please the ears of the groundling" has become "to play to the gallery".
"I do not suggest that an actor should be a Corialanus, who, through his pride in his own integrity, should never speak the soft word that will win the heart. But I do say that though the audience may bring a stronger pressure on him than either his author, his producer or his own artistic conscience, it should never force him to be faithless to these three." (Michael Redgrave: *The Actor's Ways and Means*; Heinemann, 1953; pp. 33–34.)
2   I have discussed this, and related questions, more fully in my essay The Idea of Culture, in *Essays in Criticism*; Basil Blackwell, Oxford; Vol III, No 3, July 1953; pp. 239–266.
3   Letter to Edmund Gosse, quoted in *Archer's Introduction to Emperor and Galilean* (Collected Works, Heinemann, Vol. V).
4   Preface to Lady Julie, in *Lucky Peter's Travels and other Plays*; Cape, 1930; p. 174.
5   *Drama in Performance*; Muller, 1954.

3

The Masses

From Raymond Williams (1958) Culture and Society *London: Chatto and Windus*

The history of the idea of culture is a record of our reactions, in thought and feeling, to the changed conditions of our common life. Our meaning of culture is a response to the events which our meanings of industry and democracy most evidently define. But the conditions were created and have been modified by men. Record of the events lies elsewhere, in our general history. The history of the idea of culture is a record of our meanings and our definitions, but these, in turn, are only to be understood within the context of our actions.

The idea of culture is a general reaction to a general and major change in the conditions of our common life. Its basic element is its effort at total qualitative assessment. The change in the whole form of our common life produced, as a necessary reaction, an emphasis on attention to this whole form. Particular change will modify an habitual discipline, shift an habitual action. General change, when it has worked itself clear, drives us back on our general designs, which we have to learn to look at again, and as a whole. The working-out of the idea of culture is a slow reach again for control.

Yet the new conditions, which men have been striving to understand, were neither uniform nor static. On the contrary, they have, from the beginning, contained extreme diversity of situation, in a high and moving tension. The idea of culture describes our common inquiry, but our conclusions are diverse, as our starting points were diverse. The word, culture, cannot automatically be pressed into service as any kind of social or personal directive. Its emergence, in its modern meanings, marks the effort at total qualitative assessment, but what it indicates is a process, not a conclusion. The arguments which can be grouped under its heading do not point to any inevitable action or affiliation. They define, in a common field, approaches and conclusions. It is left to us to decide which, if any, we shall take up, that will not turn in our hands.

In each of the three major issues, those of Industry, of Democracy and of Art, there have been three main phases of opinion. In industry, there was the first rejection, alike of machine-production and of the social relations embodied in the factory system. This was succeeded by a phase of growing sentiment against the machine as such, in isolation. Thirdly, in our own period, machine production came to be accepted, and major emphasis transferred to the problem of social relations within an industrial system of production.

In the question of democracy, the first phase was one of concern at the threat to minority values with the coming of popular supremacy: a concern which was emphasized by general suspicion of the power of the new masses. This, in turn, was succeeded by a quite different tendency, in which emphasis fell on the idea of community, of organic society, as against the dominant individualistic ethic and practice. Thirdly, in our own century, the fears of the first phase were strongly renewed, in the particular context of what came to be called mass democracy in the new world of mass communications.

In the question of art, the first emphasis fell, not only on the independent value of art, but on the importance to the common life of the qualities which it embodied. The contingent element of defiant exile passed into the second phase, in which the stress fell on art as a value in itself, with at times an open separation of this value from common life. Thirdly, emphasis came to be placed on a deliberate effort towards the reintegration of art with the common life of society: an effort which centred around the word 'communication'.

In these three questions I have listed the phases of opinion in the order in which they appeared, but of course opinion is persistent, and whether in relation to industry, to democracy or to art, each of the three phases could easily be represented from the opinions of our own day. Yet it is possible in retrospect to see three main periods, within each of which a distinct emphasis is paramount. In the first period, from about 1790 to 1870, we find the long effort to compose a general attitude towards the new forces of industrialism and democracy; it is in this period that the major analysis is undertaken and the major opinions and descriptions emerge. Then, from about 1870 to 1914, there is a breaking-down into narrower fronts, marked by a particular specialism in attitudes to art, and, in the general field, by a preoccupation with direct politics. After 1914 these definitions continue, but there is a growing preoccupation, approaching a climax after 1945, with the issues raised not only by the inherited problems but by new problems arising from the development of mass media of communication and the general growth of large-scale organizations.

A great deal of what has been written in each of these three periods retains its relevance and importance. In particular, it is impossible to over-emphasize our debt to the first great critical period which gave us, in relation to these problems, the greater part of our language and manner of approach. From all the periods, indeed, certain decisive statements stand. Yet even as we learn, we realize that the world we see through such eyes is not, although it resembles, our world. What we receive from the tradition is a set of meanings, but not all of these will hold their significance if, as we must, we return them to immediate experience. I have tried to make this return, and I will set down the variations and new definitions that have followed from this, as a personal conclusion.

Mass and Masses

We now regularly use both the idea of 'the masses', and the consequent ideas of 'mass-civilization', 'mass-democracy', 'mass-communication' and others. Here, I think, lies a central and very difficult issue which more than any other needs revision.

Masses was a new word for mob, and it is a very significant word. It seems probable that three social tendencies joined to confirm its meaning. First, there was the concentration of population in the industrial towns, a physical massing of persons which the great increase in total population accentuated, and which has continued with continuing urbanization. Second, there was the concentration of workers into factories: again, a physical massing, made necessary by machine-production; also, a social massing, in the work-relations made necessary by the development of large-scale collective production. Third, there was the consequent development of an organized and self-organizing working class: a social and political massing. The masses, in practice, have been any of these particular aggregates, and because the tendencies have been interrelated, it has been possible to use the term with a certain unity. And then, on the basis of each tendency, the derived ideas have arisen: from urbanization, the mass meeting; from the factory, in part in relation to the workers, but mainly in relation to the things made, mass-production; from the working class, mass-action. Yet, masses was a new word for mob, and the traditional characteristics of the mob were retained in its significance: gullibility, fickleness, herd-prejudice, lowness of taste and habit. The masses, on this evidence, formed the perpetual threat to culture. Mass-thinking, mass-suggestion, mass-prejudice would threaten to swamp considered individual thinking and feeling. Even democracy, which had both a classical and a liberal reputation, would lose its savour in becoming mass-democracy.

Now mass-democracy, to take the latest example, can be either an observation or a prejudice; sometimes, indeed, it is both. As an observation, the term draws attention to certain problems of a modern democratic society which could not have been foreseen by its early partisans. The existence of immensely powerful media of mass-communication is at the heart of these problems, for through these public opinion has been observable moulded and directed, often by questionable means, often for questionable ends. I shall discuss this issue separately, in relation to the new means of communication.

But the term mass-democracy is also, evidently, a prejudice. Democracy, as in England we have interpreted it, is majority rule. The means to this, in representation and freedom of expression, are generally approved. But, with universal suffrage, majority rule will, if we believe in the existence of the masses, be mass-rule. Further, if the masses are, essentially, the mob, democracy will be mob-rule. This will hardly be good government, or a good society; it will, rather, be the rule of lowness or mediocrity. At this point, which it is evidently very satisfying to some thinkers to reach, it is necessary to ask again: who are the masses? In practice, in our society and in this context, they can hardly be other than the working people. But if this is so, it is clear that what is in question is not only gullibility, fickleness, herd-prejudice, or lowness of taste and habit. It is also, from the open record, the declared intention of the working people to alter society, in many of its aspects, in ways which those to whom the franchise was formerly restricted deeply disapprove. It seems to me, when this is considered, that what is being questioned is not mass-democracy, but democracy. If a majority can be achieved in favour of these changes, the democratic criterion is satisfied. But if you disapprove of the changes you can, it seems, avoid open opposition to democracy as such by inventing a new category, mass democracy, which is not such a good thing at all. The submerged opposite is class-democracy, where democracy will merely describe the processes by which a ruling class conducts its business of ruling. Yet democracy, as interpreted in England in this century, does not mean this. So, if change reaches the point where it deeply hurts and cannot be accepted, either democracy must be denied or refuge taken in a new term of opprobrium. It is clear that this confusion of the issue cannot be tolerated. Masses = majority cannot be glibly equated with masses = mob.

A difficulty arises here with the whole concept of masses. Here, most urgently, we have to return the meanings to experience. Our normal public conception of an individual person, for example, is 'the man in the street'. But nobody feels himself to be only the man in the street; we all know much more about ourselves than that. The man in the street is a collective image, but we know, all the time, our own difference from him. It is the same with 'the public', which includes us, but yet is not us. 'Masses' is a little more complicated, yet similar. I do not think of my relatives, friends, neighbours, colleagues, acquaintances, as masses; we none of us can or do. The masses are always the others, whom we don't know, and can't know. Yet now, in our kind of society, we see these others regularly, in their myriad variations; stand, physically, beside them. They are here, and we are here with them. And that we are with them is of course the whole point. To other people, we also are masses. Masses are other people.

There are in fact no masses; there are only ways of seeing people as masses. In an urban industrial society there are many opportunities for such ways of seeing. The point is not to reiterate the objective conditions but to consider, personally and collectively, what these have done to our thinking. The fact is, surely, that a way of seeing other people which has become characteristic of our kind of society, has been capitalized for the purposes of political or cultural exploitation. What we see, neutrally, is other people, many others, people unknown to us. In practice, we mass them, and interpret them, according to some convenient formula. Within its terms, the formula will hold. Yet it is the formula, not the mass, which it is our real business to examine. It may help us to do this if we remember that we ourselves are all the time being massed by others. To the degree that we find the formula inadequate for ourselves, we can wish to extend to others the courtesy of acknowledging the unknown.

I have mentioned the political formula by means of which it seems possible to convert the majority of one's fellow human beings into masses, and thence into something to be hated or feared. I wish now to examine another formula, which underlies the idea of mass-communication.

Mass-communication

The new means of communication represent a major technical advance. The oldest, and still the most important, is printing, which has itself passed through major technical changes, in particular the coming of the steam-driven machine press in 1811, and the development of ever faster cylinder and rotary presses from 1815. The major advances in transport, by road, rail, sea and air, themselves greatly affected printing: at once in the collection of news and in the wide and quick distribution of the printed product. The development of the cable, telegraph and telephone services even more remarkably faciliated the collection of news. Then, as new media, came sound broadcasting, the cinema and television.

We need to look again at these familiar factual elements if we are to be able adequately to review the idea of 'mass-communication' which is their product. In sum, these changes have given us more and normally cheaper books, magazines and newspapers; more bills and posters; broad-casting and television programmes; various kinds of film. It would be difficult, I think, to express a simple and definite judgement of value about all these very varied products, yet they are all things that need to be valued. My question is whether the idea of 'mass-communication' is a useful formula for this.

Two preliminary points are evident: first, that there is a general tendency to confuse the techniques themselves with the uses to which, in a given society, they have been put; second, that, in considering these uses, our argument is commonly selective, at times to an extreme degree.

The techniques, in my view, are at worst neutral. The only substantial objection that is made to them is that they are relatively impersonal, by comparison with older techniques serving the same ends. Where the theatre presented actors, the cinema presents the photographs of actors. Where the meeting presented a man speaking, the wireless presents a voice, or television a voice and a photograph. Points of this kind are relevant, but need to be carefully made. It is not relevant to contrast an evening spent watching television with an evening spent in conversation, although this is often done. There is, I believe, no form of social activity which the use of these techniques has replaced. At most, by adding alternatives, they have allowed altered emphases in the time given to particular activities. But these alterations are obviously conditioned, not only by the techniques, but mainly by the whole circumstances of the common life. The point about impersonality often carries a ludicrous rider. It is supposed, for instance, that it is an objection to listening to wireless talks or discussions that the listener cannot answer the speakers back. But the situation is that of almost any reader; printing, after all, was the first great impersonal medium. It is as easy to send an answer to a broadcast speaker or a newspaper editor as to send one to a contemporary author; both are very much easier than to try to answer Aristotle, Burke or Marx. We fail to realize, in this matter, that much of what we call communication is, necessarily, no more in itself than transmission: that is to say, a one-way sending. Reception and response, which complete communication, depend on other factors than the techniques.

What can be observed as a fact about the development of these techniques is a steady growth of what I propose to call *multiple transmission*. The printed book is the first great model of this, and the other techniques have followed. The new factor, in our own society, is an expansion of the potential audience for such transmissions, so great as to present new kinds of problem. Yet it is clear that it is not to this expansion that we can properly object, at least without

committing ourselves to some rather extraordinary politics. The expansion of
the audience is due to two factors: first, the growth of general education, which
has accompanied the growth of democracy; second, the technical improve-
ments themselves. It is interesting, in the light of the earlier discussion of
'masses', that this expansion should have been interpreted by the phrase
'mass-communication'.

A speaker or writer, addressing a limited audience, is often able to get to
know this audience well enough to feel a directly personal relationship with
them which can affect his mode of address. Once this audience has been
expanded, as with everything from books to televised parlour-games it has
been expanded, this is clearly impossible. It would be rash, however, to assume
that this is necessarily to his and the audience's disadvantage. Certain types of
address, notably serious art, argument and exposition, seem indeed to be
distinguished by a quality of impersonality which enables them frequently to
survive their immediate occasion. How far this ultimate impersonality may be
dependent on a close immediate relationship is in fact very difficult to assess.
But it is always unlikely that any such speaker or writer will use, as a model for
communication, any concept so crude as 'masses'. The idea of mass-communication, it would seem, depends very much more on the intention of the
speaker or writer, than on the particular technique employed.

A speaker or writer who knows, at the time of his address, that it will reach
almost immediately several million persons, is faced with an obviously difficult
problem of interpretation. Yet, whatever the difficulty, a good speaker or
writer will be conscious of his immediate responsibility to the matter being
communicated. He cannot, indeed, feel otherwise, if he is conscious of himself
as the source of a particular transmission. His task is the adequate expression of
this source, whether it be of feeling, opinion or information. He will use
for this expression the common language, to the limit of his particular skill.
That this expression is then given multiple transmission is a next stage, of
which he may well be conscious, but which cannot, of its nature, affect the
source. The difficulties of expressing this source – difficulties of common
experience, convention and language – are certainly always his concern. But
the source cannot in any event be denied, or he denies himself.

Now if, on this perennial problem of communication, we impose the idea of
masses, we radically alter the position. The conception of persons as masses
springs, not from an inability to know them, but from an interpretation of
them according to a formula. Here the question of the intention of the
transmission makes its decisive return. Our formula can be that of the rational
being speaking our language. It can be that of the interested being sharing our
common experience. Or – and it is here that 'masses' will operate – it can be
that of the mob: gullible, fickle, herdlike, low in taste and habit. The formula,

in fact, will proceed from our intention. If our purpose is art, education, the giving of information or opinion, our interpretation will be in terms of the rational and interested being. If, on the other hand, our purpose is manipulation – the persuasion of a large number of people to act, feel, think, know, in certain ways – the convenient formula will be that of the masses.

There is an important distinction to be drawn here between source and agent. A man offering an opinion, a proposal, a feeling, of course normally desires that other persons will accept this, and act or feel in the ways that he defines. Yet such a man may be properly described as a source, in distinction from an agent, whose characteristic is that his expression is subordinated to an undeclared intention. He is an agent, and not a source, because the intention lies elsewhere. In social terms, the agent will normally in fact be a subordinate – of a government, a commercial firm, a newspaper proprietor. Agency, in the simple sense, is necessary in any complex administration. But it is always dangerous unless its function and intention are not only openly declared but commonly approved and controlled. If this is so, the agent becomes a collective source, and he will observe the standards of such expression if what he is required to transmit is such that he can wholly acknowledge and accept it – re-create it in his own person. Where he cannot thus accept it for himself, but allows himself to be persuaded that it is in a fit form for others – presumably inferiors – and that it is his business merely to see that it reaches them effectively, then he is in the bad sense an agent, and what he is doing is inferior to that done by the poorest kind of source. Any practical denial of the relation between conviction and communication, between experience and expression, is morally damaging alike to the individual and to the common language.

Yet it is certainly true, in our society, that many men, many of them intelligent, accept, whether in good or bad faith, so dubious a rôle and activity. The acceptance in bad faith is a matter for the law, although we have not yet gone very far in working out this necessary common control. The acceptance in good faith, on the other hand, is a matter of culture. It would clearly not be possible unless it appeared to be ratified by a conception of society which relegates the majority of its members to mob-status. The idea of the masses is an expression of this conception, and the idea of mass-communication a comment on its functioning. This is the real danger to democracy, not the existence of effective and powerful means of multiple transmission. It is less a product of democracy than its denial, springing from that half-world of feeling in which we are invited to have our being. Where the principle of democracy is accepted, and yet its full and active practice feared, the mind is lulled into an acquiescence, which is yet not so complete that a fitful conscience, a defensive irony, cannot visit it. 'Democracy would be all right,' we can come to say, 'it is indeed what we personally would prefer, if it were not for the actual people.

So, in a good cause if we can find it, in some other if we can not, we will try to get by at a level of communication which our experience and training tell us is inferior. Since the people are as they are, the thing will do.' But it is as well to face the fact that what we are really doing, in such a case, is to cheapen our own experience and to adulterate the common language.

Mass-observation

Yet the people are as they are, the objection is returned. Of course the masses are only other people, yet most other people are, on the evidence, a mob. In principle, we would wish it not to be so; in practice, the evidence is clear.

This is the negative side of the idea of mass-communication. Its evidence is collected under the title of mass-culture, or popular culture. It is important evidence, and much of it is incontrovertible. There remains, however, the question of its interpretation. I have said that our arguments on this matter are normally selective, often to an extreme degree. [. . .]

Communication and Community

Any governing body will seek to implant the 'right' ideas in the minds of those whom it governs, but there is no government in exile. The minds of men are shaped by their whole experience, and the most skilful transmission of material which this experience does not confirm will fail to communicate. Communication is not only transmission; it is also reception and response. In a transitional culture it will be possible for skilful transmission to affect aspects of activity and belief, sometimes decisively. But, confusedly, the whole sum of experience will reassert itself, and inhabit its own world. Mass-communication has had its evident successes, in a social and economic system to which its methods correspond. But it has failed, and will continue to fail, when its transmissions encounter, not a confused uncertainty, but a considered and formulated experience.

Observing this, the practitioners of mass-communication turn to the improvement of what they call their science: that is to say, to scraps of applied psychology and linguistic. It is of the greatest importance to attend to what they are doing, but at the same time any real theory of communication is a theory of community. The techniques of mass-communication will be irrelevant to a genuine theory of communication, to the degree that we judge them to be conditioned, not by a community, but by the lack or incompleteness of a community. It is very difficult to think clearly about communication, because the pattern of our thinking about community is, normally, dominative. We tend, in consequence, if not to be attracted, at least to be preoccupied by dominative techniques. Communication becomes a science of penetrating the mass mind and of registering an impact there. It is not easy to think along different lines.

It is easy to recognize a dominative theory if, for other reasons, we think it to be bad. A theory that a minority should profit by employing a majority in wars of gain is easily rejected. A theory that a minority should profit by employing a mass of wage-slaves is commonly rejected. A theory that a minority should reserve the inheritance of human knowledge to itself, and deny it to the majority, is occasionally rejected. But (we say) nobody, or only a few bad people, can be found to support such theories. We are all democrats now, and such things are unthinkable. As a matter of fact, mass-communication has served and is in some places still serving all the theories I have mentioned. The whole theory of mass-communication depends, essentially, on a minority in some way exploiting a majority. We are not all democrats now.

Yet 'exploiting', of course, is a tendentious word. What of the case where a minority is seeking to educate a majority, for that majority's ultimate good? Such minorities abound, seeking to educate majorities in the virtues of capitalism, communism, culture, contraception. Surely here mass-communication is necessary and urgent, to bring news of the good life, and of the ways to get it, and the dangers to avoid in getting it, to the prejudiced, servile, ignorant and multiplying masses? If workmen are impoverishing themselves and others by restrictive practices; if peasants are starving themselves and others by adhering to outdated ways; if men and women are growing up in ignorance, when so much is known; if families are breeding more children than can be fed: surely, urgently, they must be told this, for their own good?

The objection, as a matter of fact, is not to telling anyone anything. It is a question of how one tells them, and how one would expect to be told oneself. Nor is this merely a matter of politeness, of politeness being the best policy. It is really a matter of how one would be told oneself: telling as an aspect of living; learning as an element of experience. The very failure of so many of the items of transmission which I have listed is not an accident, but the result of a failure to understand communication. The failure is due to an arrogant preoccupation with transmission, which rests on the assumption that the common answers have been found and need only to be applied. But people will (damn them, do you say?) learn only by experience, and this, normally, is uneven and slow. A governing body, in its impatience, will often be able to enforce, by any of a number of kinds of pressure, an apparent conformity. This can on occasion be made substantial by subsequent experience; such a fact is the sharpest temptation to any dominative policy – that events will substantiate what at first people would not accept. As a matter of politics, this is perhaps the most difficult contemporary issue. As a matter of communication, however, such a point only substantiates what has already been said; it will be the experience that teaches. In a society which lacks the experience of democratic practice, a zealous reforming minority will often be forced to take this kind of chance. Yet, even here, it has great dangers; the process of learning depends so much on the conscious need to learn, and such a need is not easily imposed on anyone.

It is clear, on the other hand, that even in contemporary democratic communities the dominative attitude to communication is still paramount. Almost every kind of leader seems to be genuinely afraid of trusting the processes of majority discussion and decision. As a matter of practice this is usually whittled away to the merest formula. For this, the rooted distrust of the majority, who are seen as masses or more politely as the public, is evidently responsible. Democratic theory remains theory, and this practical scepticism breeds the theoretical scepticism which is again becoming, even in our own society, dangerously marked. The consequences are unsatisfactory from most points of view. If people cannot have official democracy, they will have unofficial democracy, in any of its possible forms, from the armed revolt or riot, through the 'unofficial' strike or restriction of labour, to the quietest but most alarming form – a general sullenness and withdrawal of interest. Faced with this set of facts, it is always possible to fall back on the other part of the 'mass' interpretation; to see these symptoms as 'proving' the unfitness of the masses – they *will* riot, they *will* strike, they *will not* take an interest – such is the nature of that brute, the mob. I am arguing, on the contrary, that these characteristic marks of our civilization are not interpretable in this mode; that they are, rather, symptoms of a basic failure in communication. It is possible to say this, and to conclude that the answer lies in educational projects, the feeding of information, or a new publicity drive. But this is to go on thinking of communication as transmission alone, a renewal, perhaps by new means, of the long dominative effort. The point is very difficult to see, in practice, when a group is certain that its case is right and urgent, and that for their own good, and urgently, people must be brought to recognize this.

Yet the uneasy symptoms are, precisely, a response to a dominative organization. In a revolt, in most riots, in many strikes, it is a positive response: the assertion of a different kind of answer. The answer that is then finally adopted will depend on the balance of power. But often it is less formulated than this: a confused, vague reaction against the dominative habit. What I have called sullenness is the obvious example of this. I think it is now a very prevalent reaction to the dominative kinds of mass-communication. People don't, of course, believe all they read in the newspapers, and this, often, is just as well. But for one small area of discriminating reading, almost always the product of training, there is a huge area of general suspicious disbelief, which, while on particular occasions it may be prophylactic, is as a general habit enfeebling. Inertia and apathy have always been employed by the governed as a comparatively safe weapon against their governors. Some governing bodies will accept this, as at least being quiet. But in our own society, because of the way we produce, there is so large a degree of necessary common interest and mutual effort that any widespread withdrawal of interest, any general mood of disbelief, can quite certainly be disastrous. The answer to it, however, does not lie in exhortation. It lies, rather, in conceding the practice of democracy, which alone can substantiate the theory. It lies, in terms of communication, in adopting a different attitude to transmission, one which will ensure that its origins are genuinely multiple, that all the sources have access to the common channels. This is not possible until it is realized that a transmission is always an offering, and that this fact must determine its mood: it is not an attempt to dominate, but to communicate, to achieve reception and response. Active reception, and living response, depend in their turn on an effective community of experience, and their quality, as certainly, depends on a recognition of practical equality. The inequalities of many kinds which still divide our community make effective communication difficult or impossible. We lack a genuinely common experience, save in certain rare and dangerous moments of crisis. What we are paying for this lack, in every kind of currency, is now sufficiently evident. We need a common culture, not for the sake of an abstraction, but because we shall not survive without it.

I have referred to equality, but with some hesitation, for the word is now commonly confusing. The theoretical emphasis on equality, in modern society, is in general an opponent response; it is less a positive goal than an attack on inequality, which has been practically emphasized in exact proportion to equalitarian ideas. The only equality that is important, or indeed conceivable, is equality of being. Inequality in the various aspects of man is inevitable and even welcome; it is the basis of any rich and complex life. The inequality that is evil is inequality which denies the essential equality of being. Such inequality, in any of its forms, in practice rejects, depersonalizes, degrades in grading, other human beings. On such practice a structure of cruelty, exploitation and the crippling of human energy is easily raised. The masses, the dominative mood, the rejection of culture, are its local testaments in human theory.

A common culture is not, at any level, an equal culture. Yet equality of being is always necessary to it, or common experience will not be valued. A common culture can place no absolute restrictions on entry to any of its activities: this is the reality of the claim to equality of opportunity. The claim to such opportunity is of course based on the desire to become unequal, but this can mean any of a number of things. A desired in equality which will in practice deny the essential equality of being, is not compatible with a culture in common. Such inequalities, which cannot be afforded, have continually to be defined, out of the common experience. But there are many inequalities which do not harm this essential equality, and certain of these are necessary, and need to be encouraged. The point becomes practical in examples, and I would suggest these. An inequality in other than personal property – that is to say an inequality in ownership of the means of life and production – may be found intolerable because in practice it may deny the basic processes of equality of being. Inequality in a particular faculty, however, or unequal developments of knowledge, skill and effort, may not deny essential equality: a physicist will be glad to learn from a better physicist, and will not, because he is a good physicist, think himself a better man than a good composer, a good chess-player, a good carpenter, a good runner. Nor, in a common culture, will he think himself a better human being than a child, an old woman, or a cripple, who may lack the criterion (in itself inadequate) of useful service. The kind of respect for oneself and one's work, which is necessary to continue at all, is a different matter from a claim to inequality of being, such as would entitle one to deny or dominate the being of another. The inequalities which are intolerable are those which lead to such denial or domination.

But some activities *are* better than others, the objection is returned. An insistence on equality may be, in practice, a denial of value. I have followed the course of this objection with some care, for it is important indeed. Is not a teacher to dominate a child, so that he may learn? Some facts will be right, and others wrong: the teacher must insist on their distinction, whether or not it is right to dominate. I agree, but most good teaching, in fact, is a transmission of the skills of discrimination alongside statements of the conclusions and judge-ments which have been received, and which have, provisionally, to be used. This offering, alike of a statement to be confirmed, and of the means of decision, is the proper working of general communication. A child will only learn the skills if he practises them; a teacher will only be skilled if he is aware of the process while offering the product. The utmost emphasis on distinctions of value, in all the things that man makes and does, is not an emphasis on inequality of being. It is, rather, a common process of learning, which, indeed, will only ever be undertaken if the primary concession of equality of being, which alone can remove such a process from the dominative sphere, is made. Nobody can raise anybody else's cultural standard. The most that can be done is to transmit the skills, which are not personal but general human property, and at the same time to give open access to all that has been made and done. You cannot stop a child reading a horror comic, or a man reading a strip newspaper, by order (unless you attempt the indignity of physical power over him), or even by argument, by telling him that it is bad. You can only give him the opportunity of learning what has been generally and commonly learned about reading, and see that he has access to all that is available to be read. In the end, and rightly, his choice will in any case be his own. A man's concern for value – for standards, as we say – properly expresses itself in the effort towards a community of experience on which these standards can rest. Further, if his concern for value is something more than dogma, he will hold himself open to learn other values, in the shaping of a new common experience. The refusal of either course is a petulant timidity. If one cannot believe in men, and in their common efforts, it is perhaps only in caricature that one can believe in oneself.

Culture and Which Way of Life?

We live in a transitional society, and the idea of culture, too often, has been identified with one or other of the forces which the transition contains. Culture is the product of the old leisured classes who seek now to defend it against new and destructive forces. Culture is the inheritance of the new rising class, which contains the humanity of the future; this class seeks, now, to free it from its restrictions. We say things like this to each other, and glower. The one good thing, it seems, is that all the contending parties are keen enough on culture to want to be identified with it. But then, we are none of us referees in this; we are all in the game, and playing in one or other direction.

I want to say something about the idea of 'working-class culture', because this seems to me to be a key issue in our own time, and one in which there is a considerable element of misunderstanding. I have indicated already that we cannot fairly or usefully describe the bulk of the material produced by the new means of communication as 'working-class culture'. [. . .] The working class does not become bourgeois by owning the new products, any more than the bourgeois ceases to be bourgeois as the objects he owns change in kind. Those who regret such a development among members of the working class are the victims of a prejudice. An admiration of the 'simple poor' is no new thing, but it has rarely been found, except as a desperate rationalization, among the poor themselves. It is the product either of satiety or of a judgement that the material advantages are purchased at too high a human cost. The first ground must be left to those who are sated; the second, which is more important, is capable of a false transference. If the advantages were 'bourgeois' because they rested on economic exploitation, they do not continue to be 'bourgeois' if they can be assured without such exploitation or by its diminution. The worker's envy of the middle-class man is not a desire to be that man, but to have the same kind of possessions. We all like to think of ourselves as a standard, and I can see that it is genuinely difficult for the English middle class to suppose that the working class is not desperately anxious to become just like itself. I am afraid this must be unlearned. The great majority of English working people want only the middle–class material standard and for the rest want to go on being themselves. One should not be too quick to call this vulgar materialism. It is wholly reasonable to want the means of life in such abundance as is possible. This is the materialism of material provision, to which we are all, quite rightly, attentive. The working people, who have felt themselves long deprived of such means in any adequacy, intend to get them and to keep them if they can. It would need more evidence than this to show that they are becoming vulgar materialists, or that they are becoming 'bourgeois'.

The question then, perhaps, is whether there is any meaning left in 'bourgeois'? Is there any point, indeed, in continuing to think in class terms at all? Is not industrialism, by its own momentum, producing a culture that is best described as classless? Such questions, today, command a significant measure of assent, but again, while drawing support from the crudities of certain kinds of class interpretation, they rest, essentially, on an external attitude alike to culture and to class. If we think of culture, as it is important to do, in terms of a body of intellectual and imaginative work, we can see that with the extension of education the distribution of this culture is becoming more even, and, at the same time, new work is being addressed to a public wider than a single class. Yet a culture is not only a body of intellectual and imaginative work; it is also and essentially a whole way of life. The basis of a distinction between bourgeois and working-class culture is only secondarily in the field of intellectual and imaginative work, and even here it is complicated, as we have seen, by the common elements resting on a common language. The primary distinction is to be sought in the whole way of life, and here, again, we must not confine ourselves to such evidence as housing, dress and modes of leisure. Industrial production tends to produce uniformity in such matters, but the vital distinction lies at a different level. The crucial distinguishing element in English life since the Industrial Revolution is not language, not dress, not leisure – for these indeed will tend to uniformity. The crucial distinction is between alternative ideas of the nature of social relationship.

'Bourgeois' is a significant term because it marks that version of social relationship which we usually call individualism: that is to say, an idea of society as a neutral area within which each individual is free to pursue his own development and his own advantage as a natural right. The course of recent history is marked by a long fighting retreat from this idea in its purest form, and the latest defenders would seem to the earliest to have lost almost the entire field. Yet the interpretation is still dominant: the exertion of social power is thought necessary only in so far as it will protect individuals in this basic right to set their own course. The classical formula of the retreat is that, in

certain defined ways, no individual has a right to harm others. But, characteristically, this harm has been primarily interpreted in relation to the individual
pursuit – no individual has a right to prevent others from doing *this kind of
thing.*

The reforming bourgeois modification of this version of society is the idea of
service, to which I shall return. But both this idea and the individualist idea can
be sharply contrasted with the idea that we properly associate with the working
class: an idea which, whether it is called communism, socialism or cooperation,
regards society neither as neutral nor as protective, but as the positive means for
all kinds of development, including individual development. Development and
advantage are not individually but commonly interpreted. The provision of the
means of life will, alike in production and distribution, be collective and
mutual. Improvement is sought, not in the opportunity to escape from one's
class, or to make a career, but in the general and controlled advance of all. The
human fund is regarded as in all respects common, and freedom of access to it
as a right constituted by one's humanity; yet such access, in whatever kind, is
common or it is nothing. Not the individual, but the whole society, will move.

The distinction between these versions of society has been blurred by two
factors: the idea of service, which is the great achievement of the Victorian
middle class, and is deeply inherited by its successors; and the complication of
the working- class idea by the fact that England's position as an imperial power
has tended to limit the sense of community to national (and, in the context,
imperialist) lines. Further, the versions are blurred by a misunderstanding of the
nature of class. The contending ideas, and the actions which follow from them,
are the property of that part of a group of people, similarly circumstanced,
which has become conscious of its position and of its own attitude to this
position. Class feeling is a mode, rather than a uniform possession of all the
individuals who might, objectively, be assigned to that class. When we speak,
for instance, of a working-class idea, we do not mean that all working people
possess it, or even approve of it. We mean, rather, that this is the essential idea
embodied in the organizations and institutions which that class creates: the
working-class movement as a tendency, rather than all working-class people as
individuals. It is foolish to interpret individuals in rigid class terms, because class
is a collective mode and not a person. At the same time, in the interpretation of
ideas and institutions, we can speak properly in class terms. It depends, at any
time, on which kind of fact we are considering. To dismiss an individual
because of his class, or to judge a relationship with him solely in class terms,
is to reduce humanity to an abstraction. But, also, to pretend that there are no
collective modes is to deny the plain facts.

We may now see what is properly meant by 'working-class culture'. It is not
proletarian art, or council houses, or a particular use of language; it is, rather,

the basic collective idea, and the institutions, manners, habits of thought and intentions which proceed from this. Bourgeois culture, similarly, is the basic individualist idea and the institutions, manners, habits of thought and intentions which proceed from that. In our culture as a whole, there is both a constant interaction between these ways of life and an area which can properly be described as common to or underlying both. The working class, because of its position, has not, since the Industrial Revolution, produced a culture in the narrower sense. The culture which it has produced, and which it is important to recognize, is the collective democratic institution, whether in the trade unions, the cooperative movement or a political party. Working-class culture, in the stage through which it has been passing, is primarily social (in that it has created institutions) rather than individual (in particular intellectual or imaginative work). When it is considered in context, it can be seen as a very remarkable creative achievement.

To those whose meaning of culture is intellectual or imaginative work, such an achievement may be meaningless. The values which are properly attached to such work can, at times, seem overriding. On this, I would only point out that while it may have seemed reasonable to Burke to anticipate the trampling down of learning by the irruption of the 'swinish multitude', this has not in fact happened, and the swinish multitude itself has done much to prevent it happening. The record of the working-class movement in its attitudes to education, to learning and to art is on the whole a good record. It has sometimes wrongly interpreted, often neglected where it did not know. But it has never sought to destroy the institutions of this kind of culture; it has, on the contrary, pressed for their extension, for their wider social recognition, and, in our own time, for the application of a larger part of our material resources to their maintenance and development. Such a record will do more than stand comparison with that of the class by which the working class has been most actively and explicitly opposed. This, indeed, is the curious incident of the swine in the night. As the light came, and we could look around, it appeared that the trampling, which we had all heard, did not after all come from them.

The Idea of Community

The development of the idea of culture has, throughout, been a criticism of what has been called the bourgeois idea of society. The contributors to its meaning have started from widely different positions, and have reached widely various attachments and loyalties. But they have been alike in this, that they have been unable to think of society as a merely neutral area, or as an abstract regulating mechanism. The stress has fallen on the positive function of society, on the fact that the values of individual men are rooted in society, and on the need to think and feel in these common terms. This was, indeed, a profound and necessary response to the disintegrating pressures which were faced.

Yet, according to their different positions, the idea of community, on which all in general agree, has been differently felt and defined. In our own day we have two major interpretations, alike opposed to bourgeois liberalism, but equally, in practice, opposed to each other. These are the idea of service, and the idea of solidarity. These have in the main been developed by the middle class and the working class respectively. From Coleridge to Tawney the idea of function, and thence of service to the community, has been most valuably stressed, in opposition to the individualist claim. The stress has been confirmed by the generations of training which substantiate the ethical practice of our professions, and of our public and civil service. As against the practice of *laissez-faire*, and of self-service, this has been a major achievement which has done much for the peace and welfare of our society. Yet the working-class ethic, of solidarity, has also been a major achievement, and it is the difference of this from the idea of service which must now be stressed.

A very large part of English middle-class education is devoted to the training of servants. This is much more its characteristic than a training for leadership, as the stress on conformity and on respect for authority shows. In so far as it is, by definition, the training of upper servants, it includes, of course, the instilling of that kind of confidence which will enable the upper servants to supervise and direct the lower servants. Order must be maintained there, by good management, and in this respect the function is not service but government. Yet the upper servant is not to think of his own interests. He must subordinate these to a larger good, which is called the Queen's peace, or national security, or law and order, or the public weal. This has been the charter of many thousands of devoted lives, and it is necessary to respect it even where we cannot agree with it.

I was not trained to this ethic, and when I encountered it, in late adolescence, I had to spend a lot of time trying to understand it, through men whom I respected and who had been formed by it. The criticism I now make of it is in this kind of good faith. It seems to me inadequate because in practice it serves, at every level, to maintain and confirm the *status quo*. This was wrong, for me, because the *status quo*, in practice, was a denial of equity to the men and women among whom I had grown up, the lower servants, whose lives were governed by the existing distributions of property, remuneration, education and respect. The real personal unselfishness, which ratified the description as service, seemed to me to exist within a larger selfishness, which was only not seen because it was idealized as the necessary form of a civilization, or rationalized as a natural distribution corresponding to worth, effort and intelligence. I could not share in these versions, because I thought, and still think, that the sense of injustice which the 'lower servants' felt was real and justified. One cannot in conscience then become, when invited, an upper servant in an establishment that one thus radically disapproves. [. . .]

The Development of a Common Culture

In its definition of the common interest as true self-interest, in its finding of individual verification primarily in the community, the idea of solidarity is potentially the real basis of a society. Yet it is subject, in our time, to two important difficulties. For it has been, basically, a defensive attitude, the natural mentality of the long siege. It has in part depended, that is to say, on an enemy; the negative elements thus produced will have to be converted into positives in a fully democratic society. This will at best be profoundly difficult, for the feelings involved are fundamental.

The issue can be defined as one in which diversity has to be substantiated within an effective community which disposes of majority power. The feeling of solidarity is, although necessary, a primitive feeling. It has depended, hitherto, on substantial identity of conditions and experience. Yet any predictable civilization will depend on a wide variety of highly specialized skills, which will involve, over definite parts of the culture, a fragmentation of experience. The attachment of privilege to certain kinds of skill has been traditionally clear, and this will be very difficult to unlearn, to the degree that is necessary if substantial community of condition is to be assured. A culture in common, in our own day, will not be the simple all- in-all society of old dream. It will be a very complex organization, requiring continual adjustment and redrawing. At root, the feeling of solidarity is the only conceivable element of stabilization in so difficult an organization. But in its issue it will have to be continually redefined, and there will be many attempts to enlist old feelings in the service of an emerging sectional interest. The emphasis that I wish to place here is that this first difficulty – the compatibility of increasing specialization with a genuinely common culture – is only soluble in a context of material community and by the full democratic process. A skill is only an aspect of a man, and yet, at times, it can seem to comprehend his whole being. This is one kind of crisis, and it can only be overcome as a man becomes conscious that the value he places on his skill, the differentiation he finds in it, can only ultimately be confirmed by his constant effort not only to confirm and respect the skills of others, but also to confirm and deepen the community which is even larger than the skills. The mediation of this lies deep in personal

feeling, but enough is known to indicate that it is possible. Further, there can
be no effective participation in the whole culture merely on the basis of the
skill which any particular man may acquire. The participation depends on
common resources, and leads a man towards others. To any individual, however gifted, full participation will be impossible, for the culture will be too
complex. Yet effective participation is certainly possible. It will, at any time, be
selective from the whole culture, and there will be difference and unevenness
in selection, as there will be in contribution. Such selection, such unevenness,
can be made compatible with an effective community of culture, but only by
genuine mutual responsibility and adjustment. This is the conversion of the
defensive element of solidarity into the wider and more positive practice of
neighbourhood. It is, in practice, for any man, a long conversion of the
habitual elements of denial; a slow and deep personal acceptance of extending
community. The institutions of cynicism, of denial and of division will perhaps
only be thrown down when they are recognized for what they are: the deposits
of practical failures to live. Failure – the jaunty hardness of the 'outsider' – will
lose its present glamour, as the common experience moves in a different
direction. Nobody will be proud any longer to be separate, to deny, or to
ratify a personal failure in unconcern.

The second difficulty, in the development of the idea of solidarity, is related
to the first: in that it is again a question of achieving diversity without creating
separation. Solidarity, as a feeling, is obviously subject to rigidities, which can
be dangerous in a period of change. The command to common action is right,
but there is always the danger that the common understanding will be inadequate, and that its enforcement will prevent or delay right action. No
community, no culture, can ever be fully conscious of itself, ever fully know
itself. The growth of consciousness is usually uneven, individual and tentative
in nature. An emphasis of solidarity which, by intention or by accident, stifles
or weakens such growth may, evidently, bring a deep common harm. It is
necessary to make room for, not only variation, but even dissidence, within the
common loyalty. Yet it is difficult to feel that, even in the English working-
class movement, with its long democratic tradition, this need has been clearly
and practically recognized.

A culture, while it is being lived, is always in part unknown, in part
unrealized. The making of a community is always an exploration, for consciousness cannot precede creation, and there is no formula for unknown
experience. A good community, a living culture, will, because of this, not
only make room for but actively encourage all and any who can contribute to
the advance in consciousness which is the common need. Wherever we have
started from, we need to listen to others who started from a different position.
We need to consider every attachment, every value, with our whole attention;

for we do not know the future, we can never be certain of what may enrich it; we can only, now, listen to and consider whatever may be offered and take up what we can.

The practical liberty of thought and expression is less a natural right than a common necessity. The growth of understanding is so difficult that none of us can arrogate to himself, or to an institution or a class, the right to determine its channels of advance. Any educational system will reflect the content of a society; any emphasis in exploration will follow from an emphasis of common need. Yet no system, and no emphasis, can be adequate, if they fail to allow for real flexibility, real alternative courses. To deny these practical liberties is to burn the common seed. To tolerate only this or only that, according to some given formula, is to submit to the phantasy of having occupied the future and fenced it into fruitful or unfruitful ground. Thus, in the working-class movement, while the clenched fist is a necessary symbol, the clenching ought never to be such that the hand cannot open, and the fingers extend, to discover and give a shape to the newly forming reality.

We have to plan what can be planned, according to our common decision. But the emphasis of the idea of culture is right when it reminds us that a culture, essentially, is unplannable. We have to ensure the means of life, and the means of community. But what will then, by these means, be lived, we cannot know or say. The idea of culture rests on a metaphor: the tending of natural growth. And indeed it is on growth, as metaphor and as fact, that the ultimate emphasis must be placed. Here, finally, is the area where we have most need to reinterpret.

To rid oneself of the illusion of the objective existence of 'the masses', and to move towards a more actual and more active conception of human beings and relationships, is in fact to realize a new freedom. Where this can be experienced, the whole substance of one's thinking is transformed. There is a further shift in experience, cognate with this, when we think again about human growth, and its human tending, in a spirit other than that of the long dominative mode. The forces which have changed and are still changing our world are indeed industry and democracy. Understanding of this change, this long revolution, lies at a level of meaning which it is not easy to reach. We can in retrospect see the dominative mood as one of the mainsprings of industry: the theory and practice of man's mastering and controlling his natural environment. We are still rephrasing this, from experience, as we learn the folly of exploiting any part of this environment in isolation. We are learning, slowly, to attend to our environment as a whole, and to draw our values from that whole, and not from its fragmented parts, where a quick success can bring long waste. In relation to this kind of learning, we come to realize, again slowly, that where the dominative mood extends to man himself, where human beings also are isolated and exploited, with whatever temporary success, the issue in the long run is a cancelling in spirit of the full opportunities offered by the material gains. A knot is tied, that has come near to strangling our whole common life, in this century. We live in almost overwhelming danger, at a peak of our apparent control. We react to the danger by attempting to take control, yet still we have to unlearn, as the price of survival, the inherent dominative mode. The struggle for democracy is the pattern of this revaluation, yet much that passes as democratic is allied, in spirit, with the practice of its open enemies. It is as if, in fear or vision, we are now all determined to lay our hands on life and force it into our own image, and it is then no good to dispute on the merits of rival images. This is a real barrier in the mind, which at times it seems almost impossible to break down: a refusal to accept the creative capacities of life; a determination to limit and restrict the channels of growth; a habit of thinking, indeed, that the future has now to be determined by some ordinance in our own minds. We project our old images into the future, and take hold of ourselves and others to force energy towards that substantiation. We do this as conservatives, trying to prolong old forms; we do this as socialists, trying to prescribe the new man. A large part of contemporary resistance to certain kinds of change, which are obviously useful in themselves, amounts to an inarticulate distrust of this effort at domination. There is the hostility to change of those who wish to cling to privilege. There is also the hostility to one's life being determined, in a dominative mood masked by whatever idealism or benevolence. This latter hostility is valuable, and needs to be distinguished from the former with which it is often crudely compounded. It is the chafing of any felt life against the hands which seek to determine its course, and this, which was always the democratic impulse, remains essential within the new definitions of society. There are still major material barriers to democracy, but there is also this barrier in our minds, behind which, with an assumption of virtue, we seek to lay hands on others, and, from our own constructions, determine their course. Against this the idea of culture is necessary, as an idea of the tending of *natural* growth. To know, even in part, any group of living processes, is to see and wonder at their extraordinary variety and complexity. To know, even in part, the life of man, is to see and wonder at its extraordinary multiplicity, its great fertility of value. We have to live by our own attachments, but we can only live fully, in common, if we grant the attachments of others, and make it our common business to keep the channels of growth clear. Never yet, in the great pattern of inheritance and response, have two wholly identical individuals been formed. This, rather than any particular image of virtue, is our actual human scale. The idea of a common culture brings together, in a particular form of social relationship, at once the idea of natural growth and that of its tending. The former alone is a type of romantic individualism; the latter alone a type of authoritarian training. Yet each, within a whole view, marks a necessary emphasis. The struggle for democracy is a struggle for the recognition of equality of being, or it is nothing. Yet only in the acknowledgement of human individuality and variation can the reality of common government be comprised. We stress natural growth to indicate the whole potential energy, rather than the selected energies which the dominative mode finds it convenient to enlist. At the same time, however, we stress the social reality, the tending. Any culture, in its whole process, is a selection, an emphasis, a particular tending. The distinction of a culture in common is that the selection is freely and commonly made and remade. The tending is a common process, based on common decision, which then, within itself, comprehends the actual variations of life and growth. The natural growth and the tending are parts of a mutual process, guaranteed by the fundamental principle of equality of being.

The evident problems of our civilization are too close and too serious for anyone to suppose that an emphasis is a solution. In every problem we need hard, detailed inquiry and negotiation. Yet we are coming increasingly to realize that our vocabulary, the language we use to inquire into and negotiate our actions, is no secondary factor, but a practical and radical element in itself. To take a meaning from experience, and to try to make it active, is in fact our process of growth. Some of these meanings we receive and re-create. Others we must make for ourselves, and try to communicate. The human crisis is always a crisis of understanding: what we genuinely understand we can do. I have written this book because I believe the tradition it records is a major contribution to our common understanding, and a major incentive to its necessary extensions. There are ideas, and ways of thinking, with the seeds of life in them, and there are others, perhaps deep in our minds, with the seeds of a general death. Our measure of success in recognizing these kinds, and in naming them making possible their common recognition, may be literally the measure of our future.

4

Individuals and Societies

From Raymond Williams (1961) The Long Revolution. *London: Chatto and Windus*

WE are seeking to define and consider one central principle: that of the essential relation, the true interaction, between patterns learned and created in the mind and patterns communicated and made active in relationships, conventions, and institutions. Culture is our name for this process and its results, and then within this process we discover problems that have been the subject of traditional debate and that we may look at again in this new way. Among such problems, that of the relationship between an individual and his society is evident and crucial. It has been discussed through the whole series of systems of thinking that compose our tradition, and it is still widely discussed, from current experience, since it seems to be agreed that precisely this issue is at the centre of the conflicts of our time. Yet of course we approach the experience through the descriptions we have learned: in a more or less conscious way if we know parts of the vast body of accumulated theory in the matter; still, in effect, if we know none of the theory directly, yet find it embedded in the very language and forms of relationship through which we are bound to live. When we examine actual relationships, we start from the descriptions we have learned. When we speak of 'the individual' and of 'society', we are using descriptions which embody particular interpretations of the experience to which they refer: interpretations which gained currency at a particular point in history, yet which have now virtually established themselves in our minds as absolutes. By a special effort, we may become conscious of 'the individual' and 'society' as 'no more than descriptions', yet still so much actual experience and behaviour is tied to them that the realization can seem merely academic. There are times, however, when there is so high a tension between experience and description that we are forced to examine the descriptions, and to seek beyond them for new descriptions, not so much as a matter of theory but as literally a problem of behaviour. It has seemed to me for some years that our ways of thinking about 'the individual and society' are inadequate, confusing, and at times sterile. In thinking about culture, rather than directly about this issue as named, I have found my own descriptions of this kind of experience changing quite radically. I want to see if it is possible, from what I have said about the creative mind and about culture, to reconsider this traditional debate. I propose to review the main descriptions historically, to examine the effect on them of recent work in a number of disciplines, and to offer some amendments and possible new descriptions.

I

We can conveniently begin the historical examination at the point where 'individual' emerged as the description we now have. It is always difficult to date an experience by dating a concept, but when a word appears – either a new word or a new sense of a word – a particular stage has been reached that is the nearest we can get to a consciousness of change. 'Individual' meant 'inseparable', in medieval thinking, and its main use was in the context of theological argument about the nature of the Holy Trinity. The effort was to explain how a being could be thought of as existing in his own nature yet existing by this nature as part of an indivisible whole. The logical problem extended to other fields of experience, and 'individual' became a term used to indicate a member of some group, kind, or species. The complexity of the term is at once apparent in this history, for it is the unit that is being defined, yet defined in terms of its membership of a class. The separable entity is being defined by a word that has meant 'inseparable': an identity – a particular name – is conferred by a realization of identity – the fact of common status. The crucial history of the modern description is a change in emphasis which enabled us to think of 'the individual' as a kind of absolute, without immediate reference, by the very structure of the term, to the group of which he is a member. And this change, so far as we can now trace it in the imperfectly recorded history of the word itself, seems to have taken place in England in the late sixteenth and early seventeenth centuries. Slowly, and with many ambiguities, since that time, we have learned to think of 'the individual in his own right', where previously to describe an individual was to give an example of the group of which he was a member, and so to offer a particular description of that group and of the relationships within it.

This semantic change, in itself very difficult to trace, seems clearer in its context of an actual change in relationships, in our long and uneven growth from the medieval world. In describing this we are of course reducing a whole area of complicated experience to a few simple patterns, but our sense of the general change is within these limits probably accurate. The basis of the new sense of 'individual' can be interestingly explored in the history of the idea of the individual soul, and we are probably right to see in the controversies of the Reformation an extension of ideas inherent in the Christian tradition, by which it was possible to pass from seeing the soul's destiny within an ordered structure, of God and the Church, to seeing this destiny as in a different way personal: a man's direct and individual relationship with God. In either way of thinking, the problem of personal destiny was real, but at one extreme this could be seen as an example of common destiny, important primarily as indicating this common destiny, while at the other extreme it was the ind-ividual destiny, in its own right, which claimed primary attention. One destiny was apprehended through the complicated structure of relationships of a total order; the other through one direct relationship, between the individual and his God. When we speak of the 'individualism' of Protestant thinking, we do not mean that the fact of a personal destiny is more real than in previous systems, but that the relationships within which the destiny is realized are differently defined. A change in the conception of relationships – crudely from man-church-God to man-God – is recorded by the new sense of what it is to be 'an individual'.

There is a similar and related change in the conception of man's individual 'position' in life. To speak of a position implies relationships, and we are still very conscious of this. But there is an evident change, between medieval and modern thinking, in this difficult conception of 'man in society'. Most accounts of medieval society stress the way in which a man was defined by his position in the social order: an 'individual' in the old sense, defined by his membership of a group. As Erich Fromm has put it: 'a person was identical with his role in society; he was a peasant, an artisan, a knight, and not *an individual* who *happened* to have this or that occupation'. We can see that this must to a large extent have been true, in a rigid society in which the possibility of 'becoming something else' was comparatively very limited. As mobility increased, and at least some men could change their status, the idea of being an individual in a sense separable from one's social role obviously gained in strength. The growth of capitalism, and the great social changes associated with it, encouraged certain men to see 'the individual' as a source of economic activity, by his 'free enterprise'. It was less a matter of performing a certain function within a fixed order than of initiating certain kinds of activity, choosing particular directions. The social and geographical mobility to which in some cases these changes gave rise led to a redefinition of the individual – 'what I am' – by extension to 'what I want to be' and 'what by my own efforts I have become'. Yet this is still a definition of an individual in his social or economic role, and we can all observe that this kind of definition has persisted into our own times. I think, among many examples, of the magistrate's question to William Morris in the dock, in 1885:

Mr Saunders: What are you?
Prisoner.   I am an artist, and a literary man, pretty well known, I think, throughout Europe.

The curtness of the question, and yet Morris's immediate understanding of it, stick in my mind, for I know my own reaction, that the only answer to 'what are you?' is 'a man', yet with the certainty that the answer would be considered insolent, as I consider the question insolent. And in rejecting the question 'what are you?', thinking of the more acceptable question 'who are you?' and then 'what is your work?', I am living out this particular history, in which we have become increasingly conscious of individual existence as a thing separable from, more important than, an occupation, a social function, a social rank. I can think of some people who would have answered the magistrate's question with the proud 'an Englishman', and indeed that kind of consciousness is a stage in the development. We have at our command, now, a number of ways of defining our existence, in terms of nationality, class, occupation and so on, in which we in fact offer a personal description in terms of membership of a group. Yet for most of us, when all these terms have been used, an area of conscious and valued existence remains, which in this mode of description could not be expressed at all. It is in relation to this area of existence that the problem of 'the individual and society' takes shape.

Thus we can trace our concept of 'the individual' to that complex of change which we analyse in its separable aspects as the Renaissance, the Reformation, the beginnings of capitalist economy. In essence it is the abstraction of the individual from the complex of relationships by which he had hitherto been normally defined. The counterpart of this process was a similar abstraction of 'society', which had earlier indicated an actual relationship – 'the society of his fellows' – but which in the late sixteenth century began to develop the more general modern sense of 'the system of common life' – society as a thing in itself. 'Community' reached the same stage of development in the seventeenth century, and 'State' had reached this stage rather earlier, having added to its two earlier meanings – the condition of the common life, as now in 'state of the nation'; the signs of a condition or status, as in 'the King's state' – the sense of the 'apparatus' of the common life, its framework or set order. Thus we see the terms of relationship separating out, until 'individual' on the one hand, 'society', 'community', and 'state' on the other, could be conceived as abstractions and absolutes.

The major tradition of subsequent social thinking has depended on these descriptions. In England, from Hobbes to the Utilitarians, a variety of systems share a common starting-point: man as a bare human being, 'the individual', is the logical starting-point of psychology, ethics, and politics. It is rare, in this tradition, to start from the fact that man is born into relationships. The abstraction of the bare human being, as a separate substance, is ordinarily taken for granted. In other systems of thinking, the community would be the axiom, and individual man the derivative. Here individual man is the axiom, and society the derivative. Hobbes virtually drops all middle terms between separate individuals and the State, and, seeing the individuals as naturally selfish, sees society as a rational construction to restrain the destructive elements in individuals and to enforce co-operation. Locke sees the rational and co-operative elements as natural, but similarly postulates separate individuals who create society by consent or contract, for the protection of their individual interests. The whole Liberal tradition, following from this, begins with the individual and his rights and, judging society as an arrangement to ensure these abstract rights, argues normally for only the necessary minimum of government. It is clear that much human good resulted from this emphasis, in the actual liberation of men from arbitrary and oppressive systems. Yet it rested on descriptions which, while corresponding to the experience of man breaking out from obsolete social forms, came to conflict with experience of the difficulties of new kinds of organization.

While the abstract individual was idealized in this tradition, an alternative tradition, sharing some but not all of its terms, moved in the direction of the idealization of society. Rousseau, arguing that 'we begin properly to become men only after we have become citizens', saw the community as the source of values and hence as 'a moral person'. Hegel, beginning from the similar emphasis that man becomes an individual through society and civilization, saw the State as the organ of the highest human values – an embodiment of what Matthew Arnold called 'our best self'. Yet both Rousseau and Hegel, with differences of emphasis, saw the importance of actual communities and forms of association as the necessary mediating element between individuals and the large Society. It is from this line of thinking that an important revision of the descriptions has followed. We preserve, from the early Liberalism, the absolutes of 'individual' and 'society', but we add to these, as mediating terms, 'community' and 'association', to describe local and face-to-face relationships through which the great abstractions of Individual and Society operate in detail. A particular and crucial addition was the concept of 'class', which is quite different from the static concepts of 'order' and 'rank' because it includes this kind of middle term between 'the individual' and 'society' – the individual relates to his society through his class. Yet 'class' carries an emphasis different from 'community' or 'association', because it is not a face-to-face grouping but, like 'society' itself, an abstraction. Marx argued that by their common membership of a particular class, men will think and act in certain common ways even though they do not belong to the same actual communities, and that the processes of 'society' are in fact best understood in terms of the interaction of these classes. Thus, in the nineteenth century, while the abstract descriptions of 'individual' and 'society' retained their force, a number of new descriptions were made and emphasized, their general import being the indication of particular kinds of relationship. It is on this whole range – rising, as we have seen, from a complex of historical changes and rival intellectual traditions – that certain twentieth-century disciplines have acted.

II

The influence of Freud, as an analyst of personal and social behaviour, has been very great, and has reinforced one part of the tradition that we have been examining. For Freudian theory assumes a basic division between the individual and society, and hence basic division between the individual and such mediating forms as 'community', or 'class', which are seen simply as social agents which operate on the individual. Man, the 'bare human being', has certain fundamental drives which are also fundamentally anti-social. Some of these society must restrain; others it must refine and divert into socially acceptable or valuable channels. Society is a mechanism of restraint and diversion, and civilization is the product, through 'sublimation', of suppressed natural impulses. Man as a bare human being is thus fundamentally alienated from society, and the best that can be hoped for is a reasonably adjusted balance between the conflicting needs of individual and society, the process of sublimation being the mechanism of balance, and breakdown being due to faulty adjustment of this kind.

Yet if Freud's account of the individual and society is, in its basic terms, merely an item in an old tradition, his actual inquiries led to a highly significant emphasis on relationships. Indeed he introduced, in a wholly new way, a new mediating term, the family, and thus remarkably extended the study of actual social growth. It was not that the family, as a first form of association, had not always been available as a concept, but that Freud's emphasis on the radical importance, in all human behaviour, of the patterns of relationship established in infancy, transformed its significance. Freud's descriptions are contained and limited by his theoretical separation of 'the individual' and 'society', yet in different hands they have been differently developed. In dogmatic Freudianism very little of interest to the study of social relationships has emerged, since such relationships are always construed as of secondary importance. In other hands, the possibility of linking our deeply personal relationships with the whole network of social relationships has been interestingly explored. The work of Fromm seems particularly useful, since he has developed one new mediating description, that of the 'social character'. This offers to describe the process by which social behaviour becomes part of an individual personality: not by regular processes of restraint and diversion, as in Freud, but by a shaping process which can include many kinds of relationship. The 'social character' is a selective response to experience, a learned system of feeling and acting, in a majority of the community into which the child is born. The family is then the community's agent in creating this desired social character in individuals. If it is successful, the individual's social activity will be at one with his personal desires, for the social character 'internalizes external necessities and thus harnesses human energy for the task of a given economic and social system'. The individual, in such a case, comes to 'act according to what is necessary for him from a practical standpoint, and also to give him satisfaction for his activity psychologically'. Instead of a permanent human nature, which society restrains or modifies, individual psychology is then a matter of 'the particular kind of relatedness of the individual towards the world'. This relatedness can correspond with the current social character, or can diverge from it.

In this we can see Freud playing the role of Hobbes, and Fromm that of Locke: in both cases with a greatly refined description of the actual process of relationship between an individual and society. Fromm has advanced considerably in showing how 'society' can become truly embodied in individuals, so that we need not think of them as separate and absolute but always in terms of relationships. The real problem arises, however, when we ask what is the source of the individual character that can diverge from the social character, or, more accurately, what kinds of relationship affect the individual character that are not forms of social relationship? If 'social character' is reserved to a particular construction which may or may not adequately interpret the real relationships which the individual forms, then its function is clearer, and the possibility of variant individual response has an obvious theoretical basis. Yet it is then a question whether 'social character' is a finally useful term, since it seems only a partial explanation of how relationships (society) create psychology (the individual).

The concept of 'social character' is similar to the anthropological concept of a 'pattern of culture'. Comparative studies of different societies have added to our historical evidence to show how various are the learned systems of behaviour and attitudes which groups of human beings adopt. Each of these systems, while it lasts, is the form of a society, a pattern of culture to which most of its individual members are successfully trained. Comparison of the systems has done much to transform traditional arguments about the individual and society, for it has shown how various are the feelings and forms of behaviour that bring individual and common satisfaction. Instead of asking the relationship between an ideally identified individual, with a standard equipment of desires and attitudes, and an ideally identified society, with standard purposes, it has been possible to look at real and changing relation-ships, with an amount of detail that has broken up the standard prescriptions. Yet, in extending the evidence, it has made theoretical inquiry more difficult. Perhaps the main result has been an enormous strengthening of the tradition which emphasized the extent to which individual personality is formed by social processes, even at very deep levels. This has been wholly valuable, as a way of correcting the false emphasis on the abstract 'individual', which we can now see to be a product of a particular social and historical situation rather than a correct reading of the general human condition. Yet this is not, rightly interpreted, a denial of the importance of individuals. As Benedict argues:

No culture yet observed has been able to eradicate the differences in the temperaments of the persons who compose it. It is always a give-and-take. The problem of the individual is not clarified by stressing the antagonism between culture and the indi-vidual, but by stressing their mutual reinforcement. This *rapport* is so close that it is not possible to discuss patterns of culture without considering specifically their relation to individual psychology.

A 'pattern of culture', like a 'social character', is a selective response to experience, a learned system of feeling and acting, in a particular society. Benedict argues that this pattern will be 'congenial' to a majority of the members of the society, and that therefore they can be trained to it, in such a way that by becoming members of the society they will adequately express their individuality. But to others, the pattern will not be 'congenial', and these will either not conform, or conform at a possibly heavy price to their individual desires. It is difficult to know what weight to put on 'congenial': the variations Benedict actually describes – different reactions to frustration and grief – look very like what others would call 'learned responses', although the problem then arises that these are 'learned' and yet are different from those the particular society teaches and approves. If they are not learned but innate, we are back to 'human nature', to be understood now not as a single thing, but as comprising an innate range of temperaments: the relation between the individual and society thus becomes a kind of lottery, in which an individual of particular temperament draws a winning or losing card in the society in which he happens to be born. We do not yet know nearly enough to prove or disprove this hypothesis, but it represents one attempted solution in a direction rather different from the general trend in social psychology. Another anthropologist, Linton, finds it

safe to conclude that innate, biologically·determined factors cannot be used to account for personality configurations as wholes or for the various response patterns included within such configurations. They operate simply as one among several sets of factors responsible for the formation of these.

Linton goes on to describe, in the now familiar way, the creation of mature individuals by learned culture patterns, and emphasizes

the fact that most human behaviour is taught in the form of organized configurations rather than simply developed by the individual on the basis of experience.

Included in this teaching, as parts of a whole pattern, are some elements serving 'to meet individual needs' and others 'to satisfy social necessities'. But the carrier of these patterns is simply acting as a 'unit in the social organism', and he has other resources which constitute his individuality. The social function of this individuality is that, in the changing world in which the society lives, the individual, by using his own resources, can help to change the pattern, in order to meet new problems.

   Yet what, precisely, is the process of this individuation? The ordinary emphases of social psychology show how far we have moved, at one level of our thinking, from the idea that the individual in some way *precedes* his society – the society being a secondary creation through restraint or contract. Most social psychologists now stress the way in which awareness of oneself as a separate individual has to be learned by the infant: 'the infant has no idea of himself as a separate individual'. As G. H. Mead has put it:

The self, as that which can be object to itself, is essentially a social structure, and it arises in social experience.

This definition implies different levels of individuality. We can distinguish between the primary individual organism and the 'self' which is socially created. This is useful, but it is only by using very difficult terms that we can clarify the distinction, since the word 'individual' ordinarily and naturally includes these theoretically separable elements. Perhaps the most useful stress is that which describes the social process of making 'selves' in terms of individuation: the conscious differences between individuals arise in the social process. To begin with, individuals have varying innate potentialities, and thus receive social influence in varying ways. Further, even if there is a common 'social character' or 'culture pattern', each individual's social history, his actual network of relationships, is in fact unique. These are the basic individualizing factors, but again, as the unique potentialities and the unique history interact, the very fact of the growth of self-consciousness produces a distinct organization, capable both of self-scrutiny and self-direction. This 'autonomous' self grows within a social process which radically influences it, but the degree of gained autonomy makes possible the observed next stage, in which the individual can help to change or modify the social process that has influenced and is influencing him.

To this vital description must be added another distinction, greatly stressed in recent sociology. The abstraction implicit in 'society' can make it difficult for us to recognize theoretically what in practice we see quite clearly: that even in a very simple society it is hardly ever one single 'social character' or 'culture pattern' that the individual encounters. In complex societies like our own, the variations encountered are so marked that we can speak of them as alternative systems within 'a society'. This is obviously very important. If the analysis of 'the individual' has returned an abstraction to its actual processes of growth, so analysis of 'society' has returned an abstraction to the actual complex of real relationships. Instead of thinking of 'society' as a single and uniform object, we look at actual groups and the relationships between them. Since these relationships can be not only those of co-operation but also of tension and conflict, the individual with his sense of particular directions finds material in the alternative directions of his society making it possible for him to express variant growth in social terms.

The recognition of 'groups' within a society is thus a considerable step forward. But of course it is possible merely to shift the ground of the abstraction, making the group in its turn a uniform absolute. Even in the simplest group, there are, as in 'society', relations of tension and conflict as well as of co-operation. This is as true of a face-to-face group like a family or a village as a common-interest group like a trade union or a social class. Each of these will have its distinct 'social character' or 'culture pattern', to which it will seek to train its members. Yet enclosing this will be the constant interaction of particular individuals, and in such groups, as in 'society', new directions will emerge. Again, since the group will be in real relations with other groups, the processes of training and amendment within the group will be part of the processes of training and amendment of the larger 'society'. A group may be a convenient mark on the scale, but it is only a mark, and the fact of continuity, over the whole scale, is fundamental.

III

We have briefly traced, first the traditional discussion of 'the individual and society', second the main directions of certain contemporary disciplines. We must now turn again to experience, and to the fact that we normally find ourselves, in thinking about 'the individual and society', limited in practice to a very simple model: that of the individual's conformity or nonconformity, and of the society's attitude to either of these courses. We have a number of names for conformity, which enable us to approve it as 'responsible' and 'law-abiding', or to condemn it as 'timidly conventional' or 'servile'. We have also a number of names for non-conformity and some of these, such as 'independence' and 'the free spirit' are approving, while others, such as 'lawlessness' and 'eccentricity' are damning. Some of us move to one side or other of these lines, and try to make a consistent position. More commonly we make a virtue out of either, as it seems to us at the moment. Such valuations may be real, but while they depend, ultimately, on the simple model — conformity or nonconformity — they are relatively very weak. I want to try to get past this model, and by examining some actual relationships between individuals and their societies extend our practical vocabulary for discussing this issue.

We can take first the description *member*. In its modern sense this is a useful way of describing an individual's positive identification with the society in which he lives. The member of a society feels himself to belong to it, in an essential way: its values are his values, its purposes his purposes, to such an extent that he is proud to describe himself in its terms. He is of course conscious of himself as *a* member — an individual within the society to which he belongs — but it is of the essence of membership that the individual, so far from feeling that the society is opposed to him, looks upon it as the natural means by which his own purposes will be forwarded. If change is necessary, he will contribute to its discussion and coming into effect, for he is confident of the values, attitudes and institutions of the society, accepts the ways in which its life is conducted, and sees even conflicts and tensions within the society as soluble by reference to these fundamental ways and values, in such a manner that the essential unity of the society will be preserved.

This experience of membership is probably much more common than is normally allowed theoretically. It is true that in many modern societies it has become much more difficult, and indeed it is when it significantly breaks down that the *problem* of 'the individual and society' is most apparent. Yet that membership can be real seems certain, and to omit its significance is to falsify the whole subsequent argument.

But if we have identified the member, we must go on to identify other relationships which apparently resemble it, and which have, by displacement, led to criticism of it. Existentialist thinkers have made an important distinction between the 'authentic self' and the 'unauthentic self', and their ordinary description of the 'unauthentic self' has been of a man who is 'the creature' of his heredity, his environment and his society. Thus Kierkegaard argues that society presses us to be 'objective' and 'typical', and that we must break through this to our own existence. Jaspers sees modern society as offering the 'unauthentic self' as a whole version of man; we are the creatures of heredity, environment and society until some basic experience (suffering, guilt, death) enables us to break through these offered versions to an authentic realization of our true existence. Nietzsche, similarly, sees the acceptance of social typification as Philistine, and Sartre emphasizes the danger of such social concepts as 'function' or 'duty', which can only be valid to the 'unauthentic' man. The central observation, in this whole tradition, is of great value, but the tendency to equate 'social man' with 'unauthentic man' is highly misleading. For what is being described as a social process is not the experience of the *member*, but of the *subject* or the *servant*. Any society will put pressure on the individuals who are born into it to think and behave in certain ways, but this need not be only the conversion of individuals to social purposes; it is also, in very many cases, an expression of the society's desire to see those individuals survive and grow, according to the best experience the society has.

We must start by recognizing that individuals could not survive and grow except within a social process of some kind. Given this, the real crisis of the 'authentic' and the 'unauthentic' is both an individual and a social process. The valuable element in the existentialist emphasis is the insistence on choice and commitment. It is true that unless an individual, in the process of his growth, achieves a real personal identity, he is incomplete and can be dismissed as 'unauthentic'. He must become deeply conscious of the validity of his ways of thinking and acting, so that he is not merely 'a creature' of the society, but also an individual, a man in his own right. Yet this process, in actual individuals and in different societies, will be exceptionally varied. It is only very rarely limited to conscious appraisal; its ordinary process, while including conscious appraisal in some cases, is a matter of the individual's whole organization: his nervous system, his body, as well as the conscious activities of his brain. In actual growth, the whole complex of feeling and behaviour that constitutes his individuality will stand in a certain relation to the complex of feeling and behaviour that is his society. The stages in his growth which constitute his integration as a particular individual will inevitably be forms of relationship with the whole organization of his society. But these forms of relationship can include what I have called the experience of membership. Particular individuals, in particular societies, can become 'authentic', can deeply commit themselves, in terms of their whole organization, to the living organization of the society to which they belong. The 'social' is not necessarily the 'unauthentic'; it is capable of being the 'authentic' and the 'individual'. But it is then necessary to distinguish the kinds of relationship which give existentialist arguments their substance. It is clearly possible for an individual to acquiesce in a way of living which in fact fails to correspond with or satisfy his own personal organization. He will obey authorities he does not personally accept, carry out social functions that have no personal meaning to him, even feel and think in ways so foreign to his actual desires that damage will be done to his own being – often deep emotional disorders, often physical damage to his own organic processes. The marks of this false conformity have been very evident in our social experience, but it is wrong to interpret them in terms of the old 'individual' and 'society' dichotomy. We can best describe them as the roles of *subject* and *servant*, in contrast with *member*.

The *subject*, at whatever violence to himself, has to accept the way of life of his society, and his own indicated place in it, because there is no other way in which he can maintain himself at all; only by this kind of obedience can he eat, sleep, shelter, or escape being destroyed by others. It is not *his* way of life, in any sense that matters, but he must conform to it to survive. In the case of the *servant*, the pressure is less severe, though still, to him, irresistible. The subject has no choice; the servant is given the illusion of choice, and is invited to identify himself with the way of life in which his place is defined. It is an illusion of choice, because again, like the subject, he has no obvious way of maintaining his life if he refuses. Yet the illusion is important, for it allows him to pretend to an identification with the society, as if the choice had been real. The subject will have few illusions about the relationship which is determining him; he will know that the way of life is not his but must be obeyed. The servant, on the other hand, may come to identify himself with the way of life that is determining him; he may even, consciously, think of himself as a member (indeed the old sense of 'member' allows this, for if the individual is an organ of the organism that is society, particular individuals will be higher or lower organs yet still feel themselves as true parts). Yet at many levels of his life, and particularly in certain situations such as solitude and age, the discrepancy between the role the individual is playing and his actual sense of himself will become manifest, either consciously or in terms of some physical or emotional disturbance. Given the right conditions, he can play the role as if it were really his, but alone, or in situations evoking his deepest personal feelings, the identification breaks down. It seems probable, from the experience that has been widely recorded, that this situation of the servant is crucial in our own kind of society. The subject is a more extreme case, theoretically, though in history, and in modern undeveloped countries, it is common experience enough. And in modern Europe and the United States there are still subjects, though the experience of the servant is much more frequently recorded. It is that we are told we are free, and that we are shaping our common destiny; yet, with varying force, many of us break through to the conviction that the pattern of public activity has, in the end, very little to do with our private desires. Indeed the main modern force of the distinction between 'the individual' and 'society' springs from this feeling. It is only from the servant complex that we can both maintain this conviction and yet repeatedly pretend that we believe, wholeheartedly, in the purposes of our society.

The existentialist refuses this complex, and asserts the centrality of personal choice. From this position, with the reality of membership virtually excluded as a possibility, the whole rich repertory of modern individualism proceeds. Yet it is obvious, when we survey this range, that the modes of nonconformity are at least as varied as the modes of conformity. Where we had not only the member but also the subject and the servant, we have now not only the rebel but also the exile and the vagrant. The idea of the *rebel* still carries a strong positive valuation, though in fact rebels are few. The rebel resembles the member in that he has made a strong personal commitment to certain social purposes, a positive identification of his personal existence with a particular pattern of social effort. The ways of his society are not his ways, but in rebelling against one social form he is seeking to establish another. There are obviously important distinctions to be drawn here, between the revolutionary on the one hand, and the reformer or critic on the other. For the reformer and the critic are, in the definition I have given, members. A sincere desire to change this or that aspect of the general way of life is perfectly compatible with adherence to its general values, and with that kind of insistence on the essential continuity and unity of the society to which reformers and critics ordinarily adhere. The revolutionary, by contrast, lacks that sense of membership of a particular society which makes it possible for the reformer and critic to suppose that their own ends can in fact be achieved within the society's existing forms. The revolutionary's relationship with his society is one of declared opposition and struggle, but it is characteristic of him that he opposes the society in terms of the struggle for a different society. This is obvious in the case of political revolutionaries, but the same pattern is evident in rebels of other kinds, in art, morality, religion. The rebel fights the way of life of his society because to him personally it is wrong, but in art, morality and religion, as more obviously in politics, the new reality he proposes is more than personal; he is offering it as a new way of life.

This indeed is his distinction from *exile* and *vagrant*, which are the more truly individual forms. The exile is as absolute as the rebel in rejecting the way of life of his society, but instead of fighting it he goes away. Often he is like the subject in that unless he conforms he will be destroyed or will be unable to maintain his life. But he is unlike the subject in that he has managed to escape, or has been allowed to get away. In some cases, indeed, he will get away to membership of another society, in which he finds his personal reality, his vital system of values and attitudes, confirmed. More usually, perhaps, he will remain an exile, unable to go back to the society that he has rejected or that has rejected him, yet equally unable to form important relationships with the society to which he has gone. This is a tragic and characteristic condition which has been reached again and again in our century. The rebel, while more exposed to real danger in that he is attacking his society at its crucial points, has a degree of positive relationship by the very fact that he is actively living out his personal values. The true exile, on the other hand, is committed to waiting: when his society changes, then he can come home, but the actual process of change is one in which he is not involved.

We have been used to thinking of exiles as men driven from their society, but an equally characteristic modern figure is the self-exile. The self-exile could, if he chose, live at ease in his society, but to do so would be to deny his personal reality. Sometimes he goes away, on principle, but as often he stays, yet still, on principle, feels separate. The Bolsheviks had a useful term for this, in 'internal émigré', and if we realize that this is not confined to politics we can use it to describe a very important modern relationship. This kind of self-exile lives and moves about in the society into which he was born, but rejects its purposes and despises its values, because of alternative principles to which his whole personal reality is committed. Unlike the rebel, he does not fight for these principles, but watches and waits. He knows himself to be different, and the pressure of his activity is to preserve this difference, to maintain the individuality which is the term of his separateness. There is great tension in this condition, for theoretically, at least, the self-exile wants the society to change, so that he can start belonging to it, and this involves him, at least notionally, in relationships. But since, unlike the rebel, his personal dissent has remained fixed at an individual stage, it is difficult for him to form adequate relationships, even with other dissenters. He may support the principles of dissenting causes, but he cannot join them: he is too wary of being caught and compromised. What he has principally to defend is his own living pattern, his own mind, and almost any relationship is a potential threat to this. He has become or remained his 'authentic self', but this authenticity cannot be shared with or communicated to others, or, if the effort at communication is made, the commitment involved in it will be characteristically minimal. Whatever he may come to say or do, he continues, essentially, to walk alone in his society, defending a principle in himself.

This condition must be distinguished, finally, from that of the *vagrant*, which in some ways it resembles. The vagrant also stays in his own society, though he finds its purposes meaningless and its values irrelevant. Yet he lacks the exile's pride and his firm attachment to principle. There is nothing in particular that the vagrant wants to happen; his maximum demand is that he should be left alone. Where the exile is usually articulate in distinguishing his personal position, the vagrant often finds as little meaning in himself as in his society. Indeed it is not *his* society to which he objects, but, essentially, the condition of society as such. Whereas to others the society comes through as a particular set of relationships which can be accepted or rejected, to the vagrant society is a meaningless series of accidents and pressures, which as far as possible he evades. He will do anything that is necessary to survive within this, but this activity will have neither personal nor social meaning; it is merely a temporary way of keeping alive, or 'getting by'. For the vagrant has gone so far that he cannot even acknowledge society, even to oppose it. The events that others interpret as 'society' are to him like such natural events as storm or sun; the farthest principle he can see is one of bad luck or good luck, by which he stumbles on money or warmth, endures until he can move away from constraint and cold. These are, moreover, not incidents on a journey, for he is not going anywhere, in the sense of having a particular direction; his life is just happening to be passing this way. When we think of the vagrant we think naturally of such people as tramps and the fringe of society to which many criminals belong, but the condition of the vagrant – the essential negation of relationships which he embodies – is not confined to these obvious examples. In some societies it is possible to live out this condition with considerable material success, and there are signs, in some modern thinking, that the condition of the vagrant is the only available condition of man in society: whatever a man does, this is how he feels, and, given a particular social atmosphere, there is no need even to pretend otherwise. Conformity and rebellion, service and exile, are all alike irrelevant. A man does what he likes, but does not fight for change; serves any master, for immediate convenience, or leaves any service, again as convenience and not principle dictates. The one thing the vagrant is certain of is that all the others who are not vagrants are fools, killing themselves for meaningless meanings, pretending to meanings whereas the only thing that matters is oneself: not even a meaningful self, but simply an organism, as such, keeping going.

We need descriptions such as member, subject and servant, or rebel, exile and vagrant, if we are to get past the impasse of simple conformity or non-conformity. But, like other descriptions, these are not absolutes; they are simply analyses of particular forms of relationship. There is no single 'society' to which these are varying forms of adjustment; indeed 'society' itself takes on the same variations, according to the particular relationship that is embodied. To the member, society is his own community; the members of other communities may be beyond his recognition or sympathy. To the servant, society is an establishment, in which he finds his place. To the subject, society is an imposed system, in which his place is determined. To the rebel, a particular society is a tyranny; the alternative for which he fights is a new and better society. To the exile, society is beyond him, but may change. To the vagrant, society is a name for other people, who are in his way or who can be used. Nor are these merely 'subjective' valuations; real societies will necessarily vary according to the kinds of individual organization which compose them. The member and the community, the servant and the establishment, the subject and the imposed system, the rebel and the tyranny, the exile and the lost society, the vagrant and the meaningless society are all forms of active organization, of action and interaction. Further, within actual societies the relationships described are almost always complicated by the existence of different groups and scales. It is possible to be a member of a particular community, yet because of that community's relation to some larger society, to be in the position of a servant or a subject, a rebel or a vagrant, in certain areas of social experience. The rebel or the exile, as we have seen, can in certain conditions find social membership in an alternative group. In fact, because the groups and the alternatives interlock, the total reality of an individual's relations to society is often a compound of the particular kinds of organization described. Moreover, at certain stages of his growth, the individual may move through various kinds of organization; indeed it is commonplace in some societies for adolescents to move through the stages of rebel, exile or vagrant before becoming members or servants. Because it is a form of organization, and not a single substance, the individual's relationship with society will be a complicated embodiment of a wide area of real relationships although within this certain forms of organization such as those described may be determining.

IV

From the early descriptions of 'the individual' and 'society' to the more refined descriptions of the contemporary debate we can trace a persistent tendency to describe living processes in terms that confer on them the apparent status of fixed and separable objects. The terms we need, to describe the experience adequately, must be essentially active, yet every new description we invent seems to turn, more or less rapidly, into an object, and it is then very difficult both to clarify experience and to remain faithful to it. The crucial fact is that every description, every offered interpretation, is a term of growth. [...]

In the case of the individual and society we need to learn ways of thinking and feeling which will enable us genuinely to know each in the other's terms, which is as near as we can ordinarily get to saying that we are studying forms of organization in a continuous process: the brain, the nervous system, the body, the family, the group, the society, man. There is no real point at which we can break off this process, to isolate an independent substance. Yet equally we cannot select any one of them and make the others dependent on it. If the old individualism artificially isolated the 'bare human being', there is equal danger in certain trends in the new sociology which isolate the group, the society or the culture as an absolute point of reference. The continuous process of our human organization is itself a continuous action and adjustment in relation to all that is not human, and the central fact of this action and adjustment is a process of learning and communication which has grown through continual variation and the effort to transmit variation. We must not think only of society or the group acting on the unique individual, but also of many unique individuals, through a process of communication, creating and where necessary extending the organization by which they will continue to be shaped. It is right to recognize that we became human individuals in terms of a social process, but still individuals are unique, through a particular heredity expressed in a particular history. And the point about this uniqueness is that it is creative as well as created: new forms can flow from this particular form, and extend in the whole organization, which is in any case being constantly renewed and changed as unique individuals inherit and continue it. This recognition of individual uniqueness, and of the relation of its creativity to general human patterns, is, of course, the permanent basis of the case for democracy as a system of government. It is true that the value and effect of any particular uniqueness will vary considerably, for it will emerge only in a system of real relationships, which will set terms to its degree of communicability and relevance, and beyond this there will be widely varying degrees of success, between individuals, in self- realization and capacity to describe. The fact remains, however, that all human individuals are unique: it was one of the worst results of the old individualism that in asserting the importance of certain individuals, it moved, consciously or unconsciously, to denying the importance of others. When we get past this to realize that individuation is in fact the general process of our humanity, and that it is through individuation and communication that we have learned and are learning to live, we must recognize and respect the true scale and complexity of the process, which no one of us, and no group, is in a position to understand, let alone seek to control. If man is essentially a learning, creating and communicating being, the only social organization adequate to his nature is a participating democracy, in which all of us, as unique individuals, learn, communicate and control. Any lesser, restrictive system is simply wasteful of our true resources; in wasting individuals, by shutting them out from effective participation, it is damaging our true common process.

The long conflict between 'the individual' and 'society' resolves itself, as we reach out in these ways, into the difficulty of stating this interlocking process of organism and organization, which are not new terms for individual and society but ways of describing a continuous process within which both are contained. The worst result of abstracting 'the individual' and 'society' is that it limits our thinking to questions of relationship between them. We say this individual is good because he lives in a way that his society values; this society is good because it allows individuals to do these kinds of thing. Yet an individual, in being directed by the norms of his society, may be suppressing a variation which could become generally valuable, or a society, by permitting certain variations, may destroy itself, or other societies, or parts of its environment. These real issues can only be looked at adequately if we recognize the continuity between the many kinds of organization which compose the whole living process. To abstract certain fixed states, and then argue from them, which has been the normal method of approaching this question, is wholly inadequate. Difficult as any new conception may be, it seems absolutely necessary to try to formulate it, and then to learn from it possibly adequate new approaches. In practical terms I think such approaches will be the kind of study of patterns and relationships, in a whole process, which we have defined as the analysis of culture. There, in the practice of creation, communication, and the making of institutions is the common process of personal and social growth.

Part II

Countering the Canon
(1962–71)

Part II: Introduction

As Terry Eagleton has observed, the usual term 'critic' is 'a problematic description' for Williams (Eagleton 1984: 108). Moving with facility from the intricate detail of historical semantics to the conceptual complexities of Marxist cultural theory, writing on politics, ecology and nuclear disarmament with the same verve and attention to detail as he gave to his analyses of pastoral poetry, the nineteenth-century novel and the history of dramatic form, and equally at home with creative as with critical writing, Williams was always more than just a literary critic.

Always more than a critic; but also first and foremost a critic. No less than ten of Williams's twenty-odd scholarly books are devoted to literary criticism, from the early *Reading and Criticism* (1950), through the major studies of the 1960s and 1970s (*Modern Tragedy* (1966), *The English Novel from Dickens to Lawrence* (1970), *The Country and the City* (1973)) to later works such as *Cobbett* (1983b), *Writing in Society* (1984) and *The Politics of Modernism* (1989a), while his thinking in his other scholarly works is always clearly indebted to his literary criticism, whether in the realm of cultural studies (*Communications* (1962a), *Television: Technology and Cultural Form* (1974), or in his more directly political writing (*May Day Manifesto* (1968), *Towards 2000* (1983a)). Yet there is a necessary paradox to this achievement in literary criticism: it was largely constituted by the detailed and principled rejection of criticism as the specific academic discipline that it usually took itself to be. Although this challenge to the self-image and self-understanding of literary criticism was only fully developed, on the level of theory, in works such as *Marxism and Literature* (1977a) and *Culture* (1981), the practical challenges to it and the tensions around it had been present from the beginning.[1] By 1977, he declared that he no longer believed, 'in any simple way, in the specialization of literature', wryly noting that this turn away from literary criticism had been 'developing over a long time' (Williams 1977b: 14). Over a long time indeed: a whole lifetime of academic writing and research.

The essays and extracts presented in this section of the *Reader* – 'Countering the Canon' – are all taken from the second major phase in Williams's development, the decade or so of teaching and writing which followed his appointment as a lecturer in the English Faculty at Cambridge University in 1961. This was by far the period of his most intense engagement with literary criticism. 1966 saw the publication of *Modern Tragedy*, while in 1968 substantially revised and extended versions of his earlier works on drama, *Drama in Performance* and *Drama from Ibsen to Brecht* appeared. In 1969 *The Pelican Book of English Prose: Volume 2, From 1780 to the Present Day* was published, and, in 1970, his riposte to F.R. Leavis's *The Great Tradition*, *The English Novel from Dickens to Lawrence*. The powerful monograph *Orwell* came out in 1971 and was followed by his masterpiece, *The Country and the City* in 1973. Throughout, Williams wrote to counter the canon, perpetually challenging the received ideas of English studies, and working to transform the discipline from within.

Each essay selected here presents Williams countering canonical thinking in one of its various forms. In **Tragedy and Revolution**, he questions the notion of the apparently stable and unitary idea of the tragic tradition, and the consequent ideological orthodoxy which had gathered around George Steiner's influential *The Death of Tragedy* (Steiner 1961). **Literature and Rural Society** represents, in its attack on the idea of a neutral literary history, the earliest formulation of the key insights which drove *The Country and the City*, while **Thomas Hardy and the English Novel** exemplifies the central arguments against the apparently aesthetic evaluation of the novelistic canon as first established in F.R. Leavis's *The Great Tradition* (Leavis [1948] 1983). Part 2 closes with an extract from Williams's reassessment of George Orwell, perhaps the most ideologically contested figure of the postwar era.

The best introduction to *Modern Tragedy* (from which we take **Tragedy and Revolution**) is to be found in 'A Dialogue on Tragedy', first published in the *New Left Review* (Williams 1962b). The 'Dialogue' presents a spectrum of opinion on tragedy, stretched between the opposing ideas and conceptions of the two main protagonists, Ridyear and Clark. While Ridyear's views are essentially those that Williams will develop in *Modern Tragedy*, Clark's ideas bear a strong resemblance to those offered in *The Death of Tragedy*. For Clark, as for Steiner, tragic drama is no longer possible in a modern, secular society.

'When man is his own measure, or, worse, when the attributes of God are transferred to man or to life, you simply cannot have tragedy', he asserts (Williams 1962b: 26). Consequently, the whole of modern tragic writing can only represent 'the dwindling of tragedy to the problem play' (p. 30). Most seriously of all, from Ridyear's point of view, Clark rules the political dimension outside the bounds of tragedy altogether. When Ridyear insists that the case of Stalin represents the main instance of genuine tragedy in the twentieth century (a point embodied in the inclusion of William's own play about Stalin, 'Koba', in the first edition of *Modern Tragedy*), Clark replies that all modern political ideologies deny 'the tragic response altogether' (p. 31). If, as Clark argues, both Marxism and liberalism claim, 'man can change himself and his condition, tragedy is merely irrelevant' (p. 31).

Merely irrelevant? Certainly not in Williams's view. For the cultural historian, though tragedy may be 'a single and powerful word' (**Tragedy and Revolution**, p. 97), it is always a word with a history; and every tradition that the critic locates is necessarily a selective one, 'not the past, but an interpretation of the past: a selection and valuation' (p. 96). Such acts of interpretation are, he argues, firmly grounded in the present, and it comes as no surprise to find that the 'most striking fact about modern tragic theory' is 'that it is rooted in very much the same structure of feeling as modern tragedy itself' (1966: 46). A paradox then follows in the common 'denial that modern tragedy is possible, after almost a century of important and continuous tragic art' (1966: ibid). Why this denial? Williams here supersedes the usual procedures of literary criticism by placing its own apparently neutral arguments firmly in their own sociopolitical context.

While Part Two of *Modern Tragedy*, 'Modern Tragic Literature', presents seven case studies which refute any idea of the contemporary 'death of tragedy', Part One, from which we take **Tragedy and Revolution**, argues the case more theoretically. It seeks to account for the denial of modern tragedy in terms of the occluded centrality of revolution in the contemporary social thinking of the 1960s. Throughout, he takes issue with both liberal and leftist attitudes towards revolution, arguing that 'the received ideas no longer describe our experience'. In its ordinary liberal form, the idea of tragedy 'excludes especially that tragic experience which is social', while 'the idea of revolution', in the orthodox Marxist form, 'excludes especially that social experience which is tragic' (**Tragedy and Revolution**, p. 98). The need is to get beyond the 'contemporary reflex' in which 'the taking of rational control over our social destiny is defeated...by our inevitable irrationality' (p. 101) while also avoiding the revolutionary optimism in which the 'more general and abstract, the more truly mechanical, the process of human liberation is ordinarily conceived to be, the less any actual suffering really counts, until even death is a paper currency' (p. 101). As Williams stressed, in an argument which embodied just that broader public relevance and address which made his criticism always something more than just literary criticism, if 'we find a particular idea of tragedy, in our own time, we find also a way of interpreting a very wide area of our own experience; relevant certainly to literary criticism but relevant also to very much else' (1966: 61).

The Country and the City – Williams's single greatest achievement – is best read as a whole, for the broad sweep of argument and analysis that takes the reader from the interpretation of the long literary tradition of writing about the country and the city through to the analysis of contemporary forms of imperialism and resistance. No single text better illustrates his commitment to a form of criticism which, by combining historical with theoretical analysis, goes beyond the usual limits of literary criticism to mutate into a powerful form of cultural critique. Rather than offering a single extract from the book, I have selected two items which give something of the distinctive flavour of the project as a whole. **Literature and Rural Society** presents the project in its earliest extant form, as a broadcast lecture from 1967, while **Thomas Hardy and the English Novel**, while taken here from *The English Novel from Dickens to Lawrence*, forms, in a lightly revised version, a section from *The Country and the City*

In **Literature and Rural Society** Williams recalled how his new critical project was grounded in the ideological dynamics of his own academic formation. 'When I first went to Cambridge, I was offered the interpretation I am now rejecting: a convention of rural order, of Old England, against industrial disorder and the modern world. I had the strongest personal reasons for doubting it', he continues, 'but it has taken me years to reach the point where I can try to say, intellectually, where it was wrong' (**Literature and Rural Society**, p. 117); it was to take several more to complete the project. This interpretation was the apparently neutral account of a literary history which had, in reality, its own contemporary agenda. Though by the 1960s it had long since settled into the orthodox underpinnings of literary criticism, the case had first been fully made as early as 1932, when F.R. Leavis had argued for the need for a minority culture of intellectuals trained in the discriminations of literary criticism to resist the forces of the new mass civilization. Arguably, Leavis's formulation of the case had, despite some queries, questions and challenges, remained the principle justification for the discipline of English.

As Williams argued, in part from the evidence offered by his own country upbringing and experience, in part from his developing theoretical and methodological resources, the key to the whole minority civilization argument rested in the assertion that an authentic and homogeneous rural civilization had only now just vanished, in the first few decades of the twentieth century.

He insisted that this claim be read against the long literary history of just such claims. 'If we mount a kind of historical escalator' he writes, in a curiously powerful figure, 'and begin to move back in time, we see that this "now" is everywhere' – present not only in George Sturt's *Change in the Village* (1923) but in the novels of Thomas Hardy and George Eliot, and, earlier, in the poetry of John Clare and William Goldsmith, and earlier still, in the '17th century and the plays of Philip Massinger' (**Literature and Rural Society**, p. 110–11). In the end, he wryly notes, the argument can only come to a halt at the gates of Eden.

Clearly, writes Williams, what is at stake in such an argument is no 'simple difference of objective fact or even of historical conditions. It's a question, rather, of a way of seeing and of a consequent literary convention' (**Literature and Rural Society**, p. 112). Importantly, two positions regarding the relations between history and literature are rejected here. The first is the rejection of the idea that literature can provide, in any unproblematic way, an accurate record of actual historical events and, along with this, the implication that literature exists as the reflection of a pre- existing social reality. The second is the turning aside of any idea that literature stands somehow outside history: Williams's emphasis is placed on the necessary historicity of literature, grounded as convention in the broader social discourses of any period, and the 'ways of seeing' which these provide. Literature, in other words, not as presentation but as representation. With this complication of the usual internal form of literary history, Williams once again worked to shift literary criticism towards the form of cultural criticism he later referred to as a cultural materialism.

This forceful response to the ways in which the literary canon was still taught in the 1960s continued in William's writing on the English novel. *The English Novel from Dickens to Lawrence* was published in 1970, bringing together a series of lectures which he had given each year for the Cambridge English Faculty. On one level, *The English Novel* may appear to offer simply a counter-canon to F. R. Leavis's influential study, *The Great Tradition*: Dickens is not important for Leavis, but he is for Williams; Williams prefers early Lawrence and early George Eliot while Leavis's preference is for the later works of both writers; Hardy is the central figure in Williams's canon, but marginal in Leavis's terms. But considerably more is at stake in the discussion than just the contents of the canon: Williams offers a major reconsideration of the relations between form and evaluation as these come together in the question of style.

Already, in his introduction to the *Pelican History of English Prose*, he had argued for a conception of style grounded in the relations between author and audience rather than in terms of aesthetic appreciation. 'One of the marks of a conservative society', he noted in 1969, 'is that it regards style as an absolute. A style of writing or speech is judged as a question of manners, and appreciation of this style as a question of breeding and taste' (Williams 1984: 73). Against this, he argued for a conception of style as 'inseparable from the substance and feelings expressed' and inseparable also from 'the precise relationship of which it is a form' (p. 74). 'Good prose and style are not things but relationships', he concludes (p. 118) and this holds for the novel just as it does for other forms of prose writing.

Discussion of Thomas Hardy's work holds a central place in the Pelican 'Introduction', as in *The English Novel from Dickens to Lawrence*. Leavis had famously restricted his comments on Hardy to a disparaging quotation from Henry James ('chock-full of faults and falsity, and yet... a singular charm' (cited in Leavis [1948] 1983: 146); he could never be allotted a central place in the canon because of his faults in style and failures of tone. Against Leavis, Williams argued that no one had better expressed the central dilemmas of the novel as a form than Thomas Hardy. Hardy always writes and 'sees as a participant who is also an observer' (**Thomas Hardy and the English Novel**, p. 135); his novels exemplify 'the recurring problem of the social consciousness of the writer' (1970: 77). Long before the writings of Mikhail Bakhtin became the common currency for understanding the ideological and the stylistic dynamics of the novel, Williams had insisted on the need to understand their interaction as the result or play of an author's social position-ality.[2] This same dynamic of observation and participation, of writing and representation was exemplified in the work of George Orwell, and we close this section of the *Reader* with an extract from the monograph on *Orwell*, first published in 1971.

If Hardy's novels exemplified the 'problem of the social consciousness of the writer', Orwell's writing did its best to avoid or repress it. Williams had already discussed his work in *Culture and Society*, dismissing orthodox Marxist critiques of Orwell as 'mere partisan debate... arrogant and crass' (Williams 1958: 286, 294). Returning to the subject in 1971, his judgements are somewhat sharper as he seeks to combat the increasingly central place Orwell's work had come to hold in liberal and conservative ideology. As he later put it, 'if you engaged in any kind of socialist argument, there was an enormously inflated statue of Orwell warning you to go back. Down to the late sixties political editorials in newspapers would regularly admonish younger socialists to read their Orwell and see where all this led to' (Williams 1979: 384).

He focused his challenge on what is generally understood as the strongest point of Orwell's appeal: the force and integrity of his plain style, which he read as Orwell's 'impersonation of the plain man who bumps into experience in an unmediated way and is simply telling the truth about it' (Williams 1979: 383). Countering this, Williams points to the fact of mediation present in all forms of representation, including those which assume the rhetoric of objecti-vity so strongly associated with Orwell. In the end, he argues, 'the problem of standpoint... is the key to any critical judgement' and, despite his frequent recourse to the figure of 'an isolated individual observer and the objects of his observation', the reality is that, for Orwell just as much as for Hardy, 'it is impossible to observe anything without being in some relationship to it' (**Orwell**, p. 144). What is paradoxically neglected or repressed in Orwell's documentary realist mode is precisely the fact of social relationship, nonetheless present in the act of composition and selection. Writing is always writing in society, the literary act always an act of representation.

By the beginning of the 1970s, Williams's work as a critic had considerably shifted the meaning of what it meant to be a critic, and redefined the focal points and perspectives associated with traditional literary criticism and its account of the canon. Evaluation was necessarily ideological as well as aesthetic; questions of style were best addressed historically, as questions of social identity and positionality; all writing embodied questions of representation and mediation. As Orwell's case exemplified, there could be no such thing as 'natural seeing': 'direct and unmediated contact with reality' was an impossibility (1979: 167). This juxtaposition of social and historical analysis with textual analysis – an act of intellectual montage – produced a third dimension of enquiry: the theoretical. And it was precisely questions of theory – problems regarding mediation, representation, and the concept of the subject – which powered the next phase of Williams's work in which he returned to address the relations between Marxism and literature in the context of the new critical structuralism.

Notes

1   This case is argued at length in Higgins 1999, especially Ch. 1 'The Tight Place: Marxism or literature? 1947–50'.

2   See, for instance, the various discussions in the essays which make up *The Dialogic Imagination* (Bakhtin 1981). Bakhtin's argument that language 'is not a neutral medium that passes freely and easily into the private property of the speaker's intentions; it is populated – overpopulated – with the intentions of others. Expropriating it, forcing it to submit to one's own intentions and accents, is a difficult and complicated process' (Bakhtin 1981: 294) seems particularly relevant to Hardy's work; while his further comment that 'Consciousness finds itself inevitably facing the necessity of *having to choose a language*. With each literary-verbal performance, consciousness must actively orient itself amidst heteroglossia...' (p. 295) seems interestingly comparable to Williams's own analysis.

5

Tragedy and Revolution

From Raymond Williams (1966) Modern Tragedy. *London: Chatto and Windus*

We come to tragedy by many roads. It is an immediate experience, a body of literature, a conflict of theory, an academic problem. This book is written from the point where the roads cross, in a particular life.

In an ordinary life, spanning the middle years of the twentieth century, I have known what I believe to be tragedy, in several forms. It has not been the death of princes; it has been at once more personal and more general. I have been driven to try to understand this experience, and I have drawn back, baffled, at the distance between my own sense of tragedy and the conventions of the time. Thus I have known tragedy in the life of a man driven back to silence, in an unregarded working life. In his ordinary and private death, I saw a terrifying loss of connection between men, and even between father and son: a loss of connection which was, however, a particular social and historical fact: a measurable distance between his desire and his endurance, and between both and the purposes and meanings which the general life offered him. I have known this tragedy more widely since. I have seen the loss of connection built into a works and a city, and men and women broken by the pressure to accept this as normal, and by the deferment and corrosion of hope and desire. I have known also, as a whole culture has known, a tragic action framing these worlds, yet also, paradoxically and bitterly, breaking into them: an action of war and social revolution on so great a scale that it is continually and understandably reduced to the abstractions of political history, yet an action that cannot finally be held at this level and distance, by those who have known it as the history of real men and women, or by those who know, as a quite personal fact, that the action is not yet ended.

Tragedy has become, in our culture, a common name for this kind of experience. Not only the examples I have given, but many other kinds of event – a mining disaster, a burned-out family, a broken career, a smash on the road – are called tragedies. Yet tragedy is also a name derived from a particular kind of dramatic art, which over twenty-five centuries has a complicated yet arguably continuous history. The survival of many great works which we call tragedies makes this presence especially powerful. This coexistence of meanings seems to me quite natural, and there is no fundamental difficulty in both seeing their relations and distinguishing between them. Yet it is very common for men trained in what is now the academic tradition to be impatient and even contemptuous of what they regard as loose and vulgar uses of 'tragedy' in ordinary speech and in the newspapers.

To begin a discussion of modern tragedy with the modern experiences that most of us call tragic, and to try to relate these to tragic literature and theory, can provoke literal amazement, or the simpler and more conventional cry of incompetence. The word, we are given to understand, is being simply and perhaps viciously misused. And of course it is natural to hesitate, at this point. In a partly educated society, we are understandably nervous about using a word or a description wrongly. But then it becomes clear, as we listen, that what is in question is not only a word. Tragedy, we are told, is not simply death and suffering, and it is certainly not accident. Nor is it simply any response to death and suffering. It is, rather, a particular kind of event, and kind of response, which are genuinely tragic, and which the long tradition embodies. To confuse this tradition with other kinds of event and response is merely ignorant.

But again, as we listen, we see that what is in question is not only the use of 'tragedy' to describe something other than a work of dramatic literature: the extension we have already noted. What is more deeply in question is a particular kind and particular interpretation of death and suffering. Certain events and responses are tragic, and others are not. By sheer authority, and from our natural eagerness to learn, it is possible for this to be said and repeated, without real challenge. And to be half inside and half outside such a system is to be reduced to despair. For there are two questions which still need to be asked. Is it really the case that what is called the tradition carries so clear and single a meaning? And, whatever our answer to this, what actual relations are we to see and live by, between the tradition of tragedy and the kinds of experience, in our own time, that we ordinarily and perhaps mistakenly call tragic?

It takes, I believe, many years, to move from first shaping these questions, in a personal uncertainty about the implications of what is being taught, to putting them at all precisely and being in any position to try to answer them. The difficulties are in any case so severe that no time is really long enough. But the moment comes when it is necessary to make a beginning. I propose to examine the tradition, with particular reference to its actual historical development, which I see as crucial to an understanding of its present status and implications. I can then offer what I believe to be an explanation of the separation between 'tragedy' and tragedy, and try, in different ways, to describe the relations and connections which this formal separation hides.

The separation of 'tragedy' and tragedy is in one sense inevitable. Our thinking about tragedy is important because it is a point of intersection between tradition and experience, and it would certainly be surprising if the intersection turned out to be a coincidence. Tragedy comes to us, as a word, from a long tradition of European civilization, and it is easy to see this tradition as a continuity in one important way: that so many of the later writers and thinkers have been conscious of the earlier, and have seen themselves as contributing to a common idea or form. Yet 'tradition' and 'continuity', as words, can lead us into a wholly wrong emphasis. When we come to study the tradition, we are immediately aware of change. All we can take quite for granted is the continuity of 'tragedy' as a word. It may well be that there are more important continuities, but we can certainly not begin by assuming them.

There is a common pressure, in the ordinary verbal contrast between traditional and modern, to compress and unify the various thinking of the past into a single tradition, 'the' tradition. In the case of tragedy, there are additional pressures of a particular kind: the assumption of a common Graeco Christian tradition, which has shaped Western civilization. Tragedy is at first sight one of the simplest and most powerful illustrations of this cultural continuity. Tragedy is the Greeks and the Elizabethans, in one cultural form; Hellenes and Christians, in a common activity. It is easy to see how convenient, how indispensable, an idea of tragedy this is. Most study of tragedy has been unconsciously determined by just this assumption, and indeed by a desire to teach and propagate it. At particular stages of our own history, the revival of tragedy has been a strategy determined by this consciousness of a necessary tradition. In our own century, especially, when there has been a widespread sense of that civilization being threatened, the use of the idea of tragedy, to define a major tradition threatened or destroyed by an unruly present, has been quite obvious. And then it is not a question of mere counter-assumption: that there is no such significant continuity. It is a question, rather, of realising that a tradition is not the past, but an interpretation of the past: a selection and valuation of ancestors, rather than a neutral record. And if this is so, the present, at any time, is a factor in the selection and valuation. It is not the contrast but the relationship between modern and traditional that concerns the cultural historian.

To examine the tragic tradition, that is to say, is not necessarily to expound a single body of work and thinking, or to trace variations within an assumed totality. It is to look, critically and historically, at works and ideas which have certain evident links, and which are associated in our minds by a single and powerful word. It is, above all, to see these works and ideas in their immediate contexts, as well as in their historical continuity, and to examine their place and function in relation to other works and ideas, and to the variety of actual experience.

I shall hope to show, if only in outline, an historical development of the idea of tragedy, which may enable us to escape the deadlock of the contemporary contrast between 'Tragedy, proper, so-called, as known from the tradition', and the forms and pressures of our own tragic experience. What we have really to see, in what is offered to us as a single tradition, is a tension and variation so significant, on matters continually and inevitably important to us, that we gain not only relief from a contemporary deadlock, but a positive historical insight. [...]

We are not looking for a new universal meaning of tragedy. We are looking for the structure of tragedy in our own culture. Once we begin to doubt, in experience and then in analysis, the ordinary twentieth-century idea, other directions seem open.

Since the time of the French Revolution, the idea of tragedy can be seen as in different ways a response to a culture in conscious change and movement. The action of tragedy and the action of history have been consciously connected, and in the connection have been seen in new ways. The reaction against this, from the mid-nineteenth century, has been equally evident: the movement of spirit has been separated from the movement of civilisation. Yet even this negative reaction seems, in its context, a response to the same kind of crisis. The academic tradition, on the whole, has followed the negative reaction, but it is difficult to hear its ordinary propositions and feel that they are only about a set of academic facts. They sound, insistently, like propositions about contemporary life, even when they are most negative and most consciously asocial. The other nineteenth-century tradition, in which tragedy and history were consciously connected, seems then deeply relevant. In experience and in theory we have to look again at this relation.

We must ask whether tragedy, in our own time, is a response to social disorder. If it is so, we shall not expect the response to be always direct. The disorder will appear in very many forms, and to articulate these will be very complex and difficult. A more immediate difficulty is the ordinary separation of social thinking and tragic thinking. The most influential kinds of explicitly social thinking have often rejected tragedy as in itself defeatist. Against what they have known as the idea of tragedy, they have stressed man's powers to change his condition and to end a major part of the suffering which the tragic ideology seems to ratify. The idea of tragedy, that is to say, has been explicitly opposed by the idea of revolution: there has been as much confidence on the one side as on the other. And then to describe tragedy as a response to social disorder, and to value it as such, is to break, apparently, from both major traditions.

The immediate disturbance is radical, for the fault in the soul was a recognition of a kind; it was close to the experience, even when it added its ordinary formulas. From the other position, from the recognition of social disorder, there is a habit of easy abstraction which the scale of the disorder almost inevitably supports. As we recognise history, we are referred to history, and find it difficult to acknowledge men like ourselves. Before, we could not recognise tragedy as social crisis; now, commonly, we cannot recognise social crisis as tragedy. The facts of disorder are caught up in a new ideology, which cancels suffering as it finds the name of a period or a phase. From day to day we can make everything past, because we believe in the future. Our actual present, in which the disorder is radical, is as effectively hidden as when it was merely politics, for it is now only politics. It seems that we have jumped from one blindness to another, and with the same visionary confidence. The new connections harden, and no longer connect.

What seems to matter, against every difficulty, is that the received ideas no longer describe our experience. The most common idea of revolution excludes too much of our social experience. But it is more than this. The idea of tragedy, in its ordinary form, excludes especially that tragic experience which is social, and the idea of revolution, again in its ordinary form, excludes especially that social experience which is tragic. And if this is so, the contradiction is significant. It is not a merely formal opposition, of two ways of reading experience, between which we can choose. In our own time, especially, it is the connections between revolution and tragedy – connections lived and known but not acknowledged as ideas – which seem most clear and significant.

The most evident connection is in the actual events of history, as we all quite simply observe them. A time of revolution is so evidently a time of violence, dislocation and extended suffering that it is natural to feel it as tragedy, in the everyday sense. Yet, as the event becomes history, it is often quite differently regarded. Very many nations look back to the revolutions of their own history as to the era of creation of the life which is now most precious. The successful revolution, we might say, becomes not tragedy but epic: it is the origin of a people, and of its valued way of life. When the suffering is remembered, it is at once either honoured or justified. That particular revolution, we say, was a necessary condition of life.

Contemporary revolution is of course very different. Only a post-revolutionary generation is capable of that epic composition. In contemporary revolution, the detail of suffering is insistent, whether as violence or as the reshaping of lives by a new power in the state. But further, in a contemporary revolution, we inevitably take sides, though with different degrees of engagement. And a time of revolution is ordinarily a time of lies and of suppressions of truths. The suffering of the whole action, even when its full weight is acknowledged, is commonly projected as the responsibility of this party or that, until its very description becomes a revolutionary or counter- revolutionary act. There is a kind of indifference which comes early whenever the action is at a distance. But there is also an exposure to the scale of suffering, and to the lies and campaigns that are made from it, which in the end is also indifference. Revolution is a dimension of action from which, for initially honourable reasons, we feel we have to keep clear.

Thus the social fact becomes a structure of feeling. Revolution as such is in a common sense tragedy, a time of chaos and suffering. It is almost inevitable that we should try to go beyond it. I do not rely on what is almost certain to happen: that this tragedy, in its turn, will become epic. However true this may be, it cannot closely move us; only heirs can inherit. Allegiance to even a probable law of history, which has not, however, in the particular case, been lived through, becomes quite quickly an alienation. We are not truly responding to this action but, by projection, to its probable composition.

The living alternative is quite different in character. It is neither the rejection of revolution, by its simple characterisation as chaos and suffering, nor yet the calculation of revolution, by laws and probabilities not yet experienced. It is, rather, a recognition; the recognition of revolution as a whole action of living men. Both the wholeness of the action, and in this sense its humanity, are then inescapable. It is this recognition against which we ordinarily struggle.

As we have reduced tragedy to the death of the hero, so we have reduced revolution to its crisis of violence and disorder. In simple observation, these are often the most evident effects, but in the whole action they are both preceded and succeeded, and much of their meaning depends on this fact of continuity. Thus it is strange that from our whole modern history revolution should be selected as the example of violence and disorder: revolution, that is, as the critical conflict and resolution of forces. To limit violence and disorder to the decisive conflict is to make nonsense of that conflict itself. The violence and disorder are in the whole action, of which what we commonly call revolution is the crisis.

The essential point is that violence and disorder are institutions as well as acts. When a revolutionary change has been lived through, we can usually see this quite clearly. The old institutions, now dead, take on their real quality as systematic violence and disorder; in that quality, the source of the revolutionary action is seen. But while such institutions are still effective, they can seem, to an extraordinary extent, both settled and innocent. Indeed they constitute, commonly, an order, against which the very protest, of the injured and oppressed, seems the source of disturbance and violence. Here, most urgently, in our own time, we need to return the idea of revolution, in its ordinary sense of the crisis of a society, to its necessary context as part of a whole action, within which alone it can be understood.

Order and disorder are relative terms, although each is experienced as an absolute. We are aware of this relativism, through history and comparative studies: intellectually aware, though that is often not much use to us, under the pressure of fear or interest or in the simple immediacy of our local and actual world. In the ideas of both tragedy and revolution, this dimension and yet also these difficulties are at once encountered. I have already argued that the relation between tragedy and order is dynamic. The tragic action is rooted in a disorder, which indeed, at a particular stage, can seem to have its own stability. But the whole body of real forces is engaged by the action, often in such a way that the underlying disorder becomes apparent and terrible in overtly tragic ways. From the whole experience of this disorder, and through its specific action, order is recreated. The process of this action is at times remarkably similar to the real action of revolution.

Yet revolution, at least in its feudal form as rebellion, is often, in many valued tragedies, the disorder itself. The restoration of 'lawful' authority is there literally the restoration of order. But the essential consideration lies deeper than this, below the false consciousness of feudal attitudes to rebellion. It is not difficult to see that the feudal definitions of lawful authority and rebellion are, at the political level, at worst timeserving, at best partisan. The majesty of kings is usually the political façade of successful usurpers and their descendants. What challenges it, as an action, is of the same human kind as what established it. Yet the investment of political power with religious or magical sanctions is also, in its most important examples, a vehicle for the expression of a fundamental conception of order, and indeed of the nature of life and of man. Characteristically, this is a conception of a static order, and of a permanent human condition and nature. Around such conceptions, real values are formed, and the threat to them overrides the temporary and arbitrary association of them with a particular figure or system. When connections of this kind are a living reality, the tragic action, whatever its local form, can have the widest human reference. [. . .]

It is here that the relation between revolution and tragedy is inescapable and urgent. It may still be possible, for some thinkers, to interpret actual revolution in the received ideology of rationalism. We can all see the constructive activity of the successful revolutionary societies, and we can take this as evidence of the simple act of human liberation by the energy of reason. I know nothing I welcome more than this actual construction, but I know also that the revolutionary societies have been tragic societies, at a depth and on a scale that go beyond any ordinary pity and fear. At the point of this recognition, however, where the received ideology of revolution, its simple quality as liberation, seems most to fail, there is waiting the received ideology of tragedy, in either of its common forms: the old tragic lesson, that man cannot change his condition, but can only drown his world in blood in the vain attempt; or the contemporary reflex, that the taking of rational control over our social destiny is defeated or at best deeply stained by our inevitable irrationality, and by the violence and cruelty that are so quickly released when habitual forms break down. I do not find, in the end, that either of these interpretations covers enough of the facts, but also I do not see how anyone can still hold to that idea of revolution which simply denied tragedy, as an experience and as an idea.

Socialism, I believe, is the true and active inheritor of the impulse to human liberation which has previously taken so many different forms. But in practice, I also believe, it is an idea still forming, and much that passes under its name is only a residue of old positions. I do not mean only such a movement as Fabianism, with its cast of utilitarianism and its mechanical conceptions of change. I mean also a man current in Marxism, which though Marx may at times have opposed it is also profoundly mechanical, in its determinism, in its social materialism, and in its characteristic abstraction of social classes from human beings. I can see that it is possible, with such habits of mind, to interpret revolution as only constructive and liberating. Real suffering is then at once non-human: is a class swept away by history, is an error in the working of the machine, or is the blood that is not and never can be rose water. The more general and abstract, the more truly mechanical, the process of human liberation is ordinarily conceived to be, the less any actual suffering really counts, until even death is a paper currency.

But then I do not believe, as so many disillusioned or broken by actual revolution have come to believe, that the suffering can be laid to the charge of the revolution alone, and that we must avoid revolution if we are to avoid suffering. On the contrary, I see revolution as the inevitable working through of a deep and tragic disorder, to which we can respond in varying ways but which will in any case, in one way or another, work its way through our world, as a consequence of any of our actions. I see revolution, that is to say, in a tragic perspective, and it is this I now seek to define.

Marx's early idea of revolution seems to me to be tragic in this sense:

A class must be formed which has *radical chains*, a class in civil society which is not a class of civil society, a class which is the dissolution of all classes, a sphere of society which has a universal character because its sufferings are universal, and which does not claim a *particular redress* because the wrong which is done to it is not a *particular wrong* but *wrong in general*. There must be formed a sphere of society which claims no *traditional* status but only a *human* status…a sphere finally which cannot emancipate itself without emancipating itself from all the other spheres of society, without therefore emancipating all these other spheres; which is, in short, a *total loss* of humanity and which can only redeem itself by a *total redemption of humanity*.

(*Zur Kritik der Hegelschen Rechts-Philosophie: Einleitung*)

So absolute a conception distinguishes revolution from rebellion, or, to put it another way, makes political revolution into a general human revolution:

In all former revolutions the form of activity was always left unaltered, and it was only a question of redistributing this activity among different people, of introducing a new division of labour. The communist revolution, however, is directed against the former *mode* of activity, does away with *labour*, and abolishes all class rule along with the classes themselves. . . .

(*Die Deutsche Ideologie*)

The *social life* from which the worker is shut out . . . is *life* itself, physical and cultural life, human morality, human activity, human enjoyment, real human existence. . . . As the irremediable exclusion from this life is much more complete, more unbearable, dreadful, and contradictory, than the exclusion from political life, so is the ending of this exclusion, and even a limited reaction, a *revolt* against it, more fundamental, as *man* is more fundamental than the *citizen, human life* more than *political life*.

(*Vorwärts* (1844))

This way of seeing revolution seems to me to stand. Whatever we have learned, since Marx wrote, about actual historical development, and thence about the agencies and tactics of revolution, does not affect the idea itself. We need not identify revolution with violence or with a sudden capture of power. Even where such events occur, the essential transformation is indeed a long revolution. But the absolute test, by which revolution can be distinguished, is the change in the *form* of activity of a society, in its deepest structure of relationships and feelings. The incorporation of new groups of men into the pre- existing form and structure is something quite different, even when it is accompanied by an evident improvement of material conditions and by the ordinary changes of period and local colour. In fact the test of a pre-revolutionary society, or of a society in which the revolution is still incomplete, is in just this matter of incorporation. A society in which revolution is necessary is a society in which the incorporation of all its people, *as whole human beings*, is in practice impossible without a change in its fundamental form of relationships. The many kinds of partial 'incorporation' – as voters, as employees, or as persons entitled to education, legal protection, social services and so on – are real human gains, but do not in themselves amount to that full membership of society which is the end of classes. The reality of full membership is the capacity to direct a particular society, by active mutual responsibility and co-operation, on a basis of full social equality. And while this is the purpose of revolution, it remains necessary in all societies in which there are, for example, subordinate racial groups, landless landworkers, hired hands, the unemployed, and suppressed or discriminate minorities of any kind. Revolution remains necessary, in these circumstances, not only because some men desire it, but because there can be no acceptable human order while the full humanity of any class of men is in practice denied.

This idea of 'the total redemption of humanity' has the ultimate cast of resolution and order, but in the real world its perspective is inescapably tragic. It is born in pity and terror: in the perception of a radical disorder in which the humanity of some men is denied and by that fact the idea of humanity itself is denied. It is born in the actual suffering of real men thus exposed, and in all the consequences of this suffering: degeneration, brutalisation, fear, hatred, envy. It is born in an experience of evil made the more intolerable by the conviction that it is not inevitable, but is the result of particular actions and choices.

And if it is thus tragic in its origins – in the existence of a disorder that cannot but move and involve – it is equally tragic in its action, in that it is not against gods or inanimate things that its impulse struggles, nor against mere institutions and social forms, but against other men. This, throughout, has been the area of silence, in the development of the idea. What is properly called utopianism, or revolutionary romanticism, is the suppression or dilution of this quite inevitable fact.

There are many reasons why men will oppose such a revolution. There are the obvious reasons of interest or privilege, for which we have seen men willing to die. There is the deep fear that recognition of the humanity of others is a denial of our own humanity, as our whole lives have known it. There is the flight in the mind from disturbance of a familiar world, however inadequate. There is the terror, often justified, of what will happen when men who have been treated as less than men gain the power to act. For there will of course be revenge and senseless destruction, after the bitterness and deformity of oppression. And then, more subtly, there are all the learned positions, from an experience of disorder that is as old as human history and yet also is continually re-enacted: the conviction that any absolute purpose is delusion and folly, to be corrected by training, by some social ease where we are, or by an outright opposition to this madness which would destroy the world.

From all these positions, revolution is practically opposed, in every form from brutal suppression and massive indoctrination to genuine attempts to construct alternative futures. And all our experience tells us that this immensely complicated action between real men will continue as far ahead as we can foresee, and that the suffering in this continuing struggle will go on being terrible. It is very difficult for the mind to accept this, and we all erect our defences against so tragic a recognition. But I believe that it is inevitable, and that we must speak of it if it is not to overwhelm us.

In some Western societies we are engaged in the attempt to make this total revolution without violence, by a process of argument and consensus. It is impossible to say if we shall succeed. The arrest of humanity, in many groups and individuals, is still severe and seems often intractable. At the same time, while the process has any chance of success, nobody in his senses would wish to alter its nature. The real difficulty, however, is that we have become introverted on this process, in a familiar kind of North Atlantic thinking, and the illusions this breeds are already of a tragic kind.

Thus we seek to project the result of particular historical circumstances as universal, and to identify all other forms of revolution as hostile. The only consistent common position is that of the enemies of revolution everywhere, yet even they, at times, speak a liberal rhetoric. It is a very deep irony that, in ideology, the major conflict in the world is between different versions of the absolute rights of man. Again and again, men in Western societies act as counter-revolutionaries, but in the name of an absolute liberation. There are real complexities here, for revolutionary regimes have also acted, repeatedly and brutally, against every kind of human freedom and dignity. But there are also deep and habitual forms of false consciousness. Only a very few of us, in any Western society, have in fact renounced violence, in the way that our theory claims. If we believe that social change should be peaceful, it is difficult to know what we are doing in military alliances, with immense armament and weapons of indiscriminate destruction. The customary pretence that this organised violence is defensive, and that it is wholly dedicated to human freedom, is literally a tragic illusion. It is easy to move about in our own comparatively peaceful society, repeating such phrases as 'a revolution by due course of law', and simply failing to notice that in our name, and endorsed by repeated majorities, other peoples have been violently opposed in the very act of their own liberation. The bloody tale of the past is always conveniently discounted, but I am writing on a day when British military power is being used against 'dissident tribesmen' in South Arabia, and I know this pattern and its covering too well, from repeated examples through my lifetime, to be able to acquiesce in the ordinary illusion. Many of my countrymen have opposed these policies, and in many particular cases have ended them. But it is impossible to believe that as a society we have yet dedicated ourselves to human liberation, or even to that simple recognition of the absolute humanity of all other men which is the impulse of any genuine revolution. To say that in our own affairs we have made this recognition would also be too much, in a society powered by great economic inequality and by organised manipulation. But even if we had made this recognition, among ourselves, it would still be a travesty of any real revolutionary belief. It is only when the recognition is general that it can be authentic, for in practice every reservation, in a widely communicating world, tends to degenerate into actual opposition.

Our interpretation of revolution as a slow and peaceful growth of consensus is at best a local experience and hope, at worst a sustained false consciousness. In a world determined by the struggle against poverty and against the many forms of colonial and neo-colonial domination, revolution continually and inescapably enters our society, in the form of our own role in those critical areas. And here it is not only that we have made persistent errors, and that we comfort ourselves with the illusion of steady progress when the gap between wealth and poverty is actually increasing in the world, and when the consciousness of exploitation is rapidly rising. It is also that the revolutionary process has become, in our generation, the ordinary starting point of war. It is very remarkable, in recent years, how the struggles for national liberation and for social change, in many different parts of the world, have involved the major powers in real and repeated dangers of general war. What are still, obtusely, called 'local upheavals', or even 'brushfires', put all our lives in question, again and again. Korea, Suez, the Congo, Cuba, Vietnam, are names of our own crisis. It is impossible to look at this real and still active history without a general sense of tragedy: not only because the disorder is so widespread and intolerable that in action and reaction it must work its way through our lives, wherever we may be; but also because, on any probable estimate, we understand the process so little that we continually contribute to the disorder. It is not simply that we become involved in this general crisis, but that we are already, by what we do and fail to do, participating in it.

There is, here, a strange contradiction. The two great wars we have known in Europe, and the widespread if still limited awareness of the nature of nuclear war, have induced a kind of inert pacifism which is too often self-regarding and dangerous. We say, understandably, that we must avoid war at all costs, but what we commonly mean is that we will avoid war at any cost but our own. Relatively appeased in our own situation, we interpret disturbance elsewhere as a threat to peace, and seek either to suppress it (the 'police action' to preserve what we call law and order; the fire brigade to put out the 'brushfire'), or to smother it with money or political manoeuvres. So deep is this contradiction that we regard such activities, even actual suppression, as morally virtuous; we even call it peacemaking. But what we are asking is what, in a limited consciousness, we have ourselves succeeded in doing: to acquiesce in a disorder and call it order; to say peace where there is no peace. We expect men brutally exploited and intolerably poor to rest and be patient in their misery, because if they act to end their condition it will involve the rest of us, and threaten our convenience or our lives.

In these ways, we have identified war and revolution as the tragic dangers, when the real tragic danger, underlying war and revolution, is a disorder which we continually re-enact. So false a peacemaking, so false an appeal to order, is common in the action of tragedy, in which, nevertheless, all the real forces of the whole situation eventually work themselves out. Even if we were willing to change, in our attitudes to others and even more in our real social relations with them, we might still not, so late in the day, avoid actual tragedy. But the only relevant response, to the tragedy of this kind that we have already experienced, is that quite different peacemaking which is the attempt to resolve rather than to cover the determining tragic disorder. Any such resolution would mean changing ourselves, in fundamental ways, and our unwillingness to do this, the certainty of disturbance, the probability of secondary and unforeseen disorder, put the question, inevitably, into a tragic form.

The only consciousness that seems adequate in our world is then an exposure to the actual disorder. The only action that seems adequate is, really, a participation in the disorder, as a way of ending it. But at this point another tragic perspective opens. I find that I still agree with Carlyle, when he wrote in *Chartism*:

Men who discern in the misery of the toiling complaining millions not misery, but only a raw material which can be wrought upon and traded in, for one's own poor hide-bound theories and egoisms; to whom millions of living fellow-creatures, with beating hearts in their bosoms, beating, suffering, hoping, are 'masses', mere 'explosive masses for blowing-down Bastilles with', for voting at hustings for *us*: such men are of the questionable species.

I have already argued the questionable nature of our many kinds of failure to commit ourselves to revolution. I would now repeat, with Carlyle, and with much real experience since he wrote, the questionable nature of a common kind of commitment. It is undoubtedly true that a commitment to revolution can produce a kind of hardening which even ends by negating the revolutionary purpose. Some people make the false commitment – the use of the misery of others – from the beginning. The most evident example is in Fascism, which is false revolution in just this sense. But, under real historical pressures, this hardening and negation occur again and again in authentic revolutionary activity, especially in isolation, under fire, and in scarcity so extreme as to threaten survival. The enemies of the revolutionary purpose then seize on the evidence of hardening and negation: either to oppose revolution as such, or to restore the convenient belief that man cannot change his condition, and that aspiration brings terror as a logical companion.

But this tragic aspect of revolution, which we are bound to acknowledge, cannot be understood in such ways. We have still to attend to the whole action, and to see actual liberation as part of the same process as the terror which appals us. I do not mean that the liberation cancels the terror; I mean only that they are connected, and that this connection is tragic. The final truth in this matter seems to be that revolution – the long revolution against human alienation – produces, in real historical circumstances, its own new kinds of alienation, which it must struggle to understand and which it must overcome, if it is to remain revolutionary.

I see this revolutionary alienation in several forms. There is the simple and yet bloody paradox that in the act of revolution its open enemies are easily seen as 'not men'. The tyrant, as he is killed, seems not a man but an object, and his brutality draws an answering brutality, which can become falsely associated with liberation itself. But it is not only a matter of the open enemies. Under severe pressure, the revolutionary purpose can become itself abstracted and can be set as an idea above real men. The decisive connection between present and future, which can only be a connection in experience and in continuing specific relations, is at once suppressed and replaced. There is then the conversion of actual misery and actual hope into a merely tactical 'revolutionary situation'. There is the related imposition of an idea of the revolution on the real men and women in whose name it is being made. The old unilinear model, by which revolution is abstractly known, is imposed on experience, including revolutionary experience. Often only this abstracted idea can sustain men, at the limits of their strength, but the need to impose it, in just such a crisis, converts friends into enemies, and actual life into the ruthlessly moulded material of an idea. The revolutionary purpose, born in what is most human and therefore most various, is negated by the single and often heroic image of revolutionary man, arrested at a stage in the very process of liberation and, persistent, becoming its most inward enemy.

In such ways, the most active agents of revolution can become its factual enemies, even while to others, and even to themselves, they seem its most perfect embodiment. But while we see this merely as accident, as the random appearance of particular evil men, we can understand nothing, for we are evading the nature of the whole action, and projecting its general meaning on to individuals whom we idealise or execrate. Elevating ourselves to spectators and judges, we suppress our own real role in any such action, or conclude, in a kind of indifference, that what has happened was inevitable and that there is even a law of inevitability. We see indeed a certain inevitability, of a tragic kind, as we see the struggle to end alienation producing its own new kinds of alienation. But, while we attend to the whole action, we see also, working through it, a new struggle against the new alienation: the comprehension of disorder producing a new image of order; the revolution against the fixed consciousness of revolution, and the authentic activity reborn and newly lived. What we then know is no simple action: the heroic liberation. But we know more also than simple reaction, for if we accept alienation, in ourselves or in others, as a permanent condition, we must know that other men, by the very act of living, will reject this, making us their involuntary enemies, and the radical disorder is then most bitterly confirmed.

The tragic action, in its deepest sense, is not the confirmation of disorder, but its experience, its comprehension and its resolution. In our own time, this action is general, and its common name is revolution. We have to see the evil and the suffering, in the factual disorder that makes revolution necessary, and in the disordered struggle against the disorder. We have to recognize this suffering in a close and immediate experience, and not cover it with names. But we follow the whole action: not only the evil, but the men who have fought against evil; not only the crisis, but the energy released by it, the spirit learned in it. We make the connections, because that is the action of tragedy, and what we learn in suffering is again revolution, because we acknowledge others as men and any such acknowledgement is the beginning of struggle, as the continuing reality of our lives. Then to see revolution in this tragic perspective is the only way to maintain it.

6

Literature and Rural Society

From The Listener *78, 16 November 1967*

Country life has been an image and even a commonplace of natural virtue and order in many literatures, and in English as powerfully as anywhere. Often it's a simple image: of the peace and quiet of the country as against the rush and ambition and worldliness of the city and the court; or in modern times, as against the ugly mechanism of the industrial town. But country life has also been seen, repeatedly, as the life of the past: of the writer's childhood, or of man's childhood, in Eden and the Golden Age. And it is here that the image becomes confused with history, so that many writers come to set dates, periods and historical formulations to the long habit of rural retrospect.

We're told this, for example, in a book published only last year: 'A way of life that has come down to us from the days of Virgil has suddenly ended.' And again we're told that since the beginning of this century, 'a whole culture that had preserved its continuity from earliest times had now received its quietus.' And in *Culture and Environment*, that critically influential book by Leavis and Thompson which was published in 1932, we find this sentence, about the disappearance of the 'organic community' of 'Old England': 'its destruction is very recent indeed.'

This account of a recently vanished rural civilisation was based on the books of George Sturt, which appeared between 1907 and 1923. Sturt wrote of the rural England 'that is dying out now', as he put it in his *Change in the Village*.

But if we mount a kind of historical escalator and begin to move back in time, we see that this 'now' is everywhere. Sturt traced the change to two periods: enclosure after 1861 and residential settlement after 1900. But that takes us back to the period of Thomas Hardy's novels, written between 1871 and 1896, but referring back to rural England since the 1840s. And hasn't everyone insisted that it was Hardy who recorded the great climacteric change in rural civilisation: the disturbance and destruction of what one writer has called the 'timeless rhythm of agriculture and the seasons'? This is also the period of Richard Jefferies, when in the 1870s he looks back to 'Old Hodge' and says that there'd been more change in rural England in the previous half-century – that is, since the 1820s – than in any previous time. And wasn't George Eliot, in *The Mill on the Floss* and in *Felix Holt*, both written in the 1860s, also looking back to the old rural England of the 1820s and early 1830s?

But the early 1830s were the last years of Cobbett's life. Cobbett was directly in touch with the rural England of that time, but he looks back to the happier country of his boyhood, during the 1770s and 1780s. And Thomas Bewick, writing his *Memoir* during the 1820s, was also recalling the happier village of *his* boyhood in the 1770s. Both these men argued that the decisive change had happened in their lifetimes. And the poet John Clare wrote of the 'far-fled pasture, long-evanish'd scene' in another retrospect on a vanishing rural order: 'Oh, happy Eden of those golden years.'

The escalator takes us back still further, for the years of Cobbett's boyhood are the years of Crabbe's poem *The Village* and Goldsmith's *The Deserted Village*. Goldsmith was writing in the late 1760s:

> E'en now the devastation is begun,
> And half the business of destruction done,
> E'en now, methinks, as pondering here I stand,
> I see the rural virtues leave the land.

The memory of 'sweet Auburn', by ordinary arithmetic, takes us back to the 1750s.

It's clear of course, as this escalator moves, that something more than ordinary arithmetic – sometimes more, too, than ordinary history – is in question. Clearly we need the sharpest scepticism against the sentimental and intellectualised accounts of an unlocalised 'Old England'. But at least some of these witnesses are writing from direct experience.

All we've done so far is to move 'Old England' and its so-called timeless agricultural rhythms back from the early 20th century to the middle of the 18th century. When we remember 'our mature, settled 18th century', we may not, after all, have made much difference to the ordinary accounts. Shall we go back, then, to the early 17th century and the plays of Philip Massinger, *The City Madam* and *A New Way to Pay Old Debts?* Here the new commercialism was breaking the old landed settlement and its virtues. Here is the enclosing and engrossing Sir Giles Overreach, and the corruption of an older rural civilisation. Shall we go back to Bastard's *Chrestoleros*, in 1598, where the same complaints were made? Or to Thomas More's *Utopia*, where another old order is being destroyed: 'Thei inclose all into pastures; their throw downe houses; thei plucke downe townes, and leave nothing standynge, but only the churche to be made a shepe-house.'

But then, of course, we find ourselves referred back to the settled Middle Ages, an organic society if ever there was one. To the 1730s, for instance, when Langland's *Piers Plowman* sees the dissatisfaction of the labourers, who won't eat yesterdays's vegetables, but must have fresh meat, who blame God and curse the king, but who didn't complain when Hunger made the Statues. Must we go back beyond the Black Death to the beginning of the Game Laws – beyond Magna Carta? Or shall we find the timeless rhythm in Domesday, when four out of five were villeins, bordars, cotters or slaves? Or in a free Saxon world before the Norman rape and yoke? In a Celtic world before the Saxons came with their gilded barbarism? Where indeed shall we reach before the escalator stop?

One answer, of course, is Eden. But let us return for the moment to Goldsmith and Crabbe. First Goldsmith, remembering sweet Auburn:

> Sweet Auburn! loveliest village of the plain,
> Where health and plenty cheer'd the labouring swain,
> Where smiling spring its earliest visit paid,
> And parting summer's lingering blooms delayed:
> Dear lovely bowers of innocence and ease,
> Seats of my youth, when every sport could please:
> How often have I loiter'd o'er thy green,
> Where humble happiness endear'd each scene!
> How often have I paused on every charm,
> The shelter'd cot, the cultivated farm,
> The never-failing brook, the busy mill,
> The decent church that topt the neighbouring hill,
> The hawthorn bush, with seats beneath the shade,
> For talking age and whispering lovers made!

And here, by contrast, is Crabbe:

> I grant indeed that fields and flocks have charms
> For him that grazes or for him that farms;
> But when amid such pleasing scenes I trace

The poor laborious natives of the place,
And see the midday sun, with fervid ray,
On their bare heads and dewy temples play;
While some, with feebler heads and fainter hearts,
Deplore their fortune, yet sustain their parts-
Then shall I dare these real ills to hide
In tinsel trappings of poetic pride?
No; cast by fortune on a frowning coast,
Which neither groves nor happy valleys boast;
Where other cares than those the Muse relates,
And other shepherds dwell with other mates;
By such examples taught I paint the cot,
As Truth will paint it, and as Bards will not.

What is clear at once is that this isn't a simple difference of objective fact, or even of historical conditions. It's a question, rather, of a way of seeing, and of a consequent literary convention. Whatever we may say about Crabbe's England, the contrast in his mind is not between rural England past and present, but between true and false ways of writing. He is forcing a contrast between a tradition of pastoral poetry and his own intention of realism. He assumes, certainly, there was once a time for what he knew as pastoral, but in classical times, not in his own or recent England:

Fled are those times, when in harmonious strains,
The rustic poet praised his native plains:
No shepherds now, in smooth alternate verse,
Their country's beauty or their nymphs' rehearse:

Crabbe is formally rejecting the literary tradition of the neo-classical pastoral: 'mechanical echoes of the Mantuan song'.

So the escalator has another destination, but we can properly get off before Mantua. English pastoral verse is of two main kinds: the first is the reflective, contemplative verse of so many 17th and 18th – century poets. They celebrate a real countryside as a place of innocence and retreat, but at the same time as a piece of modest property, with sufficient hired help.

The earlier kind of pastoral is more formal, as in Sidney or Spenser: a conventional Arcadia in which all shepherds are lovers, and pastoral care is all Christian virtue. It's ironic that Sydney's *Arcadia*, which can stand as one type for this pretty and conventional fantasy, was written in a park which had been made by enclosing a whole village and evicting its tenants. But let's visit Penshurst, the country house of the Sidneys where Spenser wrote parts of his *Shepheard's Calendar*. Here the argument takes on another dimension, for some

modern critics have held up Ben Johnson's poem, 'To Penshurst', as a celebra-
tion not only of a natural order but of a convincingly organic rural economy.
It's worth looking at the opening lines:

> Thou are not, Penshurst, built to envious show,
> Of touch, or marble; nor canst boast a row
> Of polish'd pillars, or a roof of gold:
> Thou hast no lantherne, whereof tales are told;
> Of staire, or courts; but stand'st an ancient pile,
> And these grudg'd at, art reverenc'd the while.

This procedure of definition by negatives ought to be enough in itself to warn
us that here is no simple eulogy to a whole order. The virtues of Penshurst
shine by explicit contrast with the manners of other country houses – and even
these virtues need a critical examination. There is a splendid account of the
spontaneous plenty of the estate:

> Each bank doth yield thee conies...

In another country-house poem, Thomas Carew's 'To Saxham' there is a
rather cruder statement of the same theme.

These poems are not difficult to understand, as literature. Their method is
one of conscious hyperbole: a complimentary and elegant wit. And then this is
not so much a natural order with metaphysical dimensions, as a natural order
on its way to the table, at the polite and consuming centre of the country-
house. Behind the wit, of course, is a well-remembered image: the image of
the Garden of Eden. This country, brimming with plenty, in which the animals
and the fish, no less than the fruit, offer themselves to be eaten, is the simple
fantasy of a provident nature in which man lives without the curse of labour.
But this traditional image is given a precise social dimension: it's to the lord, the
proprietor of the country estate, that nature yields its plenty. The rural folk,
the people who might be supposed to have something to do with the rearing
and tending and killing of the animals, with the preparation and gathering of
the harvest, are simply not seen in this dimension of labour. They come as
dependants with their offerings, but more crucially they come to be fed, from
the bounty of their lord; they come to partake humbly of a charitable feast,
based in fact on their own produce. This is not then a natural order, but a social
order: an economy of the post-feudal landlords, ratified by a mystification of
natural providence.

The originality of Crabbe is social quite as much as literary. The change in
literary convention arises out of a different way of seeing the world. It's not

only that Crabbe includes the 'poor laborious natives of the place' in what had previously been an empty, miraculously self-provident landscape, but that he also raises crucial questions about plenty and its distribution. Crabbe grew up in a hard countryside. He set the realities of 'a length of burning sand' against the pretty hypocrisies of simplicity in the conventional pastoral. But he went further:

> But these are scenes where Nature's niggard hand
> Gave a spare portion to the famish'd land;
> Her's is the fault, if here mankind complain
> Of fruitless toil and labour spent in vain;
> But yet in other scenes more fair in view,
> Where plenty smiles – alas! She smiles for few –
> And those who taste not, yet behold her store,
> Are as the slaves that dig the golden ore –
> The wealth around them makes them doubly poor.

Crabbe hasn't only put in the figure of the labourer: he has also included the social relations between the labourer and his employer – a reality normally omitted from the conventional images of rural harmony, but crucial in any real consideration of what is called a rural civilisation. And it's here that the real history enters. It's possible to relate Crabbe's harder view to what is supposed to be a new spirit of class antagonism – between employer and worker – in the coming of the Industrial Revolution. This way of seeing the problem supports a very common later view – a view of a pre- industrial, rural England which was more human, more integrated, more in touch with permanent realities than the noisy, embittered, mechanical and urban world which succeeded it. Certainly if the contrast is between Eden and Coketown, it has some force. But that's been the trouble: a failure to read the literature as literature, and then the making of a false history out of a false reading. What needs saying – for it has much to do with the character of our later response to industrialism – is that in England, more clearly than in any other country, a class society began on the land. By a class society I mean a society based on private property in the means of production and on wage labour – as opposed to a hierarchical society based on hereditary ownership and customary obligations.

Capitalism is now so often identified with industrial production, but in England it is at first a rural phenomenon: beginning at least as early as the 16th century. During the 17th and 18th centuries it created a highly productive and modernised agriculture, which was in fact a base for the Industrial Revolution. And it had as its social cost two long-term effects: the steady exclusion and suppression of small hereditary owners and common rights, and the consequent creation of a rural proletariat – landless wage-labourers who had no option, as the methods of production changed, but to go in their thousands to the new industrial towns and to the colonies. What we call a peasantry in other countries virtually ceased to exist in England. It was replaced, in our country-side, by a predominant system of capitalist farming, based on landlord, tenant farmer and wage-labourer. It's true this process was very long-drawn- out: through the successive phases of enclosure and engrossing, and of still higher concentrations of capital and agricultural machinery. In fact, we're still living in its last phase, as the remaining small farmers are squeezed out of business.

As we look back over 400 years, what we're seeing is not the destruction of a timeless order, but the bitter disturbance of the making of a new order – the order of rural capitalism. Against this reality, you can almost understand the wishful images of Eden and the Golden Age, whether they're projected in the fantasies of a benevolent aristocrat, or in the idylls of the small proprietor, or in the idylls of the small proprietor, or in the romantic medievalism of Cobbett: almost understand, but with the 19th-century novel ahead we must come to grips with a different and more complicated reality.

By the time of George Eliot and Jefferies and Hardy, we have a predominantly commercial countryside; the new industrial towns are its markets; it is subject to trading crises, to changes of national and imperial policy, and to continuing changes in capital accumulation, in rents, and in methods of production. All this together created a social crisis of a specifically modern kind: of low wages and high prices for the labourer; of shortage of capital and increasing rents for the tenant farmer; of eventual decline and transfer of interest elsewhere for the larger landlord. This is the real world of Hardy, and it's astonishing how we continue to fail to see it. [. . .]

Hardy's novels are histories. But they contain powerful images that stand on their own. Here is the description of the threshing-machine in *Tess of the D'Urbervilles*:

Close under the eaves of the stack, and as yet barely visible, was the red tyrant that the women had come to serve – a timber-framed construction, with straps and wheels appertaining – the threshing-machine which, whilst it was going, kept up a despotic demand upon the endurance of their muscles and nerves.

A little way off there was another indistinct figure; this one black, with a sustained hiss that spoke of strength very much in reserve. The long chimney running up beside an ash-tree, and the warmth which radiated from the spot, explained without the necessity of much daylight that here was the engine which was to act as the *primum mobile* of this little world. By the engine stood a dark motionless being, a sooty and grimy embodiment of tallness, in a sort of trance, with a heap of coals by his side: it was the engineman. The isolation of his manner and colour lent him the appearance of a creature from Tophet . . .

This powerful symbolism of an alien machine mustn't blind us to the fact that this is also an action in a story – the action of a real threshing-machine. It stands in that field and works those hours because it's hired not by industrialism but by a farmer. And there are whole human beings trying to keep up with it and with him:

> Thus the afternoon dragged on. The wheatrick shrank lower, and the straw-rick grew higher and the corn-sacks were carted away. At six o'clock the wheat-rick was about shoulder- high from the ground. But the unthreshed sheaves remaining untouched seemed countless still, notwithstanding the enormous numbers which had been gulped down by the insatiable swallower, fed by the man and Tess, through whose two young hands the greater part of them had passed. And the immense stack of straw where in the morning these had been nothing, appeared as the faeces of the same buzzing red glutton. From the west sky a wrathful shine – all that wild March could afford in the way of sunset – had burst forth after the cloudy day, flooding the tired and sticky faces of the threshers, and dyeing them with a coppery light, as also the flapping garments of the women, which clung to them like dull flames.

We can see here the relation to Crabbe, but also the development from him. This is Tess the worker and the girl: the break between her consciousness and her actions is as much a part of her emotional life as her working life. Hardy shows us the intensity of labour and the intensity of desire; and he shows us the thwarting ignorance and lack of consciousness in rural society. That is why he could say this, in his fine essay on the 'Dorsetshire Labourer', about change in the countryside and its people: 'They are losing their individuality, but they are widening the range of their ideas, and gaining in freedom. It is too much to expect them to remain stagnant and old-fashioned for the pleasure of romantic spectators.' Hardy neither diminished the crisis of his time nor fitted it simplemindedly to a pastoral retrospect. When he comes to write of the essential social history of rural England, soon after this episode in *Tess*, his touch and insight are extraordinarily sure.

Here the important literature is also the important history: the history of a rural tradition, itself defensive, which is broken from within by a conscious policy of new use and ownership, in the maturity of capitalist farming and in the crises of an essentially similar world outside it.

As it happens, I grew up in a society of that kind. I was the son of a family of farm labourers, in a village determined and changing in just those ways – I tried to describe it in my first novel, *Border Country*. When I first went to Cambridge, I was offered the interpretation I am now rejecting: a convention of rural order, of Old England, against industrial disorder and the modern world. I had the strongest personal reasons for doubting it, but it has taken me many years to reach the point where I can try to say, intellectually, where it was wrong. And I can still listen with respect and sympathy to George Eliot's version of that journey we've all made, in her introduction to *Felix Holt*:

But there were trim cheerful villages too, with a neat or handsome parsonage and grey church set in the midst; there was the pleasant tinkle of the blacksmith's anvil, the patient cart- horses waiting at his door; the basket-maker peeling his willow wands in the sunshine; the wheelwright putting the last touch to a blue cart with red wheels; here and there a cottage with bright transparent windows showing pots full of bloom- ing balsams or geraniums, and little gardens in front all double daisies or dark wall- flowers; at the well, clean and comely women carrying yoked buckets, and towards the free school small Britons dawdling on, and handling their marbles in the pockets of their patched corduroys adorned with brass buttons. The land around was rich and marly, great corn-stacks stood in the rick-yards – for the rick-burners had not found their way hither; the homesteads were those of rich farmers who paid no rent, or had the rare advantage of a lease, and could afford to keep their corn till prices had risen. The coach would be sure to overtake some of them on their way to their outlying fields or to the market-town, sitting heavily on their well-groomed horses, or weighing down on the side of an olive-green gig. They probably thought of the coach with some contempt, as an accomodation for people who had not their own gigs, or who, wanting to travel to London and such distant places, belonged to the trading and less solid part of the nation. The passenger on the box could see that this was the district of protuberant optimists, sure that old England was the best of all possible countries, and that if there were any facts which had not fallen under their own observation, they were facts not worth observing: the district of clean little market towns without manufactures, of fat livings, an aristocratic clergy, and low poor-rates.

This is warm and intelligent, but who are you, who am I, that 'passenger on the box'? Are the low poor-rates, for example, a comfort or an irony?

But as the day wore on the scene would change: the and would begin to be blackened with coal-pits, the rattle of handlooms to be heard in hamlets and villages. Here were powerful men walking queerly with knees bent outward from squatting in the mine, going home to throw themselves down in their blackened flannel and sleep through the daylight, then rise and spend much of their high wages at the ale-house with their fellows of the Benefit Club; here the pale eager faces of handloom-weavers, men and women, haggard from sitting up late at night to finish the week's work: hardly begun on the Wednesday. Everywhere the cottages and small children were dirty, for the languid mothers gave their strength to the loom; . . .

The breath of the manufacturing toil which made a cloudy day and a red gloom by night on the horizon, diffused itself over all the surrounding country, filling the air with eager unrest. Here was a population not convinced that old England was as good as possible.

'Not convinced that old England was as good as possible'. That scepticism, that eager unrest is indeed double-edged. In the industrial towns, and in the villages, there has hardly ever been an easy satisfaction with the way people had to live. Yet when it becomes 'Old England' – the past of childhood and of memory – the perspective seems always to alter. A novelist like George Eliot draws on this feeling creatively; the warmth of the memory can be heard. And, read as literature, there is no question of quarreling with it. What we have to distinguish is the transformation of that imaginative vision into another thing, in other hands: a false history, and a false theory of the present and the past. In the 19th century, in the shock of change, the countryside was used in new ways, as a human critique of industrialism; understandably but at the cost of misrepresenting the long and difficult history of actual rural society.

7

Thomas Hardy and the English Novel

From Raymond Williams (1970) The English Novel From Dickens to Lawrence. *London: Chatto and Windus*

I keep thinking about those twenty months, in 1847 and 1848, in which these novels were published: *Dombey and Son, Wuthering Heights, Vanity Fair, Jane Eyre, Mary Barton, Tancred, Town and Country, The Tenant of Wildfell Hall.*

What was it just then that emerged in England? It was of course no sudden process of just a few months. But we can see, looking back, those months as decisive. The English novel before then had its major achievements; it had Defoe and Fielding, Richardson and Jane Austen and Walter Scott. But now in the 1840s it had a new and major *generation*. For the next eighty years the novel was to be the major form in English literature. And this was unprecedented. What these months seem to mark above all is a new kind of consciousness, and we have to learn to see what this is, and some ways of relating it to the new and unprecedented civilisation in which it took shape.

The changes in society had been long in the making: the Industrial Revolution, the struggle for democracy, the growth of cities and towns. But these also, in the 1840s, reached a point of consciousness which was in its turn decisive. The twelve years from Dickens's first novel to his radically innovating *Dombey and Son* were also the years of the crisis of Chartism. The first industrial civilisation in the history of the world had come to a critical and defining stage. By the end of the 1840s the English were the first predominantly urban people in the long history of human societies. The institutions of an urban culture, from music-halls and popular Sunday newspapers to public parks, museums and libraries, were all decisively established in these years. There was critical legislation on public health and on working-hours in factories. A major economic decision, on free trade and the repeal of the corn laws, had begun a long realignment of politics. In the struggle and disturbance of those years the future, of course, was not known. But the sense of crisis, of major and radical issues and decisions, was both acute and general. It is then not surprising that in just this decade a particular kind of literature – already known and widely read, but still not very highly regarded – should come to take on new life, a newly significant and relevant life. Here, in these hands, a generation of writers, in very different ways, found the common forms that mattered, in response to a new and varied but still common experience.

There were of course immediate and related reasons for the new importance of the novel. Reading of all kinds was increasing. Between the 1820s and 1860 the annual number of new books rose from 580 to over 2,600, and much of the increase was in novels. New methods of binding and printing had brought book-prices down. In the period in which these novels were published there were new cheap libraries: the Parlour and the Railway: not led, of course, by the new generation, but by others: Lytton, Marryat, G. P. R. James. The reading of newspapers and magazines was increasing rapidly, though the major period of expansion was still twenty years ahead. In every way the reading-public was still a minority, and the book-reading public especially so. But serial publication of fiction, in the new family magazines, was significantly expanding the number of readers of novels. Direct market factors were important to writers in more pressing and evident ways.

But this is no simple case, in the end, of demand and supply. Several of the best new writers were involved in the market, and with their eyes wide open to it: Dickens above all. But what was written and what had to be written had many other sources. The crisis of the society and the expansion of reading were themselves related. More and more people felt the need for this kind of knowledge and experience, as customary ways broke down or receded. But beyond even this, as we can see most clearly from the novels themselves, the new pressures and disturbances were not simple moulds out of which new forms came. The men and women who were writing – some at the centre of opinion-forming and the market, some distant and isolated – took from the disturbance of these years another impetus: a crisis of experience, often quite personally felt and endured, which when it emerged in novels was much more than a reaction to existing and acknowledged public features. It was a creative working, a discovery, often alone at the table; a transformation and innovation which composed a generation out of what seemed separate work and experience. It brought in new feelings, people, relationships; rhythms newly known, discovered, articulated; defining the society, rather than merely reflecting it; defining it in novels, which had each its own significant and particular life. It was not the society or its crisis which produced the novels. The society and the novels – our general names for those myriad and related primary activities – came from a pressing and varied experience which was not yet history; which had no new forms, no significant moments, until these were made and given by direct human actions.

What then can we define that emerged from those months: those twenty months in which, looking back, we can see so clearly a particular achievement: a confirmation of a generation; confirmation of a new importance, a new relevance and new forms? From the many possibilities in those varied reading experiences I would choose one bearing as central: the exploration of community: the substance and meaning of community.

From Dickens to Lawrence, over nearly a hundred years, this bearing seems to me decisive. What community is, what it has been, what it might be; how community relates to individuals and relationships; how men and women, directly engaged, see within them or beyond them, for but more often against them, the shape of a society: these related themes are the dominant bearings. For this is a period in which what it means to live in a community is more uncertain, more critical, more disturbing as a question put both to societies and to persons than ever before in history. The underlying experiences of this powerful and transforming urban and industrial civilisation are of rapid and inescapable social change; of a newly visible and conscious history but at the same time, in most actual communities and in most actual lives, of a newly complicated and often newly obscure immediate process. These are not opposite poles: they are the defining characteristics of the change itself. People became more aware of great social and historical changes which altered not only outward forms – institutions and landscapes – but also inward feelings, experiences, self-definitions. These facts of change can be seen lying deep in almost every imagination.

And then of course it was right that the novel should be used to explore and to realise this process, in unprecedented ways. In the great eighteenth-century realists, in the precise social world of Jane Austen and in the historically conscious imagination of Scott, its powers and its possibilities were already evident. But though they drew some of their strength, their starting strength, from their great individual predecessors, these new novelists of a rapidly changing England had to create, from their own resources, forms adequate to the experience at the new and critical stage it had reached.

Two features of this development stand out. The historical novel, as Scott had developed it, has almost run its course – its fashionable course – before this generation began. Dickens used it occasionally; George Eliot went back to it once. But in the main line it had become a separate form: from history as change, eating into human consciousness, to history as spectacle, the spectacular past, as most clearly in Lytton. Each of these possibilities can be seen in Scott: the romantic use of the past to transcend the present had many colourful opportunities in fiction. But the permanent achievement of the romantic imagination, at the point of its deepest engagement with its own time, was not this kind of transcendence. It was the establishment of a position in human experience which was capable of judging – not incidentally but totally – the very society that was forming and changing it. Society from being a framework could be seen now as an agency, even an actor, a character. It could be seen and valued in and through persons: not as a framework in which they were defined; not as an aggregate of known relationships; but as an apparently independent organism, a character and an action like others. Society, now, was not just a code to measure, an institution to control, a standard to define or to change. It was a process that entered lives, to shape or to deform; a process personally known but then again suddenly distant, complex, incomprehensible, over-whelming.

In what had been learned of process in the historical novel, the new novel of social change – of the valuation of change – found its impetus, its initiative, its decisive and eagerly taken opportunity. Thomas Carlyle, who did more than anyone else in his generation to communicate this sense of history – of historical process as moral substance and challenge – came to think that the novel was outdated, that it could be replaced by history. He was of course to be proved wrong, but only by the transformation of the novel in very much the direction of his central argument. It was by becoming history, contemporary history – but a history of substance, of process, of the interaction of public and private life – that one important kind of novel went to the heart of its time. When Balzac, in France, learned from Scott, he went back not to the Middle Ages, at a distance which was bound to be spectacle, but as Scott had done in his best work to the recent and connecting history of Scotland; to the decisive origin of his own epoch: to the years of the French Revolution. He learned in this way, in the search for origins, how to go on to write the continuing history of his time. The new English novelists learned in comparable ways: going back to the decisive origins of their own epoch, in the crises of the Industrial Revolution, of democratic reform and of the movement from country to town: from Charlotte Brontë on the Luddites in *Shirley* to George Eliot on the years before 1832 and on town and country in *Middlemarch* and in *Felix Holt*. It was in this kind of use of the historical imagination, rather than in the fanciful exercises of a *Romola* or a *Tale of Two Cities*, that the real growth took place. And it was in these ways that novelists learned to look, historically, at the crises of their own immediate time: at Chartism, at the industrial struggle, at debt and speculation, at the complicated inheritance of values and of property.

That was one very important line of development, but there is another, even more important, which enters even more deeply into the substance and form of the novel. Most novels are in some sense knowable communities. It is part of a traditional method – an underlying stance and approach – that the novelist offers to show people and their relationships in essentially knowable and communicable ways. Much of the confidence of this method depends on a particular kind of social confidence and experience. In its simplest form this amounts to saying – though at its most confident it did not have to be said – that the knowable and therefore known relationships compose and are part of a wholly known social structure, and that in and through the relationships the persons themselves can be wholly known. Thus from the middle term, of visible and comprehensible relationship, both societies and persons are knowable; indeed certain fundamental propositions about them can even be taken for granted, in terms of a received and mutually applicable social and moral code.

Many factors combined to destroy this confidence, in the process of extraordinary change through which the new novelists were living. One effect of this change has been widely recognised. It has indeed become a dogma – more properly, a half-truth – that persons are only partially knowable in and through relationships; that some part of the personality precedes and survives – is in a way unaffected by – relationships; that in this special sense persons are not knowable, are indeed fundamentally and crucially unknowable. And this is a belief which in itself forces new and very radical experiments in the novel; experiments which have been more active and more exclusive in every subsequent generation.

What is not so often recognised in this well-known effect is that at the other end of the scale a similar process has been evident: an increasing scepticism, disbelief, in the possibility of understanding society; a structurally similar certainty that relationships, knowable relationships, so far from composing a community or a society, are the positive experience that has to be *contrasted* with the ordinarily negative experience of the society as a whole (or of the society as opposed to the local and immediate community). An important split takes place between knowable relationships and an unknown, unknowable, overwhelming society. The full seriousness of this split and of its eventual consequences for the novel can be traced only towards the end of the century. But its pressure is evident from this first period of crisis: Dicken's response to it – a very early and major response – is perhaps the key to understanding him, and especially to understanding his very original and creative use of the novel as a form.

Now we have only to name this particular crisis – the crisis of the knowable community – to see how deeply it is related to the changes through which these novelists were living. We can see its obvious relation to the very rapidly increasing size and scale and complexity of communities: in the growth of towns and especially of cities and of a metropolis; in the increasing division and complexity of labour; in the altered and critical relations between and within social classes. In these simple and general senses, any assumption of a knowable community – a whole community, wholly knowable – becomes harder and harder to sustain. And we have to remember, with this, that there is a direct though very difficult relationship between the knowable community and the knowable person. Wordsworth, in *The Prelude*, had got through to this relationship very early. In the great seventh book – *Residence in London* – he directly related the new phenomenon of the urban crowd – not the occasional but the regular crowd, the new crowd of the metropolitan streets – to problems of self-identity, self- knowledge, self-possession:

> *How often in the overflowing Streets,*
> *Have I gone forward with the Crowd, and said*
> *Unto myself, the face of every one*
> *That passes by me is a mystery...*
> *...And all the ballast of familiar life,*
> *The present, and the past; hope, fear; all stays,*
> *All laws of acting, thinking, speaking man*
> *Went from me, neither knowing me, nor known.*

It is from this critical conjunction – the unknowable crowd and the unknowing and unknown individual – that he created the image of the blind beggar with the label telling his history and his identity:

> *It seemed*
> *To me that in this Label was a type,*
> *Or emblem, of the utmost that we know*
> *Both of ourselves and of the universe.*

It is a familiar romantic conclusion; but it is important that the insight occurred where it did: in the crowded street of a city. It is a related alienation, of a community and of persons, of the kind which Blake also had seen, with a sharper emphasis on power, in his poem *London*.

The problem of the knowable community, with its deep implications for the novelist, is then clearly a part of the social history of early nineteenth-century England and of the imaginative penetration and recoil which was the creative response. But what is knowable is not only a function of objects — of what is there to be known. It is also a function of subjects, of observers — of what is desired and what needs to be known. A knowable community, that is to say, is a matter of consciousness as well as of evident fact. Indeed it is to just this problem of knowing a community — of finding a position, a position convincingly experienced, from which community can begin to be known — that one of the major phases in the development of the novel must be related.

It is so often taken for granted that a country community, most typically a village, is an epitome of direct relationships: of face-to-face contacts, within which the novelist can find the substance of a fiction of personal relationships. Certainly this aspect of its difference from the city and the suburb is important. Most English novels before Dickens are centred in rural communities, and it is because he is centred in the city — and not only a city but a metropolis — that he has to find strength and basis in an alternative tradition: in the popular culture of urban industrial society. [...]

But, even within rural communities the problem of what is known — what is desired and needs to be known — is very active and critical. This is the real key to a very important development of the country novel from Jane Austen to George Eliot and then again from George Eliot to Hardy. [...]

Some years ago a British Council critic described George Eliot, Hardy and Lawrence as 'our three great autodidacts', and as it happens his prejudice serves to indicate a very crucial fact. Why, we must ask, 'autodidact'? For all three of these writers were actively interested in learning and while they read a good deal for themselves had also a significant formal education. Their fathers were a bailiff, a builder and a miner. George Eliot was at school till sixteen and left only because her mother died and she had to go home to look after her father, though she still took regular lessons there. Hardy was at Dorchester High School till the same age and then completed his professional training as an architect. Lawrence went into the sixth form at Nottingham High School and after a gap went on to Nottingham University College. It is not only that by their contemporary standards these levels of formal education are high. It is also that they are higher, absolutely, than those of four out of five people in mid-twentieth-century Britain. The flat patronage of 'autodidact' can then be related to only one fact: that none of the three was in the pattern of board-ing-school and Oxbridge which in the late nineteenth century came to be regarded not simply as a kind of education but as education itself. To have missed that circuit was to have missed being 'educated' at all. In other words a 'standard' education was that received by one or two per cent of the popula-tion. All the rest were seen as 'uneducated' or else as 'autodidacts' (the later phrase was grammar-school-boy and will soon, no doubt, be comprehensive.)

They were seen also, of course, as either comically ignorant or when they pretended to learning as awkward, overearnest, fanatical.

The effects of this on the English imagination have been deep. To many of us, now, George Eliot, Hardy and Lawrence are important because they connect directly with our own kind of upbringing and education. They belong to a cultural tradition much older and more central in this country than the comparatively modern and deliberately exclusive circuit of what are called the public schools. And the point is that they continue to connect in this way, into a later period in which some of us have gone to Oxford or Cambridge; to myself, for instance, who came from that kind of family to Cambridge and now teach here. For it is not the education, the developed intelligence, that is really in question. How many people, if it came to it, on the British Council or anywhere else, could survive a strictly intellectual comparison with George Eliot? It is a question of the relation between education – not the marks or degrees but the substance of a developed intelligence – and the actual lives of a continuing majority of our people: people who are not, by any formula, objects of record or study or concern, but who are specifically, literally, our own families. George Eliot is the first major novelist in whom this question is active. That is why we speak of her now with a connecting respect, and with a hardness – a sort of family plainness – that we have learned from our own and common experience.

It is also why we come to Hardy with interest and respect. The more I read Hardy the surer I am that he is a major novelist, but also that the problem of describing his work is central to the problem of understanding the whole development of the English novel. It is good that so many people still read him, and also that English students are reading him increasingly and with increasing respect. Yet some influential critical accounts have tried to push him aside, and even some of those who have praised him have done so in ways that reduce him. Thus he can very easily be praised as what we now call a regional novelist: the incomparable chronicler of his Wessex. Or he can be taken as the last voice of an old rural civilisation. The acknowledgement, even the warm tribute, comes with the sense that the substance of his work is getting further and further away from us: that he is not a man of our world but the last representative of old rural England or of the peasantry.

Actually, the very complicated feelings and ideas in Hardy's novels, including the complicated feelings and ideas about country life and people, belong very much, I think, in a continuing world. He writes more consistently and more deeply than any of our novelists about something that is still very close to us wherever we may be living: something that can be put, in abstraction, as the problem of the relation between customary and educated life; between customary and educated feeling and thought. This is the problem we already saw in George Eliot and that we shall see again in Lawrence. It is the ground of their significant connection.

Most of us, before we get any kind of literary education, get to know and to value – also to feel the tensions of – a customary life. We see and learn from the ways our families live and get their living; a world of work and of place, and of beliefs so deeply dissolved into everyday actions that we don't at first even know they are beliefs, subject to change and challenge. Our education, quite often, gives us a way of looking at that life which can see other values beyond it: as Jude saw them when he looked across the land to the towers of Christminster. Often we know in ourselves, very deeply, how much those educated values, those intellectual pursuits, are needed urgently where custom is stagnation or where old illusions are still repeated as timeless truths. We know especially how much they are needed to understand *change* – change in the heart of the places where we have lived and worked and grown up.

The ideas, the values, the educated methods are of course made available to us if we get to a place like Christminster: if we are let in as Jude was not. But with the offer, again and again, comes another idea: that the world of everyday work and of ordinary families is inferior, distant; that now we know this world of the mind we can have no respect – and of course no affection – for that other and still familiar world. If we retain an affection Christminster has a name for it: nostalgia. If we retain respect Christminster has another name: politics or the even more dreaded sociology.

But it is more than a matter of picking up terms and tones. It is what happens to us, really happens to us, as we try to mediate those contrasted worlds: as we stand with Jude but a Jude who has been let in; or as we go back to our own places, our own families, and know what is meant, in idea and in feeling, by the return of the native.

The Hardy country is of course Wessex: that is to say mainly Dorset and its neighbouring counties. But the real Hardy country, I feel more and more, is that border country so many of us have been living in: between custom and education, between work and ideas, between love of place and an experience of change. This has a special importance to a particular generation, who have gone to the university from ordinary families and have to discover, through a life, what that experience means. But it has also a much more general importance; for in Britain generally this is what has been happening: a moving out from old ways and places and ideas and feelings; a discovery in the new of certain unlooked-for problems, unexpected and very sharp crises, conflicts of desire and possibility.

In this characteristic world, rooted and mobile, familiar yet newly conscious and self-conscious, the figure of Hardy stands like a landmark. It is not from an old rural world or from a remote region that Hardy now speaks to us; but from the heart of a still active experience, of the familiar and the changing, which we can know as an idea but which is important finally in what seem the personal pressures – the making and failing of relationships, the crises of physical and mental personality – which Hardy as a novelist at once describes and enacts.

But of course we miss all this, or finding it we do not know how to speak of it and value it, if we have picked up, here and there, the tone of belittling Hardy.

I want to bring this into the open. Imagine if you will the appearance and the character of the man who wrote this:

When the ladies retired to the drawing-room I found myself sitting next to Thomas Hardy. I remember a little man with an earthy face. In his evening clothes, with his boiled shirt and high collar, he had still a strange look of the soil.

Not the appearance and the character of Thomas Hardy; but of the man who could write that about him, that confidently, that sure of his readers, in just those words.

It is of course Somerset Maugham, with one of his characteristic tales after dinner. It is a world, one may think, Hardy should never have got near; never have let himself be exposed to. But it is characteristic and important, all the way from that dinner-table and that drawing-room to the 'look of the soil', in that rural distance. All the way to the land, the work, that comes up in silver as vegetables, or to the labour that enters that company – that customary civilised company – with what is seen as an earthy face.

In fact I remember Maugham, remember his tone, when I read Henry James on 'the good little Thomas Hardy' or F. R. Leavis saying that *Jude the Obscure* is impressive 'in its clumsy way'. For in several ways, some of them unexpected, we have arrived at that place where custom and education, one way of life and another, are in the most direct and interesting and I'd say necessary conflict.

The tone of social patronage, that is to say, supported by crude and direct suppositions about origin, connects interestingly with a tone of literary patronage and in ways meant to be damaging with a strong and directing supposition about the substance of Hardy's fiction. If he was a countryman, a peasant, a man with the look of the soil, then this is the point of view, the essential literary standpoint, of the novels. That is to say the fiction is not only about Wessex peasants, it is by one of them, who of course had managed to get a little (though hardly enough) education. Some discriminations of tone and fact have then to be made.

First, we had better drop 'peasant' altogether. Where Hardy lived and worked, as in most other parts of England, there were virtually no peasants, although 'peasantry' as a generic word for country people was still used by writers. The actual country people were landowners, tenant farmers, dealers, craftsmen and labourers, and that social structure – the actual material, in a social sense, of the novels – is radically different, in its variety, its shading, and many of its basic human attitudes from the structure of a peasantry. Secondly, Hardy is none of these people. Outside his writing he was one of the many professional men who worked within this structure, often with uncertainty about where they really belonged in it. A slow gradation of classes is characteristic of capitalism anywhere, and of rural capitalism very clearly. Hardy's father was a builder who employed six or seven workmen. Hardy did not like to hear their house referred to as a cottage, because he was aware of this employing situation. The house is indeed quite small but there is a little window at the back through which the men were paid, and the cottages down the lane are certainly smaller. At the same time, on his walk to school, he would see the mansion of Kingston Maurward (now happily an agricultural college) on which his father did some of the estate work, and this showed a sudden difference of degree which made the other distinction comparatively small though still not unimportant. In becoming an architect and a friend of the family of a vicar (the kind of family, also, from which his wife came) Hardy moved to a different point in the social structure, with connections to the educated but not the owning class, and yet also with connections through his family to that shifting body of small employers, dealers, craftsmen and cottagers who were themselves never wholly distinct, in family, from the labourers. Within his writing his position is similar. He is neither owner nor tenant, dealer nor labourer, but an observer and chronicler, often again with uncertainty about his actual relation. Moreover he was not writing for them, but about them, to a mainly metropolitan and unconnected literary public. The effect of these two points is to return attention to where it properly belongs, which is Hardy's attempt to describe and value a way of life with which he was closely yet uncertainly connected, and the literary methods which follow from the nature of this attempt. As so often when the current social stereotypes are removed the critical problem becomes clear in a new way.

It is the critical problem of so much of English fiction, since the actual yet incomplete and ambiguous social mobility of the nineteenth century. And it is a question of substance as much as of method. It is common to reduce Hardy's fiction to the impact of an urban alien on the 'timeless pattern' of English rural life. Yet though this is sometimes there the more common pattern is the relation between the changing nature of country living, determined as much by its own pressures as by pressures from 'outside', and one or more characters who have become in some degree separated from it yet who remain by some tie of family inescapably involved. It is here that the social values are dramatised in a very complex way and it is here that most of the problems of Hardy's actual writing seem to arise.

One small and one larger point may illustrate this argument, in a preliminary way. Nearly everyone seems to treat Tess as simply the passionate peasant girl seduced from outside, and it is then surprising to read quite early in the novel one of the clearest statements of what has become a classical experience of mobility:

Mrs. Durbeyfield habitually spoke the dialect; her daughter, who had passed the Sixth Standard in the National School under a London-trained mistress, spoke two languages: the dialect at home, more or less; ordinary English abroad and to persons of quality.

Grace in *The Woodlanders*, Clym in *The Return of the Native* represent this experience more completely, but it is in any case a continuing theme, at a level much more important than the trivialities of accent. And when we see this we need not be tempted, as so often and so significantly in recent criticism, to detach *Jude the Obscure* as a quite separate kind of novel.

A more remarkable example of what this kind of separation means and involves is a description of Clym in *The Return of the Native* which belongs in a quite central way to the argument I traced in *Culture and Society*:

Yeobright loved his kind. He had a conviction that the want of most men was knowledge of a sort which brings wisdom rather than affluence. He wished to raise the class at the expense of individuals rather than individuals at the expense of the class. What was more, he was ready at once to be the first unit sacrificed.

The idea of sacrifice relates in the whole action to the familiar theme of a vocation thwarted or damaged by a mistaken marriage, and we shall have to look again at this characteristic Hardy deadlock. But it relates also to the general action of change which is a persistent social theme. As in all major realist fiction the quality and destiny of persons and the quality and destiny of a whole way of life are seen in the same dimension and not as separable issues. It is Hardy the observer who sets this context for personal failure:

In passing from the bucolic to the intellectual life the intermediate stages are usually two at least, frequently many more; and one of these stages is sure to be worldly advance. We can hardly imagine bucolic placidity quickening to intellectual aims without imagining social aims as the transitional phase. Yeo-bright's local peculiarity was that in striving at high thinking he still cleaved to plain living – any, wild and meagre living in many respects, and brotherliness with clowns. He was a John the Baptist who took ennoblement rather than repentance for his text. Mentally he was in a provincial future, that is, he was in many points abreast with the central town thinkers of his date. . . . In consequence of this relatively advanced position, Yeobright might have been called unfortunate. The rural world was not ripe for him. A man should be only partially before his time; to be completely to the vanward in aspirations is fatal to fame. . . . A man who advocates aesthetic effort and deprecates social effort is only likely to be understood by a class to which social effort has become a stale matter. To argue upon the possibility of culture before luxury to the bucolic world may be to argue truly, but it is an attempt to disturb a sequence to which humanity has been long accustomed.

The subtlety and intelligence of this argument from the late 1870s come from a mind accustomed to relative and historical thinking, not merely in the abstract but in the process of observing a personal experience of mobility. This is not country against town, or even in any simple way custom against conscious intelligence. It is the more complicated and more urgent historical process in which education is tied to social advancement within a class society, so that it is difficult, except by a bizarre personal demonstration, to hold both to education and to social solidarity ('he wished to raise the class'). It is the process also in which culture and affluence come to be recognised as alternative aims, at whatever cost to both, and the wry recognition that the latter will always be the first choice, in any real history (as Morris also observed and indeed welcomed).

The relation between the migrant and his former group is then exceptionally complicated. His loyalty drives him to actions which the group can see no sense in, its overt values supporting the association of education with personal advancement which his new group has already made but which for that very reason he cannot accept.

'I am astonished, Clym. How can you want to do better than you've been doing?'
   'But I hate that business of mine. . . . I want to do some worthy things before I die.'
   'After all the trouble that has been taken to give you a start, and when there is nothing to do but keep straight on towards affluence, you say you . . . it disturbs me, Clym, to find you have come home with such thoughts. . . . I hadn't the least idea you meant to go backward in the world by your own free choice. . . .'
   'I cannot help it,' said Clym, in a troubled tone.
   'Why can't you do . . . as well as others?'
   'I don't know, except that there are many things other people care for which I don't. . . .'
   'And yet you might have been a wealthy man if you had only persevered. . . . I suppose you will be like your father. Like him, you are getting weary of doing well.'
   'Mother, what is doing well?'

The question is familiar but still after all these years no question is more relevant or more radical. Within these complex pressures the return of the native has a certain inevitable nullity, and his only possible overt actions can come to seem merely perverse. Thus the need for social identification with the labourers produces Clym's characteristic negative identification with them; becoming a labourer himself and making his original enterprise that much more difficult: 'the monotony of his occupation soothed him, and was in itself a pleasure'.

All this is understood and controlled by Hardy but the pressure has further and less conscious effects. Levin's choice of physical labour, in *Anna Karenina*, includes some of the same motives but in the end is a choosing of people rather than a choosing of an abstract Nature – a choice of men to work with rather than a natural force in which to get lost. This crucial point is obscured by the ordinary discussion of Hardy's attachment to country life, which would run together the 'timeless' heaths or woods and the men working on them. The original humanist impulse – 'he loved his kind' – can indeed become anti-human: men can be seen as creatures crawling on this timeless expanse, as the imagery of the health and Clym's work on it so powerfully suggests. It is a very common transition in the literature of that period but Hardy is never very comfortable with it, and the original impulse, as in *Jude the Obscure*, keeps coming back and making more precise identifications.

At the same time the separation of the returned native is not only a separation from the standards of the educated and affluent world 'outside'. It is also to some degree inevitably from the people who have not made his journey; or more often a separation which can mask itself as a romantic attachment to a way of life in which the people are merely instrumental: figures in a landscape or when the literary tone fails in a ballad. It is then easy, in an apparently warm-hearted way, to observe for the benefit of others the crudity and limitations but also the picturesqueness, the rough humour, the smocked innocence of 'the bucolic' The complexity of Hardy's fiction shows in nothing more than this: that he runs the whole gamut from an external observation of customs and quaintnesses, modulated by a distinctly patronising affection (as in *Under the Greenwood Tree*), through a very positive identification of intuitions of nature and the values of shared work with human depth and fidelity (as in *The Woodlanders*), to the much more impressive but also much more difficult humane perception of limitations, which cannot be resolved by nostalgia or charm or an approach to mysticism, but which are lived through by all the characters, in the real life to which all belong, the limitations of the educated and the affluent bearing an organic relation to the limitations of the ignorant and the poor (as in parts of *Return of the Native* and in *Tess* and *Jude*). But to make these distinctions and to see the variations of response with the necessary clarity we have to get beyond the stereotypes of the autodidact and the countryman and see Hardy in his real identity: both the educated observer and the passionate participant, in a period of general and radical change.

Hardy's writing, or what in abstraction can be called his style, is obviously affected by the crisis – the return of the native – which I have been describing.

We know that he was worried about his prose and was reduced by the ordinary educated assumptions of his period to studying Defoe, Fielding, Addison, Scott and *The Times*, as if they could have helped him. His complex position as an author, writing about country living to people who almost inevitably saw the country as empty nature or as the working-place of their inferiors, was in any case critical in this matter of language. What have been seen as his strengths — the ballad form of narrative, the prolonged literary imitation of traditional forms of speech — seem to me mainly weaknesses. This sort of thing is what his readers were ready for: a 'tradition' rather than human beings. The devices could not in any case serve his major fiction where it was precisely disturbance rather than continuity which had to be communicated. It would be easy to relate Hardy's problem of style to the two languages of Tess: the consciously educated and the unconsciously customary. But this comparison, though suggestive, is inadequate, for the truth is that to communicate Hardy's experience neither language would serve, since neither in the end was sufficiently articulate: the educated dumb in intensity and limited in humanity; the customary thwarted by ignorance and complacent in habit. The marks of a surrender to each mode are certainly present in Hardy but the main body of his mature writing is a more difficult and complicated experiment. For example:

The season developed and matured. Another year's instalment of flowers, leaves, nightingales, thrushes, finches, and such ephemeral creatures, took up their positions where only a year ago others had stood in their place when these were nothing more than germs and inorganic particles. Rays from the sunrise drew forth the buds and stretched them into long stalks, lifted up sap in noiseless streams, opened petals, and sucked out scents in invisible jets and breathings.

Dairyman Crick's houschold of maids and men lived on comfortably, placidly, even merrily. Their position was perhaps the happiest of all positions in the social scale, being above the line at which neediness ends, and below the line at which the *convenances* begin to cramp natural feeling, and the stress of threadbare modishness makes too little of enough.

Thus passed the leafy time when arborescence seems to be the one thing aimed at out of doors. Tess and Clare unconsciously studied each other, ever balanced on the edge of a passion, yet apparently keeping out of it. All the while they were converging, under an irresistible law, as surely as two streams in one vale.

This passage is neither the best nor the worst of Hardy. Rather it shows the many complicated pressures working within what had to seem a single intention. 'The leafy time when arborescence' is an example of mere inflation to an 'educated' style, but the use of '*convenances*', which might appear merely fashionable, carries a precise feeling. 'Instalment' and 'ephemeral' are also uses of a precise kind, within a sentence which shows mainly the strength of what must be called an educated point of view. The consciousness of the natural process, in 'germs and inorganic particles' (he had of course learned it from Darwin who with Mill was his main intellectual influence) is a necessary accompaniment, for Hardy's purpose, of the more direct and more enjoyed sights and scents of spiring. It is loss not gain when Hardy reverts to the simpler and cruder abstraction of 'Dairyman Crick's household of maids and men', which might be superficially supposed to be the countryman speaking but is actually the voice of the detached observer at a low level of interest. The more fully Hardy uses the resources of the whole language, as a precise observer, the more adequate the writing is. There is more strength in 'unconsciously studied each other', which is at once educated and engaged, than in the 'two streams in one vale', which shares with the gesture of 'irresistible law' a synthetic quality, here as of a man playing the countryman novelist.

Hardy's mature style is threatened in one direction by a willed 'Latinism' of diction or construction, of which very many particular instances can be collected (and we have all done it, having taken our education hard), but in the other direction by this much less noticed element of artifice which is too easily accepted, within the patronage we have discussed, as the countryman speaking (sometimes indeed it is literally the countryman speaking, in a con-trived picturesqueness which is now the novelist's patronage of his rural characters). The mature style itself is unambiguously an educated style, in which the extension of vocabulary and the complication of construction are necessary to the intensity and precision of the observation which is Hardy's essential position and attribute.

The gray tones of daybreak are not the gray half-tones of the day's close, though the degree of their shade may be the same. In the twilight of the morning, light seems active, darkness passive; in the twilight of evening, it is the darkness which is active and crescent, and the light which is the drowsy reverse.

This is the educated observer, still deeply involved with the world he is watching, and the local quality of this writing is the decisive tone of the major fiction.

The complication is that this is a very difficult and exposed position for Hardy to maintain. Without the insights of consciously learned history and of the educated understanding of nature and behaviour he cannot really observe at all, at a level of extended human respect. Even the sense of what is now called the 'timeless' – in fact the sense of history, of the barrows, the Roman remains, the rise and fall of families, the tablets and monuments in the churches – is a function of education. That real perception of tradition is available only to the man who has read about it, though what he then sees through it is his native country, to which he is already deeply bound by memory and experience of another kind: a family and a childhood; an intense association of people and places, which has been his own history. To see tradition in both ways is indeed Hardy's special gift: the native place and experience but also the education, the conscious inquiry. Yet then to see living people, within this complicated sense of past and present, is another problem again. He sees as a participant who is also an observer; this is the source of the strain. For the process which allows him to observe is very clearly in Hardy's time one which includes, in its attachment to class feelings and class separations, a decisive alienation.

If these two noticed Angel's growing social ineptness, he noticed their growing mental limitations. Felix seemed to him all Church; Cuthbert all College. His Diocesan Synod and Visitations were the mainsprings of the world to the one; Cambridge to the other. Each brother candidly recognized that there were a few unimportant scores of millions of outsiders in civilized society, persons who were neither University men nor Church-men; but they were to be tolerated rather than reckoned with and respected.

This is what is sometimes called Hardy's bitterness, but in fact it is only sober and just observation. What Hardy sees and feels about the educated world of his day, locked in its deep social prejudices and in its consequent human alienation, is so clearly true that the only surprise is why critics now should still feel sufficiently identified with that world – the world which coarsely and coldly dismissed Jude and millions of other men – to be willing to perform the literary equivalent of that stalest of political tactics: the transfer of bitterness, of a merely class way of thinking, from those who exclude to those who protest. We did not after all have to wait for Lawrence to be shown the human nullity of that apparently articulate world. Hardy shows it convincingly again and again. But the isolation which then follows, while the observer holds to educated procedures but is unable to feel with the existing educated class, is severe. It is not the countryman awkward in his town clothes but the more significant tension – of course with its awkwardness and its spurts of bitterness and nostalgia – of the man caught by his personal history in the general structure and crisis of the relations between education and class, relations which in practice are between intelligence and fellow-feeling. Hardy could not take the James way out, telling his story in a 'spirit of intellectual superior-ity' to the 'elementary passions'. As he observes again of the Clare brothers:

Perhaps, as with many men, their opportunities of observation were not so good as their opportunities of expression.

That after all is the nullity, in a time in which education is used to train members of a class and to divide them from other men as surely as from their own passions (for the two processes are deeply connected). And yet there could be no simple going back.

They had planted together, and together they had felled; together they had, with the run of the years, mentally collected those remoter signs and symbols which seen in few are of runic obscurity, but all together made an alphabet. From the light lashing of the twigs upon their faces when brushing through them in the dark, they could pronounce upon the species of tree whence they stretched; from the quality of the wind's murmur through a bough, they could in like manner name its sort afar off.

This is the language of the immediate apprehension of 'nature', for in that form, always, Hardy could retain a directness of communication. But it is also more specifically the language of shared work, in 'the run of the years', and while it is available as a memory, the world which made it possible is, for Hardy, at a distance which is already enough to detach him: a closeness, paradoxically, that he is still involved with but must also observe and 'pronounce upon'. It is in this sense finally that we must consider Hardy's fundamental attitudes to the country world he was writing about. The tension is not between rural and urban, in the ordinary senses, nor between an abstracted intuition and an abstracted intelligence. The tension, rather, is in his own position, his own lived history, within a general process of change which could come clear and alive in him because it was not only general but in every detail of his feeling observation and writing immediate and particular.

Every attempt has of course been made to reduce the social crisis in which Hardy lived to the more negotiable and detachable forms of the disturbance of a 'timeless order'. But there was nothing timeless about nineteenth-century rural England. It was changing constantly in Hardy's lifetime and before it. It is not only that the next village to Puddletown is Tolpuddle, where you can look from the Martyrs' Tree back to what we know through Hardy as Egdon Heath. It is also that in the 1860s and 1870s, when Hardy was starting to write, it was what he himself described as

a modern Wessex of railways, the penny post, mowing and reaping machines, union workhouses, lucifer matches, labourers who could read and write, and National school children.

Virtually every feature of this modernity preceded Hardy's own life (the railway came to Dorchester when he was a child of seven). The effects of the changes of course continued. The country was not timeless but it was not static either;

indeed, it is because the change was long (and Hardy knew it was long) that the crisis took its particular forms.

We then miss most of what Hardy has to show us if we impose on the actual relationships he describes a pastoral convention of the countryman as an age-old figure, or a vision of a prospering countryside being disintegrated by Corn Law repeal or the railways or agricultural machinery. It is not only that Corn Law repeal and the cheap imports of grain made less difference to Dorset: a county mainly of grazing and mixed farming in which the coming of the railway gave a direct commercial advantage in the supply of milk to London: the economic process described with Hardy's characteristic accuracy in *Tess*:

They reached the feeble light, which came from the smoky lamp of a little railway station; a poor enough terrestial star, yet in one sense of more importance to Talbothays Dairy and mankind than the celestial ones to which it stood in such humiliating contrast. The cans of new milk were unladen in the rain, Tess getting a little shelter from a neighbouring holly tree. . . .

. . . 'Londoners will drink it at their breakfasts tomorrow, won't they?', she asked. 'Strange people that we have never seen? . . . who don't know anything of us, and where it comes from, or think how we two drove miles across the moor tonight in the rain that it might reach 'em in time?'

It is also that the social forces within his fiction are deeply based in the rural economy itself: in a system of rent and trade; in the hazards of ownership and tenancy; in the differing conditions of labour on good and bad land and in socially different villages (as in the contrast between Talbothays and Flintcomb Ash); in what happens to people and to families in the interaction between general forces and personal histories – that complex area of ruin or survival, exposure or continuity. This is his actual society, and we cannot suppress it in favour of an external view of a seamless abstracted country 'way of life'.

It is true that there are continuities beyond a dominant social situation in the lives of a particular community (though two or three generations, in a still partly oral culture, can often sustain an illusion of timelessness). It is also obvious that in most rural landscapes there are very old and often unaltered physical features, which sustain a quite different time-scale. Hardy gives great importance to these, and this is not really surprising when we consider his whole structure of feeling. But all these elements are overridden, as for a novelist they must be, by the immediate and actual relationships between people, which occur within existing contemporary pressures and are at most modulated and interpreted by the available continuities.

The pressures to which Hardy's characters are subjected are then pressures from within the system of living, not from outside it. It is not urbanism but the hazard of small-capital farming that changes Gabriel Oak from an independent farmer to a hired labourer and then a bailiff. Henchard is not destroyed by a new and alien kind of dealing but by a development of his own trade which he has himself invited. It is Henchard in Casterbridge who speculates in grain as he had speculated in people; who is in every sense, within an observed way of life, a dealer and a destructive one; his strength compromised by that. Grace Melbury is not a country girl 'lured' by the fashionable world but the daughter of a successful timber merchant whose own social expectations, at this point of his success, include a fashionable education for his daughter. Tess is not a peasant girl seduced by the squire; she is the daughter of a lifeholder and small dealer who is seduced by the son of a retired manufacturer. The latter buys his way into a country house and an old name. Tess's father and, under pressure, Tess herself, are damaged by a similar process, in which an old name and pride are one side of the coin and the exposure of those subject to them the other. That one family fell and one rose is the common and damaging history of what had been happening, for centuries, to ownership and to its consequences in those subject to it. The Lady Day migrations, the hiring fairs, the intellectually arrogant parson, the casual gentleman farmer, the landowner spending her substance elsewhere: all these are as much parts of the country 'way of life' as the dedicated craftsman, the group of labourers and the dances on the green. It is not only that Hardy sees the realities of labouring work, as in Marty South's hands on the spars and Tess in the swede field. It is also that he sees the harshness of economic processes, in inheritance, capital, rent and trade, within the continuity of the natural processes and persistently cutting across them. The social process created in this interaction is one of class and separation, as well as of chronic insecurity, as this capitalist farming and dealing takes its course. The profound disturbances that Hardy records cannot then be seen in the sentimental terms of a pastoral: the contrast between country and town. The exposed and separated individuals, whom Hardy puts at the centre of his fiction, are only the most developed cases of a general exposure and separation. Yet they are never merely illustrations of this change in a way of life. Each has a dominant personal history, which in psychological terms bears a direct relation to the social character of the change.

One of the most immediate effects of mobility, within a structure itself changing, is the difficult nature of the marriage choice. This situation keeps recurring in terms which are at once personal and social: Bathsheba choosing between Boldwood and Oak; Grace between Giles and Fitzpiers; Jude between Arabella and Sue. The specific class element, and the effects upon this of an insecure economy, are parts of the personal choice which is after all a choice primarily of a way to live, of an identity *in* the identification with this or that other person. And here significantly the false marriage (with which Hardy is so regularly and deeply concerned) can take place either way: to the educated coldness of Fitzpiers or the coarseness of Arabella. Here most dramatically the condition of the internal migrant is profoundly known. The social alienation enters the personality and destroys its capacity for any loving fulfilment. The marriage of Oak and Bathsheba is a case of eventual stability, after so much disturbance, but even that has an air of inevitable resignation and lateness. It is true that Hardy sometimes, under pressure, came to generalise and project these very specific failures into a fatalism for which in the decadent thought of his time the phrases were all too ready. In the same way, seeing the closeness of man and the land being broken by the problems of working the land, he sometimes projected his insistence on closeness and continuity into the finally negative images of an empty nature and the tribal past of Stonehenge and the barrows, where the single observer, at least, could feel a direct flow of know-ledge. Even these, however, in their deliberate hardness – the uncultivable health, the bare stone relics – confirm the human negatives, in what looks like a deliberate reversal of pastoral. In them the general alienation has its characteris-tic monuments, though very distant in time and space from the controlling immediate disturbance.

But the most significant thing about Hardy, in and through these difficulties, is that more than any other major novelist since this difficult mobility began he succeeded, against every pressure, in centering his major novels in the ordinary process of life and work. For all his position as an educated observer, he still took his actions from where the majority of his fellow- countrymen were living. Work enters his novels more decisively than in any English novelist of comparable importance. And it is not merely illustrative; it is seen as it is, as a central kind of learning. Feeling very acutely the long crisis of separation, and in the end coming to more tragically isolated catastrophes than any others within this tradition, he yet created continually the strength and the warmth of people living together: in work and in love; in the physical reality of a place.

To stand working slowly in a field, and feel the creep of rain-water, first in legs and shoulders, then on hips and head, then at back, front, and sides, and yet to work on till the leaden light diminishes and marks that the sun is down, demands a distinct modicum of stoicism, even of valour. Yet they did not feel the wetness so much as might be supposed. They were both young, and they were talking of the time when they lived and loved together at Talbothays Dairy, that happy green tract of land where summer had been liberal in her gifts: in substance to all, emotionally to these.

The general structure of feeling in Hardy would be much less convincing if there were only the alienation, the frustration, the separation and isolation, the final catastrophes. What is defeated but not destroyed at the end of *The*

Woodlanders or the end of *Tess* or the end of *Jude* is a warmth, a seriousness, an endurance in love and work that are the necessary definition of what Hardy knows and mourns as loss. Vitally – and it is his difference from Lawrence . . . a difference of generation and of history but also of character – Hardy does not celebrate isolation and separation. He mourns them, and yet always with the courage to look them steadily in the face. The losses are real and heartbreaking because the desires were real, the shared work was real, the unsatisfied impulses were real. Work and desire are very deeply connected in his whole imagination. That the critical emotional decisions by Tess are taken while she is working – as in the ache and dust of the threshing-machine where she sees Alec again – is no accident of plot; it is how this kind of living connects. The passion of Marty or of Tess or of Jude is a positive force coming out of a working and relating world; seeking in different ways its living fulfilment. That all are frustrated is the essential action: frustrated by very complicated processes of division, separation and rejection. People choose wrongly but under terrible pressures: under the confusions of class, under its misunderstandings, under the calculated rejections of a divided separating world.

It is important enough that Hardy keeps to an ordinary world, as the basis of his major fiction. The pressures to move away from it, to enter a more negotiable because less struggling and less divided life, were of course very strong. And it is even more important, as an act of pure affirmation, that he stays, centrally, with his central figures; indeed moves closer to them in his actual development, so that the affirmation of Tess and of Jude – an affirmation in and through the defeats he traces and mourns – is the strongest in all his work.

Beginning with a work in which he declared his hand – *The Poor Man and the Lady, by the Poor Man*; finding that rejected as mischievous, and getting advice, from Meredith, to retreat into conventional plots; letting the impulse run underground where it was continually disturbing but also always active; gaining a growing certainty which was a strengthening as well as a darkening of vision: Hardy ran his course to an exceptional fidelity.

'Slighted and enduring': not the story of man as he was, distant, limited, picturesque; but slighted in a struggle to grow – to love, to work with meaning, to learn and to teach; enduring in the community of this impulse, which pushes through and beyond particular separations and defeats. It is not only the continuity of a country but of a history that makes me now affirm, with his own certainty and irony: Hardy is our flesh and our grass.

8

Orwell

From *Raymond Williams (1971)* Orwell *London: Collins*

Orwell's writing in the thirties can be conventionally divided into the 'documentary' and 'factual' work on the one hand, and the 'fictional' and 'imaginative' work on the other. The surface distinction is evident enough: on the one hand *Down and Out in Paris and London, The Road to Wigan Pier, Homage to Catalonia,* and such sketches as 'The Spike', 'A Hanging', 'Shooting an Elephant'; on the other hand the four novels *Burmese Days, A Clergyman's Daughter, Keep the Aspidistra Flying,* and *Coming Up for Air.* Yet nothing is clearer, as we look into the work as a whole, than that this conventional division is secondary. The key problem, in all this work, is the relation between 'fact' and 'fiction': an uncertain relation which is part of the whole crisis of 'being a writer'.

Literature used not to be divided in these external ways. The rigid distinction between 'documentary' and 'imaginative' writing is a product of the nineteenth century, and most widely distributed in our own time. Its basis is a naïve definition of the 'real world', and then a naïve separation of it from the observation and imagination of men. If there is real life and its recording, on the one hand, and a separable imaginative world on the other, two kinds of literature can be confidently distinguished, and this is much more than a formal effect. In naturalist and positivist theories this effective dualism of 'the world' and 'the mind' is at least clearly recognisable. But the conventional dualism of most orthodox literary theory has scarcely been noted, let alone challenged. Terms like 'fiction' and 'non-fiction', 'documentary' and 'imaginative', continue to obscure many of the actual problems of writing.

The unity of Orwell's 'documentary' and 'imaginative' writing is the very first thing to notice. There were many problems of method, but at least Orwell got past the conventional division, if only in practice. And he saw the division as it actually presented itself to him as something more than a formal problem. He saw it, correctly, as a problem of social relationships.

English fiction on its higher levels is for the most part written by literary gents about literary gents for literary gents; on its lower levels it is generally the most putrid 'escape' stuff – old maids' fantasies about Ian Hay male virgins, or little fat men's visions of themselves as Chicago gangsters. Books about ordinary people behaving in an ordinary manner are extremely rare, because they can only be written by someone who is capable of standing both inside and outside the ordinary man, as Joyce for instance stands inside and outside Bloom; but this involves admitting that you yourself *are* an ordinary person for nine-tenths of the time, which is exactly what no intellectual ever wants to do. (CEJL, I, 230[1])

There is still some unnoticed class feeling in this. Orwell is still seeing from far enough outside to suppose that there are people – a class of people – who are 'ordinary' ten-tenths of the time. But to have got as far as he did is something.

I think the interest of Bloom is that he is an ordinary uncultivated man described from within by someone who can also stand outside him and see him from another angle. Not that Bloom is an absolutely typical man in the street. . . .

The man in the street is usually described in fiction either by writers who are themselves intellectually men in the street, tho' they may have great gifts as novelists (e.g. Trollope), or by cultivated men who describe him *from outside* (e.g. Samuel Butler, Aldous Huxley). (CEJL, I, 128)

Cultivated men who describe the man in the street from outside. It is in and through this social deformity, inflicted on him by his class and education, that Orwell reaches for the idea of an extended or even common humanity. His writing in the thirties is an exploration, in experience and in books, towards such a humanity.

The problem of social relationship is, then, a problem of form. *Down and Out in Paris and London* is in effect a journal. What is put in is the experience of being without money in a modern city: the experience of dish-washers and tramps, of filthy rooms, dosshouses, casual wards. The author is present, but only insofar as these things are happening to him along with others. His own character and motivations are sketched as briefly as those of anyone else met in the kitchen or on the road. He is neither 'inside' nor 'outside'; he is simply drifting *with* others – exceptionally close to them but within the fact that they are drifting, that this is *happening to* their bodies and minds.

But then compare *A Clergyman's Daughter*. It is a novel about a repressed girl who has a breakdown, goes vagrant, and eventually returns, via teaching, to where she started. Anyone who reads Orwell's other writing of the time will find most of the experiences of the novel elsewhere in other forms. The 'Church Times' and the glue-and-brown-paper theatrical armour, and even the 'moribund hag who stinks of mothballs and gin, and has to be more or less carried to and from the altar' are to be found in Chapter One of the novel and in Orwell's letters about himself (CEJL, I, 103, 105, 101–2). Or the girl going vagrant, the hop-picking, Ginger and Deafie, sleeping rough in Trafalgar Square: these are to be found in Chapter Two and the beginning of Chapter Three, also in Orwell's diary, 'Hop- Picking' (CEJL, I, 52–71). The point is not the external relation between the writer's 'material' and his 'process of creation'. The interest is almost entirely in the method of handling the author's own presence: the intermediary character of the girl – 'inside' when she is caught in the routines of church and teaching; 'outside', even amnesiac, when she is drifting on the road. The attempted characterisation of the girl as more than a surrogate presence is at times serious and detailed, at times merely functional. But a *sustained* identity, through diversity and dislocation of experience, cannot yet be realised. And it is interesting that at one point – the night scene in Trafalgar Square, in the first section of Chapter Three – Orwell makes a conscious literary experiment of a different, impersonal kind, which is very evidently derived from the night- town chapter in *Ulysses* – the novel that had been so much in his mind as an example. He remained pleased with this experiment, though coming to reject the book as a whole.

Orwell's affinity to Joyce – or attempted affinity – is not in our usual reading. The modern writers Orwell mentions most often, in his earlier period, are Wells, Bennett, Conrad, Hardy, Kipling. In 1940 he makes a different list – Joyce, Eliot, and Lawrence. This change of emphasis through the 1930s is quite normal and representative. Among earlier writers on his 1940 list, he names Shakespeare, Swift, Fielding, Dickens, Reade, Butler, Zola, and Flaubert. The critical interest in Shakespeare, Swift, and Dickens can be seen from his essays. But in the development of his own writing there are two opposite emphases: the detailed interest in *Ulysses* (notably in a letter to Brenda Salkeld, CEJL, I, 125–9) at just the time of working on *A Clergyman's Daughter*, and also, as he said in 1940, 'I believe the modern writer who has influenced me most is Somerset Maugham, whom I admire immensely for his power of telling a story straightforwardly and without frills' (CEJL, II, 24).

The names as such do not greatly matter. Literary influence is a secondary business. What is important is the problem of standpoint, which is the key to any critical judgment of Orwell. It is easy to say that *Down and Out in Paris and London* is better than *A Clergyman's Daughter*, but this ought not to be reduced to the plausible generalisation that he is a better 'observer' than 'novelist'. The real problem lies deeper, in the available conceptions of 'the novel'.

'Telling a story straightforwardly and without frills.' 'Story', after all, is the whole question. Maugham is the characteristic Edwardian 'storyteller': that is to say, the collector and retailer of human episodes. Orwell had the material for this (it is usually collected at a distance, and in other lands), but only his first novel, *Burmese Days*, is at all of its kind. Even there, while the plot concerns personal intrigue among an isolated European group on an Eastern station, the stress is on the complicated social consequences of imperialism and within this there is what we can now recognise as the deep Orwell pattern: the man who tries to break from the standards of his group but who is drawn back into it and, in this case, destroyed. What is unique about the novel in Orwell's work is that he creates an entire social and physical milieu within which the social criticism and the personal break are defined elements. In all his later novels, the essential form is shaped by what became separated elements: the personal break, and social criticism through it, in the novels of the thirties; the social criticism, with the personal break inside it, in *Nineteen Eighty-Four*.

That seems a clear development, but what it omits is the material of 'observation'. Having found one form for this, in the journal of *Down and Out in Paris and London*, Orwell clearly wanted to incorporate it in a novel. This is the developmental significance of *A Clergyman's Daughter*, where the direct observation and the fiction are unusually close. But from then on he seems to have accepted the division between 'documentary' and 'fiction'. A possible reshaping of the novel was evaded, or proved too difficult: not, I would say, because he was 'not really a novelist' but because a problem of consciousness, which he shared with other writers of his time, emerged as a problem of form.

For Orwell the interest of Joyce had been his direct realisation of 'ordinary' experience. It is Bloom he selects from *Ulysses*: that recording 'inside' and 'outside' the ordinary man. But this description conceals the problem of the relationship of the novelist to his character, which is always a form of relationship of the writer to his world. And the relationship that matters here can be alternatively described as 'acceptance' or 'passivity'. It is an impersonal form, the logical consequence of James's emphasis on the artist's 'handling' of 'matter'. It is 'the artist refined out of existence', observing, recording. Except that in practice it is impossible to observe anything without being in some relationship to it. The apparent relationship, that which is recommended and publicised, is the 'aesthetic'; the 'handling' of the matter, the preoccupation with words, that is Joyce's actual development. But the 'matter' can only be handled in this way – can only be abstracted, stay still to be 'written' – if a particular relationship is in fact assumed. 'Acceptance' or 'passivity': the difference between the positive and negative descriptions is less important than the fact of the relationship itself – a refraining from intervention, or, more, a seeing no need to intervene, since the availability of the 'matter' is the artist's primary and only concern.

Orwell's artistic failure, in his novels of the thirties, is in a way and paradoxically due to his social achievement. He had known passivity at least, very closely, as he describes in *Down and Out in Paris and London*. But he had known it not in his capacity as a writer but as its victim, and insofar as it was 'matter' it was matter of a kind that concerned him personally rather than as a writer. What we have seen him describe as an 'invasion' is the growth of that social consciousness which required his intervention, which made either acceptance or passivity impossible (though he went back to the idea of acceptance and passivity, in *Inside the Whale*, at a time when the social intervention could be held to have failed).

And then in shaping a literary form, he created the figure of the intermediary (the 'shock-absorber of the bourgeoisie' as he once referred to people like himself). Instead of direct realisation of what was observed, he created the intermediary figure who goes around and to
whom things happen. This figure, in the novels, is not himself, and this is very important. The figure has his experiences, in *A Clergyman's Daughter* and then in a different way in *Keep the Aspidistra Flying*. The figure is passive; things happen to Dorothy, or *to* Comstock. And this pattern releases one element of Orwell's experience – the things that had 'happened' to him – but not or only partly why they had happened, not the intervening or 'invading' consciousness. Dorothy, certainly, is the more passive figure. Comstock, in *Keep the Aspidistra Flying*, is given some of Orwell's whole consciousness: not only trying to live without money but declaring war on money and its system. Comstock is an active and critical figure in all the initial exploration, but increasingly there is a contradiction within the mode of observation. The active and resourceful persistence of Orwell, the impressive survival and remaking of an active self, is steadily cut out, as the accepting observation continues. What begins as a protest becomes a whine, and the reabsorption of Comstock into a world of manipulable objects is accomplished with a kind of perverse triumph: the 'character' of the intermediary (like the 'character' of Flory or of Dorothy) being the 'justification' of the eventual submission or defeat.

This is the strange transmutation of 'acceptance' or 'passivity'. In Orwell, because of his uncertainties, it is neither an artistic discipline nor an acceptable worldview. His final attempt at a Bloom figure is Bowling in *Coming Up For Air*, written at a recollecting and abstracting distance and perhaps for that reason more consistent internally. Bowling breaks from an orthodox routine, like the others, though not into exposure, where things happen to him; but instead into the past, an old England and his childhood; and then the experience is of loss, disillusion, disenchantment. *Coming Up For Air* came after Orwell's crucial political experience in Spain and its consequences . . . But elements of the literary decision are continuous: observation through a limited intermediary, with the limit as the basis for a deeper pattern: a selfproving of both the need and the impossibility of a sustained break, so that active intervention dwindles to a temporary protest or self-assertion. The significance of this pattern in the altered world of *Nineteen Eighty-Four* will need further analysis, when the other changes have been taken into account.

Having failed to solve his profoundly difficult problem in the novel, Orwell turned to other forms which were in practice more available. His social and political writing was a direct release of consciousness, the practical consequence of intervention. 'Shooting an Elephant', for example, is more successful than anything in *Burmese Days* not because it is 'documentary' rather than fiction – the fiction, as we have seen, similarly relied on things that had happened to him – but because instead of a Flory an Orwell is present: a successfully created character in every real sense. Instead of diluting his consciousness through an intermediary, as the mode of fiction had seemed to require, he now writes directly and powerfully about his whole experience. The prose is at once strengthened, as the alternation between an anxious impersonation and a passively impersonal observation gives way to a direct voice, in which there is more literary creation than in all the more conventionally 'imaginative' attempts.

'Shooting an Elephant' is not a document; it is a literary work. The distinction between 'fiction' and 'nonfiction' is not a matter of whether the experience happened to the writer, a distinction between 'real' and 'imaginary'. The distinction that matters is always one of range and consciousness. Written human experience of an unspecialised and primary kind must always be recognised as literature. Particular forms, and the origins of the material, are secondary questions. Orwell began to write literature, in the full sense, when he found this 'non-fictional' form: that is, when he found a form capable of realising his experience directly.

Realising *his* experience – not only what had happened to him and what he had observed, but what he felt about it and what he thought about it, the self-definition of 'Orwell', the man inside and outside the experience. Perhaps the best example is *The Road to Wigan Pier*. As it happens Orwell's diary notes for this book have been published (CEJL, I, 170–214). A comparison of the diary and the book is interesting, for a number of reasons. It is easy enough to find in the notes the sources of many of the descriptions: of the Brookers' lodging house, for example, in the opening chapter. But what is also evident, comparing the two, is the literary process. There is the expected and necessary development of a scene, in the published version: a fuller and more fluent description, details recollected from memory. But there is also a saturation of the scene with feeling. Orwell is present and responding, indeed directing response, in a way that is only there towards the end in the diary notes. He seems also to have shifted the lodgers around a bit: Joe, at the Brookers', is described in the notes as a lodger at a previous house – a house which is not in the book. So in the book the Brookers' house is not only given the emphasis of the first place but treated as a first, representative experience ('it struck me that this palce must be fairly normal as lodging-houses in the industrial areas go') when in the diary there is a preceding and rather different experience.

This is just one small example to illustrate the point about 'documentary' experience. The writer shapes and organises what happened to produce a particular effect, based on experience but then created out of it. The overall organisation of *The Road to Wigan Pier* is a major example. In the first part, the 'observation' of the industrial north, one of the key points, in literary terms, is that Orwell is the isolated observer going around and seeing for himself. This created character is then used to important effect in the second half, the argument about socialism, where the man who has gone and seen for himself is contrasted with the jargon-ridden bourgeois socialists: 'The first thing that must strike any outside observer is that Socialism in its developed form is a theory confined entirely to the middle class' (RWP, 152).

The external political point is not what is most important here: 'in its developed form' is an infinitely saving clause. The key point is the persona, the 'outside observer' – that is, Orwell. An essential link between the two parts is indeed this character: 'inside' and then 'outside' the experience.

We learn from the diary notes that after some days wandering on his own through the Midlands Orwell was given some political contacts in Lancashire and met working-class socialists and members of the Unemployed Workers' Movement. Through one of these contacts he got the chance to go down a mine; and through the NUWM collectors he obtained facts about housing conditions. It is important that he omits most of this experience – an actual social and political network – in *The Road to Wigan Pier*. Even in the diary, some of the difficulties are apparent. A local trade union official and his wife, 'both... working-class people', are seen as living (in a twelve or fourteen-shilling- a-week estate house) in an 'entirely middle-class' atmosphere (CEJL, I, 173). Orwell has his own definition of what the working class is like. That is, presumably, why he could say, after meeting these people (who had embarrassed him by calling him 'comrade') and 'an electrician who takes a prominent part in the Socialist movement', that 'socialism' was a middle-class affair. If a working man is a socialist he is already, presumably, middle-class, the character of the working- class being already known.

But here the political point *is* the literary point. What is created in the book is an isolated independent observer and the objects of his observation. Intermediate characters and experiences which do not form part of this world – this structure of feeling – are simply omitted. What is left in is 'documentary' enough, but the process of selection and organisation is a literary act: the character of the observer is as real and yet created as the real and yet created world he so powerfully describes.

All of Orwell's writing until 1937 is, then, a series of works and experiments around a common problem. Instead of dividing them into 'fiction' and 'documentaries' we should see them as sketches towards the creation of his most successful character, 'Orwell'. It would not be so successful if it had not been so intensely and painfully lived. The exposure to poverty and suffering and filth and waste was as real as it was deliberate, and the record of the exposure is a remarkable enlargement of our literature. But in and through the exposure a character is being created, who is real in the precise sense that he becomes this writer, this shaping presence. Flory and Dorothy and Comstock, or the later Bowling, are aspects of this character but without its centrality. The only literary form which can contain the full character at this stage is the 'non-fiction journal' of an isolated writer exposed to a suffering but unconnecting world. The need to intervene, to force active connections, is the road away from Wigan Pier, back to an indifferent and sleepy and uncaring world, which has to be told about the isolation and the suffering.

At just this point, between the diary and the book, the Spanish war broke out. The writing, and the character, moved into a different dimension.

Note

1   CEJL I = *The Collected Essays, Journalism and Letters of George Orwell I: An Age Like This, 1920–1940*, eds. Sonia Orwell and Ian Angus, Harmondsworth: Penguin 1970. Further abbreviations in the text include:
CEJL II = *The Collected Essays, Journalism and Letters of George Orwell II: My Country Right or Left 1940–1943*, eds. Sonia Orwell and Ian Angus, Harmondsworth: Penguin 1970.
RWP = George Orwell *The Road to Wigan Pier*, Harmondsworth: Penguin, 1984.

Part III

Theory and Representation (1972–80)

Part III: Introduction

At first glance, Raymond Williams's relations to Marxism appear highly contradictory. In 1947, in one of his first reviews, Williams wrote in disdainful tones of Marxist criticism's failure to 'emerge from theory into respectable practice' (1947: 52). A decade later in his seminal work *Culture and Society*, he scathingly described the work of Marxist critic Christopher Caudwell as 'not even specific enough to be wrong' (1958: 277); and stated that Marxist theories of culture were 'confused' (p. 274). Yet, a further twenty years on, he came to describe Marxism as 'the single most important advance in modern thought', asserting that he 'wouldn't want to write on any question without tracing the history of it in Marxist thought' (1979: 316). How are we to understand or account for such evident contradiction in Williams's accounts of Marxism?

One way of accounting for this contradiction has been for critics to divide his work into two distinct phases – anti- and pro-Marxist – and then to read the shift between them as the product of a conceptual maturing on his part, in a welcome reversal of the usual trajectory from communist youth to conservative middle-age. So it is that the editors of *Marxist Literary Theory: A Reader* suggest, in somewhat relieved tones, that 'William's critical distance from Marxism had, by the 1970s, developed into a more explicit *rapprochement* with Marxism' (Eagleton and Milne 1996: 242) while another Marxist critic, Aijaz Ahmad, writes approvingly of the way in which his intellect 'kept moving leftward' (Ahmad 1994: 48), and welcomes his adoption of 'increasingly Marxist perspectives' (p. 47). This is explanation by parallax, where a change in the observer's position results in a difference of appearance in the object: Williams's differing assessments of Marxism are attributed to shifts in his viewpoint, while Marxism itself remains unchanged.

Any such assumption makes it difficult to chart with any accuracy the actual development of Williams's relations to Marxism. In reality, the changes in assessment are best understood dialectically: they were the consequences of his shifting attitudes towards a body of work which was in itself unstable, and liable to quite varied interpretations and even contradictory emphases. Even in his earliest account, Williams was keen to distinguish between what had come through in Britain as Marxist literary criticism, and the implications of Marx's own work. While rejecting the received ideas of Marxist literary theory, he is quick to point out that Marx himself was never the practitioner of 'what we would now know as Marxist literary criticism' (1958: 265) and to argue that, at the most, he had 'outlined, but never fully developed a cultural theory' (1958: 265). Though such an emphasis on the fragmentary and incomplete nature of Marx's thinking may have been anathama to the orthodox, it did keep open a space for the further elaboration and development of Marxist theory. In a Cold War context in which both Marxists and anti-Marxists seemed paradoxically to agree on the essential unity and internal coherence of Marx's work, this emphasis on the essentially unfinished nature of his theories was no mean achievement.[1]

Base and Superstructure in Marxist Cultural Theory (1973) is undoubtedly one of Williams's finest single essays, and is often singled out as evidence for his 'rapprochement with Marxism' (Eagleton and Milne 1996: 242). In reality, it marks a point of continuity rather than rupture in his relations to Marxism, looking back to the arguments of *Culture and Society* (1958) but also forward to the arguments of *Marxism and Literature* (1977a). As a Prefatory Note, we include a section from his memorial tribute to fellow literary and cultural critic, Lucien Goldmann, who had died in the autumn of 1970 after visiting Cambridge earlier that year. The encounter with Goldmann, in which Williams had evidently warmed to 'this smiling man in his open-necked shirt, more concerned with a cigarette than with notes but concerned above all with the challenge of his argument' (Williams 1971b: 14), pushed him to articulate the reasons for the general renewal in Britain of interest in Marxist theory. Along with the work of newly translated thinkers such as Georg Lukács, Jean-Paul Sartre and Antonio Gramsci, Goldmann's thought belonged to what Williams termed 'Marxism's alternative tradition'. This alternative tradition was 'radically different from what most people in Britain understand as Marxist', particularly in its 'account of consciousness' (**Base and Superstructure**, p. 159). Against the orthodox Marxist view of the determination of consciousness by the economic base these thinkers emphasized the power of human agency and intention even in circumstances not of their own choosing.

In particular – and here lies continuity as well as development in Williams's thinking – he saw this alternative tradition as endorsing his own questioning of the figure of a determining economic base and a determined ideological superstructure. This figure or analogy had taken on all the apparent explanatory force of a received idea in Marxist literary and cultural analysis. In 1958, he had described base and superstructure as the 'terms of an analogy [which] express at once an absolute and a fixed relationship', and insisted that 'the reality which Marx and Engels recognize is both less absolute and less clear' than the figure suggested (1958: 267–8). By 1973, this cautionary note had developed into a much fuller and considered critique, in which Williams re-examined the whole grammar of determination, in the end insisting that each term in the classic figure 'has to be revalued':

We have to revalue 'determination' towards the setting of limits and the exertion of pressure, and away from a predicted, prefigured and controlled content. We have to revalue 'superstructure' towards a related range of cultural practices, and away from a reflected, reproduced or specifically dependent content. And, crucially, we have to revalue 'base' away from the notion of a fixed economic or technological abstraction, and towards the specific activities of men in real social and economic relationships, containing fundamental contradictions and variations and therefore always in a state of dynamic process.

(Base and Superstructure in Marxist Cultural Theory, p. 165)

With this emphasis on dynamic process rather than known and settled state ('when we talk of "the base", we are talking of a process and not a state' (p. 165)), he is rejecting both the Marxist literary criticism he had known in the 1950s, but also issuing a challenge to the emerging theories of power and ideology associated with structuralist and post-structuralist theory.

Television and Representation was first published as part of the groundbreaking study, *Television: Technology and Cultural Form* (1974). The study exemplified Williams's resolve to extend the boundaries of critical analysis from canonical literature to broader forms of cultural expression, while preserving the simple but powerful modes of formal analysis associated with literary criticism. At the same time, it worked to give the flesh of example to the bones of his theoretical critique of absolute senses of determination. Technological determinism was, for instance, the key feature of Marshall McLuhan's influential work on television: and, as Williams warned in a useful extension of his reservations regarding base and superstructure theory, 'if the medium – whether print or television – is the cause, all other causes, all that men ordinarily see as history, are at once reduced to effects' (1974: 127). It was now necessary to restore the category of '*intention* to the process of research and development'

(p. 14), and to offer 'a social history of communications technology' (p. 19) as a counter to determinist models such as McLuhan's.[2]

At the formal level of textual analysis, Williams was interested in the standard ways in which television constructs the terms of its social authority. Even in the most ordinary news broadcast 'the visual presence of a familiar presenter is bound to affect the whole communication situation' (**Television and Representation**), he notes. Similarly, the dominant 'television impression of "seeing the event for oneself" is', he points out dryly, 'at times and perhaps always deceptive', noting – with the characteristic force of a simple example – just how important it is in the reporting of any riot or demonstration 'whether "the camera" is looking over the heads of the police being stoned or over the heads of the demonstrators being tear-gassed' (p. 182).

More broadly, on the level of direct political coverage, he argues that while television has 'markedly broadened the forms of public argument and discussion' ('Television and Representation', p. 183), it has also worked to contain them. What usually happens in any coverage of significant political debate 'is that a public process, at the level of response and interrogation, is *represented* for us by the television intermediaries'. Television does not only report on events and decisions in the political sphere, it also works to shape public response to them. The 'best evidence of the deadness of the familiar and now orthodox routines of displacement' lies, he argues, in the 'shock of vitality, when other conceptions of argument and discussion occasionally break through' (p. 187). That television can at times be defamiliarized in this way indicates the real limits to the general fact of social determination stressed in most Marxist theories.

Language as Sociality is taken from the classic *Marxism and Literature* (1977a). More than just a survey of the encounter between Marxist cultural theory and literary analysis, the study presented 'a critique and an argument' regarding their conjunction (1977a:1). While the argument was directed 'against the limits of the newly dominant mode of critical structuralism' which Williams saw in danger of 'being taken as Marxist literary theory all over Western Europe and North America' (1979: 339), the critique came to bear on a central absence in Marxist theory itself. 'Marxism does not have a theory of language', as he put it in an early discussion of his new study; because of this 'it goes wrong again and again' (1977b: 15–16). Absent from early drafts of the book, language theory can arguably be seen as a new focus for Williams's own work, superseding the earlier and less fully theorized concern with 'communication'.

In the writings of the critical structuralists, the term 'subject' took on a new currency as the crux or point of intersection between ideological and linguistic theory, threatening at times a linguistic idealism in which changes in discourse would guarantee transformations in the structures of social oppression. Thinkers as diverse in their disciplinary genres as Louis Althusser, Roland Barthes, Michel Foucault, Julia Kristeva, Jacques Derrida and Jacques Lacan all tended to agree that language had long been misunderstood in the Western philosophical tradition. In this tradition, language was generally taken as the tool or instrument of an autonomous self and held to work best at its most scientific, when acting as a mirror to, or reflection of, an independently existing reality. But, as Emile Benveniste – whose work is a common point of reference for the critical structuralists – argued, to speak of language as an instrument sets up an opposition between nature and humanity which ignores the fundamentally constitutive role that language plays in founding human consciousness and identity. While humans make and use tools which exist independently of them, language 'is in the nature of man, who did not fabricate it . . . It is in and through language that man is constituted as *subject*' (Benveniste 1966: 259, my translation).

'A definition of language is always,' argued Williams, 'a definition of human beings in the world' (**Language as Sociality**, p. 188). Framed in this way what representation of the social subject did the claims of critical structuralism imply? Within the terms of its own definitions, language is 'a fixed, objective, and in these senses "given" system' (p. 193), one which 'had theoretical and practical priority over what were described as "utterances" '. In this model, 'the living speech of human beings in their specific social relationships in the world was theoretically reduced to instances and examples of a system which lay beyond them' (p. 194). Implicit and at times explicit in critical structuralist theory was a corresponding idea of society as 'a controlling "social" system which is *a priori* inaccessible to "individual" acts of will and intelligence' (p. 194). Against this, Williams set the crucial but neglected work of V. N. Voloshinov, whose *Marxism and the Philosophy of Language* had first appeared in 1929, but which had not been translated into English until 1973.[3]

Williams read this as a text which anticipated and vigorously challenged many of the tenets of critical structuralism. In Voloshinov's work we find

not a reified 'language' and 'society' but an active *social language*. Nor . . . is this language a simple 'reflection' or 'expression' of 'material reality'. What we have, rather, is a grasping of this reality through language, which as practical consciousness is saturated by and saturates all social activity, including productive activity.

(**Language as Sociality**, p. 202)

This insistence on language as 'practical consciousness' was important since it allowed Williams to bring together and consolidate his objections to critical structuralism with his rejection of orthodox Marxist cultural theory. Rejecting in both cases the thesis of the absolute structural determination of human subjectivity, it stressed instead the precise constituted materiality of human agency.

The question of agency is also taken up in the final essay in this Part, **The Writer: Commitment and Alignment**, first delivered to the Socialist Society as the Marx Memorial lecture for 1980. Here he argued the need for a total reassessment of commitment. Rejecting its received idea as the writer's submission to an authoritarian party line, he suggests that commitment can only be defended if it is understood as a form of conscious resistance to the determining pressures of alignment. It is interesting to see how the notion of alignment embodies many of the insights of the critical structuralist blending of Marxism with psychoanalysis which reached its high point in Louis Althusser's theory of ideology. 'Marxism', he argues,

more clearly than any other kind of thinking, has shown us that we are in fact aligned long before we realize that we are aligned. For we are born into a social situation, into social relationships, into a family, all of which have formed what we can later abstract as ourselves as individuals. Much of this formation occurs before we can be conscious of any individuality.

(**The Writer: Commitment and Alignment**, p. 216)

Where Williams differs from Althusser and the critical structuralists is in his insistence that consciousness of alignment means the possibility of overcoming it: critical structuralist theory seemed to suggest a form of alignment and ideological determination so powerful that it seemed impossible to resist. The 'most serious case for commitment' is given by the need to become 'conscious of our own real alignments' and 'the social pressures on our own thinking' (**The Writer: Commitment and Alignment**, p. 217). 'To be committed to that is nothing whatever to do with submission to anybody', he concludes: it is simply 'the discovery of those social relationships which are in any case there' (p. 217). It is only in this discovery that a space can be made for the formation of critical consciousness and political agency.

Writing of commitment, Williams had suggested that it is always 'a mistake, when you see an idea, to go straight into an argument about it' (**The Writer: Commitment and Alignment**, p. 215). This cautionary note is characteristic, and might even be said to constitute something like a methodological principle for Williams's work as a whole. It should at least be sounded with regard to Marxism, and to any account of the relations between Williams and Marxism. Like any other complex body of thought, any particular form of Marxism can be no more than the selective reading and interpretation of an internally diverse and very likely contradictory body of work, even or especially if it presents itself as a unified and coherent body of doctrine, as an orthodoxy, or, in its most extreme form, as an unchallengeable dogma.

It was Williams's signal virtue to have insisted on challenging the dogmas of orthodox Marxism, and in so doing to keep open a space for the self-critical development of Marxist theory. As he wrote in *Marxism and Literature*, while in the 1950s it was possible to assume that Marxism was 'a settled body of theory or doctrine' (1977a: 1), by the 1970s this was no longer possible and it was now necessary to see Marxism 'as itself a historical development, with highly variable and even alternative positions' (1977a: 3). No one contributed more to this historical development than Williams himself as he wrote to unsettle Marxism.

Notes

1 See, for instance, Paul Thomas's comment: 'cold war warriors on both sides were ... quick to develop vested interests in a caricature of Marx's beliefs ... The cold war gave rise to a remarkably unitary view of Marx as the progenitor of Stalin that was useful to both sides for different reasons ... Rescuing Marx from the high cold war is going to take a lot of hard work' (Thomas 1991: 52).

2 See McLuhan 1964 and Williams 1968b.

3 I follow Williams in making no attempt to adjudicate whether or to what extent Mikhail Bakhtin may be regarded as the author of the work here attributed to Voloshinov. For a useful discussion, see Clark and Holquist 1984: 146–51; and especially their conclusion that 'a conclusive answer to the question of Bakhtin's authorship cannot be found' (p. 148).

9

Base and Superstructure in Marxist Cultural Theory

Prefatory Note: Lucien Goldmann and Marxism's Alternative Tradition

From The Listener 87, 23 March 1972

In the autumn of 1970 Lucien Goldmann died, in his late fifties. Less than a year later, Georg Lukacs died, in his eighties. I cannot easily explain my sense of loss at these two deaths. In public terms there is an obvious description: Lukacs and Goldmann were the two most significant modern figures in the Marxist tradition of the sociology of literature. But to say that, in Britain, and to most people over thirty, is to say very little. In the student generation of the last ten years there has been an active rediscovery of Marxism, but this has been very little understood by most of their elders: for many reasons, social and political, but in part at least because most of their interested elders already know, or think they know, what Marxism is, from memories of the Thirties. They may in part be right, for though Marxism is in fact a very complicated tradition, there is at least a case for saying that the variety of Marxism which emerged into significant practice, in the Soviet Union and in its associated Communist Parties, was the one that mattered, whatever intellectual variations might then be obscured. Yet if that is said, it has more than intellectual significance. In its simplification to a single major trend it cuts short the possibility of any significant Marxist analysis of Soviet Communism. More seriously, it prevents understanding of the political movements and ideas of the new post-war generation whose first voices were being heard, in Poland and in Britain and in France, in the late Fifties, and who became a public generation, in many countries with significant effect, in the Sixties.

Of the two men who died, Georg Lukacs was clearly the more widely significant figure. His *History and Class- Consciousness*, a collection of essays written in the early Twenties, is the most important single work of what can be seen – in part against the disavowal of its author – as the alternative tradition of Marxism. In the scale of its contemporary influence it is joined only by the *Prison Notebooks*, from the late Twenties, of Antonio Gramsci, and by the work of Sartre in the Fifties and Sixties. As we look at the range of this work, from fundamental philosophical problems to questions of strategy, tactics and political organisation, we can properly call it, over a very wide field, a tradition. But I am interested here in only one of its aspects, which happens to be close to my own work. This is in part a professional limitation, but I would say also that the most significant feature of this alternative Marxist tradition is its account of consciousness: a social analysis which seems to me radically different from what most people in Britain understand as Marxist.

Often, to understand where we are, we have to bring together, to force into consciousness, what appear unrelated experiences. The difficulties of Marxism, in just this area, have been very significant. [. . .]

Lucien Goldmann's attempts are especially interesting. When he came to Cambridge, only a few months before his death, we talked in a friendly way but across a gap between different cultural and philosophical traditions. That gap had oepned around the beginning of this century. In philosophy, in sociology, in political theory and in theories of literature and art, there was a loss of contact, a loss of dialogue, between Britain and the Continental European tradition. It is ironic to remember how close we once were, in the time of Coleridge and Carlyle, and the further irony for me was that, learning from that tradition, which I'd described in *Culture and Society*, I'd found myself out of sympathy with the modern English tradition, while at the same time, necessarily, I wasn't part of its cultural alternatives. This had come out strongly in the way my next book, *The Long Revolution*, was read in Britain. For me it had followed clearly from the inquiry in *Culture and Society*: it was an attempt, indeed, to extend, and so change, that tradition. But I am not likely to forget the reaction. Here was a book that, to its author's surprise, had broken the Highway Code of conventional English culture, because it included and combined theory, history and analysis in literature, sociology and politics.

The agitated waving of flags at one frontier after another, the announcement of property rights and local standards of cultivation in one field after another, made me think for some years that I was in a strange, even enemy country, though it was of the particular experience of that country that I was writing. And it was then very important, reading Lukacs, reading and meeting Gold-mann, to find an identity of interests – not just particular interests but also ways of combining them – which was not a matter of influence either way. To meet in Goldmann a man who wrote literary theory and analysis, sociology and cultural history – not as a range of interests, and certainly not as a profession and its side-lines, but as a single intellectual enterprise – was like coming home and knowing one's own country, though in detail we belonged to very different cultural milieux and traditions.

That may give some background to my sense of loss at his death. But, to put it more generally, there had been the exciting prospect of finding new colla-borative ways of stating an essential position: not so much the learning of new concepts as the deep interest of recognising still difficult concepts in another language, another tradition, and, in just this recognition, seeing some familiar ground from a different point of view.

Consciousness is restored as a primary activity: that is the central result of this alternative Marxist tradition. But this consciousness is still social, and it is centred in history. And what is most challenging is that this is held to be true not only of what is called ordinary consciousness – which in practice is related to society and history by people of many beliefs – but also, and even especially, of creative consciousness: that area which in orthodox studies is always seen as essentially different and as 'beyond' society.

There's a distinction made by both Lukacs and Goldmann between 'actual' consciousness and 'possible' consciousness. It's often a difficult distinction but it can be put like this. Within the complex of pressures and limits, in any particular social formation, a kind of consciousness emerges which can indeed be said to reflect its determining world, though almost always confusedly and with many internal contradictions. it's a consciousness, an experience, half-thought, half-felt, contradictory, unfinished: not a simple superstructure on a simple base; not a false consciousness either, but that half- built, half-inherited, uncertain house in which, at most times and in most places, most of us live and feel and think. In contrast with this, certain ideas, certain works of art, certain theories, emerge from the shared limits and pressures with a sudden clarify and intensity: internally consistent, fully-thought, fully-felt, having a power which seems to take them, then or later, into a different dimension. Not because they get beyond the pressures and limits: indeed often, as time passes, they show these most clearly and memorably. But in a different dimension, because out of the unfinished run of ordinary consciousness – how we think and feel on any ordinary day, natives of our world, remembering, feeling, trying to imagine ourselves beyond it – out of what consciousness feels like when it's being ordinarily lived, come these particular forms, these successful shapings, these sudden higher orgnaisations. They are at times familiar, what we have half-known and felt, but now clear and intense; at other times strange, hard to recognise, but finding some image, some rhythm, some expression, some form, which past its initial strangeness can slowly take on the contours of truth, our truth, the truth as far as we can reach.

In Lukacs, deeply influenced by Hegel and by the Romantic tradition in art, this creative consciousness is still often seen through a theory of permanent forms, and of the emergence within them of the world-historical individual, the world-historical thinker or artist. That can then be translated, though it would lose his meaning, into a familiar idea of the limited public and the transcending genius. But what Goldmann was arguing – and for 15 years this has been my own argument – puts the emphasis on the forms which this creative consciousness finds, forms which characteristically emerge as the work of a generation: what we mean when we say the Elizabethan dramatists, the Romantic poets, the Impressionist painters.

These are groups of men of genius and talent, but what has emerged, in and through these men, is a way of seeing the world that is also a very particular artistic form. And to understand them we have first to analyse this form, and then, if we can – but by no simple formula – the relation of this form – its organisation, its emphases, its omissions, its limits – to the social experience, the social relationships, of its shaping time. Not so much the day-to-day history, or the miscellaneity of what is called background, but, if we can find it, the structural moment, the social crisis in its quite deepest sense. For these forms are not reflections of existing consciousness or reality. They are responses, active responses: ways of organising a way of seeing the world for which, already, all the materials exist – for it is a common world – but which now, in being formed, can itself be intensely seen.

I have put these ideas in my own words. At some points, I know, Goldmann would have wanted to put them differently – has already put them differently, in *The Hidden God*, in *Towards a Sociology of the Novel*, in another tradition and language. But this difference is less important than the ideas themselves. Goldmann's emphasis on form goes along with an emphasis on what he called 'the transindividual subject': a way of describing what I see as the social process of creation, in many activities from art to institutions, in which we can't properly speak of individual and society, individual and class, in separate ways, as if these were two abstractions confronting each other: Individual and Society; Individual or Society.

In most things that matter the real process of our living is beyond these abstractions. We are true subjects, bearers of consciousness, making as well as reflecting our society, and we can act together, as ourselves, or as groups against other groups, in decisive ways: often most deeply in ourselves when we are acting, thinking, feeling with others. What we can make is ours and yet goes beyond us, as indeed it often preceded us: a form we have made, often not knowing we were making it, often in temporary isolation, until others see what we have done.

There are still many unsolved problems in this alternative tradition. Not only of detailed work, but also in seeing the tradition, in bringing it into focus, in making it common. All I can say now, but with his early death it needs to be said, is that Lucien Goldmann was one of the essential contributors: that his work helped to give us a new possible consciousness.

Base and Superstructure

From New Left Review, 82, 1973, pp. 3–16

Any modern approach to a Marxist theory of culture must begin by considering the proposition of a determining base and a determined superstructure. From a strictly theoretical point of view this is not, in fact, where we might choose to begin. It would be in many ways preferable if we could begin from a proposition which originally was equally central, equally authentic: namely the proposition that social being determines consciousness. It is not that the two propositions necessarily deny each other or are in contradiction. But the proposition of base and superstructure, with its figurative element, with its suggestion of a fixed and definite spatial relationship, constitutes, at least in certain hands, a very specialized and at times unacceptable version of the other proposition. Yet in the transition from Marx to Marxism, and in the development of mainstream Marxism itself, the proposition of the determining base and the determined superstructure has been commonly held to be the key to Marxist cultural analysis.

It is important, as we try to analyse this proposition, to be aware that the term of relationship which is involved, that is to say 'determines', is of great linguistic and theoretical complexity. The language of determination and even more of determinism was inherited from idealist and especially theological accounts of the world and man. It is significant that it is in one of his familiar inversions, his contradictions of received propositions, that Marx uses the word which becomes, in English translation, 'determines' (the usual but not invariable German word is *bestimmen*). He is opposing an ideology that had been insistent on the power of certain forces outside man, or, in its secular version, on an abstract determining consciousness. Marx's own proposition explicitly denies this, and puts the origin of determination in men's own activities. Nevertheless, the particular history and continuity of the term serves to remind us that there are, within ordinary use – and this is true of most of the major European languages – quite different possible meanings and implications of the word 'determine'. There is, on the one hand, from its theological inheritance, the notion of an external cause which totally predicts or prefigures, indeed totally controls a subsequent activity. But there is also, from the experience of social practice, a notion of determination as setting limits, exerting pressures.[1]

Now there is clearly a difference between a process of setting limits and exerting pressures, whether by some external force or by the internal laws of a particular development, and that other process in which a subsequent content is essentially prefigured, predicted and controlled by a pre-existing external force. Yet it is fair to say, looking at many applications of Marxist cultural analysis, that it is the second sense, the notion of prefiguration, prediction or control, which has often explicitly or implicitly been used.

Superstructure: Qualifications and Amendments

The term of relationship is then the first thing that we have to examine in this proposition, but we have to do this by going on to look at the related terms themselves. 'Superstructure' (*Überbau*) has had most attention. In common usage, after Marx, it acquired a main sense of a unitary 'area' within which all cultural and ideological activities could be placed. But already in Marx himself, in the later correspondence of Engels, and at many points in the subsequent Marxist tradition, qualifications were made about the determined character of certain superstructural activities. The first kind of qualification had to do with delays in time, with complications, and with certain indirect or relatively distant relationships. The simplest notion of a superstructure, which is still by no means entirely abandoned, had been the reflection, the imitation or the reproduction of the reality of the base in the superstructure in a more or less direct way. Positivist notions of reflection and reproduction of course directly supported this. But since in many real cultural activities this relationship cannot be found, or cannot be found without effort or even violence to the material or practice being studied, the notion was introduced of delays in time, the famous lags; of various technical complications; and of indirectness, in which certain kinds of activity in the cultural sphere – philosophy, for example – were situated at a greater distance from the primary economic activities. That was the first stage of qualification of the notion of superstructure: in effect, an operational qualification. The second stage was related but more fundamental, in that the process of the relationship itself was more substantially looked at. This was the kind of reconsideration which gave rise to the modern notion of 'mediation', in which something more than simple reflection or reproduction – indeed something radically different from either reflection or reproduction – actively occurs. In the later twentieth century there is the notion of 'homologous structures', where there may be no direct or easily apparent similarity, and certainly nothing like reflection or reproduction, between the superstructural process and the reality of the base, but in which there is an essential homology or correspondence of structures, which can be discovered by analysis. This is not the same notion as 'mediation', but it is the same kind of amendment in that the relationship between the base and the superstructure is not supposed to be direct, nor simply operationally subject to lags and complications and indirectnesses, but that of its nature it is not direct reproduction.

These qualifications and amendments are important. But it seems to me that what has not been looked at with equal care is the received notion of the 'base' (*Basis, Grundlage*). And indeed I would argue that the base is the more important concept to look at if we are to understand the realities of cultural process. In many uses of the proposition of base and superstructure, as a matter of verbal habit, 'the base' has come to be considered virtually as an object, or in less crude cases, it has been considered in essentially uniform and usually static ways. 'The base' is the real social existence of man. 'The base' is the real relations of production corresponding to a stage of development of the material productive forces. 'The base' is a mode of production at a particular stage of its development. We make and repeat propositions of this kind, but the usage is then very different from Marx's emphasis on productive activities, in particular structural relations, constituting the foundation of all other activities. For while a particular stage of the development of production can be discovered and made precise by analysis, it is never in practice either uniform or static. It is indeed one of the central propositions of Marx's sense of history that there are deep contradictions in the relationships of production and in the consequent social relationships. There is therefore the continual possibility of the dynamic variation of these forces. Moreover, when these forces are considered, as Marx always considers them, as the specific activities and relationships of real men, they mean something very much more active, more complicated and more contradictory than the developed metaphorical notion of 'the base' could possibly allow us to realize.

The Base and the Productive Forces

So we have to say that when we talk of 'the base', we are talking of a process and not a state. And we cannot ascribe to that process certain fixed properties for subsequent translation to the variable processes of the superstructure. Most people who have wanted to make the ordinary proposition more reasonable have concentrated on refining the notion of superstructure. But I would say that each term of the proposition has to be revalued in a particular direction. We have to revalue 'determination' towards the setting of limits and the exertion of pressure, and away from a predicted, prefigured and controlled content. We have to revalue 'superstructure' towards a related range of cultural practices, and away from a reflected, reproduced or specifically dependent content. And, crucially, we have to revalue 'the base' away from the notion of a fixed economic or technological abstraction, and towards the specific activities of men in real social and economic relationships, containing fundamental contradictions and variations and therefore always in a state of dynamic process.

It is worth observing one further implication behind the customary definitions. 'The base' has come to include, especially in certain twentieth-century developments, a strong and limiting sense of basic industry. The emphasis on heavy industry, even, has played a certain cultural role. And this raises a more general problem, for we find ourselves forced to look again at the ordinary notion of 'productive forces'. Clearly what we are examining in the base is primary productive forces. Yet some very crucial distinctions have to be made here. It is true that in his analysis of capitalist production Marx considered 'productive work' in a very particular and specialized sense corresponding to that mode of production. There is a difficult passage in the *Grundrisse* in which he argues that while the man who makes a piano is a productive worker, there is a real question whether the man who distributes the piano is also a productive worker; but he probably is, since he contributes to the realization of surplus value. Yet when it comes to the man who plays the piano, whether to himself or to others, there is no question: he is not a productive worker at all. So piano-maker is base, but pianist superstructure. As a way of considering cultural activity, and incidentally the economics of modern cultural activity, this is very clearly a dead-end. But for any theoretical clarification it is crucial to recognize that Marx was there engaged in an analysis of a particular kind of production, that is capitalist commodity production. Within his analysis of this mode, he had to give to the notion of 'productive labour' and 'productive forces' a specialized sense of primary work on materials in a form which produced commodities. But this has narrowed remarkably, and in a cultural context very damagingly, from his more central notion of *productive forces*, in which, to give just brief reminders, the most important thing a worker ever produces is himself, himself in the fact of that kind of labour, or the broader historical emphasis of men producing themselves, themselves and their history. Now when we talk of the base, and of primary productive forces, it matters very much whether we are referring, as in one degenerate form of this proposition became habitual, to primary production within the terms of capitalist economic relationships, or to the primary production of society itself, and of men themselves, the material production and reproduction of real life. If we have the broad sense of productive forces, we look at the whole question of the base differently, and we are then less tempted to dismiss as superstructural, and in that sense as merely secondary, certain vital productive social forces, which are in the broad sense, from the beginning, basic.

Uses of Totality

Yet, because of the difficulties of the ordinary proposition of base and super-structure, there was an alternative and very important development, an emphasis primarily associated with Lukács, on a social 'totality'. The totality of social practices was opposed to this layered notion of base and a consequent superstructure. This concept of a totality of practices is compatible with the notion of social being determining consciousness, but it does not necessarily interpret this process in terms of a base and a superstructure. Now the language of totality has become common, and it is indeed in many ways more acceptable than the notion of base and superstructure. But with one very important reservation. It is very easy for the notion of totality to empty of its essential content the original Marxist proposition. For if we come to say that society is composed of a large number of social practices which form a concrete social whole, and if we give to each practice a certain specific recognition, adding only that they interact, relate and combine in very complicated ways, we are at one level much more obviously talking about reality, but we are at another level withdrawing from the claim that there is any process of determination. And this I, for one, would be very unwilling to do. Indeed, the key question to ask about any notion of totality in cultural theory is this: whether the notion of totality includes the notion of intention.

If totality is simply concrete, if it is simply the recognition of a large variety of miscellaneous and contemporaneous practices, then it is essentially empty of any content that could be called Marxist. Intention, the notion of intention, restores the key question, or rather the key emphasis. For while it is true that any society is a complex whole of such practices, it is also true that any society has a specific organization, a specific structure, and that the principles of this organization and structure can be seen as directly related to certain social intentions, intentions by which we define the society, intentions which in all our experience have been the rule of a particular class. One of the unexpected consequences of the crudeness of the base/superstructure model has been the too easy acceptance of models which appear less crude – models of totality or of a complex whole – but which exclude the facts of social intention, the class character of a particular society and so on. And this reminds us of how much we lose if we abandon the superstructural emphasis altogether. Thus I have great difficulty in seeing processes of art and thought as superstructural in the sense of the formula as it is commonly used. But in many areas of social and political thought – certain kinds of ratifying theory, certain kinds of law, certain kinds of institution, which after all in Marx's original formulations were very much part of the superstructure – in all that kind of social apparatus, and in a decisive area of political and ideological activity and construction, if we fail to see a superstructural element we fail to recognize reality at all. These laws, constitutions, theories, ideologies, which are so often claimed as natural, or as having universal validity or significance, simply have to be seen as expressing and ratifying the domination of a particular class. Indeed the difficulty of revising the formula of base and superstructure has had much to do with the perception of many militants – who have to fight such institutions and notions as well as fighting economic battles – that if these institutions and their ideologies are not perceived as having that kind of dependent and ratifying relationship, if their claims to universal validity or legitimacy are not denied and fought, then the class character of the society can no longer be seen. And this has been the effect of some versions of totality as the description of cultural process. Indeed I think we can properly use the notion of totality only when we combine it with that other crucial Marxist concept of 'hegemony'.

The Complexity of Hegemony

It is Gramsci's great contribution to have emphasized hegemony, and also to have understood it at a depth which is, I think, rare. For hegemony supposes the existence of something which is truly total, which is not merely secondary or superstructural, like the weak sense of ideology, but which is lived at such a depth, which saturates the society to such an extent, and which, as Gramsci put it, even constitutes the substance and limit of common sense for most people under its sway, that it corresponds to the reality of social experience very much more clearly than any notions derived from the formula of base and super-structure. For if ideology were merely some abstract, imposed set of notions, if our social and political and cultural ideas and assumptions and habits were merely the result of specific manipulation, of a kind of overt training which might be simply ended or withdrawn, then the society would be very much easier to move and to change than in practice it has ever been or is. This notion of hegemony as deeply saturating the consciousness of a society seems to me to be fundamental. And hegemony has the advantage over general notions of totality, that it at the same time emphasizes the facts of domination.

Yet there are times when I hear discussions of hegemony and feel that it too, as a concept, is being dragged back to the relatively simple, uniform and static notion which 'superstructure' in ordinary use had become. Indeed I think that we have to give a very complex account of hegemony if we are talking about any real social formation. Above all we have to give an account which allows for its elements of real and constant change. We have to emphasize that hegemony is not singular; indeed that its own internal structures are highly complex, and have continually to be renewed, recreated and defended; and by the same token, that they can be continually challenged and in certain respects modified. That is why instead of speaking simply of 'the hegemony', 'a hegemony', I would propose a model which allows for this kind of variation and contradiction, its sets of alternatives and its processes of change.

For one thing that is evident in some of the best Marxist cultural analysis is that it is very much more at home in what one might call *epochal* questions than in what one has to call *historical* questions. That is to say, it is usually very much better at distinguishing the large features of different epochs of society, as commonly between feudal and bourgeois, than at distinguishing between different phases of bourgeois society, and different moments within these phases: that true historical process which demands a much greater precision and delicacy of analysis than the always striking epochal analysis which is concerned with main lineaments and features.

The theoretical model which I have been trying to work with is this. I would say first that in any society, in any particular period, there is a central system of practices, meanings and values, which we can properly call dominant and effective. This implies no presumption about its value. All I am saying is that it is central. Indeed I would call it a corporate system, but this might be confusing, since Gramsci uses 'corporate' to mean the subordinate as opposed to the general and dominant elements of hegemony. In any case what I have in mind is the central, effective and dominant system of meanings and values, which are not merely abstract but which are organized and lived. That is why hegemony is not to be understood at the level of mere opinion or mere manipulation. It is a whole body of practices and expectations; our assignments of energy, our ordinary understanding of the nature of man and of his world. It is a set of meanings and values which as they are experienced as practices appear as reciprocally confirming. It thus constitutes a sense of reality for most people in the society, a sense of absolute because experienced reality beyond which it is very difficult for most members of the society to move, in most areas of their lives. But this is not, except in the operation of a moment of abstract analysis, in any sense a static system. On the contrary we can only understand an effective and dominant culture if we understand the real social process on which it depends: I mean the process of incorporation. The modes of incorporation are of great social significance. The educational institutions are usually the main agencies of the transmission of an effective dominant culture, and this is now a major economic as well as a cultural activity; indeed it is both in the same moment. Moreover, at a philosophical level, at the true level of theory and at the level of the history of various practices, there is a process which I call the *selective tradition*: that which, within the terms of an effective dominant culture, is always passed off as '*the* tradition', '*the* significant past'. But always the selectivity is the point; the way in which from a whole possible area of past and present, certain meanings and practices are chosen for emphasis, certain other meanings and practices are neglected and excluded. Even more crucially, some of these meanings and practices are reinterpreted, diluted, or put into forms which support or at least do not contradict other elements within the effective dominant culture. The processes of education; the processes of a much wider social training within institutions like the family; the practical definitions and organization of work; the selective tradition at an intellectual and theoretical level: all these forces are involved in a continual making and remaking of an effective dominant culture, and on them, as experienced, as built into our living, its reality depends. If what we learn there were merely an imposed ideology, or if it were only the isolable meanings and practices of the ruling class, or of a section of the ruling class, which gets imposed on others, occupying merely the top of our minds, it would be – and one would be glad – a very much easier thing to overthrow.

It is not only the depths to which this process reaches, selecting and organizing and interpreting our experience. It is also that it is continually active and adjusting; it isn't just the past, the dry husks of ideology which we can more easily discard. And this can only be so, in a complex society, if it is something more substantial and more flexible than any abstract imposed ideology. Thus we have to recognize the alternative meanings and values, the alternative opinions and attitudes, even some alternative senses of the world, which can be accommodated and tolerated within a particular effective and dominant culture. This has been much under-emphasized in our notions of a superstructure, and even in some notions of hegemony. And the under-emphasis opens the way for retreat to an indifferent complexity. In the practice of politics, for example, there are certain truly incorporated modes of what are nevertheless, within those terms, real oppositions, that are felt and fought out. Their existence within the incorporation is recognizable by the fact that, whatever the degree of internal conflict or internal variation, they do not in practice go beyond the limits of the central effective and dominant definition. This is true, for example, of the practice of parliamentary politics, though its internal oppositions are real. It is true about a whole range of practices and arguments, in any real society, which can by no means be reduced to an ideological cover, but which can nevertheless be properly analysed as in my sense corporate, if we find that, whatever the degree of internal controversy and variation, they do not in the end exceed the limits of the central corporate definitions.

But if we are to say this, we have to think again about the sources of that which is not corporate; of those practices, experiences, meanings, values which are not part of the effective dominant culture. We can express this in two ways. There is clearly something that we can call alternative to the effective dominant culture, and there is something else that we can call oppositional, in a true sense. The degree of existence of these alternative and oppositional forms is itself a matter of constant historical variation in real circumstances. In certain societies it is possible to find areas of social life in which quite real alternatives are at least left alone. (If they are made available, of course, they are part of the corporate organization.) The existence of the possibility of opposition, and of its articulation, its degree of openness, and so on, again depends on very precise social and political forces. The facts of alternative and oppositional forms of social life and culture, in relation to the effective and dominant culture, have then to be recognized as subject to historical variation, and as having sources which are very significant as a fact about the dominant culture itself.

Residual and Emergent Cultures

I have next to introduce a further distinction, between *residual* and *emergent* forms, both of alternative and of oppositional culture. By 'residual' I mean that some experiences, meanings and values, which cannot be verified or cannot be expressed in terms of the dominant culture, are nevertheless lived and practised on the basis of the residue – cultural as well as social – of some previous social formation. There is a real case of this in certain religious values, by contrast with the very evident incorporation of most religious meanings and values into the dominant system. The same is true, in a culture like Britain, of certain notions derived from a rural past, which have a very significant popularity. A residual culture is usually at some distance from the effective dominant culture, but one has to recognize that, in real cultural activities, it may get incorporated into it. This is because some part of it, some version of it – and especially if the residue is from some major area of the past – will in many cases have had to be incorporated if the effective dominant culture is to make sense in those areas. It is also because at certain points a dominant culture cannot allow too much of this kind of practice and experience outside itself, at least without risk. Thus the pressures are real, but certain genuinely residual meanings and practices in some important cases survive.

By 'emergent' I mean, first, that new meanings and values, new practices, new significances and experiences, are continually being created. But there is then a much earlier attempt to incorporate them, just because they are part – and yet not a defined part – of effective contemporary practice. Indeed it is significant in our own period how very early this attempt is, how alert the dominant culture now is to anything that can be seen as emergent. We have then to see, first, as it were a temporal relation between a dominant culture and on the one hand a residual and on the other hand an emergent culture. But we can only understand this if we can make distinctions, that usually require very precise analysis, between residual- incorporated and residual not incorporated, and between emergent- incorporated and emergent not incorporated. It is an important fact about any particular society, how far it reaches into the whole range of human practices and experiences in an attempt at incorporation .. It may be true of some earlier phases of bourgeois society, for example, that there were some areas of experience which it was willing to dispense with, which it was prepared to assign as the sphere of private or artistic life, and as being no particular business of society or the state. This went along with certain kinds of political tolerance, even if the reality of that tolerance was malign neglect. But I am sure it is true of the society that has come into existence since the last war, that progressively, because of developments in the social character of labour, in the social character of communications, and in the social character of decision, it extends much further than ever before in capitalist society into certain hitherto resigned areas of experience and practice and meaning. Thus the effective decision, as to whether a practice is alternative or oppositional, is often now made within a very much narrower scope. There is a simple theoretical distinction between alternative and oppositional, that is to say between someone who simply finds a different way to live and wishes to be left alone with it, and someone who finds a different way to live and wants to change the society in its light. This is usually the difference between individual and small-group solutions to social crisis and those solutions which properly belong to political and ultimately revolutionary practice. But it is often a very narrow line, in reality, between alternative and oppositional. A meaning or a practice may be tolerated as a deviation, and yet still be seen only as another particular way to live. But as the necessary area of effective dominance extends, the same meanings and practices can be seen by the dominant culture, not merely as disregarding or despising it, but as challenging it.

Now it is crucial to any Marxist theory of culture that it can give an adequate explanation of the sources of these practices and meanings. We can understand, from an ordinary historical approach, at least some of the sources of residual meanings and practices. These are the results of earlier social formations, in which certain real meanings and values were generated. In the subsequent default of a particular phase of a dominant culture, there is then a reaching back to those meanings and values which were created in real societies in the past, and which still seem to have some significance because they represent areas of human experience, aspiration and achievement, which the dominant culture under-values or opposes, or even cannot recognise. But our hardest task, theoretically, is to find a non-metaphysical and non-subjectivist explanation of emergent cultural practice. Moreover, part of our answer to this question bears on the process of persistence of residual practices.

Class and Human Practice

We have indeed one source to hand from the central body of Marxist theory. We have the formation of a new class, the coming to consciousness of a new class. This remains, without doubt, quite centrally important. Of course, in itself, this process of formation complicates any simple model of base and superstructure. It also complicates some of the ordinary versions of hegemony, although it was Gramsci's whole purpose to see and to create by organization that hegemony of a proletarian kind which would be capable of challenging the bourgeois hegemony. We have then one central source of new practice, in the emergence of a new class. But we have also to recognize certain other kinds of source, and in cultural practice some of these are very important. I would say that we can recognize them on the basis of this proposition: that no mode of production, and therefore no dominant society or order of society, and there-fore no dominant culture, in reality exhausts the full range of human practice, human energy, human intention (this range is not the inventory of some original 'human nature' but, on the contrary, is that extraordinary range of variations, both practised and imagined, of which human beings are and have shown themselves to be capable). Indeed it seems to me that this emphasis is not merely a negative proposition, allowing us to account for certain things which happen outside the dominant mode. On the contrary, it is a fact about the modes of domination that they select from and consequently exclude the full range of actual and possible human practice. The difficulties of human practice outside or against the dominant mode are, of course, real. It depends very much whether it is in an area in which the dominant class and the dominant culture have an interest and a stake. If the interest and the stake are explicit, many new practices will be reached for, and if possible incorporated, or else extirpated with extraordinary vigour. But in certain areas, there will be in certain periods practices and meanings which are not reached for. There will be areas of practice and meaning which, almost by definition from its own limited character, or in its profound deformation, the dominant culture is unable in any real terms to recognize. This gives us a bearing on the observable difference between, for example, the practices of a capitalist state and a state like the contemporary Soviet Union in relation to writers. Since from the whole Marxist tradition literature was seen as an important activity, indeed a crucial activity, the Soviet state is very much sharper in investigating areas where different versions of practice, different meanings and values, are being attempted and expressed. In capitalist practice, if the thing is not making a profit, or if it is not being widely circulated, then it can for some time be overlooked, at least while it remains alternative. When it becomes oppositional in an explicit way, it does, of course, get approached or attacked.

I am saying then that in relation to the full range of human practice at any one time, the dominant mode is a conscious selection and organization. At least in its fully formed state it is conscious. But there are always sources of actual human practice which it neglects or excludes. And these can be different in quality from the developing and articulate interests of a rising class. The can include, for example, alternative perceptions of others, in immediate personal relationships, or new perceptions of material and media, in art and science, and within certain limits these new perceptions can be practised. The relations between the two kinds of source – the emerging class and either the dominatively excluded or the more generally new practices – are by no means necessarily contradictory. At times they can be very close, and on the relations between them much in political practice depends. But culturally and as a matter of theory the areas can be seen as distinct.

Now if we go back to the cultural question in its most usual form – what are the relations between art and society, or literature and society? – in the light of the preceding discussion, we have to say first that there are no relations between literature and society in that abstracted way. The literature is there from the beginning as a practice in the society. Indeed until it and all other practices are present, the society cannot be seen as fully formed. A society is not fully available for analysis until each of its practices is included. But if we make that emphasis we must make a corresponding emphasis: that we cannot separate literature and art from other kinds of social practice, in such a way as to make them subject to quite special and distinct laws. They may have quite specific features as practices, but they cannot be separated from the general social process. Indeed one way of emphasizing this is to say, to insist, that literature is not restricted to operating in any one of the sectors I have been seeking to describe in this model. It would be easy to say, it is a familiar rhetoric, that literature operates in the emergent cultural sector, that it re-presents the new feelings, the new meanings, the new values. We might persuade ourselves of this theoretically, by abstract argument, but when we read much literature, over the whole range, without the sleight-of-hand of calling Literature only that which we have already selected as embodying certain meanings and values at a certain scale of intensity, we are bound to recognize that the act of writing, the practices of discourse in writing and speech, the making of novels and poems and plays and theories, all this activity takes place in all areas of the culture.

Literature appears by no means only in the emergent sector, which is always, in fact, quite rare. A great deal of writing is of a residual kind, and this has been deeply true of much English literature in the last half-century. Some of its fundamental meanings and values have belonged to the cultural achievements of long-past stages of society. So widespread is this fact, and the habits of mind it supports, that in many minds 'literature' and 'the past' acquire a certain identity, and it is then said that there is now no literature: all that glory is over. Yet most writing, in any period, including our own, is a form of contribution to the effective dominant culture. Indeed many of the specific qualities of literature – its capacity to embody and enact and perform certain meanings and values, or to create in single particular ways what would be otherwise merely general truths – enable it to fulfil this effective function with great power. To literature, of course, we must add the visual arts and music, and in our own society the powerful arts of film and of broadcasting. But the general theore-tical point should be clear. If we are looking for the relations between literature and society, we cannot either separate out this one practice from a formed body of other practices, nor when we have identified a particular practice can we give it a uniform, static and ahistorical relation to some abstract social for-mation. The arts of writing and the arts of creation and performance, over their whole range, are parts of the cultural process in all the different ways, the different sectors, that I have been seeking to describe. They contribute to the effective dominant culture and are a central articulation of it. They embody residual meanings and values, not all of which are incorporated, though many are. They express also and significantly some emergent practices and meanings, yet some of these may eventually be incorporated, as they reach people and begin to move them. Thus it was very evident in the sixties, in some of the emergent arts of performance, that the dominant culture reached out to transform, or seek to transform, them. In this process, of course, the dominant culture itself changes, not in its central formation, but in many of its articulated features. But then in a modern society it must always change in this way, if it is to remain dominant, if it is still to be felt as in real ways central in all our many activities and interests.

Critical Theory as Consumption

What then are the implications of this general analysis for the analysis of particular works of art? This is the question towards which most discussion of cultural theory seems to be directed: the discovery of a method, perhaps even a methodology, through which particular works of art can be understood and described. I would not myself agree that this is the central use of cultural theory, but let us for a moment consider it. What seems to me very striking is that nearly all forms of contemporary critical theory are theories of *consumption*. That is to say, they are concerned with understanding an object in such a way that it can profitably or correctly be consumed. The earliest stage of consumption theory was the theory of 'taste', where the link between the practice and the theory was direct in the metaphor. From taste there came the more elevated notion of 'sensibility', in which it was the consumption by sensibility of elevated or insightful works that was held to be the essential practice of reading, and critical activity was then a function of this sensibility. There were then more developed theories, in the 1920s with I.A. Richards, and later in New Criticism, in which the effects of consumption were studied directly. The language of the work of art as object then became more overt. 'What effect does this work ("the poem" as it was ordinarily described) have on me?' Or, 'what impact does it have on me?', as it was later to be put in a much wider area of communication studies. Naturally enough, the notion of the work of art as *object*, as *text*, as an isolated artefact, became central in all these later consumption theories. It was not only that the practices of *production* were then overlooked, though this fused with the notion that most important literature anyway was from the past. The real social conditions of production were in any case neglected because they were believed to be at best secondary. The true relationship was seen always as between the taste, the sensibility or the training of the reader and this isolated work, this object 'as in itself it really is', as most people came to put it. But the notion of the work of art as object had a further large theoretical effect. If you ask questions about the work of art seen as object, they may include questions about the components of its production. Now, as it happened, there was a use of the formula of base and superstructure which was precisely in line with this. The components of a work of art were the real activities of the base, and you could study the object to discover these components. Sometimes you even studied the components and then projected the object. But in any case the relationship that was looked for was one between an object and its components. But this was not only true of Marxist suppositions of a base and a superstructure. It was true also of various kinds of psychological theory, whether in the form of archetypes, or the images of the collective unconscious, or the myths and symbols which were seen as the *components* of particular works of art. Or again there was biography, or psycho-biography and its like, where the components were in the man's life and the work of art was an object in which components of this kind were discovered. Even in some of the more rigorous forms of New Criticism and of structuralist criticism, this essential procedure of regarding the work as an object which has to be reduced to its components, even if later it may be reconstituted, came to persist.

Objects and Practices

Now I think the true crisis in cultural theory, in our own time, is between this view of the work of art as object and the alternative view of art as a practice. Of course it is at once argued that the work of art *is* an object: that various works have survived from the past, particular sculptures, particular paintings, particular buildings, and these are objects. This is of course true, but the same way of thinking is applied to works which have no such singular existence. There is no *Hamlet*, no *Brothers Karamazov*, no *Wuthering Heights*, in the sense that there is a particular great painting. There is no *Fifth Symphony*, there is no work in the whole area of music and dance and performance, which is an object in any way comparable to those works in the visual arts which have survived. And yet the habit of treating all such works as objects has persisted because this is a basic theoretical and practical presupposition. But in literature (especially in drama), in music and in a very wide area of the performing arts, what we permanently have are not objects but *notations*. These notations have then to be interpreted in an active way, according to the particular conventions. But indeed this is true over an even wider field. The relationship between the making of a work of art and its reception is always active, and subject to conventions, which in themselves are forms of (changing) social organization and relationship, and this is radically different from the production and consumption of an object. It is indeed an activity and a practice, and in its accessible forms, although it may in some arts have the character of a singular object, it is still only accessible through active perception and interpretation. This makes the case of notation, in arts like drama and literature and music, only a special case of a much wider truth. What this can show us here about the practice of analysis is that we have to break from the common procedure of isolating the object and then discovering its components. On the contrary we have to discover the nature of a practice and then its conditions.

Often these two procedures may in part resemble each other, but in many other cases they are of radically different kinds, and I would conclude with an observation on the way this distinction bears on the Marxist tradition of the relation between primary economic and social practices, and cultural practices. If we suppose that what is produced in cultural practice is a series of objects, we shall, as in most current forms of sociological-critical procedure, set about discovering their components. Within a Marxist emphasis these components will be from what we have been in the habit of calling the base. We then isolate certain features which we can so to say recognize *in component form*, or we ask what processes of transformation or mediation these components have gone through before they arrived in this accessible state.

But I am saying that we should look not for the components of a product but for the conditions of a practice. When we find ourselves looking at a particular work, or group of works, often realizing, as we do so, their essential community as well as their irreducible individuality, we should find ourselves attending first to the reality of their practice and the conditions of the practice as it was then executed. And from this I think we ask essentially different questions. Take for example the way in which an object – 'a text' – is related to a genre, in orthodox criticism. We identify it by certain leading features, we then assign it to a larger category, the genre, and then we may find the components of the genre in a particular social history (although in some variants of criticism not even that is done, and the genre is supposed to be some permanent category of the mind).

It is not that way of proceeding that is now required. The recognition of the relation of a collective mode and an individual project – and these are the only categories that we can initially presume – is a recognition of related practices. That is to say, the irreducibly individual projects that particular works are, may come in experience and in analysis to show resemblances which allow us to group them into collective modes. These are by no means always genres. They may exist as resemblances within and across genres. They may be the practice of a group in a period, rather than the practice of a phase in a genre. But as we discover the nature of a particular practice, and the nature of the relation between an individual project and a collective mode, we find that we are analysing, as two forms of the same process, both its active composition and its conditions of composition, and in either direction this is a complex of extending active relationships. This means, of course, that we have no built-in procedure of the kind which is indicated by the fixed character of an object. We have the principles of the relations of practices, within a discoverably intentional organization, and we have the available hypotheses of dominant, residual and emergent. But what we are actively seeking is the true practice which has been alienated to an object, and the true conditions of practice – whether as literary conventions or as social relationships – which have been alienated to components or to mere background.

As a general proposition this is only an emphasis, but it seems to me to suggest at once the point of break and the point of departure, in practical and theoretical work, within an active and self-renewing Marxist cultural tradition.

Note

1   For a further discussion of the range of meanings in 'determine' see *Keywords*, 1976, pp. 87–91.

10

Television and Representation

From Raymond Williams (1974) Television: Technology and Cultural Form. *London: Fontana*

There is a complicated interaction between the technology of television and the received forms of other kinds of cultural and social activity. Many people have said that television is essentially a combination and development of earlier forms: the newspaper, the public meeting, the educational class, the theatre, the cinema, the sports stadium, the advertising columns and billboards. The development is complicated in some cases by the earlier precedents of radio, and these will need to be considered. Yet it is clearly not only a question of combination and development. The adaptation of received forms to the new technology has led in a number of cases to significant changes and to some real qualitative differences. It is worth looking at each of the main forms with these questions in mind. But when we have done this, it will be necessary also to look at those forms which are not in any obvious way derivative, and which can usefully be seen as the innovating forms of television itself.

Combination and Development of Earlier Forms

(i) News

The newspaper had gone through all its major phases of development before the coming of broadcast news. In the early days of radio there was virtually absolute dependence on existing press agencies for the collection of news. Techniques of broadcast presentation were at first the simple transmission of news agency dispatches read by 'announcers' who were assumed to be at once authoritative and neutral, though the real 'authority' and 'neutrality' were those of the agencies. The use of special broadcasting reporters and correspondents developed mainly during the Second World War. By the time a majority television service was being developed, there were specific internal facilities for news gathering and news presentation, although the general news agencies continued to be used.

Relations between the broadcast news bulletin and the newspaper, as forms, are then complicated. They can best be analysed under four headings: sequence; priority; personal presentation; visualisation.

(a) Sequence

The printed page of the ordinary newspaper had become, before television, a mosaic of items. Earlier newspapers had followed a certain sequence, by column division. But even before this division had been broken down to the mosaic layout which was common in most papers from the 1920s, the act of reading a newspaper page involved a glancing over or scanning, and then, within the terms of the newspaper's selection, the reader's selection of items on which to concentrate. Since particular pages of the paper were specialised to certain kinds of news and related material, any particular mosaic page was then itself selected, before scanning within the mosaic began.

Some elements of this virtually simultaneous presentation of a number of news items were technically possible in broadcasting, and have to a limited extent been used. But the simplest mode of presentation in broadcasting was linear in time. In British radio it was only during the war that what were still called, from newspaper practice, 'headlines' were assembled at the beginning of the bulletin. This kind of headlining is now widely used in television newscasts, although not universally. Repetition of the main points at the end of the bulletin is again common but not universal. Yet whether or not these techniques of attention and repetition are locally employed, the main form of television news is, within its own structure, linear.

(b) Priorities

Linear presentation has necessary effects on questions of priority between news items. The mosaic newspaper page has its own techniques of catching attention and indicating relative importance, but these are to a certain extent subject to the reader's capacity to find his own way through. The broadcast news bulletin thus tends to retain more apparent editorial control of priority and attention.

It is impossible to estimate the effects of this without looking at what had happened to priorities in different kinds of newspaper. In Britain, for example, a comparison of lead stories (see *Communications*, 1975, pp. 75–80) showed marked variations of priorities in different kinds of paper. A further comparison with broadcast bulletins showed that broadcasting priorities were, on the whole, those of the minority press. In the United States the press situation is different, but the general point still holds. The world-view indicated by the selection and relative priority of news items is very similar as between broadcast bulletins and those minority newspapers which are written by and for the relatively highly educated. The distribution of interests in the more popular press, which supposedly follows the interests of its characteristic readers, is hardly to be found anywhere in broadcast news, although very similar definitions of what is popular and interesting tend to predominate in the non-news programming.

The effects of this are complex. It can be said that the broadcast bulletins impose certain priorities, and that among these are characteristic definitions of high politics, with a centralising emphasis on the acts and words of political leaders. Yet, though this is in general true, the national television news bulletins provide more public news than all but a very few newspapers. Moreover, they provide this to a very wide public, in ways that would not happen if we had only a 'minority' and a 'popular' press.

(c) Presentation

In Britain until the Second World War, the broadcast announcer was an anonymous authoritative (ruling-class) voice. Personal identification was introduced only as a security measure under the threat of invasion and capture of the stations. In television personal identification has become more marked, though in BBC bulletins it is still only lightly emphasised, while in ITN bulletins the formula is 'the news with . . . ' and then the names of the readers. This is also a common formula in American newscasts, but then there is additionally, as in most American television, immediate self-introduction.

Through any of these formulas the visual presence of a familiar presenter is bound to affect the whole communication situation. The BBC, at one extreme, tries continually to limit the presenter to a reading function, going out of its way to show him being handed papers or with the news-writers visible behind him. At the other extreme, in the mixed bulletins of local and national and international news in American television, there is a studied informality which is meant to create the effect of a group of men telling you things they happen to know. Even in the network bulletins there is less emphasis on a script and more on a personal presentation. Further, in the network bulletins, one of the presenters normally ends with a commentary, of an editorial kind, including relatively controversial points. In BBC television, commentary is strictly separated from the presenter, and specialist 'correspondents' are introduced to give what is in effect – though local neutrality is usually maintained – an editorial interpretation or point of view.

Most television news now includes a large number of reports from outside the studio, by reporters on the spot or in the wings. There is a variation of formula here also. In BBC bulletins it is 'our reporter' but it is 'his report'. In many American bulletins there is a closer identification between the central presentation and the substance of the distant report. This difference is quite marked in matters of commentary and interpretation, which at least formally, in BBC bulletins, are placed as the views of a section editor or correspondent. Though these differences are quite important, most of them are in practice overridden by the generalised authority of the presentation as a whole.

(d) Visualisation

Much of the real content of news has been altered by the facts of visual presentation. In certain kinds of report there seems to be an absolute difference between the written or spoken account and the visual record with commentary. It is true that much can be altered by selection and editing, but of course this is true also of any observer's account. It can be reasonably argued that the televisual impression of 'seeing the events for oneself' is at times and perhaps always deceptive. It matters very much, for example, in the visual reporting of a civil disturbance, whether 'the camera' is looking over the heads of the police being stoned or over the heads of the demonstrators being tear-gassed. The former is much more common, and the 'middle' view, which is often attempted in commentary, is rarely visually present – a fact which can make the 'neutrality' of the commentary essentially abstract. An intermediary is always present if not visible, and this can be more misleading than situations in which awareness of an intermediary is inevitable. Such awareness, however, is commonly absorbed, to an important degree, by habituation and routine, and indeed there are many events which come through the television camera with less processing or filtration than in any other medium. This has had important effects in the reporting of wars, natural disasters and famines. Its effect has also been important in the matter of political leaders, who are now less protected by standard communication formulas such as 'the President said...', and who, in spite of many consequent devices, are more regularly visible as whole persons. This has had complicated and controversial effects on many of the styles of politics. However, when we add the general facts of visualisation to the altered selections and priorities of the broadcast bulletins, we have to see a qualitative difference, and almost certainly a qualitative gain, in television as compared with printed news. Print, of course, retains its incomparable advantages as a way of collecting, recalling and checking information.

One significant difference between current British and American television should be noted in this context. British news bulletins now make much more intensive use of visual material beyond the immediate presentation. Indeed it is sometimes possible to feel, in British bulletins, that the item is there, or has that priority, because the film has come in. Or, if the film is not available, still photographs of people and events in the news fill the whole screen while much of the report is being read. In American bulletins, by contrast, the most obvious opportunities for this kind of visualisation – whether by film or stills – are often as it were deliberately ignored. The main visual experience of an American news bulletin is of the news readers themselves, with very simple visual background signs, and in current practice a significantly lower proportion of filmed reports, especially in regional news. Accustomed to British television news presentation, I felt after watching some weeks of American television bulletins that some new term was needed: perhaps 'visual radio'. I do not know all the reasons for this difference. There are some obvious problems of physical distance. But in regional and local bulletins many obvious opportunities for visual presentation are not taken. It presumably makes the news service very much cheaper to run. On the other hand, where there has been good visual reporting, as in some of the powerful film from Vietnam, the effect is proportionately very much more striking.

(ii) Argument and Discussion

There can be little doubt that broadcasting as a whole, and television especially, has markedly broadened the forms of public argument and discussion. All earlier forms, in large-scale societies, were more limited in character and scale. The sermon, the lecture, the political address were obviously more limited in immediate points of view. Only in certain favourable situations was there that regular choice and variety of viewpoints which is now common within even the limited range of current television argument. Public debates and meetings, or sessions of local and national government, reached many fewer people. Only a few newspapers, and some minority magazines, opened their columns to a wide range of controversy.

Yet it has been difficult to acknowledge this qualitative change because of the various restrictions still placed on the full range of argument. In some services there is a regular and virtually absolute exclusion of oppositional or minority views. When there is any change in this, as in Prague with Dubcek, the extent of the repression but also of the consequent potential for liberation can be seen as remarkable. It is then useful to compare the situation in relatively open societies such as Britain and the United States. At first glance, American television is much more open to public argument. There is a crucial difference in the fact that many public proceedings in the United States, from Senate hearings to local schools boards, are broadcast or televised, whereas in Britain there have been repeated refusals to allow the televising or broadcasting of any parliamentary proceedings. Again, there is the American use of the 'free speech message', which usually comes among the commercials. This excludes certain categories of message which are subject to law or formal vote, but includes points of view about a wide range of public actions and attitudes, given on the speaker's own responsibility. Again, there is rather more public questioning of local elected officials on American television, and this includes sharp controversy between them – a rare public situation in Britain. What can be said in general is that the transmissive elements of television are more widely used in American practice: an interpretation in terms of access.

In British television, where this kind of access and entry is much less common, there is on the other hand a much wider area of specially arranged discussion and argument. It is not only that there are many more controversial features and documentaries. It is that in prime time on majority channels there are many more discussion and argument programmes. In current (1973) American television most such programmes – and there are really not many – are in public service broadcasting, and are characteristically presented through the personality of an interviewer or interrogator (*Bill Moyers' Journal*; William Buckley's *Firing Line, The Reasoner Report, Sixty Minutes*). The British range, from *Panorama* and *Twenty-four Hours* or *Midweek* to *Man Alive, This Week* and *World in Action*, is not only very much wider; it is also more freestanding – more consistently an arranged service rather than transmitted access. This can be seen more clearly if we separate out the kind of programme which is most directly a continuation of an earlier form of public argument, the arranged and formal debate – in the United States *The Advocates*; in Britain several short-running experiments. Here the formality of the presentation as debate, with a chairman or moderator and certain declared rules of procedure, makes the special nature of the discussion explicit. In most British television discussions and arguments there are indeed some ground-rules, expressed in abstraction in the concepts of 'fairness' and 'balance', but these are normally dissolved into the actual presentation, and given little or no emphasis. What emerges, or is meant to emerge, is a representation of the state of 'informed opinion', with its own internal differences and nuances. There is then the paradox that though in British television there is more sustained and on the whole more serious discussion of public affairs than in American television, its characteristic process is at once consensual and substitutional. Certain producers try, at times successfully, to break this mode, and to develop it towards confrontation or the presentation of irreconcilable differences. But the majority tone and mode remain consensual, and the figure of the interrogator or the chairman develops into the figure of the true 'moderator'.

There is then the question of the relation of these processes of public argument and discussion to the orthodox representative political process. The most visible relation is one of tension. In the United States the Administration openly resents the power of the networks to present arguments from an independent position. In Britain there are continual allegations of party bias, this way or that. In relation to national leaders, American television still largely depends on or is limited to the form of the press conference, where the leader takes questions from the floor, and a status relation is then contained within the communication format. In Britain, by contrast, there are many more highlighted interviews and direct interrogations, often of a critical kind, where leader and interviewer are given positions of apparent equality. Directly transmitted public addresses, by leadres, are of course also used, in both kinds of television, on especially important occasions.

Yet there is quite another dimension of relationship between television discussion and the orthodox political process. To an important extent these uses of television serve to mediate the political process to its real constituencies. It is in this sense an *apparently* public form, in which there is reactive and speculative discussion of a decision-making process which is in real terms displaced or even absent. The exceptions to this are the direct American transmissions of public hearings and some of the direct British interrogations of Ministers. In these cases the public remains, evidently, beyond the screen; we are watching a proceeding which we can see as separate from us; we can then independently, though in effect silently, respond. But what more often happens is that a public process, at the level of response and interrogation, is *represented* for us by the television intermediaries. Not only the decisions and events, but what are intended to be the shaping responses to them, come through in a prepared and mediated form. These are apparently responses by 'our' representatives, though we have not selected them (as selected politicians, for their own defensive purposes, are often quick to point out). In any large and complex society this mediation of representation is especially important, since in its speed and general availability it tends towards monopoly of the reactive process, and is no less a monopoly when it includes an internally selected balance and differentiation of opinion. This is especially important in that it reinforces tendencies within the orthodox process of political representation, where representatives, between elections, acquire and claim a certain absolute character; if we do not like *them*, and through them their policies, we can change them *at the appointed times*. There is then, in these different ways, a displacement and attenuation of representation which can be felt, at times, as its absence. Oppositional elements who are outside the existing structures of representation have to find other ways to present their views: by petition or lobbying, directed towards existing representatives; or with much more difficulty, by actions and demonstrations directed towards the already 'represented' people. Characteristically, and in direct relation to the mediating nature of current television, many such efforts are governed by the attempt to become real – that is to say, to become present – in television terms. This is obviously true of the march or the 'happening', to attract the cameras. But there is then an obvious contrast, of a structural kind, between the apparently reasoned responses of the arranged studio discussion and the apparently unreasoned, merely demonstrative, responses of the arranged and marginal visual event. This is in its turn often mediated as a contrast between serious informed responses and emotional simplifying responses.

A powerful centralising medium such as television can then, in much the same way as the representative but centralising processes of government, exhaust and even claim to exhaust the necessarily manifold and irregular processes of true public argument. Orthodox politics exhausts it at a formally representative level. Television exhausts it at a reactive level. In relatively closed societies, this exhaustion can be almost total. In relatively open societies, it remains a tendency, but a very powerful tendency, since its means of arrangement and access are funded and permanently available, while alternative means are dependent on continual creation and recreation and in any case ordinarily lack its reach. The best television arguments and discussions are in fact those which open themselves towards people not assumed in advance to be already represented; for example, BBC 2's *Open Door*. Some of the worst, for all their internal skills, are those which *simulate a representation by their own criteria*. When this is, however statically, an attempted representation of public opinion, it can often be justified, within current institutions and techniques. But the criterion is more often likely to be a representation of *informed* opinion, and here a distinct social structure produces a distinguishable television form.

'Informed' is sometimes interpreted as 'having publicly attested skills'. It is more often interpreted as 'having access to real sources'. What then materialises is in effect an anteroom to a court: 'informed opinion' is the White House correspondent, the Lobby correspondent, the political editor, the financial journalist. These are literally mediators, since their skills and knowledge (and therefore the dimensions of their discussions) are determined by the fact of access. Around the centralised and only intermittently visible processes of decision there develops what is at worst a session of political gossip, at best a session of café politics. Political argument is not so much heard as overheard, and the relation of these mediators to the centres of decision is duplicated in the relation of the audience to the mediators. This most powerful medium of public presentation is then in large part limited to what is at every level an intended mediation. The shock of vitality, when other conceptions of argument and discussion occasionally break through, is the best evidence of the deadness of the familiar and now orthodox routines of displacement.

11

Language as Sociality

From Raymond Williams (1977) Marxism and Literature. *Oxford: Oxford University Press*

A definition of language is always, implicitly or explicitly, a definition of human beings in the world. The received major categories – 'world', 'reality', 'nature,' 'human' – may be counterposed or related to the category 'language', but it is now a commonplace to observe that all categories, including the category 'language', are themselves constructions in language, and can thus only with an effort, and within a particular system of thought, be separated from language for relational inquiry. Such efforts and such systems, nevertheless, constitute a major part of the history of thought. Many of the problems which have emerged from this history are relevant to Marxism, and in certain areas Marxism itself has contributed to them, by extension from its basic revaluation, in historical materialism, of the received major categories. Yet it is significant that, by comparison, Marxism has contributed very little to thinking about language itself. The result has been either that limited and undeveloped versions of language as a 'reflection' of 'reality' have been taken for granted, or that propositions about language, developed within or in the forms of other and often antagonistic systems of thought, have been synthesized with Marxist propositions about other kinds of activity, in ways which are not only ultimately untenable but, in our own time, radically limiting to the strength of the social propositions. The effects on cultural theory, and in particular on thinking about literature, have been especially marked.

The key moments which should be of interest to Marxism, in the development of thinking about language, are, first, the emphasis on language as *activity* and, second, the emphasis on the *history* of language. Neither of these positions, on its own, is enough to restate the whole problem. It is the conjunction and consequent revaluation of each position that remains necessary. But in different ways and with significant practical results, each position transformed those habitual conceptions of language which depended on and supported relatively static ways of thinking about human beings in the world.

The major emphasis on language as activity began in the eighteenth century, in close relation to the idea of men having made their own society, which we have seen as a central element in the new concept of 'culture'. In the previously dominant tradition, through all its variations, 'language' and 'reality' had been decisively separated, so that philosophical inquiry was from the beginning an inquiry into the connections between these apparently separate orders. The pre- Socratic unity of the *logos*, in which language was seen as at one with the order of the world and of nature, with divine and human law, and with reason, had been decisively broken and in effect forgotten. The radical distinction between 'language' and 'reality', as between 'consciousness' and 'the material world', corresponding to actual and practical divisions between 'mental' and 'physical' activity, had become so habitual that serious attention seemed naturally concentrated on the exceptionally complicated consequent relations and connections. Plato's major inquiry into language (in the *Cratylus*) was centred on the problem of the correctness of *naming*, in which the interrelation of 'word' and 'thing' can be seen to originate either in 'nature' or in 'convention'. Plato's solution was in effect the foundation of idealist thought: there is an intermediate but constitutive realm, which is neither 'word' nor 'thing' but 'form', 'essence', or 'idea'. The investigation of either 'language' or 'reality' was then always, at root, an investigation of these constitutive (metaphysical) forms.

Yet, given this basic assumption, far-reaching inquiries into the uses of language could be undertaken in particular and specialized ways. Language as a way of indicating reality could be studied as *logic*. Language as an accessible segment of reality, especially in its fixed forms in writing, could be studied as *grammar*, in the sense of its formal and 'external' shape. Finally, within the distinction between language and reality, language could be conceived as an *instrument* used by men for specific and distinguishable purposes, and these could be studied in *rhetoric* and in the associated poetics. Through prolonged academic and scholastic development, these three great branches of language study – *logic, grammar,* and *rhetoric* – though formally associated in the medieval *trivium*, became specific and eventually separated disciplines. Thus though they made major practical advances, they either foreclosed examination of the form of the basic distinction between 'language' and 'reality', or determined the grounds, and especially the terms, in which such an examination might be made.

This is notably the case with the important medieval concept of *sign*, which has been so remarkably readopted in modern linguistic thought. 'Sign', from Latin *signum*, a mark or token, is intrinsically a concept based on a distinction between 'language' and 'reality'. It is an interposition between 'word' and 'thing' which repeats the Platonic interposition of 'form', 'essence', or 'idea', but now in accessible linguistic terms. Thus in Buridan 'natural signs' are the universal mental counterparts of reality and these are matched, by convention, with the 'artificial signs' which are physical sounds or letters. Given this starting-point, important investigations of the activity of language (but not of language as an activity) could be undertaken: for example, the remarkable speculative grammars of medieval thought, in which the power of sentences and of the modes of construction which underlay and complicated simple empirical notions of 'naming' was described and investigated. Meanwhile, however, the *trivium* itself, and especially grammar and rhetoric, moved into relatively formal, though immensely learned, demonstrations of the properties of a given body of 'classical' written material. What was later to be known as 'literary study', and from the early seventeenth century as 'criticism', developed from this powerful, prestigious, and limited mode.

Yet the whole question of the distinction between 'language' and 'reality' was eventually forced into consciousness, initially in a surprising way. Descartes, in reinforcing the distinction and making it more precise, and in demanding that the criterion of connection should be not metaphysical or conventional but grounded in scientific knowledge, provoked new questions by the very force of his scepticism about the old answers. It was in response to Descartes that Vico proposed his criterion that we can have full knowledge only of what we can ourselves make or do. In one decisive respect this response was reactionary. Since men have not in any obvious sense made the physical world, a powerful new conception of scientific knowledge was ruled out *a priori* and was, as before, reserved to God. yet on the other hand, by insisting that we can understand society because we have made it, indeed that we understand it not abstractly but in the very process of making it, and that the activity of language is central in this process, Vico opened a whole new dimension.

It was and is difficult to grasp this dimension, initially because Vico embedded it in what can be read as a schematic account of the stages of language development: the notorious three stages of divine, heroic, and human. Rousseau, repeating these three stages as 'historical' and interpreting them as stages of declining vigour, gave a form of argument to the Romantic

Movement – the revival of literature as a revival of the 'original', 'primal' power of language. But this at once obscured the newly active sense of history (specializing it to regeneration and ultimately, as this failed, to reaction) and the newly active sense of language, which in being specialized to literature could be marked off as a special case, a special entity, a special function, leaving the 'non- literary' relations of language to reality as conventional and as alienated as before. To take Vico's three stages literally, or indeed as 'stages' at all, is to lose sight, as he did, of the dimension he had opened. For what was crucial, in his account of language, was that it emerged only at the human stage, the divine being that of mute ceremonies and rituals and the heroic that of gestures and signs. Verbal language is then distinctively human; indeed, constitutively human. This was the point taken up by Herder, who opposed any notion of language being 'given' to man (as by God) and, in effect, the apparently alternative notion of language being 'added' to man, as a special kind of acquisition or tool. Language is then, positively, a distinctively human opening of and opening to the world: not a distinguishable or instrumental but a constitutive faculty.

Historically this emphasis on language as constitutive, like the closely related emphasis on human development as culture, must be seen as an attempt both to preserve some idea of the generally human, in face of the analytical and empirical procedures of a powerfully developing natural science, and to assert an idea of human creativity, in face of the increased understanding of the properties of the physical world, and of consequently causal explanations from them. As such this whole tendency was in constant danger of becoming simply a new kind of idealism – 'humanity' and 'creativity' being projected as essences – while the tendencies it opposed moved towards a new kind of objective materialism. This specific fission, so fateful in all subsequent thought, was in effect masked and ratified by a newly conventional distinction between 'art' (literature) – the sphere of 'humanity' and 'creativity' – and 'science' ('positive knowledge') – the knowable dimension of the physical world and of physical human beings within it. Each of the key terms – 'art', 'literature', and 'science', together with the associated 'culture' and with such a newly necessary special-ization as 'aesthetic' and the radical distinction between 'experience' and 'experiment' – changed in meaning between the early eighteenth and early nineteenth centuries. The resulting conflicts and confusions were severe, but it is significant that in the new situation of the nineteenth century the issues were never really joined on the ground of language, at any radical level, though it was precisely in relation to language that the newly conventional distinctions most needed to be challenged.

What happened instead was an extraordinary advance in empirical know-ledge of languages, and a wholly remarkable analysis and classification of this knowledge in terms which set some of the basic questions aside. It is impossible to separate this movement from its political history, within the dynamic development of Western societies in a period of extending colonialism. Older studies of language had been largely contained within the model of the dead 'classical' languages (which still effectively determined 'grammar' in both its syntactic and literary senses) and of the 'derived' modern vernaculars. European exploration and colonization, meanwhile, had been dramatically expanding the available range of linguistic material. The critical encounter was between the European and Indian civilizations: not only in available languages but in European contact with the highly developed methods of Indic grammatical scholars, with their alternative body of 'classical' texts. It was as an Englishman in India that William Jones learned Sanskrit and from an observation of its resemblances to Latin and Greek began the work which led to classification of the Indo-European (Aryan) and other 'families' of languages.

This work, based on comparative analysis and classification, was procedurally very close to the evolutionary biology with which it is contemporary. It is one of the major periods of all scholarly investigation, empirically founding not only the major classifications of language families, including schemes of their evolutionary development and relationships, but also, within these schemes, discovering certain 'laws' of change, notably of sound-change. In one area this movement was 'evolutionary' in a particular sense: in its postulate of a proto-language (proto-Indo-European) from which the major 'family' had developed. But in its later stages it was 'evolutionary' also in another sense. Increasing rigour in the study of sound-changes associated one branch of language study with natural science, so that a system of linguistic phonetics marched with physical studies of the language faculty and the evolutionary origins of speech. This tendency culminated in major work in the physiology of speech and in the field significantly designated within this area as experimental *psychology*.

This identification of language-use as a problem in *psychology* was to have major effects on concepts of language. But meanwhile within general language-studies there was a new phase which reinforced inherent tendencies to objectivism. What was characteristically studied in comparative philology was a body of *records* of language: in effect, centrally, the alien written word. This assumption of the defining material of study was already present, of course, in the earlier phase of 'classical' language studies: Greek, Latin, Hebrew. But then the modes of access to a wider range of languages repeated this earlier stance: that of the privileged (scientific) observer of a body of alien written material. Methodological decisions, substantially similar to those being developed in the closely related new science of anthropology, followed from this effective situation. On the one hand there was the highly productive application of modes of systematic observation, classification, and analysis. On the other hand there was the largely unnoticed consequence of the privileged situation of the observer: that he was observing (of course scientifically) within a differential mode of contact with alien material: in texts, the records of a *past* history; in speech, the activity of an alien people in subordinate (colonialist) relations to the whole activity of the dominant people within which the observer gained his privilege. This defining situation inevitably reduced any sense of language as actively and presently constitutive. The consequent objectivism of fundamental procedure was intensely productive at the level of description, but necessarily any consequent definition of language had to be a definition of a (specialized) philological *system*. In a later phase of this contact between privileged observer and alien language material, in the special circumstances of North America where hundreds of native American (Amerindian) languages were in danger of dying out after the completion of European conquest and domination, the earlier philological procedures were indeed, characteristically, found to be not objective enough. Assimilation of these even more alien languages to the categories of Indo-European philology – the natural reflex of cultural imperialism – was scientifically resisted and checked by necessary procedures which, assuming only the presence of an alien system, found ways of studying it in its own (intrinsic and structural) terms. This approach was a further gain in scientific description, with its own remarkable results, but at the level of theory it was the final reinforcement of a concept of language as an (alien) objective system.

Paradoxically, this approach had even deeper effect through one of the necessary corrections of procedure which followed from the new phase of contact with languages without texts. Earlier procedures had been determined by the fact that a language almost invariably presented itself in specific past texts, finished monologic utterances. Actual speech, even when it was available, was seen as *derived*, either historically into vernaculars, or practically into speech acts which were instances of the fundamental (textual) forms of the language. Language-use could then hardly ever be seen as itself active and constitutive. And this was reinforced by the political relations of the observer-observed, where the 'language-habits' studied, over a range from the speech of conquered and dominated peoples to the 'dialects' of outlying or socially inferior groups, theoretically matched against the observer's 'standard', were regarded as at most 'behaviour', rather than independent, creative, self-directing life. North American empirical linguistics reversed one part of this tendency, restoring the primacy of speech in the literal absence of 'standard' or 'classical' texts. Yet the objectivist character of the underlying general theory came to limit even this, by converting speech itself to a 'text' – the characteristically persistent word in orthodox structural linguistics. Language came to be seen as a fixed, objective, and in these senses 'given' system, which had theoretical and practical priority over what were described as 'utterances' (later as 'performance'). Thus the living speech of human beings in their specific social relationships in the world was theoretically reduced to instances and examples of a system which lay beyond them.

The major theoretical expression of this reified understanding of language came in the twentieth century, in the work of Saussure, which has close affinities to the objectivist sociology of Durkheim. In Saussure the social nature of language is expressed as a system (*langue*), which is at once stable and autonomous and founded in normatively identical forms; its 'utterances' (*paroles*) are then seen as 'individual' (in abstract distinction from 'social') uses of 'a particular language code' through an enabling 'psycho-physical mechanism'. The practical results of this profound theoretical development, in all its phases, have been exceptionally productive and striking. The great body of philological scholarship has been complemented by a remarkable body of linguistic studies, in which the controlling concept of language as a formal system has opened the way to penetrating descriptions of actual language operations and many of their underlying 'laws'.

This achievement has an ironic relation with Marxism. On the one hand it repeats an important and often dominant tendency within Marxism itself, over a range from the comparative analysis and classification of stages of a society, through the discovery of certain fundamental laws of change within these systematic stages, to the assertion of a controlling 'social' system which is *a priori* inaccessible to 'individual' acts of will and intelligence. This apparent affinity explains the attempted synthesis of Marxism and structural linguistics which has been so influential a phenomenon of the mid-twentieth century. But Marxists have then to notice, first, that history, in its most specific, active, and connecting senses, has disappeared (in one tendency has been theoretically excluded) from this account of so central a social activity as language; and second, that the categories in which this version of system has been developed are the familiar bourgeois categories in which an abstract separation and distinction between the 'individual' and the 'social' have become so habitual that they are taken as 'natural' starting-points.

In fact there was little specifically Marxist work on language before the twentieth century. In their chapter on Feuerbach in *The German Ideology* Marx and Engels touched on the subject, as part of their influential argument against pure, directive consciousness. Recapitulating the 'moments' or 'aspects' of a materialist conception of history, they wrote:

Only now, after having considered four moments, four aspects of the fundamental historical relationships, do we find that man also possesses 'consciousness'; but, even so, not inherent, not 'pure' consciousnes. From the start the 'spirit' is afflicted with the curse of being 'burdened' with matter, which here makes its appearance in the form of agitated layers of air, sounds, in short of language. Language is as old as consciousness, language is practical consciousness, as it exists for other men, and for that reason is really beginning to exist for me personally as well; for language, like consciousness, only arises from the need, the necessity, of intercourse with other men. (*GI*, 19)

So far as it goes, this account is wholly compatible with the emphasis on language as practical, constitutive activity. The difficulty arises, as it had also arisen in a different form in previous accounts, when the idea of the constitutive is broken down into elements which are then temporally ordered. Thus there is an obvious danger, in the thinking of Vico and Herder, of making language 'primary' and 'original', not in the acceptable sense that it is a necessary part of the very act of human self-creation, but in the related and available sense of language as the founding element in humanity: 'in the beginning was the Word'. It is precisely the sense of language as an *indissoluble* element of human self-creation that gives any acceptable meaning to its description as 'constitutive'. To make it *precede* all other connected activities is to claim something quite different.

The idea of language as constitutive is always in danger of this kind of reduction. Not only, however, in the direction of the isolated creative word, which becomes idealism, but also, as actually happened, in objectivist materialism and positivism, where 'the world' or 'reality' or 'social reality' is categorically projected as the pre-existent formation to which language is simply a response.

What Marx and Engels actually say, in this passage, points to simultaneity and totality. The 'fundamental historical relationships' are seen as 'moments' or 'aspects', and man then 'also possesses' consciousness'. Moreover, this language is material: the 'agitated layers of air, sounds', which are produced by the physical body. It is then not a question of any temporal priority of the 'production of material life' considered as a separable act. The distinctively human mode of this primary material production has been characterized in three aspects: needs, new needs, and human reproduction – 'not of course to be taken as three different stages . . . but . . . which have existed simultaneously since the dawn of history and the first men, and still assert themselves in history today'. The distinctive humanity of the development is then expressed by the fourth 'aspect', that such production is from the *beginning* also a social relationship. It then involves from the beginning, as a necessary element, that practical consciousness which is language.

Thus far the emphasis is primarily 'constitutive', in the sense of an indissoluble totality of development. But it is easy to see how, in this direction also, what begins as a mode of analysis of aspects of a total process develops towards philosophical or 'natural' categories – simple materialist statements which retain the idealist separation of 'language' from 'reality' but simply reverse their priority – and towards historical categories, in which there is, *first*, material social production and *then* (rather than *also*) language.

In its predominantly positivist development, from the late nineteenth to the mid-twentieth century, a dominant kind of Marxism made this practical reduction: not so much directly in language theory, which on the whole was neglected, but habitually in its accounts of consciousness and in its analyses of the practical language activities which were grouped under the categories of 'ideology' and 'the superstructure'. Moreover this tendency was reinforced by the wrong kind of association with important scientific work on the physical means of language. This association was wholly compatible with an emphasis on language as mateial, but, given the practical separation of 'the world' and 'the language in which we speak about it', or in another form, of 'reality' and 'consciousness', the materiality of language could be grasped only as physical – a set of physical properties – and not as material *activity*: in fact the ordinary scientistic dissociation of the abstracted physical faculty from its actual human use. The resulting situation had been well described, in another context, by Marx, in the first 'thesis' on Feuerbach:

The chief defect of all materialism up to now (including Feuerbach's) is, that the object, reality, what we apprehend through our senses, is understood only in the form of the *object of contemplation (anschauung)*; but not as *sensuous human activity, as practice*; not subjectively. Hence in opposition to materialism the *active* side was developed abstractly by idealism – which of course does not know real sensuous activity as such. (*GI*, 197)

This was indeed the situation in thinking about language. For the active emphases of Vico and Herder had meanwhile been remarkably developed, notably by Wilhelm von Humboldt. Here the inherited problem of the origin of language had been remarkably restated. Language of course developed at some point in evolutionary history, but it is not only that we have virtually no information about this; it is mainly that any human investigation of so constitutive an activity finds language already there in itself and in its presumed object of study. Language has then to be seen as a persistent kind of creation and re-creation: a dynamic presence and a constant regenerative process. But this emphasis, again, can move in different directions. It could reasonably have been associated with the emphasis of whole, indissoluble practice, in which the 'dynamic presence' and the 'constant regenerative process' would be necessary forms of the 'production and reproduction of real life' similarly conceived. What happened instead, in Humboldt and especially after him, was a projection of this idea of activity into essentially idealist and quasi-social forms: either the 'nation', based on an abstract version of the 'folk-mind' or the (ahistorical) 'collective consciousness'; or the 'collective spirit', the abstract creative capacity – self-creative but prior to and separate from material social practice, as in Hegel; or, persuasively, the 'individual', abstracted and defined as 'creative subjectivity', the starting-point of meaning.

The influence of these various projections has been deep and prolonged. The abstract idea of the 'nation' could be readily connected with major philological work on the 'families' of languages and on the distinctive inherited properties of particular languages. The abstract idea of the 'individual' could be readily connected with the emphasis on a primary subjective reality and a consequent 'source' of meaning and creativity which emerged in the Romantic concepts of 'art' and 'literature' and which defined a major part of the development of 'psychology'.

Thus the stress on language as activity, which was the crucial contribution of this line of thinking, and which was a crucial correction of the inherent passivity, usually formalized in the metaphor of 'reflection', of positivism and objectivist materialism, was in turn reduced from specific activities (then necessarily social and material, or, in the full sense, historical) to *ideas* of such activity, categorized as 'nation' or 'spirit' or the 'creative individual'. It is significant that one of these categories, the 'individual' (not the specific, unique human being, who cannot of course be in doubt, but the generalization of the common property of all these beings as 'individuals' or 'subjects', which are already *social* categories, with immediate social implications), was prominent also within the dominant tendency of objectivist materialism. The exclusion of activity, of making, from the category of 'objective reality' left it contemplated only by 'subjects', who might in one version be ignored in the observation of objective reality – the active 'subject' replaced by the neutral 'observer' – or in another version, when it became necessary to speak about language or about other forms of practice, appeared in 'inter-subjective' relations – speaking to or at each other, passing information or a 'message' between each other, as separate or distinguishable identities, rather than ever *with* each other, the fact of language constituting and confirming their relationship. Language here decisively lost its definition as *constitutive* activity. It became a tool or an instrument or a medium taken up by individuals when they had something to communicate, as distinct from the faculty which made them, from the beginning, not only able to relate and communicate, but in real terms to be practically conscious and so to possess the active practice of language.

Against this reduction of language to instrumentality, the idea of language as expression, which was the main outcome of the idealist version of language as activity, was evidently attractive. It appeared literally to speak to an experience of language which the rival theory, confined to passing information, exchanging messages, naming objects, in effect suppressed. It could include the experience of speaking *with* others, of *participating* in language, of making and responding to rhythm or intonation which had no simple 'information' or 'message' or 'object' content: the experience, indeed, which was most evident in 'literature' and which was even, by specialization, made identical with it. Yet what actually happened was a deep split, which produced its own powerful categories of separation, some of them old terms in new forms: categorical divisions between the 'referential' and the 'emotive', between the 'denotative' and the 'connotative', between 'ordinary language' and 'literary language'. Certainly the uses towards which these categories point can be distinguished as the elements of specific practices, defined by specific situations. But their projection as categories, and then their further projection as separte entities, separate 'bodies' of language-use, permitted a dissolution and specialization which for a long time prevented the basic issues of the unfinished argument about language from becoming focused within a single area of discourse.

Marxism might have become this area of discourse, but it had developed its own forms of limitation and specialization. The most evident of these was a specialization of the whole material social process to 'labour', which was then more and more narrowly conceived. This had its effect in the important argument about the origins and development of language, which could have been reopened in the context of the new science of evolutionary physical anthropology. What happened instead was an application of the abstract concept of 'labour' as the single effective origin. Thus, in a modern authoritative account:

First labour, then articulate speech, were the two chief stimuli under the influence of which the brain of the ape gradualy changed into the human brain. (*Fundamentals of Dialectical Materialism*, ed. Schneierson, Moscow, 1967, 105)

This not only establishes an abstract, two-stage temporal development. It also converts both labour and language to 'stimuli', when the real emphasis should be on connected practice. This leads to an abstraction of evolutionary stages:

The development of labour brought the members of the community more closely together, for it enabled them to extend their joint activity and to support each other. Labour relations gave rise to the need for primitive men to speak and communicate with each other.

(Ibid. 105)

This is in effect an idealism of abstracted stimuli and needs. It must be contrasted with a properly materialist theory, in which labour and language, as practices, can be seen as evolutionarily and historically constitutive:

The argument that there could be no language without all the structure of modern man is precisely the same as the old theory that human hands made implement-making and using possible. But the implements are thousands of years older than hands of the modern human form. Modern speech-producing structures are the result of the evolutionary success of language, just as the uniquely human hand is the result of the evolutionary success of implements. (J. S. Washburn and J. B. Lancaster, *Current Anthropology*, vol. 12, No. 3, 1971)

Any constitutive theory of practice, and especially a materialist theory, has important effects beyond the question of origins, in restating the problem of the active process of language at any time: a restatement which goes beyond the separated categories of 'language' and 'reality'. Yet orthodox Marxism remained stuck in reflection theory, because this was the only plausible materialist connection between the received abstract categories. Reflection theory, in its first period, was itself specialized to crude stimulus-and-response models, adapted from positivist physiology. In its second period, in the later work of Pavlov, it added, as a way of dealing with the special properties of language, the concept of the 'second signal system', the first being the simple physical system of sensations and responses. This was better than nothing, but it assimilated language to the characteristics of a 'signal system', in relatively mechanistic ways, and was in practice unequal to problems of meaning beyond simple models of the associative. Setting out from this point, L.S. Vygotsky (*Thought and Language*, Moscow, 1934) proposed a new social theory, still named the 'second signal system', in which language and consciousness are freed from simple analogies with physical perception. His work on the development of language in children, and on the crucial problem of 'inner speech', provided a new starting-point, within a historical-materialist perspective. But for a generation, in orthodox Marxism, this was neglected. Meanwhile the work of N. S. Marr, based on older models, tied language to the 'super-structure' and even to simple class bases. Dogmatic positions, taken from other areas of Marxist thinking, limited the necessary theoretical developments. It is ironic that the influence of Marr was in effect ended by Stalin in 1950 with declarations that language was not 'part of the superstructure' and that languages did not have any essential 'class character' but rather a 'national character'. Ironic because though the declarations were necessary, in that context, they simply threw the argument back to a much earlier stage, in which the status of 'reflection' and, very specifically, the status of 'the superstructure', had, in Marxist terms, needed question. By this time, moreover, linguistics had come to be dominated by a specific and distinctive form of objectivism, which had produced the powerful systems of structuralism and semiotics. It was at this point that generally Marxist positions in other fields, especially in the popular form of objectively determined systems, were practically synthesized with theories of language which, from a fully Marxist position, needed to be profoundly opposed.

A tragic element in this history is that such theories had been profoundly opposed in the 1920s in Leningrad, where the beginnings of a school of Marxist linguistics, of a significant kind, had in fact emerged. It is best represented by the work of V.N. Vološinov, whose *Marxism and the Philosophy of Language* appeared, in two editions, in 1929 and 1930; the second edition has been translated into English (Matejka and Titunik, New York and London, 1973). Vološinov had been associated with M. M. Bakhtin, author of a study of Dostoevsky (*Problemy tvor čestva Dostoevskogo*, 1929; new version, with new title, *Problemy poetiki Dostoevskogo*, 1963); see also 'P.N. Medvedev' (author of *Formal'ny metod v literaturovedenii – kritičeskoe vvedenie v sociologičeskuju poètiku – The Formal Method in Literary Scholarship: a critical introduction to sociological poetics* – 1928). Sometime during the 1930s Vološinov disappeared. Nearly half a century was then lost, in real terms, in the development of his exceptionally important realignment of the argument.

Vološinov's decisive contribution was to find a way beyond the powerful but partial theories of expression and objective system. He found it in fundamentally Marxist terms, though he had to begin by saying that Marxist thinking about language was virtually non-existent. His originality lay in the fact that he did not seek to apply other Marxist ideas to language. On the contrary he reconsidered the whole problem of language within a general Marxist orientation. This enabled him to see 'activity' (the strength of the idealist emphasis after Humboldt) as social activity and to see 'system' (the strength of the new objectivist linguistics) in relation to this social activity and not, as had hitherto been the case, formally separated from it. Thus in drawing on the strengths of the alternative traditions, and in setting them side by side showing their connected radical weaknesses, he opened the way to a new kind of theory which had been necessary for more than a century.

Much of his effort went to recovering the full emphasis on language as activity, as practical consciousness, which had been weakened and in effect denied by its specialization to a closed 'individual consciousness' or 'inner psyche'. The strength of this tradition was still its insistence on the active creation of meanings, as distinct from the alternative assumption of a closed formal system. Vološinov argued that meaning was necessarily a social action, dependent on a social relationship. But to understand this depended on recovering a full sense of 'social', as distinct both from the idealist reduction of the social to an inherited, ready-made product, an 'inert crust', beyond which all creativity was individual, and from the objectivist projection of the social into a formal system, now autonomous and governed only by its internal laws, within which, and solely according to which, meanings were produced. Each sense, at root, depends on the same error: of separating the social from individual meaningful activity (though the rival positions then valued the separated elements differently). Against the psychologism of the idealist emphasis, Vološinov argued that 'consciousness takes shape and being in the material of signs created by an organized group in the process of its social intercourse. The individual consciousness is nurtured on signs; it derives its growth from them; it reflects their logic and laws' (13).

Normally, it is at just this point (and the danger is always increased by retaining the concept of 'sign', which Vološinov revalued but continued to use) that objectivism finds its entry. 'The material of signs' can be translated as 'system of signs'. This system can then be projected (by some notion of a theoretical 'social contract', as in Saussure, protected from examination by the assumption of the priority of 'synchronic' over 'diachronic' analysis) both beyond history and beyond any active conception of contemporary social life, in which socially related individuals meaningfully participate, as distinct from acting out the laws and codes of an inaccessible linguistic system. Each side of Vološinov's argument has a continuing relevance, but it is in his (incomplete) revaluation of the concept of 'sign' that his contemporary significance is most evident.

Vološinov accepted that a 'sign' in language has indeed a 'binary' character. (In fact, as we shall see, his retention of these terms made it easier for the radical challenge of his work to be missed.) That is to say, he agreed that the verbal sign is not equivalent to, nor simply a reflection of, the object or quality which it indicates or expresses. The relation within the sign between the formal element and the meaning which this element carries is thus inevitably conventional (thus far agreeing with orthodox semiotic theory), but it is *not* arbitrary[1] and, crucially, it is not fixed. On the contrary the fusion of formal element and meaning (and it is this fact of dynamic fusion which makes retention of the 'binary' description misleading) is the result of a real process of social development, in the actual activities of speech and in the continuing development of a language. Indeed signs can exist only when this active social relationship is posited. The usable sign – the fusion of formal element and meaning – is a product of this continuing speech-activity between real individuals who are in some continuing social relationship. The 'sign' is in this sense their product, but not simply their past product, as in the reified accounts of an 'always-given' language system. The real communicative 'products' which are usuable signs are, on the contrary, living evidence of a continuing social process, into which individuals are born and within which they are shaped, but to which they then also actively contribute, in a continuing process. This is at once their socialization and their individuation: the connected aspects of a single process which the alternative theories of 'system' and 'expression' had divided and dissociated. We then find not a reified 'language' and 'society' but an active *social language*. Nor (to glance back at positivist and orthodox materialist theory) is this language a simple 'reflection' or 'expression' of 'material reality'. What we have, rather, is a grasping of this reality through language, which as practical consciousness is saturated by and saturates all social activity, including productive activity. And, since this grasping is social and continuous (as distinct from the abstract encounters of 'man' and 'his world', or 'consciousness' and 'reality', or 'language' and 'material existence'), it occurs within an active and changing society. It is of and to this experience – the lost middle term between the abstract entities, 'subject' and 'object', on which the propositions of idealism and orthodox materialism are erected – that language speaks. Or to put it more directly, language is the articulation of this active and changing experience; a dynamic and articulated social presence in the world.

Yet it remains true that the mode of articulation is specific. This is the part of the truth which formalism had grasped. The articulation can be seen, and in some respects has to be seen, as both formal and systematic. A physical sound, like many other natural elements, may be made into a sign, but its distinction, Volosinov argued, is always evident: 'a sign does not simply exist as part of a reality – it reflects and refracts another reality'. What distinguishes it as a sign, indeed what made it a sign, is in this sense a formal process: a specific articulation of a meaning. Formalist linguistics had emphasized this point, but it had not discerned that the process of articulation is necessarily also a *material* process, and that the sign itself becomes part of a (socially created) physical and material world: 'whether in sound, physical mass, colour, movement of the body or the like'. Signification, the social creation of meanings through the use of formal signs, is then a practical material activity; it is indeed, literally, a means of production. It is a specific form of that practical consciousness which is inseparable from all social material activity. It is not, as formalism would make it, and as the idealist theory of expression had from the beginning assumed, an operation of and within 'consciousness', which then becomes a state or a process separated, *a priori*, from social material activity. It is, on the contrary, at once a distinctive material process – the making of *signs* – and, in the central quality of its distinctiveness as practical consciousness, is involved from the beginning in all other human social and material activity.

Formalist systems can appear to meet this point by referring it to the 'already-given', the 'last-instance determination of the economic structure', as in some current versions of structuralist Marxism. It is to avoid this kind of reduction that we must consider Volosinov's crucial distinction between a 'sign' and a 'signal'. In reflexive theories of language, whether positivist kinds of materialism, or such theories as psychological behaviourism, all 'signs' are in

effect reduced to 'signals', within the simple models of 'object' and 'consciousness' or 'stimulus' and 'response'. Meanings are created by (repeated) recognition of what are then in effect 'signals': of the properties of an object or the
character of a stimulus. 'Consciousness' and 'response' then 'contain' (for this is
what meaning now is) those properties or that character. The assigned passivity
and mechanism of such accounts have often been recognized. Indeed it was
against such passivity and mechanism that formalism had most to contribute, in
its insistence on the specific (formal) articulation of meanings through signs.

But it has been less often noticed that quite different theories, based on the
determinate character of systems of signs, depend, ultimately, on a comparable
idea of the fixed character of the sign, which is then in effect a displacement of
fixed content to fixed form. Intense argument between these rival schools has
allowed us to overlook the fact that the conversion of the 'sign' (as the term
itself always made possible and even likely) into either fixed content or fixed
form is a radical denial of active practical consciousness. The sign, in either
case, is moved in the direction of a signal, which Vološinov distinguishes from
a sign by the fact that it is intrinsically limited and invariant. The true quality of
a sign (one would have preferred him to say, of a signifying element of a
language) is that it is effective in communication, a genuine fusion of a formal
element and a meaning (a quality that it indeed shares with signals); but also
that as a function of continuing social activity it is capable of modification and
development: the real processes that may be observed in the history of a
language, but which the privileged priority of 'synchronic' analysis had ignored
or reduced to a secondary or accidental character.

Indeed since it exists, as a sign, by its quality of signifying relationship – both
the relation between formal element and meaning (its internal structure) and
the relations between the people who in actually using it, in practical language,
make it a sign – it has, like the social experience which is the principle of its
formation, both dialectical and generative properties. Characteristically it does
not, like a signal, have fixed, determinate, invariant meaning. It must have an
effective nucleus of meaning but in practice it has a variable range, corresponding to the endless variety of situations within which it is actively used. These
situations include new and changing as well as recurrent relationships, and this
is the reality of the sign as dynamic fusion of 'formal element' and 'meaning' –
'form' and 'content' – rather than as fixed, 'already-given' internal significance.
This variable quality, which Vološinov calls *multi-accentual*, is of course the
necessary challenge to the idea of 'correct' or 'proper' meanings, which had
been powerfully developed by orthodox philology from its studies of dead
languages, and which had been taken over both into social-class distinctions of
a 'standard' language flanked either by 'dialects' or by 'errors', and into literary
theories of a 'correct' or 'objective' reading. But the quality of variation – not

random variation but variation as a necessary element of practical consciousness – bears heavily also against objectivist accounts of the sign-system. It is one of the decisive arguments against reduction of the key fact of social determination to the idea of determination by a system. But, while it thus bears heavily against all forms of abstract objectivism, it offers a basis also for a vital reconsideration of the problem of 'subjectivity'.

The signal, in its fixed invariance, is indeed a collective fact. It may be received and repeated, or a new signal may be invented, but in either case the level at which it operates is of a collective kind: that is to say. it has to be recognized but it need not be internalized, at that level of sociality which has excluded (as reductive versions of the 'social' commonly exclude) active participation by conscious individuals. The signal, in this sense, is fixed, exchangeable, collective property; characteristically it is easily both imported and exported. The true signifying element of language must from the beginning have a different capacity: to become an inner sign, part of an active practical consciousness. Thus in addition to its social and material existence between actual individuals, the sign is also part of a verbally constituted consciousness which allows individuals to use signs of their own initiative, whether in acts of social communication or in practices which, not being *manifestly* social, can be interpreted as personal or private.

This view is then radically opposed to the construction of all acts of communication from pre-determined objective relationships and properties, within which no individual initiative, of a creative or self-generating kind, would be possible. It is thus a decisive theoretical rejection of mechanical, behaviourist, or Saussurean versions of an objective system which is beyond individual initiative or creative use. But it is also a theoretical rejection of subjectivist theories of language as individual expression, since what is internally constituted is the social fact of the sign, bearing a definite though never fixed or invariant social meaning and relationship. Great strength has been given, and continues to be given, to theories of language as individual expression, by the rich practical experience of 'inner signs' – inner language – in repeated individual awareness of 'inner language activities', whether we call them 'thought' or 'consciousness' or actual verbal composition. These 'inner' activities involve the use of words which are not, at least at that stage, spoken or written to any other person. Any theory of language which excludes this experience, or which seeks to limit it to some residue or by-product or rehearsal (though it may often be these) of manifest social language activity, is again reductive of social language as practical consciousness. What has really to be said is that the sign is social but that in its very quality as sign it is capable both of being internalized – indeed has to be internalized, if it is to be a sign for communicative relation between actual persons, initially using only their own physical powers to express it – and of being continually available, in social and material ways, in manifest communication. This fundamental relationship between the 'inner' and the 'material' sign – a relationship often experienced as a tension but always lived as an activity, a practice – needs further radical exploration. In individual developmental psychology Vygotsky began this exploration, and at once discerned certain crucially distinguishing characteristics of 'inner speech', themselves constitutive rather than, as in Vološinov, merely transferred. This is still within the perspective of a historical materialist theory. The complex relationship, from another direction, needs specifically historical exploration, for it is in the movement from the production of language by human physical resources alone, through the material history of the production of other resources and of the problems of both technology and notation then involved in them, to the active social history of the complex of communicative systems which are now so important a part of the material productive process itself, that the dynamics of social language – its development of new means of production within a basic means of production – must be found.

Meanwhile, following Vološinov, we can see that just as all social process is activity between real individuals, so individuality, by the fully social fact of language (whether as 'outer' or 'inner' speech), is the active constitution, within distinct physical beings, of the social capacity which is the means of realization of any individual life. Consciousness, in this precise sense, is social being. It is the possession, through active and specific social development and relationships, of a precise social capacity, which is the 'sign-system'. Vološinov, even after these fundamental restatements, continues to speak of the 'sign-system': the formulation that had been decisively made in Saussurean linguistics. But if we follow his arguments we find how difficult and misleading this formulation can be. 'Sign' itself – the mark or token; the formal element – has to be revalued to emphasize its variability and internally active elements, indicating not only an internal structure but an internal dynamic. Similarly, 'system' has to be revalued to emphasize social process rather than fixed 'sociality': a revaluation that was in part made by Jakobson and Tynjanov (1928), within formalist argument, with the recognition that 'every system necessarily exists as an evolution while, on the other hand, evolution is inescapably of a systemic nature'. Although this was a necessary recognition, it was limited by its perspective of determinate systems within an 'evolutionary' category – the familiar reification of objective idealism – and still requires amendment by the full emphasis of social process. Here, as a matter of absolute priority, men relate and continue to relate before any system which is their product can as a matter of practical rather than abstract consciousness be grasped or exercise its determination.

These changes will have to be made, in the continuing inquiry into language. But the last point indicates a final difficulty. Much of the social process of the creation of meanings was projected within objectivist linguistics to the formal relations – thus the systematic nature – of signs. What at the level of the sign had been abstractly and statically conceived was set into a kind of motion – albeit a frozen, determinate motion, a movement of ice-fields – in the relational 'laws' or 'structures' of the system as a whole. This extension to a relational system, including its formal aspect as grammar, is in any case inevitable. Isolation of 'the sign', whether in Saussure or Volosinov, is at best an analytical procedure, at worst an evasion. Much of the important work on relations within a whole system is therefore an evident advance, and the problem of the variability of the sign can appear to be contained within the variability of its formal relations. But while this kind of emphasis on the relational system is obviously necessary, it is limited by the consequence of the initial abstract definition of the sign. The highly complex relations of (theoretically) invariable units can never be substantive relationships; they must remain as formal relationships. The internal dynamics of the sign, including its social and material relationships as well as its formal structure, must be seen as necessarily connected with the social and material as well as the ·formal dynamics of the system as a whole. There have been some advances in this direction in recent work (Rossi-Landi, 1975).

But there has also been a move which seems to reopen the whole problem. In Chomskyan linguistics there has been a decisive step towards a conception of system which emphasizes the possibility and the fact of individual initiative and creative practice which earlier objectivist systems had excluded. But at the same time this conception stresses deep structures of language formation which are certainly incompatible with ordinary social and historical accounts of the origin and development of language. An emphasis on deep constitutive structures, at an evolutionary rather than a historical level, can of course be reconciled with the view of language as a constitutive human faculty: exerting pressures and setting limits, in determinate ways, to human development itself. But while it is retained as an exclusively evolutionary process, it moves, necessarily, towards reified accounts of 'systemic evolution': development by constituted systems and structures (the constitution now at once permitting and limiting variations) rather than by actual human beings in a continuing social practice. Here Vygotsky's work on inner speech and consciousness is theoretically crucial:

If we compare the early development of speech and of intellect – which, as we have seen, develop along separate lines both in animals and in very young children – with the development of inner speech and of verbal thought, we must conclude that the later stage is not a simple continuation of the earlier. *The nature of the development itself changes*, from biological to socio-historical. Verbal thought is not an innate, natural form of behaviour but is determined by a historical-cultural process and has specific properties and laws that cannot be found in the natural forms of thought and speech. (*Thought and Language*, 51)

Thus we can add to the necessary definition of the biological faculty of language as *constitutive* an equally necessary definition of language development – at once individual and social – as historically and socially *constituting*. What we can then define is a dialectical process: the *changing practical consciousness of human beings*, in which both the evolutionary and the historical processes can be given full weight, but also within which they can be distinguished, in the complex variations of actual language use. It is from this theoretical foundation that we can go on to distinguish 'literature', in a specific socio-historical development of writing, from the abstract retrospective concept, so common in orthodox Marxism, which reduces it, like language itself, to a function and then a (superstructural) by-product of collective labour.[2] [. . .]

Notes

1 The question of whether a sign is 'arbitrary' is subject to some local confusion. The term was developed in distinction from the 'iconic', to indicate, correctly, that most verbal signs are not 'images' of things. But other senses of 'arbitrary', in the direction of 'random' or 'causal', had developed, and it was these that Vološinov opposed.

2 References for this chapter as given by Williams are:
Jakobson, R. and Tynjanov, J.U. 'Problems in the Study of Language and Literature' in *Readings in Russian Poetics: Formalist and Structuralist Views* (eds) L. Matejka and K. Pomeska, Cambridge: MIT Press 1971, pp. 79–81.
Marx, K, and Engels, F. *The German Ideology* [GI], London 1963.
Rossi-Landi, F. *Language as Work and Exchange*, The Hague, 1975.
Saussure, F. de, *Cours de linguistique générale*, Lausanne, 1916.
Scheneierson A., (ed.) *Fundamentals of Dialectical Materialism*, Moscow, 1967.
Stalin, J., *Marxism and Linguistics*, New York, 1951.
Vico, G., *The New Science*, tr. Bergin, T, and Fisch, M., Ithaca, N.Y., 1948.
Voloshinov, V.N., *Marxism and the Philosophy of Language*, New York, 1973.
Vygotsky, L.S., *Thought and Language*, Cambridge, Mass., 1962.
Washburn, S.L. and J.B. Lancaster 'On Evolution and the Origin of Language' in *Current Anthropology* 1971 Vol 12 No 3 pp. 384–5.

12

The Writer: Commitment and Alignment

From Marxism Today, *June 1980*

Some people, when they see an idea, think the first thing to do is to argue about it. But while this passes the time and has the advantage of keeping them warm it has little else to recommend it. If there is one thing we should have learned from the Marxist tradition it is that ideas are always representations of things people are actually doing or feel themselves prevented from doing. So that the first way to look at the idea of commitment is not as at some general notion about which we can at once argue, citing this or that historical case, but rather to see why the notion of commitment was developed and against what alternative ideas it was directed.

In fact the matters at issue have been discussed in many terms. Commitment became the normal term, in our own time, because of the famous intervention by Jean-Paul Sartre at the end of the war when he wrote:

If literature is not everything it is worth nothing. This is what I mean by 'commitment'. It wilts if it is reduced to innocence or to songs. If a written sentence does not reverberate at every level of man and society then it makes no sense. What is the literature of an epoch, but the epoch appropriated by its literature?[1]

It was in this sense that a long-standing argument was concentrated around the notion of commitment. But immediately with a certain difficulty. First that

Sartre, quite wrongly in my view, said that this should only apply to prose, that poetry was something else. But it is very difficult to argue this case for one kind of writing in ways that make it clear why you should exclude the same demands on another kind of writing. The distinction between prose and poetry that Sartre tried to make confused the argument from the beginning. Second, and much more seriously, the unstated background of Sartre's intervention was a very specific historical and political context. It was within the climate of the Resistance. It was moreover at a time of real possibilities of significant movement, in France as in other parts of Western Europe, towards a new kind of democracy. The engagement of intellectuals of all kinds, and especially writers, in those great collective movements which had come from anti- fascist war and resistance, had an immediate, concentrated and urgent social resonance. On the other hand in England, by the time the idea had taken its usual inordinate time to cross the Channel (because that must be one of the longest cultural journeys in existence by comparison with the physical distance) it fell into the most difficult times.

Then it sounded like, and of course correctly sounded like, a well-known position in the 1930s. The positions of the British left writers in the thirties, although they were not normally assembled around the term 'commitment', were directed towards the same essential idea. But in the late forties and early fifties it was another time. It was the beginning of the Cold War. There were then three kinds of backlash against the idea.

First, and we should not forget this, there was a backlash against the cause to which those writers had been committed. This was the time when we had to look at the other face of that generation of the thirties. It is true that many of the best had died in Spain or in the general European war. But we had also the beginning of that extraordinary and terrible period in which one writer after another from the thirties renounced what he had then believed in, and explained in what was meant to be a charming and pathetic − anyway an apologetic − manner how he had been taken in or fooled or something of that kind. There were some writers who didn't move in this way but their views tended to be less publicized. By the early fifties you could line up a whole series of writers who said 'Yes, of course, I was like that in my foolish youth, but now I know better.' And from that it was no distance at all to saying that writers should keep out of that kind of political and especially left-political thing. That was the first reason why the argument got off to a very bad start after the war.

Second, there was one very severe problem that ought to be intellectually distinguished from this but of course was not. For there were phases, including the Stalin phase, in the Soviet Union, when the notion of commitment could easily be related to the practice of an authority above the writer which was telling him what to write and how to write. 'We know what you mean by commitment. You don't want to be a real writer, you want yourself and others to be party hacks.' And the fact that some – too many – real historical instances could be quoted to support this made clarity very difficult to sustain. Yet at its best this was always a dispute *inside* the socialist movement. There is still no better statement on this whole matter than that of Brecht, a Communist writer, in the 1930s, replying to an article by the Hungarian Marxist then in Moscow, Georg Lukács. Brecht said of that whole tendency:

They are, to put it bluntly, enemies of production. Production makes them uncomfort-able. You never know where you are with production; production is unforeseeable. You never know what is going to come out. And they themselves don't want to produce. They want to play the apparatchik and exercise control over other people. Every one of their criticisms contains a threat.[2]

So there was a principled position, inside the socialist movement, which could enable a totally committed writer like Brecht to make the necessary distinction between a commitment to production linked to a cause, and on the other hand a subservience to some version of desirable production arbitrarily decided by a party and its ideologists. This remains a crucial distinction, but it was very difficult to sustain it in the period of cold war and that mood of confession of errors which was weakening the confidence of a whole generation of writers. In practice the two very different ideas – of commitment and of subservience – were pushed together and seemed to support each other.

Third, there was a certain backlash among those few left writers who kept their heads through this difficult period. And it was an intensely difficult period, because it was so complex. There was an understandable wariness of what can quite properly be called opportunism. This, then as now, was not the reality of commitment but a careerist version of it. Commitment still meant, at its best, taking social reality, historical reality, the development of social and historical reality, as the centres of attention, and then finding some of the hundreds of ways in which all those processes can be written. On the other hand, at its worst, it could be a superficial kind of writing which took care to include the political references that went with the cry of the moment. If we want an authority on this we have in one of his grumpier moods no less an authority than Engels, who said:

It became more and more the habit, particularly of the inferior sorts of *literati*, to make up for the want of cleverness in their productions by political allusions which were sure to attract attention. Poetry, novels, reviews, the drama, every literary production teemed with what was called 'tendency'.[3]

This was only a few years after Marx had referred to work like that of Eugene Sue as 'the most wretched offal of socialist literature'.[4] And Engels, in an even grumpier mood, thirty years later, talked about 'a worthless fellow who, due to lack of talent, has gone to extremes with tendentious junk to show his convictions, but it is really in order to gain an audience'.[5] Now I don't quote these remarks because we should believe everything Marx or Engels said. In fact, in the later mood, Engels was moving, as in his literary tastes he often did, towards a slightly grumpy bourgeois position rather than necessarily towards a Marxist one. But it is very important, if we are to have honesty on the Left, that we should be quite clear that there is a kind of opportunism which can usurp the idea of commitment, by catching the political cry of the moment whether or not it has any significant reference to the central experience or the integrity of the writing. This is the false commitment of the inserted political reference. It is not what Sartre or anyone else who has taken the idea seriously can mean by commitment.

Anyway this third backlash, this wariness, developed, and in the middle of it one further fact was discovered, one which was memorably expressed by the German Marxist Adorno. He made the point that if you propose commitment you have to recognize that it is what he called 'politically polyvalent'.[6] That is to say, if you ask writers to commit themselves, you can have no certainty at all that they are going to commit themselves to any particular cause. It would have been easier if it had been true that writers of significance could never commit themselves to fascism, or to the most archaic kinds of conservatism, or to the softer kinds of liberalism. But indeed if the idea of commitment is there but undefined, as in the rhetoric it often is, such writers indeed come out, take a position about social reality, engage with political struggle. Indeed this is happening from the right all the time. Then if that is so, at whatever level it is done, in actual writing or in some more general capacity, there can of course be no guarantee that commitment is intrinsically progressive, as some people had assumed. On its own, that is to say, the usual idea of commitment is bound to be polyvalent. We used to have arguments at the end of the thirties about whether a good writer could be a fascist. It seemed to us then that there was something wrong if that could be so, and some people found themselves in quite extraordinary positions, saying either 'yes, he is a fascist but then he is not a very good writer', or 'he may be a good writer but of course he is politically naive'. It is better to recognize social reality, which in our own time as in others has produced good and even great reactionary writers, as well as all the others whom we may prefer, for different reasons, to honour and remember.

Those were bad, confused times. Yet it can happen that the bad times teach us as much as the good times. When there is intellectual confusion, when you undergo a great deal of political rhetoric, when you have all sorts of recriminations and divisions inside your own movement, there is still a chance to learn from within such developments. In the case of a general idea there is a chance to learn what is significant in it and what on the other hand is insignificant or meretricious. And that I think, although people are still nervous of it, is what has been happening in more recent thinking.

There has been a change from the sixties onwards after the end of that confused and frightened period. Actually 'commitment' is still not the word most commonly used because, given that history, there is still a lot of nervousness about it. What we have come to understand, I think, is that commitment was not, for the most part, a positive proposition. It was mainly a response to another position which had become very general and which it wanted to challenge. This was the position that the artist, by definition, must be a free individual; that to be an artist is to be a free individual. Of course there is a version of commitment which can include that, because if you are a free individual you can choose to commit yourself. This was really what Sartre was saying. But to others such commitment was a cancellation of freedom. How can you commit yourself to anything except the practice of your own heart? Is the artist then not necessarily the very type of the free individual?

Now this is an important general case. And one of the advantages of looking at it within Marxist thought is this: that we can see when the idea of the artist as a free individual arose, and this in turn throws important light on the history of the practice of writing and of its always difficult social relations. For the idea of the artist as the type of the free individual in fact arose in the late eighteenth and early nineteenth centuries; that is to say in the period of two very important changes. On the one hand there was the emergence of a new libertarianism in literature, primarily in the Romantic movement. On the other hand the conditions of writing and publishing were changing in unprecedented ways, which on the one hand gave a new professional independence to successful writers, and on the other hand marginalized certain sectors of writing to such an extent that the possibility of feeling related to and wanted by society – either as a whole or by any part of it – had for that kind of writer been in effect excluded.

Now we should not reduce this development to any one of these three factors. All three are crucial in the developing notion of the free artist. The free artist of the Romantic movement was arguing for a kind of freedom which identified itself, in many cases, with the most general human liberation. He was arguing against the tyranny of Church and State, indeed against any authority which tried to dictate to the artist what he should think or write. He was also arguing against the tyranny of artistic rules. There is a standard Romantic complaint against what they defined and opposed as classicist imitation: rules of how to write well; rules of what to write about; rules of how any particular subject should be handled; rules which had been taken to a point, at least theoretically, as definitive, so that the test of good writing was the extent to which you showed the qualities of this known craft, with all its rules and its skills. The new claim that a writer must be free to break the rules, must be free to innovate, free to create works as the experience required, whether or not this corresponded with preexisting notions: that was the important claim of the Romantic movement, and it was accompanied by a conscious revolt against any authorities which would try to seize or suppress or discriminate against new writing of such kinds.

On the other hand the literary market which was then becoming more organized had a very curious double-edged effect. If you were a certain kind of novelist, from about the 1830s, you could become a successful professional man in a way that very few writers had been before. And although this was obviously most true for the most successful, still, given the extraordinary expansion of magazine publications, the cheapening of books and the huge growth of the newspaper and periodical press, the opportunities for a very large number of writers were much wider than those in any preceding period. But of course this was a freedom to go out and compete in that market. So that what came through at this level was the professional ideology of the independent artist, who was defining freedom in this very special sense, that he must be free to compete in the market. In effect he was then taking the market as a definition of his social province, his real social relations. And since society was represented by the market, there could be no question of any other significant social commitments. This is a classic bourgeois definition of freedom.

On the other hand, in other areas of writing, and notably in poetry, the economic situation of writers was moving quite the other way. Certain kinds of writing were marginalized, for the market was replacing earlier system of patronage, and in the market such writing as poetry was at best a marginal product, at worst quite unwanted. So alongside the newly successful literary professional, claiming his professional freedom but claiming it so that he could enter the market (which would tell him what society wanted) was the unwanted writer, who was soon mythicized as the starving genius. There were indeed some of these; and the starving would-be genius, there were some of them too. But at its worst it became a model of what a serious writer ought to be. You can still find people who think it is something which proves you are a real writer. It was a myth which seemed all the more attractive in this market society in which the leading writers were becoming more and more professionally established solid citizens.

Now we can see what a very complex idea this proposition that the artist must be free is. In one sense who would wish to dissent from it? Who would suppose that we are likely to get better writing if some appointed authority is at the writer's elbow, looking over his shoulder, advising him what to do? It isn't that writers don't benefit from advice; it's that there is an almost insoluble problem of getting the right advice and the right writer together: it is always more likely that you will get the wrong writer with the wrong advice. What we have really to understand is the set of ideas that were being fused in this notion of free independence, which we have really to take apart again if we are to understand the real situation. For the acceptance of the market as the guarantee of freedom is of course largely illusory. Although it is true that, at the point of success, the independent professional writer can operate very freely in the market, becoming himself a seller with a certain real independence, the average writer, and in these conditions these were the great majority, was dependent on the market in ways which were at least as severe and sometimes more severe than the earlier dependence of writers on patrons.

Patronage itself had passed through several stages, only some of which were deeply restrictive. In the very earliest forms patronage was an obligation. In feudal society, for example, it was the obligation of a household of a certain dignity to support and to give hospitality, to sustain the livelihood, of artists, poets, painters, musicians. Later there was a different type of patronage, in which courts, households and similar authorities hired writers and artists for specific commissions. In the course of that hiring every complaint came up that was subsequently heard in the market, but in the most favourable conditions there was a certain diversity; that if you ran into trouble with this patron you could take the work to another, as indeed in the early capitalist market. It was not a comfortable situation, it was not a good situation, but it does not necessarily compare unfavourably with the market. There is also another phase of patronage, which didn't depend on monetary exchange at all but was simply the offering of social support, social protection, and where necessary early encouragement. It often happened, of course, that support and protection were only offered to certain kinds of writing, from the notion that this was a good kind of writing to have done. But this was always potentially a different calculation – let us leave aside whether it was a better calculation – from what became for the market the single criterion, of whether this writing would *sell*. As the market developed this became and is becoming the only criterion. Indeed we are passing through now the biggest change in the writing and publishing market since the early nineteenth century. The criterion of desirability is the promise to sell, and, increasingly now, to sell fast, so that there are no expensive warehousing costs and other accounting considerations. This development set up, within the very conditions which appeared to guarantee freedom to the successful, constraints of a new kind, which however could not be recognized as obstacles to freedom because this was the very competitive area which most writers had sought. A bourgeois writer could not say 'it is the market which is restricting my freedom', because for him the market was his freedom. Yet it has always been clear that the market guides writers, restricts them, pushes them this way and that. It can be a very simple or a very complex process. It is extraordinarily difficult for any of us, as writers, to be honest about it.

The situation now, for example, at a very organized late stage of the market, is often this: that you want to write a particular work which happens to be of an inconvenient length, that length being your best estimate of what handling that material would be. You talk to a publisher or an editor about it, and he often says: 'Well, it's a pity about that length. But we've got an idea for a book in one of our series. Surely you can do that meanwhile.' And suppose this is, with luck, something which you thought someday you might write, but which you wouldn't have written just then, by the time you have decided to do it – and many people do – it has become what *you* want. Indeed unless you are absolutely ruthless with yourself, ruthless in your examination of your motives and especially your more complex adaptations, these pressured decisions come to take on the plausibility of your natural wishes, of your free development as a writer. And of course people say: 'Why should you be a primadonna?' 'Why shouldn't you write what people want?' Indeed the familiar phrases of commitment come back in the rhetoric of the sharply commercial editor: 'Don't you want to write what people are interested in?' 'What's the point of writing for yourself and a few friends?' So the market comes to seem a definition of social duty, even though publishers usually know a good deal less than writers about what people will like to read, as distinct from what they *have* liked. They are at least as often wrong as they are right, but in any case the notion of what people want which has passed through the market comes back as a strange kind of freedom. Yet many writers are afraid that if they say 'the market is not really free', then they deny the accessible basis of their own freedom. So what they talk about instead, in relation to freedom, is not of where they are. They talk about other situations, where the constraints are different: where there is state support of writers, for example, but of course not the state's support of all literature, indeed the refusal to publish certain kinds of book, and that is totalitarian. So indeed it often is. We have all to recognize the faults and deformities – sometimes the crimes – of such systems. Most of them are limited by the fact that public support operates only as *state* support; that will have to be changed, by new and more open kinds of procedure. Yet in any case we have also to look at freedom, and at its enemies, where we ourselves are.

Now I said at the beginning that it is a mistake, when you see an idea, to go straight into an argument about it. The trouble with most arguments about commitment is that they confuse two pairings. Either they confuse the notion of the artist having his own autonomy, which commitment is held to undermine, with the notion of being ordered by some central authority to do something. Or they confuse both with the idea of professional independence, which has been the historical situation of fortunate writers in our own kind of society. And at that point we have to attempt a further disentangling. I put into the title of this lecture not only the word 'commitment', but also the word 'alignment'. Of course in one weak sense 'alignment' is just another word for 'commitment'. But there is another sense of alignment, which I take very seriously and from which, I think, any serious contemporary argument about commitment must begin.

Marxism, more clearly than any other kind of thinking, has shown us that we are in fact aligned long before we realize that we are aligned. For we are born into a social situation, into social relationships, into a family, all of which have formed what we can later abstract as ourselves as individuals. Much of this formation occurs before we can be conscious of any individuality. Indeed the consciousness of individuality is often the consciousness of all those elements of our formation, yet this can never be complete. The alignments are so deep. They are our normal ways of living in the world, our normal ways of seeing the world. Of course we may become intellectually aware that they are not normal in the sense that they are universal. We come to recognize that other people live differently, were born into different social relationships, see the world differently. Yet still, at certain deep levels – and this matters very much in writing – our own actual alignment is so inseparable from the constitution of our own individuality that to separate them is quite artificial. And then for a writer there is something even more specific: that he is born into a language; that his very medium is something which he will have learned as if it were natural, although of course he eventually knows that there are other very different languages. But still it is the medium in which he will work, the medium which he shares with his own people, and which has entered into his own constitution long before he begins to write. To be aligned to and by that language, with some of its deep qualities, is inevitable if he is to write at all. So, born into a social situation with all its specific perspectives, and into a language, the writer begins by being aligned.

Yet alignment goes deeper again, into the actual and available forms of writing. When I hear people talk about literature, describing what so-and-so did with that form – how did he handle the short novel? – I often think we should reverse the question and ask, how did the short novel handle him. Because anyone who has carefully observed his own practice of writing eventually finds that there is a point where, although he is holding the pen or tapping the typewriter, what is being written, while not separate from him, is not only him either, and of course this other force is literary form. Very few if any of us could write at all if certain forms were not available. And then we may be lucky, we may find forms which happen to correspond to our experience. But take the case of the nineteenth-century working-class writers, who wanted to write about their working lives. The most popular form was the novel, but though they had marvellous material that could go into the novel very few of them managed to write good or even any novels. Instead they wrote marvellous autobiographies. Why? Because the form coming down through the religious tradition was of the witness confessing the story of his life, or there was the defence speech at the trial when a man tells the judge who he is and what he has done, or of course other kinds of speech. These oral forms were more accessible, forms centred on 'I', on the single person. The novel with its quite different narrative forms was virtually impenetrable to working-class writers for three or four generations, and there are still many problems in using the received forms for what is, in the end, very different material. Indeed the forms of working-class consciousness are bound to be different from the literary forms of another class, and it is a long struggle to find new and adequate forms.

Now these are alignments of a deep type, and really I think the most serious case for commitment is that we should commit ourselves far enough to social reality to be conscious of this level of sociality. It means becoming conscious of our own real alignments. This may lead to us confirming them, in some situations. Or it can often lead to changing or shifting or amending them, a more painful process than it sounds. Some of the most publicized cases of 'commitment' are when people shift in this way from one set of beliefs and assumptions to another, and this can involve a quite radical shift in real practice. In fact even when we confirm our deepest alignments, but now very consciously and deliberately, something strange has happened and we feel quite differently committed. Because really to have understood the social pressures on our own thinking, or when we come to that wonderful although at first terrible realization that what we are thinking is what a lot of other people have thought, that what we are seeing is what a lot of other people have seen, that is an extraordinary experience. We can make this point negatively against all those people who appeal to the freedom of the individual artist within their own isolated terms. It is one of the most surprising things about most of them that they say, 'I only write as a free individual, I only write what I want to write', but in fact what they write is, in majority, already written and what everybody already knows. That of course is an illusion of freedom. But beyond it, under pressure, there is a very high kind of freedom. This is when you are free to choose, or to choose to try to alter, that which is really pressuring you, in your whole social formation, in your understanding of the possibilities of writing.

To be committed to that is nothing whatever to do with submission to anybody. It is the discovery of those social relationships which are in any case there. It is what I think Sartre meant by reverberation, resonance: that active consciousness of those social relationships which include ourselves and our practices. It is never likely to be a convenient discovery, in our kind of world. It permits very little in the way of being immediately signed up for somebody else's market or somebody else's policy. But when it really happens, in the many different ways that are possible, its sound is usually unmistakeable: the sound of that voice which, in speaking as itself, is speaking, necessarily, for more than itself. Whether we find such voices or not, it is worth committing ourselves to the attempt.

Notes

1 Jean-Paul Sartre, *Between Existentialism and Marxism*, London 1974, pp. 13–14.
2 Quoted in Walter Benjamin, 'Talking to Brecht', *NLR* 77, January–February 1973.
3 Friedrich Engels, *New York Daily Tribune*, 28 October 1851.
4 Karl Marx, 'The Holy Family', in Lee Baxandall and Stefan Marawski, eds, *Marx and Engels on Literature and Art*, St Louis 1973, p. 121.
5 Friedrich Engels, Letter to Eduard Bernstein, 17 August 1881, Baxandall and Marawski, p. 125.
6 Theodor Adorno, 'Commitment', *NLR* 87/88. September–December 1974.

Part IV

Cultural Materialism in Action (1980–88)

Part IV: Introduction

While the statement that cultural materialism makes up the substance of Williams's intellectual legacy is hardly likely to be challenged, exactly what constitutes cultural materialism is more open to dispute. The difficulties are particularly striking and present when cultural materialism is treated less as a concept and more as a 'term', that is, as a signifier whose signified content can be filled in according to the whim of the interpreter. Cultural materialism may then seem to appear something considerably less than the attempt at an ambitious programme for a new academic discipline which haunted Williams's final writings.

The problem of definition was evident at an early stage, in the very first borrowings and adaptions of Williams's concept. Dollimore and Sinfield had laid strong claim to Williams's cultural materialism in their *Political Shakespeare: New Essays in Cultural Materialism*, where it was defined as a method which combined 'historical context, theoretical method, political commitment, and textual analysis' (1985: vii). They further described the content of that political commitment as 'the transformation of a social order which exploits people on grounds of race, gender and class' (p. viii). While there is no doubt that this commitment to commitment is in line with Williams's own record of cultural and political activism, there is little sense in his work that political commitment could figure as a part of the methodological basis for cultural materialism. Indeed, as we saw in Part 3, Williams was most wary of any such assumption, and repeated Adorno's warning that commitment was always 'politically

polyvalent' in his essay **The Writer: Commitment and Alignment** (p. 211)
Something of the specificity of cultural materialism is lost or dissolved when
this emphasis is made, while in a curious way, Dollimore and Sinfield's
presentation of cultural materialism keeps it bound too narrowly within the
borders of existing literary studies.

This becomes more apparent if we examine Dollimore's further description
in his own essay in the volume, 'Shakespeare, Cultural Materialism and the
New Historicism'. Here Dollimore describes ' "cultural materialism" ' as a
'term . . . borrowed from its use by Raymond Williams', but, as the scare-
quotes around 'cultural materialism' indicate, this 'borrowing' is also something of an adaption and redefinition. In practice, Dollimore's sense of cultural
materialism is derived from 'an eclectic body of work', one which includes 'the
convergence of history, sociology and English in cultural studies, some of the
major developments in feminism, as well as continental Marxist-structuralist
and post-structuralist theory, especially that of Althusser, Macherey, Gramsci
and Foucault' (1985: 2–3).[1] The problem lies with just that eclecticism. As we
have seen, Williams spent a great deal of his time criticizing structuralist
Marxists such as Althusser and Macherey, and post-structuralist theory more
generally, and indeed intended his own theory of cultural materialism as a
conscious alternative to 'the newly dominant mode of critical structuralism'
(Williams 1979: 339). It is hardly surprising, then, that Williams, in his cautious
'Afterword' to *Political Shakespeare*, recorded a 'certain wariness, an unease,'
about the volume, centred on its 'main title' (Williams 1985: 231) but, I think,
going beyond the issue of the title alone.

For Williams, the title suggested too strong a kinship with the usual appropriations of Shakespeare around the critic's own political beliefs, especially
apparent in the 'dismal practice . . . of assembling lists of reactionary or progressive writers' (1985: 237) current in the 1930s. Thus, though he commends
the collection for the 'edge of challenge to existing confusions and certainties'
which it provides, and welcomes in particular 'the studies of contemporary
productions of Shakespeare, in education and performance' (p. 237), he nonetheless closes his essay with a recommendation for the actual procedures of his
own cultural materialism, thus intimating that these have not been followed in
the collection as a whole:

the most practical and effective new direction will be in the analysis of the historically
based conventions of language and representation; the plays themselves as socially and
materially produced, within discoverable conditions; indeed the texts themselves as
history.

(Williams 1985: 239)

Reading the 'Afterword', there is a strong sense that there is some distance —
both conceptual and practical — between William's idea of a cultural materialism and the sense given to it as a 'term' by Dollimore and others.

Indeed, in many current accounts, cultural materialism appears to add up to
little more than the politically correct and theoretically sophisticated reading of
canonical texts. In *Beginning Theory*, Peter Barry describes cultural materialism
as 'the study of historical material (which includes literary texts) within a
politicized framework, this framework including the present which those
literary texts have in some way helped to shape' (Barry 1995: 183) while
American scholar Louis Montrose represents it as 'the uses to which an
historical *present* puts its versions of the English past' (1989: 27). Both Montrose
and Barry refer for the substance of their definitions to the previous work of
Alan Sinfield and Jonathan Dollimore rather than to Williams, and this is where
the conceptual problems begin. While there can be no doubt that Williams was
always attentive to what he called the dynamics of the selective tradition (how
the present interprets the past), an awareness of these dynamics was never more
than just one aspect of the necessary work of the cultural materialist critic. The
aim of this final selection of writings is to introduce readers to some of the
complexities of Williams's own practice of cultural materialism, all the while
emphasizing, as he did, that cultural materialism was best understood as 'a
theory of the specificities of material cultural and literary production within
historical materialism' (1977a: 5).

Williams didn't use the term 'cultural materialism' until 1976; but the
method of cultural materialism had surely been developing since the introduction of the concept of 'structure of feeling', with its challenge to Marxist
orthodoxy, in the 1950s.[2] The theory of *cultural* materialism seeks to establish
the constitutive force of culture for any account of historical change and any
political practice, while respecting the necessary limits of determination; and, as
a cultural *materialism*, it stresses the historical and political determinants of any
cultural or signifying practice against a bourgeois aesthetic theory which was
usually predicated on the existence of the free individual. In this sense,
Williams's cultural materialism emerges as a third term from the juxtaposition
of two opposed theoretical positions: the economic determinism of Soviet
Marxism and the individual aesthetic freedom of bourgeois literary theory. The
four essays in this final Part demonstrate and exemplify some of the distinctive
elements of Williams's own concept of cultural materialism.

The Bloomsbury Fraction represents one of the first self-conscious
attempts to put the theory of cultural materialism into practice. Its starting
point is the problem posed to both Marxist and liberal sociological analysis by
the disproportionate influence exercised on cultural history by small groups or
movements such as the Bloomsbury Group of Virginia Woolf, Maynard

Keynes, Lytton Strachey, Clive Bell and others. While their social and cultural significance can hardly be doubted ('No history of modern culture could be written without attention to them', he says (**The Bloomsbury Fraction**, p. 229), existing sociological analysis tends to be extremely reductive. Cultural materialism proposes a finer-grained account, one which blends the findings of textual interpretation with theoretical enquiry, and places these findings firmly in the perspective offered by historical contextualization.

The focus of the cultural materialist account is the terms of the group's self-understanding, and the precise textual, theoretical and historical analysis of these terms. Williams finds a central paradox here: the key to the significance of Bloomsbury as a group lies precisely in the ways in which it 'denied its existence as a formal group' (**The Bloomsbury Fraction**, p. 243). While its diverse members accepted their deep ties of mutual friendship and intellectual affiliation, each rejected with great force any idea that their collective work was in some sense the result of an adhesion to any general theory or system. For the Bloomsbury intellectuals 'theories and systems obstructed the true organizing value of the group, which was the unobstructed free expression of the civilized individual' (p. 243–44). Yet, as Williams points out, they were collectively 'against ignorance, poverty, sexual and racial discrimination, militarism and imperialism', and collectively against them in a particular way. What Blooms-bury appealed to 'against all these evils' was, he writes, 'not any alternative idea of a whole society. Instead it appealed to the supreme value of the civilized *individual*, whose pluralization, as more and more civilized individuals, was the only acceptable social direction' (**The Bloomsbury Fraction**', p. 244). In fact, this common focus on the 'civilized individual' meant that an 'effective integration' of Bloomsbury thinking had already taken place at a pretheoretical level, on the level of unconscious assumption, and in the act of representation. The political result follows directly from this as 'the governing object of all the public interventions' becomes 'to secure this kind of autonomy' (p. 246), that of 'all the best people, secure in their autonomy but turning their free attention this way and that, as occasion requires' (p. 246). In the end, writes Williams, the 'social conscience...is to protect the private consciousness' and the Bloomsbury Group is best understood as 'a true *fraction* of the existing English upper class' (p. 236).

While **The Bloomsbury Fraction** presents a fine instance of the explanatory power of cultural materialism in action, **Crisis in English Studies** offers a succinct account of the challenges it posed to both existing literary studies and the new semiotic and post-structuralist theories of the 1970s. The paper was first read as a public lecture in Cambridge as Williams's response to what one newspaper called 'Cambridge's bitterest academic row since the bitter days of Dr. F. R. Leavis' (cited in Simpson 1990: 226). A striking feature of the account is the claim that the explanatory paradigms of Cambridge English and critical structuralism have too much in common rather than, as most disputants claimed, were too far apart.

As far as Williams was concerned, both the structuralist literary criticism of the 1960s and the older paradigm of Practical Criticism placed a common emphasis on 'the isolated internal organization' of literary texts. As we saw in Part 2 of the *Reader*, and as the lecture recalls here, *The Country and the City* had challenged the isolation of text from context characteristic of Cambridge English, and had insisted on placing all acts of writing 'within an active, conflicting historical process' (**Crisis in English Studies**, p. 263). At the same time, the cultural materialist account challenged the underlying assumptions of critical structuralism, and particularly those concerning the status of the subject in the system of language.

In **Crisis in English Studies**, Williams places cultural materialism alongside the new work in radical semiotics of Cambridge colleagues such as Stephen Heath and Colin MacCabe.[3] 'There were still radical differences, especially in their reliance on structural linguistics and psychoanalysis... but... a fully historical semiotics would be very much the same thing as cultural materialism' (**Crisis**, p. 264). 'A fully historical semiotics': as Williams had put it in *Culture*, this meant accpeting 'the social as well as the notational basis of sign-systems', and adding 'a deliberately extended social dimension' to the usual formal analyses of the purely textual criticism associated with conventional literary studies and structuralism (Williams 1981: 31).

The two final essays in this *Reader* both demonstrate the continuity through difference characteristic of Williams's work. **Writing, Speech and the 'Classical'** shows Williams returning to the skills of practical criticism he had first learned in Cambridge some forty-five years before, but using these to defend the humanities from the new attacks on education; while **Language and the Avant-Garde** reconsiders the questions of naturalism and modernism that had provided his starting point in the 1950s.

In 1984, Williams gave the Presidential Address at the annual meeting of the Classical Association. With some prescience, he addressed the ways in which the new currents of neoliberal thinking sought to turn education away from the general literacy taught in the humanities and towards a purely vocational educational emphasis.[4] Williams had long argued against this utilitarian reduction and for the need to consider literacy as a constitutive moment of citizenship – most notably in *The Long Revolution*.[5] In this regard, it is best to understand the educational and political focus of cultural materialism as simply the promotion of the extended and varied forms of critical literacy necessary to engage the politics of the modern (or postmodern) world: that, after all, had been the mission since his early days in adult education.[6]

Focusing on two exemplary passages from Tacitus, Williams urges the need to reconsider the relations between speech and writing, and stresses the need to understand how 'writing has from the beginning been a special form of privilege and social discrimination' (**Writing, Speech and the 'Classical'**, p. 274). From its beginnings as a stable medium for the recording of facts and transactions, writing soon shifted to a mode of representing events and became 'a medium of obscurantism and falsification', one in which it's always difficult to see events 'from any point of view but that of the effective conqueror' (**Writing**, p. 289). Against this pressure of writing as representation, he calls for the democratic redefinition of the skills of a 'high literacy'. This is not the high literacy of those who would oppose a minority civilization to mass culture, and maintain a rigid divide between them, but a critical literacy which:

calls the bluffs of authority, since it is a condition of all its practical work that it questions sources, closely examines offered authenticities, reads contextually and comparatively, identifies conventions to determine meanings: habits of mind which are all against, or should be all against, any and every pronunciation of a singular or assembled authority.

(**Writing**, p. 276)

One aspect of this critical literacy is the need to subject the axioms of theory to some form of historical control, and in his final writings Williams was particularly concerned to challenge the received ideas of much structuralist and post- structuralist theory.

Nowhere is this challenge more evident than in the lecture **Language and the Avant-Garde**, prepared for the conference on *The Linguistics of Writing* organized by Colin MacCabe at the University of Strathyclyde in 1986.[7] In his examination of the variety of positions on language available in the period of high modernism, he was consciously questioning the orthodox representation offered by much contemporary theory, and the ways it identified its projects with a particular version of modernism.[8] Against the grain of much contemporary theory, Williams denies that modernist writers share anything like a 'common rejection of the representational character of language and thence of writing' (**Language and the Avant-Garde**, p. 279), and he set out to challenge 'certain tendencies in applied linguistics, and to forms of literary analysis seemingly derived from them, which have appropriated a selective version of Modernism...as a way of ratifying their own much narrower positions and procedures' (p. 279). In a wide-ranging discussion of the work of writers such as Artaud, Hugo Ball, André Breton and the Russian Formalists, Williams demonstrated that 'what we have really to investigate is not some single position of language in the avant-garde or...Modernism... [but] a range of distinct and in many cases actually opposed formations... Formal analysis can contribute to this, but only if it is firmly grounded in foundational analysis' (p. 292). Genuinely modern consciousness, he writes elsewhere, 'begins by recognizing that its very modernity is historical' (1987: 4–5).

Genuine theoretical consciousness must equally begin by recognizing that the terms of its theory are genuinely historical: this is the simple but hard lesson of Williams's cultural materialism. From a brief survey of the available definitions of cultural materialism, it seems that its central lesson still remains to be learned. It may be that it is now time to reread and reconsider the theoretical implications of Williams's own, now historical, body of work. This selection of essays – both in this final section and in the *Reader* as a whole – is intended as a help and stimulus to just such a project.

Notes

1　A similar theoretical eclecticism is present in Scott Wilson's *Cultural Materialism*, which distinguishes between a 'mainstream' cultural materialism, associated with Williams, and his own development from this, which would integrate with it 'the general economic of George Bataille' and 'the work of Lacan and Derrida' (Wilson 1995: xi). For recent studies more interested in Williams's own concept of cultural materialism, see Milner 1993, Higgins 1999 and Mulhern 2000. I leave aside the question of the relations between cultural materialism and the diverse trends and writers associated with New Historicism and contemporary cultural studies. For some interesting discussion with regard to cultural materialism and New Historicism, see Ryan 1996, particularly his observation that 'New historicism and cultural materialism are united by their compulsion to relate literature to history, to treat texts as indivisible from contexts, and to do so from a politically charged perspective forged in the present. But they are divided by the different routes they take to reach this goal, and by the different conclusions they draw once they have reached it' (p. xi); and, for Williams and cultural studies, Dworkin 1993, 1997, and Mulhern 2000.

2　See Williams 1980: 243.

3　See, for instance, Rosalind Coward and John Ellis 1977, Stephen Heath 1981, 1982, Colin MacCabe 1979, 1985, and, for a useful general account, Anthony Easthope 1988.

4　For a useful comparable accounts, see Godzich 1994 and Readings 1997. See also *boundary 2* 2000 for further discussion of the now advanced crisis around education in the humanities.

5　In *The Long Revolution*, Williams writes of the central place of literacy in a participatory democracy, and he returns to this same emphasis in many later essays (see Higgins 1999: 174–7).

6 For the formative influence of Williams's years in adult education, see especially McIlroy and Westwood (1993), Inglis 1995 (especially Ch. 5 'Workers' Education in the Garden of England'), and Higgins 1999 (especially pp. 15–20, 52–6).

7 See N. Fabb, D. Attridge, A. Durant and C. MacCabe 1988.

8 MacCabe acknowledges the influence on his own work of the 'ultra-modernist positions adopted by Barthes and the *Tel Quel* group' and their 'analyses of the classic texts of French modernism' (1985: 7–8). See, for instance, Jacques Derrida's fascinating analyses of Artaud in *L'Ecriture et la Différence* (1967) and Julia Kristeva's emphasis on Mallarmé in *La Révolution du language poétique* (1974).

13

The Bloomsbury Fraction

From D. Crabtree and A. P. Thirlwall (eds.) (1980) Keynes and the Bloomsbury Group. *London: Macmillan*

There are serious problems of method in the analysis of cultural groups. When we are analysing large social groups we have some obvious and useful methods at our disposal. The large numbers allow significant statistical analysis. There are usually organized institutions and relatively codified beliefs. There are still many problems in analysis, but we can at least begin with these reasonably hard facts.

In the case of a cultural group, the number of people involved is usually much too small for statistical analysis. There may or may not be organized institutions, through which the group works or develops, but even the most organized institutions are different in scale and kind from those of large groups. The principles which unite the group may or may not be codified. Where they are codified, one kind of analysis is immediately relevant. But there are many important cultural groups which have in common a body of practice or a distinguishable ethos, rather than the principles or stated aims of a manifesto. What the group itself has not formulated may indeed be reduced to a set of formulations, but some effects of reduction – simplification, even impoverishment – are then highly probable.

The social and cultural significance of all such groups, from the most to the least organized, can hardly be doubted. No history of modern culture could be written without attention to them. Yet both history and sociology are uneasy with them. We find histories of particular groups, but little comparative or analytic history. In the sociology of culture, we find the effect of general sociology in a tendency to concentrate on groups of a more familiar kind, with relatively organized institutions: churches for the sociology of religion, an educational system for the sociology of education. In other areas of culture – writing, painting, music, theatre, and for that matter philosophy and social thought – there is usually either specialization or neglect. The group, the movement, the circle, the tendency seem too marginal or too small or too ephemeral, to require historical and social analysis. Yet their importance, as a general social and cultural fact, especially in the last two centuries, is great in what they achieved, and in what their modes of achievement can tell us about the larger societies to which they stand in such uncertain relations.

These are general considerations but they happen to be particularly important in the case of the Bloomsbury Group, if only because, influentially, they went out of their way, by assertion or innuendo, to deflect or deny them. For example, Leonard Woolf:

What came to be called Bloomsbury by the outside world never existed in the form given to it by the outside world. For 'Bloomsbury' was and is currently used as a term – usually of abuse – applied to a largely imaginary group of persons with largely imaginary objects and characteristics . . . We were and always remained primarily and fundamentally a group of friends.[1]

Of course when Leonard Woolf complained of misrepresentation, he had important things to say. But the theoretical interest of his observation is that, first, in discussing this 'largely imaginary group' he takes for granted the existence and the concept of 'the outside world', and, second, he counterposes 'a group of friends' to a group in some more general sense. But it is a central fact about many though not all such groups that they begin and develop as 'a group of friends'. What we have then to ask is whether any shared ideas or activities were elements of their friendship, contributing directly to their formation and distinction as a group, and, further, whether there was anything about the ways in which they became friends which indicate wider social and cultural factors. It is significant, for example, to continue the quotation:

We were and always remained primarily and fundamentally a group of friends. Our roots and the roots of our friendship were in the University of Cambridge.[2]

For it is especially significant of Bloomsbury that 'the University of Cambridge' can be taken, in this way, as if it were a simple location, rather than the highly specific social and cultural institution which it was and is. Moreover the social and cultural roots of that particular form of perception – the 'group' and the 'outside world' – have in their turn to be traced to a precise social position and formation.

For this is the real point of social and cultural analysis, of any developed kind: to attend not only to the manifest ideas and activities, but also to the positions and ideas which are implicit or even taken for granted. This is especially necessary in the England of the last hundred years, in which the significance of groups like Bloomsbury or, to take another relevant example, F.R. Leavis and *Scrutiny*, has been widely acknowledged but within an especially weak general perspective. For the concepts to which such groups are referred belong, essentially, to the definitions and perspectives of the groups themselves, so that any analysis which follows tends to be internal and circular.

This is so, for example, in the concept of the 'intellectual aristocracy', which Lord Annan has popularized and documented, and in the concept of 'minority culture', which Clive Bell, of Bloomsbury, and F.R. Leavis, of *Scrutiny*, in their different ways relied on. The point is not to question the intelligence or the cultivation of such self-defining groups. It is rather to relate them, in their specific forms, to those wider conditions which the concepts of an 'aristocracy' or a 'minority' both imply and obscure. This means asking questions about the social formation of such groups, within a deliberate context of a much wider history, involving very general relationships of social class and education. It means asking, further, about the effects of the relative position of any particular formation on their substantive and self-defining activities: effects which may often be presented merely as evidence of the distinction but which, viewed in a different perspective, may be seen as defining in less realized ways.

Thus Annan's presentation of an intellectual aristocracy, defined by a number of intellectually distinguished families, has to be qualified by two different considerations: first, the effect, including the generational effect, of the social position of those families on their members' *opportunities* for intellectual distinction; and, second, the facts of those families as whole numbers of persons, who need not – except on the founding assumption – be described as it were from the most eminent outwards (a method which allows virtually indefinite inclusion by relationship, where inclusion by independent distinction might present more problems) but who, if distinguished families are the *starting point*, can all, by the apparently independent criterion of intellectual achievement, be included and praised. I believe it to be true that indeed, by independent criteria, in the case of many of Annan's subjects, some remarkable clusters of distinction are evident. But these may then be open to quite different kinds of analysis and conclusion from the ideological, and ideologically derived, notion of an 'intellectual aristocracy'.

The same considerations apply to the Bloomsbury Group, especially as we now see it at some historical distance. It can be presented, reasonably, as an extraordinary grouping of talents. Yet in Bloomsbury, quite clearly, there is also now eminence by association. It is interesting to go through Leonard Woolf's list of Old Bloomsbury and its later accessions.[3] It is difficult to be certain in these matters, but it is worth asking how many people on the list would be now independently and separately remembered, in any generally significant cultural sense, apart from their membership of the group. I mean that in one kind of presentation we can lead with Virginia Woolf, E.M. Forster and J.M. Keynes, and then go on through the widening circle to others. But suppose we take the list as it comes: Vanessa Bell, Virginia Woolf, Leonard Woolf, Adrian Stephen, Karin Stephen, Lytton Strachey, Clive Bell, Maynard Keynes, Duncan Grant, Morgan Forster, Saxon Sydney Turner, Roger Fry, Desmond Mac-Carthy, Molly MacCarthy, Julian Bell, Quentin Bell, Angelica Bell, David (Bunny) Garnett. It is a list of well-known and some other names. It is indeed exactly what we would expect from Leonard Woolf's accurate description of a group of friends and relations who included some people whose work would be widely respected if the group itself were not remembered, others of whom this is quite clearly not the case, and others again in whom it is difficult to distinguish between independent reputation and the effect of group association and group memoirs.

Yet the point is emphatically not to diminish anybody. That would, indeed, be a gross surrender to some of the very modes of human judgement which Bloomsbury and similar groups effectively popularized. The real point is to see the significance of the cultural group over and above the simple empirical presentation and self-definition as 'a group of friends'. It is to ask what the group was, socially and culturally, as a question distinct from (though still related to) the achievements of individuals and their own immediately perceived relationships. It is indeed just because so many significant modern cultural groups are formed and developed in this way that we have to ask, even against the rising eyebrows of Bloomsbury, certain (heavy) theoretical questions.

For it is clear that no analysis which neglects the elements of friendship and relationship, through which they recognized and came to define themselves, would begin to be adequate. At the same time any restriction to these terms would be a clear evasion of the general significance of the group. We have therefore to think about modes of analysis which avoid collapsing one kind of definition into another, either the generalized group or the empirical assembly. For it is just because of its specific internal formation and its evident general significance – the two qualities taken together – that Bloomsbury is so inter-esting. It is also an especially important case theoretically, since it is impossible to develop a modern cultural sociology unless we can find ways of discussing such formations which both acknowledge the terms in which they saw themselves and would wish to be presented, and at the same time enable us to analyze these terms and their general social and cultural significance. And because this is so, though I shall mainly discuss Bloomsbury, I shall say something also about Godwin and his circle and the Pre-Raphaelite Brotherhood. This is partly for comparison, including historical comparison, but it also a way of beginning to find terms for the more general discussion.

The Formation of Bloomsbury

Let us then notice first that certain of the declared founding principles of Bloomsbury were of a kind which corresponded directly to their precise mode of formation and to the activities for which most of them are remembered. One account after another emphasizes the centrality of the shared values of personal affection and aesthetic enjoyment. For any conscious formulation of these values, we are regularly referred to the great influence of G.E. Moore on the original friends at Cambridge. These shared values were modulated in specific ways. There was a sustained emphasis on candour: people were to say to each other exactly what they thought and felt. There was also great emphasis on clarity: the candid avowal, or any other kind of statement, must expect to be met by the question: 'what precisely do you mean by that?'. These shared values and habits are then immediately relevant to the internal formation of the group and to some of its external effects. The values and habits which brought them so closely together soon gave them a (self-regarding) sense of being different from others, and these others, in turn, could identify them as a clique. But then, in this as in other important respects, they were also one of the advanced formations of their class:

When I went to Ceylon [*sc.* 1904] – indeed even when I returned [*sc.* 1911] – I still called Lytton Strachey Strachey and Maynard Keynes Keynes, and to them I was still Woolf. When I stayed for a week with the Stracheys in the country in 1904, or dined in Gordon Square with the Stephens, it would have been inconceivable that I should have called Lytton's or Toby's sisters by their Christian names. The social significance of using Christian instead of surnames and of kissing instead of shaking hands is curious. Their effect is greater, I think, than those who have never lived in a more formal society imagine. They produce a sense – often unconscious – of intimacy and freedom and so break down barriers to thought and feeling. It was this feeling of greater intimacy and freedom, of the sweeping away of formalities and barriers, which I found so new and so exhilarating in 1911. To have discussed some subjects or to have called a (sexual) spade a spade in the presence of Miss Strachey or Miss Stephen would seven years before have been unimaginable; here for the first time I found a much more intimate (and wider) circle in which complete freedom of thought and speech was now extended to Vanessa and Virginia, Pippa and Marjorie.[4]

This sense of liberation was a stage in the development of the original Cambridge friends. It was a local realization of their earlier bearings:

We were convinced that everyone over twenty-five, with perhaps one or two remarkable exceptions, was 'hopeless', having lost the elan of youth, the capacity to feel, and the ability to distinguish truth from falsehood... We found ourselves living in the springtime of a conscious revolt against the social, political, religious, moral, intellectual and artistic institutions, beliefs and standards of our fathers and grandfathers... We were out to construct something new; we were in the van of the builders of a new society which should be free, rational, civilized, pursuing truth and beauty.[5]

It must of course be clear that this was a very much wider movement than Bloomsbury. In this very account, with a characteristic mixture of honesty and unawareness, Leonard Woolf noted that 'we felt ourselves to be the second generation in this exciting movement', though the attitude to almost everyone over twenty-five seems to have survived this. In fact most of the attitudes and opinions were derived, as here from Ibsen

saying 'Bosh!' to that vast system of cant and hypocrisy which made lies a vested interest, the vested interest of the 'establishment', of the monarchy, aristocracy, upper classes, suburban bourgeoisie, the Church, the Army, the stock exchange.[6]

What Bloomsbury really represented, in the development of this wider movement, was a new *style*.

It was an effective style for the new critical frankness. But there were elements in its formation which brought other tones, and not only the cliquishness of the self-conscious advanced group. The frankness could modulate into tones of quite extraordinary rudeness about, and to, the 'hopeless'. There is also something very curious about the attachment to personal affections. This is difficult to estimate, at a distance and from outside, but 'affection', rather than any stronger word, does, as one reads, come to seem exact. A cool frankness as a dominant intellectual tone seems to have had its effect on certain levels of emotional life. This was, of course, already evident in Shaw, and in the related but wider Fabian formation. There is an unforgettable moment in a conversation between Virginia Woolf and Beatrice Webb in 1918:

Beatrice had asked Virginia what she intended to do now that she was married. Virginia said that she wanted to go on writing novels. Beatrice seemed to approve and warned Virginia against allowing her work to be interfered with by emotional relations.

'Marriage, we always say', she said, 'is the waste paper basket of the emotions'. To which, just as they came to the level crossing, Virginia replied: 'But wouldn't an old servant do as well?'.[7]

The fact that in her own record of this conversation Virginia Woolf has 'waste pipe' for 'waste paper basket' only deepens its ironic fascination. There is a sense in which the rationality and the candour give 'affection' a limiting though still important definition. On the other hand, what is quite evident in the group is a significant tolerance in sexual and emotional matters. This valuable tolerance and the exact weight of 'affection' seem really to be linked.

A final factor which must be added to this initial definition of the structure of feeling of the group can be precisely represented by the phrase 'social conscience'. They were not its originators, and in any case it is a more evident factor after 1918 than before 1914. It relates, certainly, to the comprehensive irreverence for established ideas and institutions, in the earliest phase. But it becomes something more. Nothing more easily contradicts the received image of Bloomsbury as withdrawn and languid aesthetes than the remarkable record of political and organizational involvement, between the wars, by Leonard Woolf, by Keynes, but also by others, including Virginia Woolf, who had a branch of the Women's Cooperative Guild meeting regularly in her home. The public record of Keynes is well enough known. That of Leonard Woolf, in his prolonged work for the League of Nations, for the Cooperative movement, and for the Labour Party, especially on anti-imperialist questions, is especially honourable.

It might then come as a surprise, to Bloomsbury and to those formed in its image, to set a mark on 'social conscience'. The phrase itself, from just this period, has become widely naturalized, and it is then very difficult to question it. One way of doing so is to note its widespread association with that other significant phrase, 'concern for the underdog'. For what has most carefully to be defined is the specific association of what are really quite unchanged class feelings – a persistent sense of a quite clear line between an upper and a lower class – with very strong and effective feelings of sympathy with the lower class as victims. Thus political action is directed towards systematic reform at a ruling-class level; contempt for the stupidity of the dominant sectors of the ruling class survives, quite unchanged, from the earliest phase. The contradiction inherent in this – the search for systematic reform at the level of a ruling class which is known to be, in majority, short-sighted and stupid – is of course not ignored. It is a matter of social conscience to go on explaining and proposing, at official levels, and at the same time to help in organizing and educating the victims. The point is not that this social conscience is unreal; it is very real indeed. But it is the precise formulation of a particular social position, in which a fraction of an upper class, breaking from its dominant majority, relates to a lower class *as a matter of conscience*: not in solidarity, nor in affiliation, but as an extension of what are still felt as personal or small-group obligations, at once against the cruelty and stupidity of the system and towards its otherwise relatively helpless victims.

The complex of political attitudes, and eventually of political and social reforms of a certain kind, that flowed from this 'social conscience' has been especially important in England. It has indeed become consensual, from the right wing of the Labour Party through the Liberal Party to a few liberal Conservatives. Bloomsbury, including Keynes, was in this as in other matters well ahead of its times. In its organs, from the *New Statesman* through to the *Political Quarterly*, it was, in its period, second in importance in this consensus only to the closely related Fabian Society. In its hostility to imperialism, where the conscientious identification with victims was more negotiable than in England itself, its contribution was very significant. In its early and sustained hostility to militarism it represented an element of the consensus which was later, and especially in the Cold War, phased out. But what now matters most, in defining the group, is the nature of the connection between these important political bearings and the small, rational, candid group. The true link term is 'conscience'. It is a sense of individual obligation, ratified among civilized friends, which both governs immediate relationships and can be extended, without altering its own local base, to the widest 'social concerns'. It can then be distinguished, as the group itself always insisted, from the unfeeling, complacent and stupid state of mind of the dominant sector of the class. It has also to be distinguished – and this the group and its successors did not see – from the 'social *consciousness*' of a self-organizing subordinate class. These very different political bearings were not so much rejected as never taken seriously. Close contact with them, which the 'social conscience' required, produced a quite un-self-conscious and in its own way quite pure patronage. For if this were not given, these new forces could not be expected to be any more rational and civilized than their present masters.

In these initial definitions of the meanings and values which made this group more than just a group of friends – meanings and values, of course, which at every point, because of what they were, sustained their self-perception as *only* a group of friends, a few civilized individuals – we have come to the edge of the central definition of the social significance of the Bloomsbury Group. They were a true *fraction* of the existing English upper class. They were at once against its dominant ideas and values and still willingly, in all immediate ways, part of it. It is a very complex and delicate position, but the significance of such fractions has been very generally underestimated. It is not only a question of this problematic relationship within any particular section of time. It is also a question of the function of such relationships and such groups in the development and adaptation, through time, of the class as a whole.

Godwin and His Circle

It is here that we can look briefly, by way of comparison, at two important earlier English groups. William Godwin and his circle, in the 1780s and 1790s, came out of a quite differently based dissent. Their religious dissent, at the moment of their formation, already carried the specific social implications: of a relatively disadvantaged religious sector, but also the effects of a social and economic position which was very sharply different from that of the ruling and upper class of the day. That is to say, Godwin and his friends were relatively poor working professionals, an emerging small-bourgeois intelligentsia, with no other means of social or political influence. In their basic attempt to establish rationality, tolerance and liberty they were opposing, and knew they were opposing, a whole class and system beyond them. Within their own group they could argue for and try to practise the rational values of civilized equality, including, it should be remembered, for in this with Mary Wollstone-craft they were especially advanced, sexual equality. In their early phase they were wholly persuaded of the powers of rational explanation and persuasion. Vice was simply error, and error could be repaired by patient inquiry. Virtue could be assured by reasonable institutions. The stupidities and dogmas which now barred the way must be met by steady and careful enlightenment.

What then happened is still very striking. They encountered a ruling class, quite beyond them, which was not only arrogant and cruel but, at just that time, was under a new kind of threat from the effects of the French Revolution. The rational and civilizing proposals were met by the crudest kind of repression: prosecution, imprisonment and transportation. Godwin's novel, *Things as They Are*, is a remarkable evocation of this crisis, in which truth became a literal risk to life, and reasonable explanation was quite ruthlessly hunted down. It is a remarkable moment in English culture, still insufficiently honoured for the bravery of its initial attempt, and this mainly because the repression broke it so thoroughly and drove it underground for a generation. Failed groups are not easily respected, yet this one should be, in the nobility of its aspirations alongside the inherent character of its illusions. What we can so easily call failure was in fact defeat, and it was defeat by a vicious repression.

More generally, and decisively, this group was not a fraction, a break from an upper class. It was an emergent sector of a still relatively subordinate class, the smaller independent commercial bourgeoisie. Questioning everything, but within the assumption of a continuing rational discourse, they were hit by people who hardly even bothered to answer their arguments but who as threat and danger mounted simply bullied or locked them up. And then what we learn theoretically is that we cannot describe any of these cultural groups simply in internal terms: of what values they stood for, what meanings they tried to live. Taken only at this level, Godwin and his circle have some striking resemblances to Bloomsbury, although they were always stronger. But the level that matters, finally, is not that of the abstracted ideas, but of the real relations of the group to the social system as a whole.

The Pre-Raphaelite Brotherhood

The social system as a whole, but of course social systems change: in their general character and in their internal relations. By the time of the Pre-Raphaelite Brotherhood, in the middle of the nineteenth century, an industrial and commercial bourgeoisie was becoming dominant, and some parts of that earlier discourse had found a limited social base. For these and other reasons, the character of this new group was quite different. What they primarily opposed was the conventional philistinism of their day. In their earliest phase they were irreverent, impatient, contemptuous of shams; they were trying to find new and less formal ways of living among themselves. For a moment, which did not last, they were part of the democratic turbulence of 1848. But the central mode of their brief unity as a group was a declaration for truth in art, and a corresponding rejection of the received conventions. Their positive aim was truth to nature, 'rejecting nothing, selecting nothing and scorning nothing'. They defined a return to the old (pre-Raphaelite) as a means to the new. As an immediate group, they practised an easy and irreverent informality, an exceptional and now 'bohemian' tolerance, and some elements of a private group language (in slang such as 'stunner' and 'crib') which deliberately marked them off. They could be described as being, in their chosen area of art, in revolt against the commercial bourgeoisie, yet in majority they came from this same class. Holman Hunt's father was a warehouse manager, William Morris's a bill broker. Moreover, to a surprising extent as they developed, they found their patrons in this same class. Of course in the end they went their separate ways: towards the new and flattering integration represented by Millais, or to the break towards revolutionary socialism – though with the same immediate commercial links – of Morris. But in their effective moment, for all their difficulties, they were not only a break from their class – the irreverent and rebellious young – but a means towards the necessary next stage of development of that class itself. Indeed this happens again and again with bourgeois fractions: that a group detaches itself, as in this case of 'truth to nature', in terms which really belong to a phase of that class itself, but a phase now overlaid by the blockages of later development. It is then a revolt against the class but for the class, and it is no surprise that its emphases of style, suitably mediated, became the popular bourgeois art of the next historical period.

The Bloomsbury Fraction

There is always advantage in historical distance, and Godwin and his circle, or the Pre-Raphaelites, are in this sense more easily placed than Bloomsbury, which in certain of its tones and styles has still significant contemporary influence and even presence. Yet the purpose of this brief reference to these earlier groups is to emphasize, past some of the more obvious points in common, not only the ideal differences but the decisive social differences. And these in their turn can be understood only by following the development of the general society. For what happened in the second half of the nineteenth century was a comprehensive development and reform of the professional and cultural life of bourgeois England. The old universities were reformed and made more serious. The administrative services were both developed and reformed, by the new needs of imperial and state administration, and by the competitive examinations which interlocked with the reformed universities. The changing character of the society and the economy built, in fact, a new and very important professional and highly educated sector of the English upper class: very different in its bearings and values from either the old aristocracy or from the directly commercial bourgeoisie. And then – indeed as we look it is no surprise – it was from this sector, and especially from its second and third generations, that novel definitions and new groups emerged; and specifically, in its full sense, Bloomsbury.

The direct connections of the Bloomsbury Group with this new sector are well known. There is a significant frequency of connection with the upper levels of colonial (usually Indian) administration, as in the Stephen family, in Lytton Strachey's father, in Leonard Woolf's early career. There are continuities before and after in this respect: the Mills in the nineteenth century; Orwell in the twentieth. But the period of the emergence of Bloomsbury was the high point of this sector, as it was also the high point of the social order which it served. The sector is distinguishable but is still very closely connected with a wider area of the class. As Leonard Woolf says of the social world of the Stephens:

That society consisted of the upper levels of the professional middle class and county families, interpenetrated to a certain extent by the aristocracy [Or more generally] The Stephens and the Stracheys, the Ritchies, Thackerays and Duckworths had an intricate tangle of ancient roots and tendrils stretching far and wide through the upper middle classes, the county families, and the aristocracy.[8]

One of the interests of Woolf's account is that he was himself entering this crucial sector from a rather different class background:

I was an outsider to this class, because, although I and my father before me belonged to the professional middle class, we had only recently struggled up into it from the stratum of Jewish shopkeepers.[9]

He was thus able to observe the specific habits of the class from which Bloomsbury was to emerge:

Socially they assumed things unconsciously which I could never assume either unconsciously or consciously. They lived in a peculiar atmosphere of influence, manners, respectability, and it was so natural to them that they were unaware of it as mammals are unaware of the air and fish of the water in which they live.[10]

But that was the class as a whole. What was decisive in the emergence of its professional sector was the social and intellectual atmosphere of the reformed ancient universities. It was here, after liberalization, after a significant recovery of seriousness, and after internal reorganization to assure coached and competitive merit, that the specific qualities of the professional sector emerged within the general assumptions of the class. This allowed some new recruits, like Woolf himself. It promoted many significant and in a sense autonomous continuities, within the old universities. This is why it can still be seen, from a deliberately selective angle, as an 'intellectual aristocracy'.

The male members of the British aristocracy of intellect went automatically to the best public schools, to Oxford and Cambridge, and then into all the most powerful and respectable professions. They intermarried to a considerable extent, and family influence and the high level of their individual intelligence carried a surprising number of them to the top of their professions. You found them as civil servants sitting in the seat of permanent under-secretaries of government departments; they became generals, admirals, editors, judges, or they retired with a KCSI or KCMG after distinguished careers in the Indian or Colonial Civil Services. Others again got fellowships at Oxford or Cambridge and ended as head of an Oxford or Cambridge college or headmaster of one of the great public schools.[11]

The confusion of this account is as remarkable as the local accuracy of its information. There is the very characteristic admission and yet blurring of the two factors in success: 'family influence', 'high level of... individual intelligence'. There is a related blurring of the 'aristocracy of intellect', supported by one range of examples (Fellows and Headmasters; Permanent Under-Secretaries and Editors) and rather different ruling-class figures (Generals, Admirals). Within each range, in fact, the proportionate effect of class provenance, including family influence, and examined or demonstrated individual intelligence would need to be very precisely estimated. For what is really being described is a sectoral composition, and the diversities within this composition need much more precise description than the self-presenting and self-recommending formula – with its deliberate and yet revealing metaphor – of an 'intellectual aristocracy'.

A further relevant point, in this significant sectoral composition, is raised by Woolf's accurate reference to 'male members'. One of the factors that was to affect the specific character of the Bloomsbury Group, as a formation distinguishable from this whole sector, was the delay in higher education for women of this class. Even in its early stages, a few women from these families were directly involved; one of the Strachey sisters, Pernel, became Principal of Newnham. Yet a persistent sexual asymmetry was an important element in the composition of the Bloomsbury Group. As Woolf again puts it:

Our roots and the roots of our friendship were in the University of Cambridge. Of the 13 persons mentioned above [as members of Old Bloomsbury] three are women and ten men; of the ten men nine had been at Cambridge.[12]

The effects of this asymmetry were ironically and at times indignantly noted by Virginia Woolf, in *A Room of One's Own* and *Three Guineas*.

What we have then to emphasize, in the sociological formation of Bloomsbury, is, first, the provenance of the group in the professional and highly educated sector of the English upper class, itself with wide and sustained connections with this class as a whole; second, the element of contradiction between some of these highly educated people and the ideas and institutions of their class as a whole (the 'intellectual aristocracy', in the narrower sense, or at least some or a few of them, were bringing their intelligence and education to bear on the 'vast system of cant and hypocrisy' sustained by many of the institutions – 'monarchy, aristocracy, upper classes, suburban bourgeoisie, the Church, the Army, the stock exchange' – which were elsewhere included as the fields of success of this same 'aristocracy of intellect'); third, the specific contradiction between the presence of highly intelligent and intellectual women, within these families, and their relative exclusion from the dominant and formative male institutions; and, fourth and more generally, the internal needs and tensions of this class as a whole, and especially of its professional and highly educated sector, in a period which, for all its apparent stability, was one of social, political, cultural and intellectual crisis.

The Bloomsbury Group, we can then say, separated out as a distinct fraction on the basis of the second and third factors: the social and intellectual critique, and the ambiguity of the position of women. Taken together, these are the modes at once of its formation and of its achievements. But the first factor, of their general provenance, must be taken as defining the particular qualities of this fraction: their significant and sustained combination of dissenting influence and influential connection. And the fourth factor indicates something of their general historical significance: that in certain fields, notably those of sexual equalization and tolerance, of attitudes to the arts and especially the visual arts, and of some private and semi-public informalities, the Bloomsbury Group was a forerunner in a more general mutation within the professional and highly educated sector, and to some extent in the English ruling class more generally. A fraction, as was noted, often performs this service for its class. There was thus a certain liberalization, at the level of personal relationships, aesthetic enjoyment and intellectual openness. There was some modernization, at the level of semi-public manners, of mobility and contact with other cultures, and of more extended and more adequate intellectual systems. Such liberalization and modernization were of course quite general tendencies, in changing social circumstances and especially after the shocks of the 1914–18 war and, later, the loss of Empire. It is not that the Bloomsbury Group *caused* it is only (but it is something) that they were prominent and relatively coherent among its early representatives and agents. At the same time, the liberalization and modernization were more strictly adaptations than basic changes in the class, which in its function of directing the central ruling-class institutions has, for all the changes of manners and after some evident recruitment of others into its modes, not only persisted, but more successfully persisted *because* these adaptations have been made and continue to be made.

The Contribution of Bloomsbury

What has then finally to be discussed is the character of Bloomsbury's cultural, intellectual and artistic contributions within this context of their specific sociological formation and their historical significance. Yet any such discussion faces severe theoretical and methodological difficulties. There can be no question of reducing a number of highly specific individual contributions to some crude general content. Cultural groups of this kind – fractions by

association rather than fractions or oppositional groups by manifesto or programme – can in any case never be treated in this way. Yet neither can the
contributions be seen in mere random association. It is in this careful mood that
we have to read Leonard Woolf's interesting summary:

There have often been groups of people, writers and artists, who were not only friends,
but were consciously united by a common doctrine and object, or purpose artistic or
social. The utilitarians, the Lake poets, the French impressionists, the English Pre-
Raphaelites were groups of this kind. Our group was quite different. Its basis was
friendship, which in some cases deepened into love and marriage. The colour of our
minds and thought had been given to us by the climate of Cambridge and Moore's
philosophy, much as the climate of England gives one colour to the face of an
Englishman while the climate of India gives a quite different colour to the face of a
Tamil. But we had no common theory, system or principles which we wanted to
convert the world to; we were not proselytizers, missionaries, crusaders or even
propagandists. It is true that Maynard produced the system or theory of Keynesian
economics which has had a great effect upon the theory and practice of economics,
finance and politics; and that Roger, Vanessa, Duncan and Clive played important
parts, as painters or critics, in what came to be known as the Post-Impressionist
Movement. But Maynard's crusade for Keynesian economics against the orthodoxy
of the Banks and academic economists, and Roger's crusade for post-impressionism and
'significant form' against the orthodoxy of academic 'representational' painters and
aestheticians were just as purely individuals as Virginia's writing of *The Waves* – they
had nothing to do with any group. For there was no more a communal connection
between Roger's 'Critical and Speculative Essays on Art', Maynard's *The General
Theory of Employment, Interest and Money*, and Virginia's *Orlando* than there was between
Bentham's *Theory of Legislation*, Hazlitt's *Principal Picture Galleries in England*, and
Byron's *Don Juan*.[13]

At the simplest empirical level this can be taken to be true, though the final
comparison is merely rhetorical: Bentham, Hazlitt and Byron were never
significantly associated, and their names beg the question. Nor is the characteristic rejection of 'common theory, system or principles' quite as convincing as
it looks; Bloomsbury's attitudes to 'system', at least, were among their most
evident common, and principled, characteristics.

Indeed there is something in the way in which Bloomsbury denied its
existence as a formal group, while continuing to insist on its group qualities,
which is the clue to the essential definition. The point was not to have any
common – that is to say, general – theory or system, not only because this was
not necessary – worse, it would probably be some imposed dogma – but
primarily, and as a matter of principle, because such theories and systems
obstructed the true organizing value of the group, which was the unobstructed

free expression of the civilized individual. The force which that adjective, 'civilized', carries or is meant to carry can hardly be overestimated.

In the decade before the 1914 war there was a political and social movement in the world, and particularly in Europe and Britain, which seemed at the time wonderfully hopeful and exciting. It seemed as though human beings might really be on the brink of becoming civilized.[14]

In this sense, at its widest range, Bloomsbury was carrying the classical values of bourgeois enlightenment. It was against cant, superstition, hypocrisy, pretension and public show. It was also against ignorance, poverty, sexual and racial discrimination, militarism and imperialism. But it was against all these things in a specific moment of the development of liberal thought. What it appealed to, against all these evils, was not any alternative idea of a whole society. Instead it appealed to the supreme value of the civilized *individual*, whose pluralization, as more and more civilized individuals, was itself the only acceptable social direction.

The profoundly representative character of this perspective and commitment can now be more clearly seen. It is today the central definition of bourgeois ideology (bourgeois practice, of course, is something else again). It commands the public ideals of a very wide range of orthodox political opinion, from modern conservatives through liberals to the most representative social democrats. It is a philosophy of the sovereignty of the civilized individual, not only against all the dark forces of the past, but against all those other and actual social forces which, in conflicts of interest, in alternative claims, in other definitions of society and relationships, can be quickly seen as enemies and can as quickly be assigned to the far side of that border which is marked by its own definition of 'civilized'. The early confidence of the position, in the period before 1914, has in its long encounter with all these other and actual social forces gone in Leonard Woolf's title – 'downhill all the way'. For all its continuing general orthodoxy, it appears now much more often as a beleagured than as an expanding position. The repetition of its tenets then in turn becomes more and more ideological.

Bloomsbury's moment in this history is significant. In its practice – as in the sensibility of the novels of Virginia Woolf and of E. M. Forster – it could offer much more convincing evidence of the substance of the civilized individual than the orthodox rallying phrase. In its theory and practice, from Keynesian economics to its work for the League of Nations, it made powerful interventions towards the creation of economic, political and social conditions within which, freed from war and depression and prejudice, individuals could be free to be and to become civilized. Thus in its personal instances and in its public interventions Bloomsbury was as serious, as dedicated and as inventive as this position has ever, in the twentieth century, been. Indeed the paradox of many retrospective judgements of Bloomsbury is that the group lived and worked this position with a now embarrassing wholeheartedness: embarrassing, that is to say, to those many for whom 'civilized individualism' is a summary phrase for a process of conspicuous and privileged consumption. It is not that we can sever the positions of Bloomsbury from these later developments: there are some real continuities, as in the cult of conspicuous-appreciative-consumption; and certain traps were sprung, as in Keynesian economics and in monetary and military alliances. But we have still to see the difference between the fruit and its rotting, or between the hopefully planted seed and its fashionably distorted tree.

But then, as we see both the connections and the differences, we have to go on to analyze the obscurities and the faults of the original position around which Bloomsbury defined itself. This can be done either seriously or light-heartedly. Let us for a moment choose the latter, in one of Bloomsbury's own modes. It can be said, it was often said, that the group had no *general* position. But why did it need one? If you cared to look, there were Virginia and Morgan for literature, Roger and Clive and Vanessa and Duncan for art, Leonard for politics, Maynard for economics. Didn't these about cover the proper interests of all civilized people? With one exception perhaps, but in the twenties, significantly, this was remedied. A number of associates and relations of the group – Adrian and Karin Stephen, James Strachey – moved into the new practice of psychoanalysis, and Leonard and Virginia Woolf's Hogarth Press – their own direct and remarkable creation – effectively introduced Freudian thinking into English. Thus to the impressive list of Virginia and Morgan for literature, Roger and Clive and Vanessa and Duncan for art, Leonard for politics and Maynard for economics they could, so to say, add Sigmund for sex.

It is tempting to turn any mode back on itself, but the underlying point is serious. The work and thought of the Bloomsbury Group, and that other work and thought which it effectively associated with itself and presented – includ-ing, it should be said, the early 'communist' poetry of the thirties – are remarkable, at first sight, for their eclecticism, for their evident *dis*connections. In this sense it is understandable that anyone should turn and ask, rhetorically, what connections there could ever be between Clive Bell on art and Keynes on employment, or Virginia Woolf on fiction and Leonard Woolf on the League of Nations, or Lytton Strachey on history and the Freudians on psychoanalysis. It is true that we cannot put all this work together and make it into a general theory. But of course that is the point. The different positions which the Bloomsbury Group assembled, and which they effectively disseminated as the contents of the mind of a modern, educated, civilized individual, are all in effect *alternatives* to a general theory. We do not need to ask, while this impression holds, whether Freud's generalizations on aggression are compatible with single-minded work for the League of Nations, or whether his generalizations on art are compatible with Bell's 'significant form' and 'aesthetic ecstasy', or whether Keynes's ideas of public intervention in the market are compatible with the deep assumption of society as a group of friends and relations. We do not need to ask because the effective integration has already taken place, at the level of the 'civilized individual', the singular definition of all the best people, secure in their autonomy but turning their free attention this way and that, as occasion requires. And the governing object of all the public interventions is to secure this kind of autonomy, by finding ways of diminishing pressures and conflicts, and of avoiding disasters. The social conscience, in the end, is to protect the private consciousness.

Where this can be assured without that kind of protection – in the privileged forms of certain kinds of art, refusing the 'sacrifice... to representation' as 'something stolen from art',[15] or of certain kinds of fiction, as in Virginia Woolf mockingly rejecting social description –

Begin by saying that her father kept a shop in Harrogate. Ascertain the rent. Ascertain the wages of shop assistants in 1878. Discover what her mother died of. Describe cancer. Describe calico. Describe...[16]

– or in the available significant forms of personal relationships and aesthetic enjoyments – there is still no conflict (in spite of the troublesome 'details') with social *conscience*. Rather this higher sensibility is the kind of life which is its aim and model, after the rational removal of ('unnecessary') conflicts and contradictions and modes of deprivation. For the sake of personal life and of art, as Clive Bell argued,

Society can do something... because it can increase liberty... Even politicians can do something. They can repeal censorious laws and abolish restrictions on freedom of thought and speech and conduct. They can protect minorities. They can defend originality from the hatred of the mediocre mob.[17]

It is not always that specific blend of sweet and sour. It is indeed never free from class connotations, as again most explicitly in Bell:

The liberation will not be complete until those who have already learned to despise the opinion of the lower-middle classes learn also to neglect the standards and the disapproval of people who are forced by their emotional limitations to regard art as an elegant amenity... Comfort is the enemy; luxury is merely the bugbear of the bourgeoisie.[18]

At its best it was brave, in its own best terms:

> The least that the State can do is to protect people who have something to say that may cause a riot. What will not cause a riot is probably not worth saying.[19]

Yet after so much saying, there were no riots. Because for all its eccentricities, including its valuable eccentricities, Bloomsbury was articulating a position which, if only in carefully diluted instances, was to become a 'civilized' norm. In the very power of their demonstration of a private sensibility that must be protected and extended by forms of public concern, they fashioned the effective forms of the contemporary ideological dissociation between 'public' and 'private' life. Awareness of their own formation as individuals within society, of that specific social formation which made them explicitly a group and implicitly a fraction of a class, was not only beyond their reach; it was directly ruled out, since the free and civilized individual was already their founding datum. Psychoanalysis could be integrated with this, while it remained an ahistorical study of specific individual formations. Public policies could be integrated with it, while they were directed to reforming and amending a social order which had at once produced these free and civilized individuals but which through stupidity or anachronism now threatened their existence and their indefinite and generalized reproduction. The final nature of Bloomsbury as a group is that it was indeed, and differentially, a group of and for the notion of free individuals. Any general position, as distinct from this special assumption, would then have disrupted it, yet a whole series of specialized positions was at the same time necessary, for the free individuals to be civilized. And the irony is that both the special assumption, and the range of specialized positions, have become naturalized – though now more evidently incoherent – in all later phases of English culture. It is in this exact sense that this group of free individuals must be seen, finally, as a (civilizing) fraction of their class.

Notes

1 *Beginning Again*, London 1964, pp. 21, 23.
2 Ibid., p. 23.
3 Ibid., p. 22.
4 Ibid., pp. 34–5.
5 Idem, *Sowing*, London 1960, pp. 160–1.
6 Ibid., p. 164.
7 *Beginning Again*, p. 117.

8   Ibid., p. 74.
9   Ibid., p. 74.
10   Ibid., p. 75.
11   *Sowing*, p. 186.
12   *Beginning Again*, p. 23.
13   Ibid., p. 26.
14   Ibid., p. 36.
15   Clive Bell, *Art*, London 1914, p. 44.
16   *Mr Bennett and Mrs Brown*, London 1924, p. 18.
17   *Art*, p. 274–5.
18   Ibid., pp. 273–4.
19   Ibid., p. 275.

14

Crisis in English Studies

From New Left Review *129, 1981, pp. 51–66*

Recent events in Cambridge, of which some of you may have heard, have persuaded me to bring forward some material which I was preparing for a course of lectures in the autumn. Because the material was originally conceived on that scale, the prospect for this crowded hour can be considered daunting. But it seems important to try to set out a general position now, rather than leave so many of these issues in the air until they can be more fully examined. My main purpose is one of identifying and briefly explaining some currently controversial positions beyond the labels which are being so loosely attached, but I have a quite different argument to put in front of that, which seems to me to go to the centre of the controversy. Within both Marxism and structuralism there are diverse tendencies, and there is further diversity in other tendencies in part influenced by them. Several of these tendencies are in sharp opposition to each other. This has to be emphasized not only to prevent reductive labelling but for a more positive reason, that some of these tendencies are compatible with the existing dominant paradigm of literary studies while others are incompatible and have for some years been challenging the dominant paradigm – and thus its profession. I am using 'paradigm' broadly in Kuhn's sense of a working definition of a perceived field of knowledge, indeed of an *object of knowledge*, based on certain fundamental hypotheses, which carries with it definitions of appropriate methods of discovering and establishing such knowledge. Now the case of Literature seems to me exactly such a paradigm. Moreover, as Kuhn argued, such paradigms are never simply abandoned. Rather they accumulate anomalies until there is eventually a breaking point, and attempts are made to shift and replace the fundamental hypothesis, its definitions and what are by this stage the established professional standards and methods of enquiry. That evidently is a moment of crisis. I think it is where we now are, although at a relatively very early stage, in literary studies in Cambridge.

Of course the definition of an object of knowledge that is perceived in certain ways becomes hopelessly confused within any dominant paradigm with the object about which the knowledge is to be gained. This is clear now in some uses of the term 'Literature', which is, after all, in its most common general sense, not often *produced* by literary departments but is still held in some way to be possessed and defended by them. This takes variable forms. Thus it is said that it is our business to teach 'the canon of English literature'. This use of 'canon', borrowed from Biblical studies, where it meant a list of sacred writings accepted as authentic, is significant. For of course the 'canon of English Literature' is not given; it is produced. It is highly selected and in practice reselected. In its simplest version it was decisively challenged by Richards in his experiments in practical criticism. He showed that even highly trained students could be taught the canon but could not in majority produce for themselves its implicit valuations. Indeed, they often preferred writing which was well outside the canon. These findings forced the most effective modern redefinition of the paradigm, though it did not replace it. In this redefinition, Literature came to be paired with Criticism. For since, by contrast with Biblical studies, scholarship could not itself *establish* the literary canon (though it could do local verification inside it), a new process – critical judgement – had to be taught as the condition of retaining the defining idea of Literature.

Literature had once meant, at least until the early nineteenth century, a body of printed writings; indeed that neutral sense survives in such contexts as 'literary supplement' or 'literature stall'. This use, obviously, had the effect of a specialization to print, and this was quite generally appropriate to the period between the seventeenth and the early twentieth centuries, but then with certain anomalies. There was drama, which was writing not to be read but to be performed. There was what was called, from earlier periods, 'oral literature' – a strange and often misleading classification. There was eventually the problematic status of writing in modern forms such as broadcasting, film and revived oral production. But then increasingly through the nineteenth century there was further specialization of the term, based on what are now evidently anomalous categories. Literature came predominantly to mean 'imaginative writing' of novels and poems, in a difficult distinction from 'factual' or 'discursive' writing. It was not only that this tended to conceal the element of *writing*, the linguistic composition of facts and arguments, in the excluded ('discursive' or 'factual') areas; it was also that the relations assumed between 'imagination' and 'facts' for the other 'literary' cases were, while at times obvious, in many cases the very problem that had to be construed. That would have been difficult enough. But there was then a further specialization in which, so to speak, the category of 'Literature' censored itself. Not all literature – novels, poems, and plays – was Literature in that capital- letter category. An actual majority of novels, poems and plays were seen as not belonging to Literature, which was now in practice the selective category, and thus the received 'canon' established by criticism.

So, if someone now says: 'Literature is more important than all the isms', it can seem a persuasive idea when the *isms* are, for example, those strangers: Marxism and structuralism. But one *ism* does not so often get mentioned: *criticism*, which is now, by this redefinition of the paradigm, actually incorporated in 'Literature' itself (is indeed what defines it and can even come to dominate it). There is often then the paradox that what most people are actually doing in literary departments is criticism or critical scholarship, and that this is seen as a proper literary activity, though it is so unlike what others – writers of novels, poems, plays – are doing, always elsewhere.

So you have in sequence, first, a restriction to printed texts, then a narrowing to what are called 'imaginative' works, and then finally a circumscription to a critically established minority of 'canonical' texts. But also growing alongside this there is another and often more potent specialization: not just Literature, but English Literature. This is itself historically a late construction, since for medieval writing, at least to the seventeenth century, it is obviously uncertain. Is 'English' then the language or the country? If it is the language, there are also fifteen centuries of native writing in other languages: Latin, Welsh, Irish, Old English, Norman French. If it is not the language but the country, is that only 'England' or is it now also Ireland, Wales, Scotland, North America, Old and New 'Commonwealths'?

The idea of a 'national literature' is a historical production of great importance for a certain period. The term *Nationalliteratur* began in Germany in the 1780s, and histories of 'national literatures', with quite new perspectives and emphases from older and more general ideas of 'humane letters', were being written in German, French and English from the same period, in which there was a major change in ideas both of 'the nation' and of 'cultural nationality'. Subsequent historical developments, especially in our own century, have made these 'national' specializations uncertain, and have created anomalies which have to be temporarily regulated year by year by examination rubrics and so on. 'For the purposes of this paper, *English* should be taken to mean . . . ' In fact this is a very potent anomaly, since the question of 'Englishness', so often adducted in English literary studies, is now for obvious social and political reasons very critical, full of tense and often highly emotional problems of traditional identity and contemporary threat. Consider some current attitudes to some recent new work as 'French' or as 'Paris fashion'. These are not just descriptive terms but are used deliberately in a marking-off sense. What is often being defended, it seems, is not just a body of writing but a major projection from this, in which the actually very diverse works of writers in English are composed into a national identity – the more potent because it is largely from the past – in which a mood, a temper, a style, or a set of immediate 'principles' (which can be contrasted not only with 'theory' but with all other forms of reasoning) are being celebrated, taught and – where possible – administratively imposed. This is a long way from literature in the sense of active and diverse writing. Rather it is a stand, a last redoubt, from which much more general notions of Englishness, of values, of tradition are defended against all comers; until even native dissidents (to say nothing of all those foreigners) are seen not merely as different but as alien – speaking not our language but some incomprehensible jargon. It is not, so far as all the English are concerned, how most of them actually feel and think in the face of related problems of identity, stress and change. But among what can be called, with precision, traditional English literary intellectuals, it is not just a profession; it is and has sounded like a calling and a campaign. In its own field it is congruent with much more general reflexes and campaigns of the English ruling class as a whole, whose talk and propagation of 'heritage' have increased in proportion with their practical present failures.

   Now, for various reasons, both Marxism and structuralism, in their different ways, have impinged directly on the paradigm and on its anomalies. Indeed the surprising thing is that in so many of their actual tendencies they have been accommodated, or have accommodated themselves, *within* the paradigm, where they can be seen as simply diverse approaches to the same object of knowledge. They can then be taken as the guests, however occasionally untidy or unruly, of a decent pluralism. However, certain other tendencies are not so assimilable and are indeed quite incongruent with the received definition. It is these that are involved, not without dust and heat, in the current crisis. For this crisis is, above all, a crisis of the dominant paradigm and of its established professional standards and methods. Yet for the reasons just given, this acquires a resonance well beyond the terms of a professional dispute. It is, in the fullest sense, one of the key areas in which a very general cultural crisis is being defined and fought out.

   I will now go on to describe, briefly, the main and very diverse tendencies in Marxism, formalism and structuralism, as they bear on what by received habit we call literary studies. To know any of these properly needs much further study, but I want at least to identify them, and then briefly indicate, because this is now the crucial point, which of these tendencies are compatible with the paradigm – and thus with established professional arrangements – and which in my view are not.

In Marxism the first area to explore is that which is centred on the idea of 'reflection', in itself a very complex notion and used differentially within the Marxist tradition. It does historically represent the earliest application of Marxism to literary studies, but in three interestingly different ways.

First, there is that most general proposition in Marxism: that the whole movement of society is governed by certain dispositions of the means of production and that when these dispositions – forces and relations in a mode of production as a whole – change through the operation of their own laws and tendencies, then forms of consciousness and forms of intellectual and artistic production (forms which have their place in orthodox Marxist definition as a 'super-structure') change also. Some shift in relatively direct ways, like politics and law; some in distant and often indirect ways – the traditional examples are religion, philosophy and aesthetics. According to this Marxist version of the history of art and thought, changes at the most basic levels of the social order resonate in the most distant areas as people become conscious of these conflicts and in various ways fight them out.

This proposition has been endlessly argued about, most of all within the Marxist tradition itself. But in its relation to literary studies we can distinguish two versions: one rather crude, though it is still widely known (and often all that is known) as Marxism in literary studies; the other a good deal more sophisticated or appearing to be more sophisticated. The first crude version is this: if it is true that literary and intellectual production is, in the broadest sense, a reflection of fundamental conflicts in the social order, then the business of Marxists engaged in such studies is to identify the conflicting forces and then to distinguish (as was commonly done in the thirties) progressive kinds of writing and reactionary kinds of writing, to take positions about these, and, above all (for the emphasis was always more on production than on criticism), to find ways of producing new kinds of writing which correspond to the needs of the fundamental conflict.

This is – and not only in caricature – a very simple position. At its weakest it amounts to branding certain kinds of literature as good or bad according to their presumed political or historical tendency. More generally the literary argument is seen as dependent on an assumed total position or class world-view. These general truths, moreover, are conceived as coming first, and then being demonstrated and illustrated in literature. Not surprisingly, when this variant of Marxist interpretation encountered a much closer kind of literary analysis in the thirties, for example in Leavis (himself engaged and embroiled in moral and cultural discriminations within literature), it suffered a rather decisive defeat. It was seen as crude and reductionist, or as at best dogmatically selective.

And yet it has still to be said that no Marxist, however he/she redefines the terms of this general proposition of social determination, can wholly give it up without abandoning the Marxist tradition. The more modern forms of this argument in fact dispense with the idea of reflection. For even after it had been allowed that there are distances, that there are lags in time and so on, it is clear that too close and direct an a priori correspondence had been assumed between those things which could be historically identified as happening elsewhere in the social order, and actual literary production. So, instead of looking for those direct and obvious connections which could support the simple labelling of works as politically good or bad, or as representing this or that tendency or class, the general position was retained but with a radical redefinition of what the variable literary and aesthetic processes actually are. Eventually that became, at a later stage, a quite complex position; but I have mentioned the older version first, both because it is the most widely known and because, existing in crude as well as some more refined forms, it is at once challenging and difficult.

Now the second position which was constructed around the idea of reflection was really very much simpler. This turns out to be one of the wholly compatible tendencies, drawing on a very long tradition in literary thought, of the general idea of reflection, and indeed of the broader and more passive version of mimesis. (There is a quite different, active sense of *mimesis*, which is not reflection at all but a process of grasping, interpreting and changing.) This tendency defines valuable literture as that which reflects social reality, and its preferred method is realism: judging works of art by their fidelity to or illumination of otherwise observable social reality. And if this is the criterion, then there must be no external labelling of progressive and reactionary works. As Marx observed of Balzac (a man at the opposite political extreme from himself): precisely because Balzac represents the realities of French society he is important. He would have been a much inferior writer if he had attempted to turn this realistic representation towards what both Marx and Engels continuously attacked as 'tendency literature', in which instead of reflecting reality you to try to turn it in the direction of some political presupposition of your own. It was thus crucial in this tendency that the work reflected reality – reality as it was, however unwelcome.

But we have to allow something, perhaps a lot, for the fact that Marxism, as a general position, claims unique insights into the nature of this reality, or rather its fundamental laws. This can be very different, in practice, from the idea of reflecting any 'reality' that happens from time to time to exist. Yet that difference tends to concern primarily questions of *historical* argument. The method of literary analysis – the demonstration of a reflection of a state or process defined as its basis or context or background – usually remains compatible. For this is after all a very familiar position in all literary studies. People again and again actually ask, in more or less sophisticated ways, how this novel or that relates to some otherwise observable reality. Indeed this forms a very large part of the most orthodox research in criticism and scholarship. Thus one kind of 'Marxist' position, defended on its own grounds, is in practice nearly always compatible with much more widely approved and justified methods.

So also, I believe, is the third version of the reflection theory, which becomes particularly apparent in the work of Lukács – the previous phases having been primarily represented by Plekhanov. Lukács argued that we can take a deceptively simple view of the relation between a work of art and reality, because the reflection of reality *in its immediately apprehensible form* may be either insufficient or indeed illusory. Hence that definition of realism which Lukács eventually embraced: a definition harder in some ways to defend theoretically than the previous positions, for it said that the task of the writer is to reflect underlying *movements*. This is where the previous point, about the privileged insights of Marxism, becomes much more salient, for the 'underlying movement' tends to belong to the 'laws', to privileged analysis, and thus looks very different from the citation of empirical detail within a Marxist or any other perspective. Yet it is also an attempt to move beyond these empirical simplicities, in a way related to other attempts to show an indirect or a penetrating or an ideal relation between 'what happened' and what writers 'have made of it'. Hence Lukács' attack on naturalism, which (it was said) simply reflects the appearance of things as they are, the immediately accessible reality. The alternative to naturalism is a *realism* which, while faithful to the contemporary reality which is its subject, is concerned above all to discern the underlying movements in it. Great stress is then put on realism as a *dynamic* rather than a static category. Lukács's accounts of the historical novel or the changing forms of drama are cast in those terms. Yet interestingly, when quite different kinds of writing were developed in the twentieth century to represent, precisely, dynamic movement – as, for example, Brecht – Lukács attacked them: indeed, he tended to remain deeply attached to that older version of realism as reflecting and illuminating a general, and generally knowable, reality.

Now, for a long time the Marxist contribution to literary studies – at least in work available in English – was represented by reflection theory. But already from the 1920s a very different definition of literary production and its social relations had been developing within Marxism. This was centred not on 'reflection' but on what appears to be the quite different concept of 'mediation.' Actually the first sense of 'mediation' is not much more than a recognition of the more refined sense of 'reflection'. It accepts that it is misleading to look in literature for the 'reflection of reality.' Necessarily, by its construction as literature, reality becomes mediated in certain definite ways. This is again a perfectly familiar and even orthodox proposition within literary studies. It is not far from Eliot's notion of an 'objective correlative', although it starts at the other end of the process. But it is concerned above all to refute the reductive versions of the earlier phases, in which you could look for untransformed content. Significantly the great arguments about 'mediation' took place about Kafka. Because here was a kind of writing which either had to be rejected on the simplest premisses of reflection theory – the 'sick fantasies of a decadent class'; 'pessimistic and subjectivist lucubrations, far removed from the active and vigorous life of the people' – or *interpreted* by different versions of the idea of mediation. I must resist the temptation to give detailed examples of the different readings of Kafka – as the fiction of alienation, of bureaucracy, of declining imperialism, of Jewishness in the diaspora, of the Oedipus complex, of fatal illness, and so on – which came out of these different versions of mediation, but they are in the record. Still, however, the earliest sense of mediation is only a refinement of the idea of reflection, and I must briefly mention three other senses.

First there is the very interesting notion developed by Walter Benjamin in the 1930s: the idea of *correspondences*. This is a decisive shift, because Benjamin does not argue that a work of literature is the literary transformation of some element of reality. Rather, there is an observable 'correspondence' between certain kinds of writing and certain other contemporary social and economic practices. The most famous example is his long analysis of Baudelaire, where he argues that certain new conditions in the city, leading to new forms of the 'crowd' and within these to the redefinition of 'the individual', produced a number of new forms of writing, including Baudelaire's. There the reference is not to an otherwise existing, otherwise observable social reality, which the literature 'reflects' or even 'mediates', but to the fact of an observed correspondence between the nature and form of the literary activity and the nature and form of other contemporary practices of a more general kind.

Benjamin came to be close to the important ideas of the Frankfurt School, though he fell out on just this point with Adorno, who went much further in use of the idea of mediation. Adorno argued that correspondences of *content*, let alone reflections or mediations of content, are basically irrelevant to art. Indeed, the presence of such correspondences or reflections is virtually a guarantee that the art is not authentic. Art is produced – and this was his contribution to the Kafka argument – by a process which he called the discovery of 'dialectical images', which had no possibility of being discovered or expressed in any other form. The 'dialectical image' arose within the processes of art, and when created, although it might by analysis be related to the whole structure within which it was formed, was never overtly or directly related. Indeed the condition of its success as art was that it achieved an *autonomous* existence.

This is a sense of mediation which eventually connects with forms of literary structuralism. Lucien Goldmann, in his studies first of the French classical drama, particularly Racine, and then in work on the nineteenth-and twentieth-century novel, produced a position which still further widened the category of mediation: correspondence was never a relation of content, but always of *form*. He said, further, that it is only in secondary or inferior literature that vulgar sociologists, as he tended to call them, look for and find their simple relations between literature and society or reality. On the contrary, he argued, what is reflected in those works is merely the contradictory and *unachieved* consciousness of the time. The deep consciousness of the time is achieved only in certain major works and is achieved by them in their form and not in their content. This is the whole thrust of the analysis of Racine, although I must say that he does not always keep to his own prescriptions. Nevertheless, the proposition is that the correspondence, the mediation, is entirely a matter of the *form*. A certain disposition of human relationships is always present as the deepest consciousness of a particular epoch, and this disposition is homologous with a specific ordering of the elements of the literary work. Goldmann called this position 'genetic structuralism'. This was a deliberate opposition to orthodox structuralism because he argued that if we are to understand such forms, we must under- stand them in their processes of building up, stabilizing and breaking down; whereas in other tendencies of structuralism, there was a rejection of any notion of that kind of *historical* genesis and dissolution.

It would now be convenient to pass at once to literary structuralism, but from the real history of the case we have to make a detour through formalism. For there can be no doubt that formalism – both the early work of the Russian formalists as well as the later developments in emigration in the United States and then France – has had a more practical effect on literary studies that are now broadly grouped as 'structuralist' than that more general structuralism which is active in other disciplines, especially in anthropology. Brevity here is especially constraining, but the key démarche of the formalists was a new definition of *literariness*. Indeed they were reacting precisely against the modes of study, or most of the modes of study, that I have previously described. At first, they were reacting within a specifically Russian context, in which these theories, Marxist and related, were very active and current. The formalists said: the crucial omission you are making is that quality which makes a work *literary*. This is not to be found in what you are enquiring into, which is the relation of the work to something else. The central question, necessarily, is what makes this precise work literary. It was thus the formalists who began to use, with a quite new emphasis, the notion of '*literary language*' which one still so often hears.

It doesn't make for clarity that there are of course also much older concepts of 'literary language': either of a kind of language appropriate to the elevated processes of literature, or of a standard of correctness by which all other usage can be judged. Those are old and often now merely conservative positions. Moreover the former, in the fixed modes into which it tended to settle down, was again and again challenged and often effectively overthrown by writers, who in certain periods consciously rejected received 'literary' or 'poetic' diction, and tried to restore relations with the popular and 'living language'. We have always in practice to look to historical evidence about actual and changing ways of writing, and about its changing social relations, if we are to get very far with the notion of a 'literary language' as distinct from the more general uses of language. It can be the problem of the relations between speech and print, or between elevated and popular forms, or, still, it can be an inherent problem in the modes of any conscious composition.

The formalist emphasis had very little to do with the more familiar positions of conservation or elevation. On the contrary, what they proposed was a revolutionary break, as the condition of any authentic literature (the most influential position) or as a condition necessary in their own time, as 'classical' modes broke down. These two arguments still need to be clearly distinguished, but what the early formalists proposed was a conscious estrangement in language, a deliberate break from ordinary language use. This is what in practice always happens when a work announces itself as literary. Either in its most specific uses of words, or in some break with the conventions and perspectives from which a particular subject matter is ordinarily seen, it makes the jump to literature, to the 'literary'. And then the business of the analyst is to trace precisely those breaks which constitute the literariness of the work.

This position is very productive. The argument between the formalists and more traditional Marxists has been, I believe, very important. Moreover, from about 1925, there is a less well- known development of formalism of a kind which has taken the argument into a quite new stage. Yet compared with people who know formalism as the early work of Eichenbaum, Shklovsky and so on, there are far fewer who are familiar with Volosinov or Bakhtin or Mukarovsky. But it was the work of these later formalists, with their inquiries into general or universal 'literariness', which transformed the whole argument about the study of literature, and in the end, the status of the paradigm itself. This late stage was indeed a social and historical formalism, because it was concerned not only with a general definition of literariness, but with the changing conditions in which 'literariness' – now in its turn a dynamic concept – is achieved by particular writers, as well as with much wider processes of historical and social development.

Consider Volosinov for example. His work remained virtually forgotten for fifty years (he was writing in the late twenties and there are many who believe that he was only ever a pen-name of Bakhtin). Deeply influenced by the new school of structural linguistics and accepting the analysis of language as analysis of a system of signs, Volosinov nevertheless insisted that language is at once a system of signs and a *socially produced* system of signs. He further argued that verbal signs are always 'multi-accentual'. He could thus reject those conceptions of a 'system' that were being offered by structural linguistics – as well as by psychoanalysis – in which certain rules of the system produce meanings and forms. For in real social and historical life there is constant systematic production and yet this is also a constantly open production. It is then possible to place 'literariness' within the open potential of a language, which is both generally and specifically available.

This is a decisive break with earlier formalism. While emphasizing what the formalists indicated as distinctive about literary language, it does not restrict linguistic generation and regeneration to works of literature. The process of language itself is a continual possibility of shift and change and initiation of meanings, and this range of possibility is embedded in the 'rules' of both the linguistic and the social system. The work of Bakhtin himself, especially in his study of Rabelais, had indicated the beginning of a certain new kind of literariness – and thus an *historical* literariness – by observing the interaction and the creative surpassing both of modes of folk literature, which had traditionally been present, and of the polite literature which had come down within a more limited and conservative social tradition. It was precisely in the interaction of those received and different traditions that a new indication of what it was to be literary was formed.

All this is very different from the early formalists with their more local stress on what makes language literary, such as the local use of 'devices'. It is an historical indication of how specific kinds of literariness come into social practice. There is then Mukarovsky, who is perhaps the most serious reviser of the original formalist positions; indeed his work points towards some of the later most incongruent and incompatible kinds of analysis. Mukarovsky argued devastatingly (although in the end not quite carrying the argument through) that aesthetic quality is not even primarily produced *within* a work of art. He thus moved away from aesthetic formalism, which had looked inside the work for indications that it was literary or was intended for aesthetic response. On the contrary, he said, the aesthetic indications, and thus the aesthetic norms and aesthetic values, are themselves always *socially* produced. There are changing indications of what is and is not to be regarded as art and of what is and is not to be regarded as art of a certain kind. Although these indications bear on the internal organization of the work, they are always much more widely operative and have a history.

It is very significant that from the late fifties in the USA and in France, the body of work that was first translated and became influential was the work of the early formalists, and the later more social and historical work was comparatively little known until much later. This had serious effects on the way in which certain formalist positions were developed in literary analysis. The most limited (though in local terms still impressive) kind of formalist analysis became the dominant form which was believed to correspond, in literature, with what was by this time called 'structuralist' methodology in anthropology, in linguistics and in psychoanalysis. This is why it is still difficult to understand the relations between structuralism, in its full general sense, and what are often much more local literary positions. Yet there were of course some connections.

One of the most common tendencies in structuralism, of notable value in anthropology and in linguistics, is that it refuses to interpret an event in its own isolated terms or in its immediate form of presentation. It seeks, rather, to locate an event, a relationship or a sign within a whole signifying system. Such systems are governed by their own *internal* rules: a position initially reached as a creative solution to the problems, in the field, of studying languages organized by quite different notions of syntax from any that were available within the Indo-European tradition. Instead of appropriating the novel event to an already known system, the attempt was made to find its meaning within a specific structural system: in practice by the relations of this unit to other units, and then the discovery of the general internal rules of the specific system.

What would such a procedure involve in literary studies? First, there is the possibility of some direct transfer from structuralist linguistics. Indeed, this has promoted certain refined techniques of analysis which are increasingly being practised, though still looked at with suspicion by the older literary departments. There is stylistics, for example, but much more important is discourse analysis, often at a certain evident distance from the ordinary language of literary analysis but often also commanding a more precise vocabulary in the analysis of syntactic forms, or in the identification of the narrator of the speaker and the relation between speakers. Some of this passed into literary studies a number of years ago and is available, as one technique among others, in fairly ordinary procedures of literary analysis.

More generally, however, the notion of an internal rule- governed system was easily applicable; indeed it was in some ways directly congruent with a position that had already been reached without reference to structuralism within literary studies itself. When this tendency in literary structuralism appeared as an import from France in the sixties, I even risked saying that it seemed strange only because it was a long-lost cousin who had emigrated from Cambridge in the late twenties and early thirties. That was not in fact its only source. Yet there is at least an indirect inheritance from the kind of thinking which Richards had been doing about the isolated internal organization of a poem. And this was especially apparent when you looked at where the cousin had been: in North American New Criticism. What had happened in Cambridge was, by contrast, a confused but striking association of moral and indeed normative judgement with these techniques of isolated internal analysis. This was regarded elsewhere as an unfortunate impurity and a deviation from the only relevant discipline, which was the analysis of a specific verbal organization; indeed the object as in itself it really is, an ironic echo in this context. Either way the local techniques were or could quickly become familiar in literary analysis, where they were directed, constitutionally and very respectably, to analysing the internal organization of *the* text, *the* poem.

This kind of literary structuralism is not only congruent with the paradigm which I began by describing. It is the paradigm itself in its most influential modern form. And indeed whether it is genuinely structuralist is a necessary question. In its usual forms it is so obstinately local and technical, so little concerned with any wide or general systemic properties, that it barely deserves the name. What can much more reasonably be called 'structuralist', in cultural studies, is that work which analyses internal organization not as an end in itself – the acquisition of competence in reading – but as the necessary way of analysing, and thus distinguishing, specific or systemic *forms*. Thus Goldmann's work on dramatic forms, and much current work on narrative forms, are attempts to discover the rules, the structural rules, of specific general forms of drama or fiction. This is very different from the more local technical analysis taken from linguistics. It is an application of the fundamental structuralist idea to problems of form which have indeed been profoundly neglected in literary studies. In Goldmann's case such analysis is at once formal and historical – there are historically changing forms. However, in many more centrally structuralist interventions it has been believed, in ways resembling much older theories of literary genres, that there are discoverable rules of general literary organization: of 'Narrative' as such, 'Drama' as such, and so on. It is an important kind of project, but typically it often unites an extremely local technicism, of internal analysis, with extremely broad categories – deliberately unhistorical and comprising aesthetic or psychological abstractions – as the 'structures' to which all detail relates.

A third kind of 'literary structuralism' is the work influenced by the largely philosophical arguments of Louis Althusser. These came into literary analysis through his pupil Pierre Macherey and are represented in this country by, for example, Terry Eagleton's *Criticism and Ideology*. This is a quite different tendency. It says: certainly society, the social order, is a rule-governed system, but above all it is a system of systems, determined in the last instance by the economy. Within this general determination each practice – such as writing – has an important relative autonomy. Yet it is still a part, and must ultimately be perceived as a part, of a wider system to which it cannot be reduced but to which it must ultimately be related. How in practice is this relation handled and demonstrated? It is through what is seen as the binding force of the whole system: ideology. Ideology is very much more, here, than the ideas and beliefs of particular classes or groups. It is in effect, with only limited exceptions, the condition of all conscious life. Thus the area to which most students of literature normally refer their reading and their judgement, that area summarized in the decisive term 'experience', has in fact to be seen as within the sphere of ideology. Indeed, experience is seen as the most common form of ideology. It is where the deep structures of the society actually reproduce themselves as conscious life. Ideology is indeed so pervasive and so impenetrable, in this account, that you wonder who is ever going to be able to analyse it. But there is a precedent, after all, in the case of the Unconscious, with which it has certain close connections and analogies. There is an absolute unconscious, psychoanalysis says, but there are also discoverable techniques of penetration and understanding. In the case of Althusser, the leading technique of penetration is theory. Only theory can fully escape ideology. But there is also, in the case of literature, a relatively privileged situation. Literature is not just a carrier of ideology, as in most forms of reflection theory. It is inescapably ideological, but its specific relative autonomy is that it is a form of writing, a form of practice, in which ideology both exists and is or can be internally distanced and questioned. Thus the value of literature is precisely that it is one of the areas where the grip of ideology is or can be loosened, because although it cannot escape ideological construction, the point about its literariness is that it is a continual questioning of it internally. So you get readings which are very similar to certain recent semiotic readings, where you construct a text and subtext, where you can say 'this is what is reproduced from the ideology'; but also, 'this is what is incongruously happening in the text which undermines or questions or in certain cases entirely subverts it'. This method has been used in very detailed and interesting analysis.

Then, finally, there is a tendency which undoubtedly has a relation to structuralism, certainly to structural linguistics, yet which – validly in my opinion – denies that it is a structuralism. This is what is now called semiotics. Semiotics in general is, without doubt, a true natural child of structuralism. It is a science of signs and a science of systems of signs (not confined to language). Meanings are construed not by their apparent content but by their relations within a general system of signification. In recent semiotics, this kind of analysis has been vigorously extended to advertising, to film, to photo- journalism and in the case of Barthes to fashion. If you have this fundamental procedure of reading a system of signs – of which the meanings do not simply disclose themselves, but have to be constructed by understanding their place in a system which is never itself disclosed, which indeed always has to be *read* – then you have something which although it begins within structuralism can become in some of its later work separable from it. Thus instead of seeing literary works as *produced* by the system of signs, which has been the central emphasis of the most orthodox structuralism, this later semiotics has on the contrary emphasized that productive systems have themselves always to be constituted and reconstituted, and that because of this there is a perpetual battle about the fixed character of the sign and about the systems which we ordinarily bring to production and interpretation. One effect of this shift is a new sense of 'deconstruction': not the technical analysis of an internal organization to show where all the parts, the components, have come from, but a much more open and active process which is continually taking examples apart, as a way of taking their *systems* apart. It is clearly in this sense a much more explosive tendency than any of the other tendencies within structuralism. It is not simply demonstrating the operation of systematic rules in ways which can settle down as competences within the paradigm. On the contrary, whether it is analysing literature or television or physical representation, it is looking not for the academically explanatory system, but for the system as a mode of formation, which as it becomes visible can be put into question or quite practically rejected. In that sense the whole impulse of this radical semiotics is very different from the structuralist version of production and reproduction which has been much more widely influential – and more welcome and at home – in literary studies.

I now want to say that in recent years there has been an observable moving together of two positions which started a long way apart. I can perhaps best illustrate this in my own case. Much of the literary work I have done, with I think two or three exceptions, can be read as compatible with what I called at the beginning the dominant literary paradigm. That is to say, it is work which may be approaching the analysis and judgement of literature with an exceptionally strong consciousness of the social determinants upon it, but the centre of literary attention is still there, and the procedures are judgement, explanation, verification in terms of historical explanation, and so on. One work, however, of which this cannot be true is *The Country and the City*, which is in fact very near that first Marxist position I described, because it sets out to identify certain characteristic forms of writing about the country and the city, and then insists on placing them not only in their historical background – which is within the paradigm – but within an active, conflicting historical process in which the very forms are created by social relations which are sometimes evident and sometimes occluded. So that is in any reading a break.

But of course there was other work, going back especially to *The Long Revolution*, which had not been perceived as within literary studies at all but which can now evidently be seen as a shift of emphasis which would end by rejecting the dominant paradigm. I mean especially the work on the social history of English writers, the social history of dramatic forms, the growth of standard English, and also the new positions on what is necessary in the analysis of culture. A further shift was apparent in the work on communications, on television, on technologies and cultural forms, and on the sociology of culture, although these were again typically seen as a separate interest outside English or literary studies. Now all this came together for me around 1970 and from that time I developed a more explicit theoretical position which I eventually described in *Marxism and Literature* as 'cultural materialism'. This is of course outside the paradigm altogether, but it is not the case that it has moved away from the ultimate common concern, the works about which knowledge is to be gained. It has moved much wider than literature in its paradigmatic sense, but it still centrally includes these major forms of writing, which are now being read, along with other writing, in a different perspective. Cultural materialism is the analysis of all forms of signification, including quite centrally writing, within the actual means and conditions of their production.

It was here, perhaps to our mutual surprise, that my work found new points of contact with certain work in more recent semiotics. There were still radical differences, especially in their reliance on structural linguistics and psycho-analysis, in particular forms; but I remember saying that a fully historical semiotics would be very much the same thing as cultural materialism, and I was glad to see certain tendencies in this direction, as distinct from some of the narrower structuralist displacements of history. I could see also that some of the simpler positions of early structural linguistics could be modified by new emphases on the social and historical production of signifying systems, as in Volosinov and the social formalists. There remained the problem of the bear-ings of psychoanalysis, where there were still radical differences, but on the other hand I knew that Marxism had been generally weak in this area of the problems of subjectivity, and there might now be a radical new dimension of enquiry, testing evidence and propositions in this area which is so evidently important in the production of meanings and values. Thus in practice two different kinds of work were now in touch with each other and were de-veloping in some cases very constructively. Perhaps we were so involved in this in Cambridge that we forgot that while we pushed on in these ways the older paradigm was still there and was still institutionally powerful, though the anomalies by this time were quite evidently disorganizing it even at the most practical levels. Some new work was being included to cover the anomalies, but the result was then incoherent from most points of view.

So I come back at last to my original argument. Most actual Marxist and structuralist tendencies are and have been, however locally unfamiliar or crudely identifiable as strange and partisan, compatible or even congruent in a broad sense with the orthodox paradigm, especially in its practically loosened and eclectically incoherent form. Certain others, however, are not; and most specifically that first position in Marxism, which instead of privileging a generalized Literature as an independent source of values insists on relating the actual variety of literature to historical processes in which fundamental *conflicts* had necessarily occurred and were still occurring. That was the sense and the challenge of the *The Country and the City*. The other positions that are not compatible with the paradigm and its professional organization are cultural materialism and radical semiotics. For these necessarily include the paradigm itself as a matter for analysis, rather than as a governing definition of the object of knowledge.

It is necessary to insist on these distinctions. What their institutional consequences may be it is much too early to say. In some other universities and in some of the new higher education institutions the shift from the old paradigm has already in whole or in part occurred. Yet it still matters very much what happens in the older, more established institutions. In Cambridge especially we have to ask a hard question: can radically different work still be carried on under a single heading or department when there is not just diversity of approach but more serious and fundamental differences about the object of knowledge (despite overlapping of the actual material of study)? Or must there be some wider reorganization of the received divisions of the humanities, the human sciences, into newly defined and newly collaborative arrangements? This is what now must be faced in what is also, for other reasons, a frozen – indeed a pinched – climate. All that we can be certain that we can and must do is to clarify, very openly, the major underlying intellectual issues.

15

Writing, Speech and the 'Classical'

From Raymond Williams (1989) What I Came to Say *(ed. F. Mulhern) London: Hutchinson Radius*

The ideal of the 'classical' has been so closely associated, historically, both with the practice of writing and with the facts of educational and civil authority, that it should not be surprising that it now faces major difficulties. To those of us whose working lives have been centrally concerned with writing, the second half of this conventionally numbered twentieth century has brought many surprises. Among some these changes have occasioned distress. The old authority of writing, and more specifically of print, has in many areas been by-passed by what seem more ephemeral or more doubtful forms. 'I saw it on television', as a warrant of authority, is now more common than the comparable 'I saw it in the newspaper', though by some the authority of either ought still to be questioned. In some areas of education, prolonged practice in composition and analysis is being reduced or replaced by oral exercises, often supplemented by tests of written or at least inscribed response which closely resemble or actually are the filling-in of forms: 'delete where appropriate'; 'tick this box'.

It is then easy to feel that a long literate tradition, carrying so many of the achievements and also the hopes of civilisation, is in real danger. Many children, it is said, are already more skilled at a computer keyboard than with a pen. Modern writing, except in certain specialised areas, has rejected what it calls the longwinded in favour of the notably short and sharp breathed. The complex constructions of many older forms of writing are rejected in favour of the running impromptu of the colloquial. And if this is so, some argue, the rising generations, again apart from a few barely tolerated specialists, will be effectively cut off from that great body of writing, in a number of languages, which we have had good reason to call 'classical'.

It was obvious that the effects of these changes would be felt first among those responsible for the learning and teaching of the old classical languages. Latin has been dislodged from its position as a general requirement for entry into higher education. Greek, which never had the same privileged connections with civil authority, in the churches and lawcourts, has been pushed even further away. Yet some comparable effects have been noticed in the teaching of even English literature, and have worked their way, though less noticed, into the teaching – or should one say the abandonment of teaching, even in the English Faculties of many universities – of the English language itself. Certainly some forms of English writing, of earlier centuries, appear to have become more difficult to understand, if only because of a general lack of terms to describe, with any accuracy, forms of writing other than the contemporary or relatively recent.

It is from this general sense of a great literate tradition now under major threat that many who once associated literacy with high liberal virtues and aspirations, to say nothing of more recognisable conservatives, whose privileged learning is readily identified, at least by themselves, as a last bastion of civilisation, and who in this sense are even proud to be known as reactionary, gather what strength they can to resist the strong tides of contemporary social development, or if that is not possible at least to preserve some areas, some places of storage of learning and practice, from what they have precedents to call the barbarian onslaught.

If I do not stand with them, in the terms which they have announced – simple adhesion to what they call the 'classical', a simple affiliation to what they significantly call the 'canon' – it is not that my educational history, and indeed much of my working life, has not been bound up with theirs. In that sense I am indeed, by presumption, of their party, and we all know that the most bitter responses are regularly reserved for those who, presumed to be of a certain party and having appeared to gain advantages from it, nevertheless refuse to join it. I have often put the charge to myself, since I know that if I had not been good at school Latin I would not, from a working-class family, have entered the kind of higher education which led to my writing *The Long Revolution* and other similarly subversive works. It was not for that, it could be said, that my Latin master took me patiently through the *Georgics*, though as it happens his choice of text – for I was by that stage his only pupil – was made because he knew that my father supplemented his earnings as a railwayman by the extensive keeping of bees and by selling their honey in Abergavenny market, just down the road from the Grammar School. I wish I could say that anything I learned improved his beekeeping. It went much more into an increasingly distancing education. Yet there was one deeper lesson, though it took many years to understand. The skills of learning and of literature were not self-evidently distant from everyday labour. If they were being made to appear so, that was a fact about our educational system and, this being construed, about our social and economic system, with which the skills and the materials of learning should not be, as so often, glibly identified. I could of course see one all too probable end of that line of thinking: that resentment of these systems might eventually lead to rejecting or diminishing the skills and materials thus traditionally identified with them. Indeed, at university, I was taught that perspective: that the masses were coming, and that they would trample and destroy the fine fields of culture. On this I can only repeat what I wrote in *Culture and Society*, recalling that curious incident of the dog in the night. For the trampling which has indeed happened, and which is of course still happening, with ever more resolute and destructive thuds, did not after all come from them. It came from very different people, seeing profit rather than privilege in the exploitation of learning and eventually, by that criterion, seeing little or no profit in that humane and literate tradition which, from their narrowed understanding of a society and even of an economy, they found increasingly irrelevant and even, in its practical offering of so many diverse and alternative values, dangerous.

Yet what might then be said is that we should, as a party, as a profession, stand also against them. Whoever may be controlling these dangerous tides, it is our plain duty to resist them. I can go along with that, some of the way, in the most immediate terms, but my most general position is quite different. I believe that what must really be done, precisely from our own learning and skills, and in a much wider collaboration of the humanities than has yet been realised or even convincingly proposed, is to understand, in some new ways, what the traditions of learning and of literacy really are, and from this to find new directions for an extending practice, which our rapidly changing, indeed dislocating, society is going, on its life, to require.

One of the central problems of this necessary and now urgent reconsideration is a better understanding of the relations between writing and speech. There is a moment in the *Annals* of Tacitus (XIV, 30) which for me, a Welshman reading it after some nineteen centuries, clearly dramatises the problem. There is also a different but even more revealing moment in his *Agricola*, xxx, to which I shall return.

The point of the confrontation between the Roman army under Suetonius and the Britons crowded on what is now the island of Anglesey is quickly registered. We are not likely to forget the contrast between the scared but disciplined soldiers and, on the opposite shore, the troop of frenzied women and the Druids lifting up their hands to heaven and pouring forth dreadful imprecations. Yet what is now most striking is that this is widely represented and read as a confrontation, a violent contrast, between civilisation and barbarism, with the Britons as the barbarians, when the truth of the local case is almost exactly the reverse. It can of course be argued that behind those soldiers, who crossed the straits to kill and burn and destroy, was a high material civilisation, stretching back to the gathered and tributary wealth of Rome. Yet what was actually being destroyed on Anglesey was a distinctive native culture, with its own highly organised order of scholars, philosophers, poets and priests. It is always very difficult to see such an event, of which we have seen a hundred examples in later imperialisms, from any point of view but that of the effective conqueror. I have sometimes tried to imagine the arrival of an alien army, black or red, on the banks of Cam or Isis, and the accounts that might be given of the curiously named Dons, pouring forth in their robes and uttering dreadful imprecations. That the implied comparison can appear absurd is my point. For while there can be little doubt that, by the standards of their time, the learned order of the Celts was highly skilled in natural philosophy and in oral poetry, what it lacked was writing, and that deficit, as in many other comparable cases, has been decisive. It is not that writing alone can be made the test of a highly developed learned and artistic culture. It is that once it is introduced it confers quite disproportionate advantages on those who possess it. Theirs, above all, is the record and, if we are not careful, the verdict of history. In the history of Britain this has been especially marked. Gildas, in the sixth century, seems not to know that there had been a life of his people before the Romans arrived. His ignorance is still echoed today, qualified only, in popular accounts, by vague images of savages in skins and woad, or even, often confused with them, comparably traduced cavemen. Through most of the Middle Ages extraordinary pseudo-histories, reaching an intensity of influence in my neighbour Geoffrey of Monmouth, took as their point of origin a misreading and then an extrapolation within a frame of reference which had been defined by a version of classical literature. The false etymology of Brut and the Britons was to be joined by the fantasy of the British Israelites, from that other body of sacred and authoritative texts, in the Judaeo/Christian tradition. It is a terrible irony that writing, until our own century incomparably the greatest skill of accurate record, should so often, within the realities of historical conquest and repression, have become a medium of obscurantism and falsification. And it is this fact which should now be a challenge to those of us who belong and are committed to the high literate tradition.

It is true that inspired, to an important degree, by classical and Judaeo/Christian texts, there is now a growing body of evidence of a different, non-literate kind. The evidence of archaeology, difficult as it must often be, is bringing us much nearer to an adequate understanding of that long and vast and diverse human history which is before and beyond writing. It is there, for example, in our own country, that we find apparent evidence of an even earlier, mathematically-skilled learned class, in the British Neolithic: two millennia before the Roman legions as they are two millennia before ourselves. All this is of great importance, and we can recall Marx and Engels saying that material evidence should always be preferred to literary records. Yet we have only to look at hard material evidence which has no written accompaniments to realise the limitations of their polemical point. The central example is that of the great cave paintings: major works of art if indeed, in a modern category, that is how they should be described; major human achievements, by any category or standard; yet liable, as we have seen, in the absence of any but the most general contextual evidence, to extraordinary variations of qualified interpretation, from primitive magic to target practice; few willing, it seems, to accept more directly what human hands find joy in making, by material practice, in paint or in stone or in ink.

Thus the point should never be to oppose literacy to the range of other major human skills, for a judgment either way. We have seen the disproportionate historical advantages of literate societies, but not all of these would have been realised, to their current extent, if they had not, to put it bluntly, been carried by force of arms. We have seen this clearly enough in the last five centuries, when European forces arrived in the rest of the world with both guns and texts. At a late point in that long and bloody process, after centuries of written tales of the eccentricities and barbarisms of those being attacked, there was an exceptionally interesting moment, in which what might be called the liberal mind, formed in the complex development of its own metropolitan culture, looked at and listened to the barbarians and found them fully human. This went through many phases: the important contacts with Sanskrit, for example, and with the Hindu grammarians, which were to be so vital an element in the great nineteenth-century development of European philology; or the methodological problems of the Amerindian languages, which contributed to a major new turn in linguistics. The more general contact, in our own time, with other great ancient cultures, including some notably literate, should have altered, permanently, our derived and limited sense of the canon of human civilisation as defined by our own texts, our 'humanities'.

Yet there is one particularly interesting phase of what I have called the liberal mind, when the effort is made, within a complex and sophisticated minority culture, to see the process the other way round, from the other side. The classic case of this, in English, is, I suppose, E. M. Forster's Passage to India. There are also the African novels of Joyce Cary. It is then worth adding at once that this liberal mind, at its best, is no substitute for the direct voice or writing which is really from the other side. We have been learning this, in interesting and deeply challenging ways, in the important and developing work of the Indian and West African and East African novelists. Yet this is at a time of a general development of literacy, in the metropolitan but also in many mother tongues. From the period of classical literature we do not have such benefits, and it is this consideration which makes puzzling for me, though it seems not for many others, that moment in the *Agricola* of Tacitus when Calgacus denounces imperialism, in words of a concentrated power which I find without equal: indeed in what can be properly called a classical statement of human values.

Raptores orbis: the Latin words still have more power than any translation I have seen: *brigands du monde*, as a French translation has it; *plunderers of the earth*, as an English. *Raptores orbis*: it is that unforgettable underlying image of hands seizing the round globe itself that, as I read it, is the source of the power. *Auferre, trucidare, rapere falsis nominibus imperium, atque ubi solitudinem faciunt, pacem appellant*. Again this surpasses the available translations. One part of the sentence has been extracted and widely quoted, with the common versions of making a wilderness of a desert and calling it peace. But it is the exposure of the double falsehood which should strike home. It is the linkage of *imperium* and *pacem*, the two false names, which should count. It goes much further than Proudhon's revolutionary challenge, *property is theft*, for here are the received conditions of civilisation, ordered government and peace, seen as covering, with false names, the real practices of theft, massacre and rape.

In their original power these are Latin words: spoken, *in hunc modum* – which may be the decisive point – by a man with a good Celtic name, Calgacus, Swordsman, before a battle somewhere west of Aberdeen, at Mons Graupius which might be Sillyean Hill east of Keith, and the Britons with their backs to the sea. Within the discriminating advantages of literacy, which archaeology in any such case can only track, that is in effect all we know.

Yet in a different sense how much it is then that we know, or can know. For what I find remarkable, within the common practice of including set speeches in narrations, is the power of this speech to surpass its occasion. It is inserted, we remember, within what is in effect a eulogy of Agricola, and nothing of that emphasis is withdrawn. Agricola's countering speech is in character with the eulogy: firm, experienced, practical, successful: prudent and moderate, as Tacitus summarises: 'a good man you would have readily believed him, and been glad to have found he was a great man'. Yet what the speech of such a man counters is not the distantly reported 'dreadful imprecations', with their impression of wild barbarism, but a close, sinewy, classical statement of the virtues of civilisation – liberty, community, justice, a plain-living self-respect – and these brought to a climax within the terrible necessity of opposing their destroyers, the *raptores orbis*.

What is usually said, as I have followed it, is that Tacitus the practised lawyer and orator is extending his skills, in this studied piece of writing, even to the speech of an enemy of Rome. Others couple this with the argument that in thus humanising the enemy, as perhaps also in the *Germania*, he is representing the old senatorial virtues against the tyranny and corruption of that stage of the Empire from which Agricola, though serving it, had suffered. I take these points, but still the actual speech of Calgacus surpasses them: his is a universal statement against the whole project that was the reputed glory of Rome. It would be good to be able to believe that what Calgacus says is really the voice of that conquered British civilisation. But we have no way of knowing that, even when we seem to hear the same voice centuries later, in the earliest Welsh poetry, where among the braggadocio of military valour and the flattery of tyrants we catch also the sad sound of a different idea of humanity, including the experience of humanity in defeat, as in Aneirin. Whether there was indeed any such continuity, or whether if there was Tacitus could have known of it, we are unable to say, barred for all time by that single deficit in writing.

Yet what we may be able to say is that we can see here, very clearly, what is really comprehended by the idea of *humanitas*. The word, as in another passage Tacitus reminds us, is easily misunderstood, in the way that *civilisation* was often misunderstood in our own late eighteenth and nineteenth centuries, leading to an important and influential if still difficult distinction between *civilisation* and *culture*. Speaking of the Britons who were adapting to Roman civilisation, by wearing the toga and frequenting the fine galleries and bath-houses and banquets of the new order, he adds, with a cutting edge: *idque apud inperitos humanitas vocabatur, cum pars servitutis esset*. We have since known very many of these eager, new-rich collaborators, but few have had the benefit of that judgment from the other side, that in their inexperience they were calling civilisation that which was a part of their submission and servitude.

It is the reach of that wider *humanitas*, against a powerful war-machine and a display of material wealth and skill, which we can at least temporarily extract. There remains, however, the specifically literary problem. As I said earlier, the insertion of speeches in historical narratives was by this time conventional. It goes back to Thucydides, whom we are not surprised, if we examine the convention, to find the contemporary of Sophocles and Euripides. In Latin it is common from Cato. Yet the imposed distance of genres, as here between drama and history, is for all its emphasis in classical literature in some important respects misleading. What we find, as we think about it, is a fundamental question about the relationships between speech and writing, which from our own period and type of education, with its accustomed predominance of print, we are rather poorly placed to understand.

So much of what is now called the literature of the world, including a large part of its greatest literature, was either written for actual speaking or in a mode of speech, that we are likely to deform it if we apply our comparatively recent norm of writing for silent reading. It is not only that so much of this work is drama or oratory (the latter including the modern forms of sermons, lectures and addresses, which as late as the nineteenth century play a most important part). It is also that through classical and medieval times, and in many cases beyond these, most reading was either aloud or silently articulated as if speaking: a habit we now recognise mainly in the slow. Most classical histories were indeed quite close to oratory, and public speech, rather than silent reading of an artefact, was the central condition of linguistic composition.

Yet within this condition and its conventions we must make distinctions, not only, as obviously, between individual writers but more decisively between functions. Thus if with the memory of the speech of Calgacus in mind we turn to the speeches of Boudicca and Suetonius, as represented in the *Annals* (XIV, 35, 36) we find a mode which is effective as an element of narration; indeed the speeches are enclosed within narrative. They are short, to the immediate point and situation, but with hardly any reference or relevance beyond these. It might then be possible to contrast the speech of Calgacus in terms of its more developed oratory, which is indeed obvious; the speech is, in that sense, evidently 'set'. But though I may be wrong I think we must see something more in the difference: something which I would myself relate to the dramatic mode. It is not only that we have to remember classical drama as a unique (though internally developing) combination of narration, speech and chorus, in which many elements are somewhere between the categories of speech and narration as we now distinguish them. It is also that remembering the dramatic mode allows me, at least, to get beyond what is otherwise the difficulty of the placing of the speech of Calgacus within a eulogy of his conqueror. For while it will not do to extract the speech as an absolute condemnation of imperialism, it will not do either to dissolve it into a eulogistic narration. What the dramatic mode made possible, in what has to be seen as a major cultural liberation, was what in fact we find here: a narration, a speech, of a number of voices; thus inherently, in its multivocal character, a way of presenting voices, which while they speak have their own and temporarily absolute power, but which because other voices will speak have to be gathered, finally, into a whole action. Of course much is changed when the narrative mode in drama is specialised from messengers and reports to a single, enclosing narrative voice: moreover, as in Tacitus, a named voice, declaring his particular relation to his subject. Yet the thrust of the mode can still be there: Calgacus can denounce imperialism, with a reference and relevance beyond the narrative occasion, yet he can then be not so much answered as followed by the very different voice of the practical, moderate, loyal servant of Empire who goes on to defeat him. And what has then to be said is that neither voice is lost; the alternative voices stick in the memory, in ways comparable to the many voices of drama.

I am not making only a technical point. The crisis of humane studies, in our own times, can be described in many ways, but one major element of it, which has been too little and sometimes not at all recognised, is the again changing relation between writing and speech. All of us likely to be taking part in the discussion have been so formed by writing and by the silent reading of print that we may come to misrepresent even our own subject, ironically in a period in which oral forms, of some new and some older kinds, are again becoming central and even decisive in our culture. To trace this full history is beyond this occasion; I have tried, several times, to write parts of it, elsewhere. But the key point is not only a change of modes. Difficult as it may be for some of us to admit it, writing has from the beginning been a special form of privilege and social discrimination. Unlike all other forms of social communication and record, it does not come to anyone in the most general processes of growing up in a particular society. It has to be carefully taught and learned, and until comparatively recently, and still in some respects today even in the most literate societies, access to this skill has been carefully and at times malignly controlled. Moreover we must remember where it started: in the bureaucratic records of centralising urban economies, and then in trading economies. What must now be seen, historically, as advantage or deficit, in this or that former culture, has to be related not to some abstraction of civilisation but to particular kinds of social order. It is then true that there developed, on this material base and again in particular kinds of social order, moving in that same centralising direction, ways of using writing which were eventually to give us what we now call the literatures of the world. Yet, given the relation of this development to the mode of public speech, what was still a minority practice had a public presence and reference.

The case was then changed with the coming of print and silent reading. Over the five centuries of print which have formed our minds, even the writing for public speaking, of earlier times, has been reclassified as what we call, barbarously, 'oral literature', and has been reified as 'texts'. Of course we would not have these at all if they had not been written down and preserved: that key function of record in writing to which scholars have primarily to attend. But there were two wider social effects.

First, when such decisive matters as history and law retreat into writing, with different degrees of retreat according to whether a dead or specialised or a vernacular language is employed, a majority of any people is cut off from knowledge of some of its most decisive conditions of life and identity. The extraordinary ignorance of the British about their own past is not mere deficit; it is again and again functional, through the effective control of print. And then none of us should really be surprised if forms of dismissal or even hatred of that book-learning spread and take effect, the more quickly of course if the print is foreign. Nor should we be surprised, though we can be right to be shocked, when these distances are demagogically exploited. We say that we are offering the great works of the ages; others say, often with justice, that these are too bound up with distance and privilege and authority to be taken or even offered innocently.

This point becomes crucial when we include the second effect. Through the agonisingly slow development of general literacy, and then significantly in the period of rising democracy and the extension of the suffrage, received written forms were modified by innovations and pressures of several kinds. As late as Fielding's *Tom Jones* lovers can speak their extended declarations in the mode of generals before a battle, and the narrative voice is still in many ways spoken. But through the nineteenth century there developed not only the composed artefact, often of an impersonal narrative, for silent reading, but wholly novel ways – though with some precedents in parts of the drama – of representing what was not now public or semi-public speech, but conversation. I have given examples of this development, and of its conventions and difficulties, in *Writing in Society*. But what was also happening, for largely political and commercial reasons, was the development, in the newspapers, of a novel representation of public speech: one which in our own century has become, though always in conventional and sometimes in highly artificial ways, increasingly colloquial and idiomatic. The narrative voice in the novel followed the same course, though usually with more integrity.

It is then into this situation that the new oral forms of cinema and radio and television, two of them combining speech with a new power of moving images, arrived. The majority response of the highly literate, at each stage, has been deep suspicion if not horror. It was not only classicists, it was also teachers of English literature – English print – who could feel their whole world threatened. The values of high literacy, privately and clubbably evidenced by long knowledge and experience of so many major works, were taken as arrayed against what was seen as a destructive and demotic – demotic was quicker to say than democratic, though some went all the way – anyway vulgar mass culture.

I have been arguing against this conclusion through the whole of my working life, and I know I still fail to persuade. But what I have still to say, and with special point within the Classical Association, is that a major ground for my argument has always been high literacy itself. It is high literacy which shows us the remarkable historical diversity of modes of address and composition. It is high literacy which shows us the extraordinary diversity – literally as wide as the world – of the meanings and values which these works carry: a diversity which again and again is their only general value, and one which is not to be reduced to plausible singularities of consideration or conclusion, or to the use of literature, in some highly selective tradition, to ratify the habits of some temporary or self-interested group. It is again high literacy, in its only real sense, which can take us beyond those local conclusions of commonsense or necessity, as common among the generally literate as anywhere else, which override the facts of actual change and diversity, and even more the profound alternatives of belief and commitment in the long human record: facts and alternatives which at any time, and under any pressures, are necessary grounds of wisdom in complex and contending socie-ties. It is high literacy, finally, which calls the bluffs of authority, since it is a condition of all its practical work that it questions sources, closely ex-amines offered authenticities, reads contextually and comparatively, identifies conventions to determine meanings: habits of mind which are all against, or should be all against, any and every pronunciation of a singular or assembled authority.

But if the classics must be separated from authority, by the very process of understanding what authentic authorities are or are not, there must equally, from disciplines based on more recent material, be an attempt at honest collaboration and convergence. It is bound to be the case that the works of the classical European languages – and that formulation is meant to emphasise that there are others – are necessary elements of human culture and under-standing, whatever else may be happening. Yet that you would properly expect me to say. What I have also to say may be more surprising. There are very many faults in our current uses of the new oral and oral-visual forms, some of them, in their control of access, repeating the early faults of print. Yet as forms they could be especially near to us. Some modes of public speech are again being directly attempted, within conditions which remove them from what must be seen as the decadence of oratory: conditions which have already multiplied the actually contributing voices, and might multiply them many times again; conditions moreover of dialogue, of the multivocal, which are repeatedly trivialised, under the pressures of a centralising system, but which include possibilities beyond those of silent reading. For close, sustained, check-able argument there are still few substitutes for print, but for direct exchange the new forms have advantages, and it is now in any case true that all these modes can be followed without specialised and discriminating access; the mother-tongue is again the common entry for all to hear, if not yet for all to speak.

At the same time, within the rapid and often reckless expansion of these forms, at a time of major social dislocations as well as persistent inequalities, the skills that have been learned in high literacy have much to contribute. Our working practices may seem much too slow to survive in that torrent, but it is already the case that many young scholars and analysts, with some success, have taken these skills through to the material of the new forms: forms which now in any case must be included among the humanities. The work is not for any one group to do. Only a very diverse community of writers and scholars and analysts can approach adequacy. But then that finally is my case for a reorganisation of the humanities, a new school and curriculum of humanities, which will undoubtedly include many workers whose terms and materials will be very strange to classicists, but which in including classicists will continue to assert its breadth, its depth, and, above all, its historical sense of humanity.

16

Language and the Avant-Garde

From N. Fabb, D. Attridge, A. Durant and C. MacCabe (eds) (1988) The Linguistics of Writing: Arguments Between Language and Literature. *Manchester: Manchester University Press.*

As to the dialogue: I have rather broken with tradition in not making my characters who sit asking foolish questions in order to elicit a smart reply. I have avoided the mathematically symmetrical construction of French dialogue and let people's brains work irregularly, as they do in actual life, where no topic of conversation is drained to the dregs, but one brain receives haphazard from the other a cog to engage with. Consequently my dialogue too wanders about, providing itself in the earlier scenes with material which is afterwards worked up, admitted, repeated, developed, and built up, like the theme in a musical composition.[1]

Again:

My souls (characters) are conglomerations from past and present stages of civilization; they are excerpts from books and newspapers, scraps of humanity, pieces torn from festive garments which have become rags – just as the soul itself is a piece of patch-work.[2]

I take these descriptions of intention in writing from an unarguably Modernist playwright who was moreover often seen, in the movements of the avant-garde, as a precedent: August Strindberg. Yet the descriptions occur in what is in effect his manifesto of Naturalism, and this is my point in quoting them: as a challenge to certain tendencies in applied linguistics, and to forms of literary analysis seemingly derived from them, which have appropriated a selective version of Modernism, and within this an internal and self-proving definition of the avant-garde, as a way of ratifying their own much narrower positions and procedures.

The most serious consequence of this appropriation is that what are actually polemical positions, some of them serious, on language and writing, can pass, however ironically, as historical descriptions of actual movements and formations: the summations *Modernism* and *avantgarde* are, in most uses, obvious examples. For suppose we say, conventionally, that Modernism begins in Baudelaire, or in the period of Baudelaire, and that the avant-garde begins around 1910, with the manifestos of the Futurists, we can still not say, of either supposed movement, that what we find in them is some specific and identifiable position about language, or about writing, of the kind offered by subsequent theoretical or pseudo-historical propositions.

Even at their most plausible – in a characteristic kind of definition by negative contrast, where the main stress is put on a common rejection of the representational character of language and thence of writing – there is not only an astonishing reduction of the diversity of actually antecedent writing practices and theories of language, but a quite falsely implied identification of actual Modernist and avant-garde writing – with convenient slippages between the two loose terms – as based on attitudes to language which can be theoretically generalized, or at least made analogous, to what, borrowing the classifications, are themselves offered as modernist or avant-garde linguistic and critical positions and methodologies.

My challenge in quoting Strindberg, in his Naturalist manifesto, is that he was evidently putting forward a version of character – as a 'conglomeration', an 'excerpt', 'pieces torn' and 'scraps' – which has been widely seen as characteristic of Modernist writing and indeed of more general theory, together with a method of irregular writing, 'built up like the theme in a musical composition', also widely identified as 'modernist', which are yet quite unmistakably based on an affiliation to, even a desire to represent, actual social processes: 'I have . . . let people's brains work irregularly, *as they do in actual life*'. One is even reminded of Ibsen's words, when he decided to abandon dramatic verse and cultivate 'the very much more difficult art of writing the genuine, plain language spoken in real life.'[3] 'My desire was to depict human beings and therefore I would not make them speak the language of the gods': Ibsen, who, if it is a question of movements, was so influential on Joyce.[4]

I am not of course saying that Modernism was a Naturalism, though dramatic Naturalism was indeed one of its major early manifestations. But I am saying, certainly of Modernism, and even, where I shall concentrate, of the avant-garde, that actual positions and practices are very much more diverse than their subsequent ideological presentations, and that we shall misunderstand and betray a century of remarkable experiments if we go on trying to flatten them to contemporary theoretical and quasi-theoretical positions.

For the present analysis I am accepting the conventional delineation of the avant-garde as a complex of movements from around 1910 to the late 1930s. In real practice there are no such convenient break-points. What is almost the only distinguishing feature, and even then incompletely, is less a matter of actual writing than of successive formations which challenged not only the art institutions but the institution of Art, or Literature, itself, typically in a broad programme which included, though in diverse forms, the overthrow and remaking of existing society. That certainly cuts it off from later formations which continued its technical practices, and its accompanying aggressiveness marks at least a change in tone from earlier formations which had pioneered some of its methods and which, in at least some cases, had comparably broad social and even political intentions. Within the irregularities and overlaps of any cultural history – its repeated co-presence of various forms of the emergent with forms of the residual and the dominant – that definition of period and type has a working usefulness.

Yet we cannot then jump to its farthest manifestations: to the phonetic poems and the automatic writing, and the body language of the Theatre of Cruelty. What we have, instead, to distinguish is a set of tendencies, in writing, which in this place and that had specific but in no way inevitable outcomes. Thus the movement of verbal composition towards what was seen as the condition of music has no predestined outcome in Dada. The movement of verbal composition towards the creation of what were seen as images has no predestined outcome in Imagist verses. Rather, in the diverse movements which are summarized as Modernism or as the avant-garde, we have to look at radical differences of practice within what can be seen, too hastily, as a common orientation, and then relate both practices and orientation to certain uses and concepts of language and writing which historically and formally belong to neither.

The central issue may be that which was defined, ideologically, by Shklovsky, as 'the resurrection of the word'.[5] At the level of summary, this idea is often now used as a core definition of literary Modernism, and is further associated with certain interpretations of the 'sign' in linguistics. Yet it was Shklovsky's colleague among the early Russian Formalists, Eikhenbaum, who wrote that 'the basic slogan uniting the initial group was the emancipation of the word from the shackles of the philosophical and religious tendencies with which the Symbolists were possessed.'[6] The local observation is just, yet it was precisely the Symbolists who had most clearly introduced the new emphasis on the intrinsic value of the poetic word. A word seen in this way was not a signal to something beyond it, but a signifier in its own material properties which, by its poetic use, embodied, rather than expressed or represented, a value. It is then true that this value, for the Symbolists, was of a particular kind: the poetic word as the ideoglyph of mystery or of myth. In some later tendencies of this sort, for example the Acmeists or the Yeats of the Dancer plays, this embodiment of the poetic word is refracted through existing literary or legendary material, a more specialized and often more exotic manifestation of the more general – and much older – use of classical myth and literature as a source of symbolic, self-valuable units of meaning. We can then go on to see the Formalist 'resurrection' or 'emancipation' of the word as a secularization, a demystification, of the 'poetic word' of the Symbolists. What was being proposed instead was still a specific 'literary language', but now defined in terms of the word as empirical phonetic material. Yet it was then not simply the specific ideological freight of the Symbolist 'poetic word' that was being rejected, but, so far as possible, not only its ideological but any or all of its received semantic freight: the poetic word then being not simply a grammatical unit but available in what came to be called a 'transrational sound image'.

Moreover this was always a matter of practice. In the early years of the century, partially in Apollinaire and more directly in the poems which became known as *bruitiste*, verse composed as pure sound was being written in several European languages. The eventual outcome, along this very specialized line of development, was the phonetic poem, evident among some of the Futurists but more especially in Dadaism. In 1917, following a common earlier analogy, Hugo Ball wrote that 'the decision to let go of language in poetry, just like letting go of the object in painting, is imminent', and he had indeed just written his *Gadji Beri Bimba*. His own account of its public reading is instructive:

> I began in a slow and solemn way
> *gadji beri bimba glandridi launa lonni cadori . . .*
> It was then that I realized that my voice, lacking other
> possibilities, was adopting the ancestral cadence of priestly
> laments, that style of chanting the mass in the
> catholic churches of East and West:
> *zimzim urallala zimzim urallala zimzim zanzibar*
> *zimzall zam.*[7]

Moreover it was done to drums and bells.

There is a sense in which the most extreme practitioners of these new theories of language and writing are markedly more acceptable than the contemporary makers of formulae. For what was being tested in practice, even where tested to destruction, was actually a major element of very old as well as very new kinds of verbal performance. The relapse to the rhythms of the mass in the middle of an outraging Dadaist spectacle is not only funny; it is, like the sudden locating appearance of Zanzibar, a reminder of how deeply constituted, socially, language always is, even when the decision has been made to abandon its identifiable semantic freight.

For of course the use of material sound and of rhythm, in both general communication and the many forms of drama, narrative, lyric, ritual and so on, is in no way a Modernist discovery and is, moreover, never reducible, in another direction, to simplified accounts of meaning in language. From the Welsh *cynghanedd* to medieval alliterative verse it has been an element not only of practice but even of rules. In less ordered forms it has been virtually a constant component of many different kinds of oral composition and of writing, from dramatic blank verse to the nonsense-poem (that significantly popular nineteenth-century English form which certain phonetic poems much resemble). What is different, in some Modernist and avant-garde theory and practice, is the attempt to rationalize it for specific ideological purposes of which the most common – though it has never been more than an element of these movements – is the deliberate exclusion or devaluing of all or any referential meaning.

We have already seen, in Hugo Ball, the false analogy with renunciation of the 'object' in painting. A true analogy would have been a decision by painters to give up paint. But we must go beyond these pleasantries to the substantial case which is at the root of so many of these diverse movements and indeed of some of their predecessors. This case is primarily historical, underlying the diverse formations and practices, but also underlying many of the developments in the study of language which, at an altogether later stage, are now used to interpret or recommend them. Yet the complexity of this history – indeed that which makes it history – is evident at once if we abstract and then offer to construe the substantial position from which so many of these initiatives were made. Indeed the difficulty of formulating it is, in a real sense, its history.

If I say, for example, as so many of these writers did, that language should be creative, as against its contemporary condition, I can be reasonably certain, given a sufficient diversity of audience, of being understood as saying at least seven different things: not only because of the manifold possibilities of 'creative' but because the 'contemporary condition' has been historically understood as at least one of the following: a state of active repression of human possibilities; a state of antiquated discourse and composition; a state in which language is dulled and exhausted by custom and habit or reduced to the merely prosaic; a state in which everyday, ordinary language makes literary composition difficult or impossible; a state in which a merely instrumental language blocks access to an underlying spiritual or unconscious reality; a state in which a merely social language obstructs the most profound individual expression. There are probably other variants and accompaniments, as there are certainly other slogans. But the extraordinary historical generalization of what may − indeed I think must − still be grasped as the underlying position is too important to allow any intellectual retreat. What is being argued, in these diverse ways, leading to so many diverse formations and practices, has to be not summarized but explored.

It is only in one special outcome of this argument, in one part of Modernism and a rather larger part of the avant-garde, that the difficulties and tensions are in effect collapsed. This is in the (themselves varied) attempts either to dispense with language altogether, as too hopelessly compromised and corrupted by this or that version of its condition, or, failing that, to do what Artaud proposed, 'substituting for the spoken language a different language of nature, whose expressive possibilities will be equated to verbal language.'[8] In straight terms this is vaudeville, but more practically we can see that a key element in both Modernism and the avant-garde was a deliberate running-together, cross-fertilization, even integration of what had been hitherto seen as different arts. Thus the aspiration to develop language towards the condition of music, or towards the immediacy and presence of visual imagery or performance could, if it failed (as it was bound to) in its original terms, be taken on into music or painting or performance art, or, significantly, into film of an avant-garde kind. These developments, however, go beyond the present argument. For though Apollinaire apostrophized 'man in search of a new language to which the grammarian of any tongue will have nothing to say',[9] and looked forward to the time when 'the phonograph and the cinema having become the only forms of "print" in use, poets will have a freedom unknown up till now',[10] he continued for his own part in his own written compositions. Even Artaud, much later in this development, continued to write, if only, as he claimed, for illiterates, years after he had conceived, in the Theatre of Cruelty, a kind of dramatic performance in which bodily presence and action, a dynamic of movement and image, would take decisive priority over what remained of dramatic language: an initiative which has been continued and even in some respects − ironically even in commercial cinema − generalized.

Thus we can return to the underlying history of direct positions in the practice of language, in relation to that almost neutral term, the 'contemporary condition'. 'Almost neutral', since for the Symbolists, for example, the so-called condition was not contemporary but permanent, though acute in the crises of their time. This is, incidentally, a way in which, with a certain effect of paradox, the Symbolists can be distinguished from one main sense of modernism. Their ways of writing verse were new, often radically so, but it was less among them than among their very different contemporaries, the Naturalists, that there came the familiar challenging rhetoric of the new, the *modern*, which required a new art: new bottles for this new wine, as Strindberg put it in his arguments for Naturalism.[11] The idealist substratum of Symbolism was the belief that the world transmitted by the senses – but then by all the senses and most profoundly in synaesthesia – should be understood as revealing a *spiritual* universe. The Symbolist poem would then be an enabling form of such revelation, a mode of realized *correspondance* in Baudelaire's sense, in which the 'poetic word' becomes a verbal symbol, at once material in embodiment and metaphysical in its revelation of a spiritual but still sensual reality.

This concept was related, linguistically, to ideas of the 'inner form' of a word – indeed its internal creative capacity – as defined, for example, by Potebnia. It was often supported from the established idea of the distinctive 'inner forms' of languages, corresponding to the inner life of their speakers, as argued as early as Humboldt. This 'inner form' had then to be, as it were, discovered, released, embodied in the 'poetic word': and especially then by poets: the basis for speaking, as they did, of a 'literary language'. Within this whole concept these are already, one can say, distinguishable metaphysical and historical bearings: distinguishable but in practice ordinarily fused and confused. For the intention is metaphysical but the occasion can still be defined as the 'contemporary', or in that loose grand way the 'modern', crisis of life and society.

Characteristically, in the Symbolists, as clearly in Baudelaire and again in Apollinaire, this form of poetic revelation involved a fusion of present synaesthetic experience with the recovery of a nameable, tangible past which was yet 'beyond' or 'outside' time. And versions of this form of practice have continued to be important in many works which do not formally carry the specific marks of Symbolism as an identifiable historical movement. It is evident, for example, in the visionary and legendary Yeats and, in a different way, in Eliot, who is so often taken, in English, as the exemplary Modernist poet but who in this respect, as in others, can be more precisely defined, in an idealist as well as a historical sense, as quintessentially Ancient and Modern.

And we have then only to go across from that whole tendency to the Futurists, with their wholesale rejection of any trace of the past, indeed, as Marinetti put it, with their campaigning 'modernolatry', to know the profound disjunctions which the usual summary of Modernism papers over. For now 'literary language', and indeed the whole institution and existing practice of literature, were the shackles which these heralds of the new time must break. Not an 'inner form' but the 'freedom' of words is what is now celebrated, for they are to be hurled in the shock of action or of play against a sclerotic literary or social order. To be sure there still can be appeal to primeval energies against the decayed forms. This goes on into the Expressionists. It is a main theme of Brecht's *Baal*.

But there are also more specific changes in the handling of language; for example, Khlebnikov's use of his studies of the linguistic history of words to propose a form of release in the coming of new verbal forms, as in the famous poem the 'Incantation to Laughter', where the whole composition is a series of variations on the Russian word *smekh* = laughter. Mayakovsky's 'A Cloud in Trousers' in a broader way offers to break up, in a single operation, the habitual expectations, collocations and connections of both existing poems and existing perceptions. Significantly, it was from this Futurist practice that the early Formalists derived their concepts not only of the word as grammatical unit – the linguistic element of their arguments – but as a 'transrational sound image' – the literary element or potential. This can be connected – though not by direct influence – with the bruitiste poems and with the phonetic poems of Dada, but it was to have much longer and wider though perhaps equally surprising effects.

For there is already an underlying dichotomy in this understanding of 'the word'. Whether as 'grammatical unit' or as 'transrational sound image' it can be projected in two quite different directions: on the one hand towards active composition, in which these units are arranged and combined, by conscious literary strategies or devices, into works; or, on the other hand, taking an ideological cue from 'transrational', into procedures much resembling traditional accounts of 'inspiration', in which the creative act occurs beyond the 'ordinary self', and more substantial, more original, energies are tapped.

It is interesting to reflect on the itinerary of this latter conception: from metaphysical notions of literal possession by gods or spirits in the moment of true utterance, through the conventional personifications of inspiring muses of great predecessors, ancestor poets, into the Romantic version of creative access to the new all-purpose personification of Nature, and finally – or is it finally? – to creative access to 'the unconscious'. Certainly we have to notice how commonly, in later Modernism and in sectors of the avant-garde, both idealist notions of the 'life force' (as in Bergson) and psychoanalytic notions of the unconscious (as derived from Freud but perhaps more commonly from Jung) functioned in practice as modernized versions of these very old assumptions and processes.

The most relevant example, in avant-garde practice, is of course the 'automatic writing' of the Surrealists, which was based on one, or perhaps several, of the positions about language and its contemporary condition which we have identified. 'Everyday' and 'ordinary' language, or sometimes 'the language of a decadent bourgeois society', blocked true creative activity, or (for another different formulation was also employed) prevented us embodying – almost one can say 'representing' – the true process of thought. Thus Breton had said, in a still general way: 'words are likely to group themselves according to particular affinities, recreating the world in accordance with its old pattern at any moment.'[12] But this still broad position was sharpened to a more sweeping rejection: 'we pretend not to notice that...the logical mechanism of the sentence appears more and more incapable of releasing the emotional shock in man which actually gives some true value to his life.'[13] And so to 'automatic writing': 'a pure psychic automatism by which one proposes to express, either verbally or in writing, or in any other way, the real functioning of thought: dictation by thought, in the absence of any control exercised by reason, and without any aesthetic or moral consideration.'[14] The terms of this rhetoric, confused and confusing as they ought to be seen, are now in many ways naturalized: that highly specific 'thought'/'reason' dichotomy, for example. Yet one can look back on 'automatic writing', for all the meagreness of its actual results, with a certain respect for its ambitions of practice, as distinguishable from its much looser though more suggestive ideological context. For language was being simultaneously identified with the blocking of 'true consciousness' and, to the extent that it could emancipate itself from its imprisoning everyday forms and, beyond that, from the received forms of 'literature', as itself the medium of the idealized 'pure consciousness'.

One way out of this contradiction was the move to Surrealist film, but most writers stayed in the double position and then of course at once encountered the obvious and ominous question of 'communication'. Theoretically it might have been said that if psychic automatism could reach 'the real functioning of thought' it would be transparently, even universally, communicable, yet the means of psychic automatism were, in practice, if not alienating, at least distancing. Artaud could go on to say: 'The break between us and the world is well established. We speak not to be understood, but to our inner selves.'[15] Thus the purpose of writing (as we have since often heard) is not communication but illumination (a contrast which seems necessarily to modify the second term to self-illumination). There can be an emphasis – which indeed became a culture – on the experience itself, rather than on any of the forms of embodying or communicating it.

Automatic writing had been achieved, by the internal account, in somnambulist or trance-like states: drugs were one group of means to this state; several varieties of esoteric, mystical and transcendental philosophy another. Breton himself distinguished the poetic process as empirical; it did not 'presuppose an invisible universe beyond the network of the visible world.' Yet this older form of contrast – which would hold as a distinction, one way or the other, as late as the Symbolists – was now insignificant, within the ideological substitution of 'the unconscious' which could comfortably embrace 'reality' and 'hidden reality', 'experience' and 'dream', 'neurosis' and 'madness', 'psychic trace' and 'primal myth', in a dazzling shift of new and old concepts which could be selected as purpose served.

What came through, at its most serious, were unforeseen yet convincing or at least striking collocations, but this much more often in visual imagery than in language. The presumptive dismissal of 'everyday' content found a later rationalization, for example in Adorno, in the idealization of form as authentic – art-defining – image. But there was also a broad highway into the process rather than the product: the drug-experience as such; the esoteric and the occult as direct, but not artistic, practices; the support looked for in mystical philosophies becoming the new practice of the meditative and transcendental rather than the 'poetic' or 'creative' word.

That was one general way, later dividing, from the proposition of the transrational sound-image. Within Surrealist practice, for all the specificity of its forms, there was still construction through, if not from, the word. The other general way took construction in language more directly, but then again in diverse ways.

For the Expressionists, in writing, the emphasis was not on transcending contradictions – as in Breton's remark that 'Surrealism would have liked nothing better than to allow the mind to jump the barrier raised by contradictions such as action- dream, reason-madness, and sensation- representation',[16] but on raising them to a principle of form: sharply polarized states of mind, angrily polarized social positions, whose conflict was then the dynamic of truth. The discursive language which they identified in Naturalism – whether as reflection or discussion of a situation or problem, or as the social process which Strindberg had defined as the irregular engagement of minds or which Chekhov had realized in his writing of failures of communication, that negative group which yet, as a group, shared a social situation of which they needed to speak and which others should see and understand – all that kind of writing of speech was rejected, within the polar contradictions, for what is in effect the language of the cry, the exclamation.

In its early stages especially, the Expressionist word is indeed 'transrational', but for conflict rather than access. The idea of primeval energy in the cry is again evident, and in some later Expressionist work – in Toller and Brecht, for example – the cry is a consciously liberating, indeed revolutionary moment: the cry can become a shout or the still inarticulate cry a protest; that cry which fights to be heard above the news bulletins, the headlines, the false political speeches of a world in crisis; even the cry which can become a slogan, a fixed form, to shout as a means to collective action. That direction in language sought, in its own terms, to intervene in the social process and to change reality by struggle. It is then at most a distant cousin of the 'transrational sound-image', though some relationship is there.

Yet this is one more case in which a specific and specializing development of actual writing practices cannot usefully be reduced to the general propositions about language which, in their own but different terms, were becoming influential. Thus we can see some relationship between certain versions of the 'poetic word' or the 'transrational sound-image' and certain modern linguistic definitions of the 'sign': indeed 'sign', as a term, with its available free associations to 'icon' or 'ideogram' or some visual representation, sometimes points us that way, and we can usefully recall Saussure's hesitations about it, since it can blur the necessary choice between 'sign' as *signifier*, a unit within an autonomous language system, and 'sign' in its very combination of 'signifier' and 'signified' as pointing both ways, to the language-system and to a reality which is not language.[17] But that is a question within the distinctive area of linguistics, and there is little point – indeed there is some obvious danger – in assimilating one or other version of the linguistic sign to the specific – and in fact diverse – concepts of the sound-image that were available to certain strategies in writing.

Thus, if we look back to the early Formalists, we find a failure to resolve this problem as it passes from linguistic definition to literary analysis or recommendation. To understand the word as empirical phonetic material is indeed a basis for a strategy of 'defamiliarization' or 'estrangement', and it is true that exclusion of received or indeed any semantic content opens possibilities of semantic exploration as well as our old friends the phonetic poem or its upstart cousin, cross- cultural assonance: 'jung and easily freudened'.

Yet the Formalist position, as it came through into an influential tendency in literary theory, was a disastrous narrowing of the very facts to which it pointed. It became tied to rejections of what were called 'content' and 'representation', and even more damagingly of 'intention', which actually missed the point of active literary uses of the very quality that Voloshinov called 'multiaccentual', an inherent semantic openness, corresponding to a still active social process, from which new meanings and possible meanings can be generated, at least in certain important classes of words and sentences.[18]

Yet even that was still a linguistic proposition. The Formalists, though tying their linguistic position to certain kinds of literary practice – kinds heavily influenced by the practice of Futurism though most of their illustrative examples were from much earlier works and, of course, from folk-tales – limited the true potential of the position by a characteristic error. Under the spell of their own selected examples, of valued but highly specific uses, they forgot that every act of composition in writing, indeed every utterance, at once moves into specific processes which are no longer in that way open: which indeed, as acts, even in the most seemingly bizarre cases, necessarily have 'content' and 'intention' and which may, in any of many thousands of ways, even in these terms 'represent'. To retain the useful abstraction of basic linguistic material, which is properly the ground of linguistic analysis, in arguments which offer to deal with what is already and inevitably a wide range of practices, in which that material is for this and that purpose being used, has been to misdirect several generations of analysts and even, though fewer in number, some writers.

And perhaps, finally, there is more than a wide range of practices; perhaps, through the many complications, overlaps and uncertainties, there have been, through this period of active innovation and experiment, two fundamental directions which we can at least provisionally distinguish.

We can begin by noticing the two active senses of 'modern' in this context: 'modern' as a historical time, with its specific and then changing features; but 'modern' also as what Medvedev and Bakhtin, criticizing it, called 'eternal contemporaneity', that apprehension of the 'moment' which overrides and excludes, practically and theoretically, the material realities of change, until all consciousness and practice are 'now'.

From the first sense, with its grasp of changes that were factually remaking society (a grasp that was of course variable, selecting this or that group of features, in this or that movement), a sense of the future, and then properly of an avant-garde, was extensively derived. From the second sense there was, and is, something else: a generalization of the human condition, including generalizations of both art and language, and through them of consciousness. The 'modern', in this sense, is then either a set of conditions which allow this universal condition to be at last recognized, after the tied ideologies of earlier times, or else, as in the earliest movements, a set of circumstances in which the universal and true nature of life is especially threatened by a modernity which must be opposed or evaded: a modernism, as so often, against modernity: not an *avant* but an *arrière* garde: the literally reactionary tendency which should have culminated in Eliot.

Correspondingly there appear to be two basic contradictory attitudes towards language: that which, engaging with received form and the possibilities of new practice, treats language as material in a social process; and that other which, as in several avant-garde movements, sees it as blocking or making difficulties for authentic consciousness: 'the need for expression . . . born from the very impossibility of expression';[19] or what Artaud seems to mean when he writes: 'my thought abandons me at every step – from the simple fact of thought to the external fact of its materialization in words.'[20]

Each of these positions is, we can say, a modernism; but we can then also say that while the first is modernist in both theory and practice, the latter is modernist in practice, but in its underlying theory, its finally intransigent idealism, at best a finding of new terms for the 'ineffable': even anti-theological, anti-metaphysical terms for that same 'ineffable', as they would of course now have to be.

The same basic contrast, within modernism, is evident in the forms of specification of 'the modern' itself: on the one hand those forms which engage with history and with specific social formations; on the other hand those which point to certain general features, approvingly or disapprovingly: features which then function in effect as 'background' to the foregrounded 'creative act'. Thus we are told, in an enumeration, of the facts of the city, of new technology, of changes in work and in class, of the weakening and collapse of traditional faiths, and so on, for the listing can be endless. Yet any or all of these probable features has to be seen as having influenced whole populations, whole social processes, whereas Modernism and the avant-garde, in any of their forms, have never involved, as producers or as publics, more than minorities; often very small minorities. To be sure there is an internal way of meeting this objection: that while 'mass life' may flow this way or that, the significant movements are always those of minorities. That conceit has been heard from embattled innovators, where it is understandable, to privileged and even institutionalized groups, which when they are also attaching themselves to an avant-garde become absurd.

What matters, still, is not general features but specification. Certainly the city is relevant, and specifically the city as a metropolis. It is a very striking feature of many Modernist and avant-garde movements that they were not only located in the great metropolitan centres but that so many of their members were immigrants into these centres, where in some new ways all were strangers. Language, in such situations, could appear as a new kind of fact: either simply as 'medium', aesthetic or instrumental, since its naturalized continuity with a persistent social settlement was unavailable; or, of course, as system: the distanced, even the alien fact. Moreover, these cities had become the capitals of imperialism. The old hegemony of capital over its provinces was extended over a new range of disparate, often wholly alien and exotic, cultures and languages. The evolutionary and family versions of language which were the basis of language studies in the period of formation of nation- states and confederacies were then replaced by studies of universal systems within which specificities were either, as in much literary practice, exotica, or were the local, momentary, and superficial features of more fundamental structures.

There was then both gain and loss: new possibilities of analysis beyond the naturalized forms; new kinds of false transfer of these analytic positions to practice and recommendations for practice. Within these specific conditions, various formations emerged; in political aspirations to a corresponding uni-versality – the revolutionary groups; or in reactionary redoubts, preserving a literary language in either of its forms – a pure national language or a language of authenticity against the banalities or repressions of everyday language use.

But finally, and still much the most difficult to analyse, there were the formations of certain special innovations, and these most marked – to use shorthand for what would need to be a very complex socio-historical analysis – in three types of group: those who had come to the metropolis from colonized or capitalized regions; those who had come from what were already linguistic borderlands, where a dominant language coexisted with the practice or the memory of an older native language; and those who came as exiles – an increasingly important kind of formation – from rejecting or rejected political regimes. For in each of these cases, though in interestingly different ways, an old language had been marginalized or suppressed, or else simply left behind, and the now dominant language either interacted with its subordinate for new language effects or was seen as, in new ways, both plastic and arbitrary: an alien but accessible system which had both power and potential yet was still not, as in most earlier formations, however experimental, the language or the possible language of a people but now the material of groups, agencies, fractions, specific works, its actual society and complex of writers and game-players, translators and signwriters, interpreters and makers of paradoxes, cross-cultural innovators and jokers. The actual social processes, that is to say, involved not only an Apollinaire, a Joyce, an Ionesco, a Beckett, but also, as Joyce recognized in Bloom, many thousands of extempore dealers and negotiators and persuaders: moreover not even, reliably, these as distinct and separate groups.

And indeed this was bound to be so, since the shift was occurring within accelerating general processes of mobility, dislocation and paranational communication which, over the decades, appeared to convert what had been an experience of small minorities to what, at certain levels, and especially in its most active sites and most notably in the United States, could be offered as a definition of modernity itself.

There was then a now familiar polarization, of an ideological kind: between on the one hand the 'old, settled' language and its literary forms and on the other hand the 'new, dynamic' language and its necessarily new forms. Yet at each of these poles there is a necessary distinction. The cultural forms of the 'old, settled' language (always, in practice, never settled, however old) were indeed, at one level, the imposed forms of a dominant class and its discourse. But this was never the only level. Uses of a language of connection and of forms of intended communication remained an emphasis and an intention of other social groups, in both class and gender, whose specific existence had been blurred or contained within the imposed 'national' forms. Similarly, the cultural forms of the 'new, dynamic' language were never only experimental or liberating. Within the real historical dynamics they could be, and were, notably and deliberately manipulative and exploiting. The widespread adoption and dilution of avant-garde visual and linguistic modes by advertising and publicity agencies is only the most evident example; overtly commercial paranational art includes many more interesting, if less obvious, cases. There is then a practical linkage of a selective definition of modernity with the asymmetries of political and economic domination and subordination. This cannot be rendered back to isolated formal or technical levels.

Thus what we have really to investigate is not some single position of language in the avant-garde or language in Modernism. On the contrary, we need to identify a range of distinct and in many cases actually opposed formations, as these have materialized in language. This requires us, obviously, to move beyond such conventional definitions as 'avant-garde practice' or 'the Modernist text'. Formal analysis can contribute to this, but only if it is firmly grounded in formational analysis.

Thus the 'multivocal' or 'polyphonic', even the 'dialogic', as features of texts, have to be referred to social practice if they are to be rigorously construed. For they can range from the innovatory inclusion of a diversity of voices and socio-linguistic relationships (as in that remarkable historical instance of English Renaissance popular drama, in an earlier period of dislocation and offered integration) to what is no more in effect, but also in intention, than the self-absorbed miming of others: a proliferation and false interaction of class and gender linguistic stereotypes from an indifferent and enclosing technical consciousness. The innovatory inclusion can be traced to its formation, but the isolated technique is more usually traceable to its agency, in direct or displaced domination. Similarly, the important inclusion, within a highly literate and culturally allusive context, of the active range and body of the everyday vernacular has to be distinguished not only formally but formationally from that rehearsal and miming of what is known in the relevant agencies as *Vox Pop*: that linguistic contrivance for political and commercial reach and control. The polar instances may be relatively easy to distinguish, but the complex range between them demands very precise analysis: some of it made more difficult by the facts of indeterminacy between 'literary texts' and 'general cultural discourse' which ironically, but then with very different intentions, elements in the avant-garde had worked to bring about.

Moreover, and finally, the work can be done only if we begin moving beyond those received theoretical positions, in applied linguistics and derived forms of literary analysis, which have now to be seen as at many levels internal to these very processes; often, indeed, repeating, in what appear more formal ways, the operational manifesto phrases of specific avant-garde formations, though they offer to be independently explanatory of them and indeed of most other practices. Such positions are not collaborators in the necessary work but in effect agents of its indefinite – its 'eternally contemporary' – postponement. On the other hand the history and practice of these same general movements, reviewed to disclose in some new ways the profound connections between formations and forms, remain sources of inspiration and of strength.

Notes

1 August Strindberg, Preface to *Lady Julie*, in *Five Plays*, Berkeley, 1981, p. 71.

2 Ibid. p. 67.

3 Henrik Ibsen, *Collected Works*, W. Archer, ed., London 1906–8, VI, p. xiv.

4 Ibid.

5 V.B. Shklovsky, in Striedter and Sempel, eds, *Texte der Russischen Formalisten*, Munich 1972, II, p. 13.

6 B.M. Eikhenbaum, 'La théorie de la "méthode formelle"', in *Théorie de la littérature*, ed. and trans., Tzvetan Todorov, Paris, 1965, p. 39.

7 Cited in M. Sanouillet, *Dada à Paris*, Paris 1965, pp. 70 ff.

8 A. Artaud, *The Theatre and its Double*, New York 1958, p. 110.

9 G. Apollinaire, *Oeuvres complètes* volume III, edited by M. Décaudin, Paris 1965–66, p. 901.

10 G. Apollinaire, 'La Victoire', in *Calligrammes* (12th edn.), Paris, 1945.

11 Strindberg, p. 64.

12 A. Breton, *Manifestes du surréalisme*; Coll. Idées, 23, Paris 1963, p. 37.

13 A. Breton, *Point du jour*, Paris 1934, p. 24.

14 *Manifestes du surréalisme*, p. 109.

15 A. Artaud, *Oeuvres complètes*, Paris 1961, I, p. 269.

16 A. Breton, *Entretiens: 1913–1952*, Paris 1952, p. 283.

17 Cf. R. Godel, *Les sources manuscrites du 'Cours de linguistique générale' de F. de Saussure*, Geneva, Paris, 1957, p. 192.

18 V. Voloshinov, *Marxism and the Philosophy of Language*, New York 1973.

19 G. Picon, *L'Usage de la lecture*, Paris 1961, II, p. 191.

20 *Oeuvres complètes*, I, p. 20.

Bibliography

The fullest existing bibliography of Williams's work and writings on Williams was prepared by Alan O'Connor, and can be found both in O'Connor 1989 and Eagleton 1989. It now stands in need of some revision, and can be usefully supplemented by the bibliography available in Higgins 1999.

Works by Raymond Williams

Williams, Raymond 1947 'Saints, Revolutionaries, Carpetbaggers', review of E. W. Martin, *The New Spirit*, and D. V. Baker (ed.) *Writers of Today* (ed.), *The Critic* 1(1): 52–4.

Williams, Raymond 1950 *Reading and Criticism*, London: Frederick Muller.

Williams, Raymond 1952 *Drama from Ibsen to Eliot*, London: Chatto and Windus.

Williams, Raymond 1953 'Film as a Tutorial Subject', *Rewley House Papers* 3:2:27–37. (Reprinted in John McIlroy and Sallie Westwood (eds) *Border Country: Raymond Williams in Adult Education*. Leicester: National Institute of Adult and Continuing Education, 1993, pp. 185–92.)

Williams, Raymond 1954 *Drama in Performance*, London: Fredrick Muller.

Williams, Raymond 1958 *Culture and Society 1780–1950*, London: Chatto and Windus. (Reprinted with a new Foreword by Williams in 1990, London: The Hogarth Press.)

Williams, Raymond 1961 *The Long Revolution*, London: Chatto and Windus. (Reprinted Harmondsworth: Penguin, 1975.)

Williams, Raymond 1962a *Communications*, Harmondsworth: Penguin. (3rd edition with new 'Reading and Retrospect 1975', Harmondsworth: Penguin, 1975.)

Williams, Raymond 1962b 'A Dialogue on Tragedy', *New Left Review* 13–14: 22–35.

Williams, Raymond 1966 *Modern Tragedy*, London: Chatto and Windus. (New edition without the play 'Koba' and with a new Afterword, London: Verso, 1979.)

Williams, Raymond 1968a *Drama from Ibsen to Brecht*, Harmondsworth: Penguin (revised and extended version of Williams 1952).

Williams, Raymond 1968b 'paradoxically, if the book works it to some extent annihilates itself' in Gerald E. Stearn (ed.) *McLuhan: Hot and Cool*, Harmondsworth: Penguin, pp. 216–19.

Williams, Raymond (ed.) 1969 *The Pelican Book of English Prose, Vol. 2: From 1780 to the Present Day*, Harmondsworth: Penguin.

Williams, Raymond 1970 *The English Novel from Dickens to Lawrence*, London: Chatto and Windus. (New edition London: The Hogarth Press, 1984.)

Williams, Raymond 1971a *Orwell*, Fontana Modern Masters Series, London: Fontana Collins. (2nd edition with new Afterword by Williams, London: Fontana/Flamingo 1984.)

Williams, Raymond 1971b 'Literature and Sociology: In Memory of Lucien Goldmann' *New Left Review* 67: 3–18. (Reprinted in R. Williams *Problems in Materialism and Culture*, London: Verso 1980, pp. 11–30.)

Williams, Raymond 1973 *The Country and the City*, London; Chatto and Windus. (2nd edition St Albans: Paladin; 1975.)

Williams, Raymond 1974 *Television: Technology and Cultural Form*, London: Fontana.

Williams, Raymond 1976 *Keywords: A Vocabulary of Culture and Society*, London: Croom Helm. (Revised and extended 2nd edition, London: Fontana, 1983.)

Williams, Raymond 1977a *Marxism and Literature*, Oxford: OUP

Williams, Raymond 1977b 'Two Interviews with Raymond Williams', *Red Shift* 2: 12–17.

Williams, Raymond 1979 *Politics and Letters: Interviews with New Left Review*, London: Verso.

Williams, Raymond 1980 *Problems in Materialism and Culture*, London: Verso.

Williams, Raymond 1981 *Culture*, London: Fontana.

Williams, Raymond 1983a *Towards 2000*, London: Chatto and Windus.

Williams, Raymond 1983b *Cobbett*, Oxford Past Masters Series, Oxford and New York: Oxford University Press.

Williams, Raymond 1984 'Notes on English Prose' in *Writing in Society*, London: Verso.

Williams, Raymond 1985 'Afterword' in J. Dollimore and A. Sinfield *Political Shakespeare: New Essays in Cultural Materialism*, Manchester: Manchester University Press

Williams, Raymond 1987 'Country and City in the Modern Novel', W. D. Thomas Memorial Lecture. (Republished in *Pretexts: Studies in Writing and Culture*, 2:1: 3–13, 1990.)

Williams, Raymond 1989a *The Politics of Modernism: Against the New Conformism*, ed. Tony Pinkney, London and New York: Verso.

Williams, Raymond 1989b *Resources of Hope: Culture, Democracy*, ed. Robin Gable, London and New York: Verso.

Williams, Raymond 1989c *What I Came to Say*, ed. Francis Mulhern, London: Hutchinson Radius.

Williams, Raymond 1989d *Raymond Williams on Television: Selected Writings*, ed. A. O'Connor, London: Routledge.

Williams, Raymond 1989e *People of the Black Mountains I: The Beginning*, London: Chatto and Windus.

Williams, Raymond 1990 *People of the Black Mountains II: The Eggs of the Eagle*, London: Chatto and Windus.

Works co-authored by Raymond Williams

Williams, Raymond, Stuart Hall, and Edward Thompson (eds.) 1968 *May Day Manifesto*, Harmondsworth: Penguin.

Williams, Raymond and Michael Orrom 1954 *Preface to Film*, London: Film Drama Limited.

Secondary sources

Adorno, Theodor and Max Horkheimer 1979 *Dialectic of Enlightenment*, trans. John Cumming, London: Verso. (First published 1944)

Ahmad, Aijaz 1994 *In Theory: Classes, Nations, Literatures*, London and New York: Verso.

Bakhtin, Mikhail 1981 *The Dialogic Imagination*, trans. C. Emerson and M. Holquist, Austin: University of Texas Press.

Barry, Peter 1995 *Beginning Theory*, Manchester: Manchester University Press.

Benveniste, Emile 1966 *Problèmes de linguistiques générales*, Paris: Gallimard.

Bernstein, Charles 1984 'Living Tissue/Dead Ideas' in C. Bernstein *Content's Dream: Selected Essays 1975–1984*, Los Angeles: Sun and Moon Press.

Bernstein, Charles 1992 *A Poetics*, Cambridge, MA and London: Harvard University Press.

Blackburn, Robin 1989 'Introduction' in Raymond Williams *Resources of Hope: Culture, Democracy, Socialism*, London and New York: Verso.

Bloom, Allan 1987 *The Closing of the American Mind*, New York: Simon and Schuster.

boundary 2, 2000 Special Issue on the University, 27(1).

Clark, Katherina and Michael Holquist 1984 *Mikhail Bakhtin*, London and Cambridge, MA: The Belknap Press of Harvard University Press.

Cooper, John Xiros 1995 *T.S. Eliot and the Ideology of the Four Quartets*, Cambridge: CUP.

Coward, Rosalind and John Ellis 1977 *Language and Materialism: Developments in Semiology and the Theory of the Subject*, London: Routledge and Kegan Paul.

Crabtree, D. and Thirlwall, A. P. (eds) 1980 *Keynes and the Bloomsbury Group*. London: Macmillan.

Derrida, Jacques 1967a 'La Parole Souflée' in *L'Ecriture et la Différence*, Paris: Editions du Seuil, pp. 253–92. (First published 1965)

Derrida, Jacques 1967b 'Le Théatre de la Cruauté et la Cloture de la Représentation' in *L'Ecriture et la Différence*, Paris: Editions du Seuil, pp. 341–68. (First published 1966)

Derrida, Jacques 1967c *L'Ecriture et la Différence*, Paris: Editions du Seuil.

Dollimore, Jonathan 1985 'Shakespeare, Cultural Materialism, and the New Historicism' in Dollimore and Sinfield *Political Shakespeare: New Essays in Cultural Materialism*, Manchester: Manchester University Press, pp. 2–17.

Dollimore, Jonathan and Alan Sinfield (eds) 1985 *Political Shakespeare: New Essays in Cultural Materialism*, Manchester: Manchester University Press.

Dworkin, Dennis L 1993 'Cultural Studies and the Crisis in British Radical Thought' in Dworkin and Roman (eds) *Views Beyond the Border Country: Raymond Williams and Cultural Politics*, New York and London: Routledge, pp. 38–54.

Dworkin, Dennis 1997 *Cultural Marxism in Postwar Britain: History, The New Left, and the Origins of Cultural Studies*, Durham, NC and London: Duke University Press.

Dworkin, Dennis L and Leslie G. Roman (eds.) 1993a *Views Beyond the Border Country: Raymond Willams and Cultural Politics*, New York and London: Routledge.

Dworkin, Dennis L and Leslie G. Roman 1993b 'Introduction: The Cultural Politics of Location' in Dworkin and Roman *Views Beyond the Border Country: Raymond Willams and Cultural Politics*, New York and London: Routledge, pp. 1–17.

Eagleton, Terry 1984 *The Function of Criticism: From the Spectator to Post-Structuralism*, London: Verso.

Eagleton, Terry (ed.) 1989 *Raymond Williams: Critical Perspectives*, Oxford: Polity Press.

Eagleton, Terry and Drew Milne (eds.) 1996 *Marxist Literary Theory: A Reader*, Oxford: Blackwell.

Easthope, Anthony 1988 *British Post-Structuralism*, London and New York: Routledge.

Eldridge, John and Lizzie Eldridge 1994 *Raymond Williams: Making Connections*, London and New York: Routledge.

Eliot, T. S. 1983 *Notes towards the Definition of Culture*, London: Faber, 1983. (First published 1948)

Fabb, N., D. Attridge, A. Durant and C. MacCabe (eds) 1988 *The Linguistics of Writing: Arguments Between Language and Literature*, Manchester: Manchester University Press.

Godzich, Wlad 1994 *The Culture of Literacy*, London and Cambridge, MA: Harvard University Press.

Gorak, Jan 1988 *The Alien Mind of Raymond Williams*, Columbia, MO: University of Missouri Press.

Graff, Gerald 1992 *Beyond the Culture Wars: How Teaching the Conflicts Can Revitalize American Education*, New York and London: Norton.

Hall, Stuart 1989 'The "First" New Left: Life and Times', in R. Archer et. al. *Out of Apathy: Voices of the New Left Thirty Years On*, London and New York: Verso, pp. 11–38.

Heath, Stephen 1981 *Questions of Cinema*, London: Macmillan.

Heath, Stephen 1982 *The Sexual Fix*, London: Macmillan.

Higgins, John 1989 'Raymond Williams 1921–1988', *Pretexts: Studies in Writing and Culture* 1(1): 79–91.

Higgins, John 1995 'Forgetting Williams' in C. Prendergast (ed.) *Cultural Materialism: Essays on Raymond Williams*, Minneapolis: University of Minnesota Press, pp. 117–39.

Higgins, John 1999 *Raymond Williams: Literature, Marxism and Cultural Materialism*, London and New York: Routledge.

Inglis, Fred 1995 *Raymond Williams*, London and New York: Routledge.

Kristeva, Julia 1974 *La Révolution du langage poétique*, Paris: Editions du Seuil.

Leavis, F. R. 1933 *For Continuity*, Cambridge: The Minority Press.

Leavis, F. R. 1983 *The Great Tradition: George Eliot, Henry James, Joseph Conrad*, Harmondsworth: Penguin, 1983. (First published 1948)

MacCabe, Colin 1979 *James Joyce and the Revolution of the Word*, London: Macmillan.

MacCabe, Colin 1985 *Theoretical Essays: Film, Linguistics, Literature*, Manchester: Manchester University Press.

MacKenzie, Norman (ed.) 1958 *Conviction*, London: MacGibbon and Kee.

McIlroy, John and Sallie Westwood (eds) 1993 *Border Country: Raymond Williams in Adult Education*, Leicester: National Institute of Adult Continuing Education.

Marshall McLuhan 1964 *Understanding Media: The Extensions of Man*, New York: McGraw Hill.

Milner, Andrew 1993 *Cultural Materialism*, Melbourne: Melbourne University Press.

Montrose, Louis 1989 'Professing the Renaissance: The Poetics and Politics of Culture' in H. A. Veeser (ed.) *The New Historicism*, London: Routledge, pp. 15–36.

Morgan, W. John and Preston, Peter (eds) 1993 *Raymond Williams: Politics, Education, Letters*, London: Macmillan.

Mulhern, Francis 2000 *Culture/Metaculture*, London and New York: Routledge.

New Formations 1988 'Editorial'. Special Issue: 'Identities' 5, Summer: 3–4.

O'Connor, Alan 1989 *Raymond Williams: Writings, Culture, Politics*, Oxford: Basil Blackwell.

Parrinder, Patrick 1988 'Diary', *London Review of Books*, February 18, p. 25.

Perelman, Bob 1996 *The Marginalization of Poetry: Language Writing and Literary History*, Princeton, NJ: Princeton University Press.

Perloff, Marjorie 1987 'The Word as Such: L=A=N-G=U=A=G=E Poetry in the Eighties' in M. Perloff *The Dance of the Intellect: Studies in the Poetry of the Pound Tradition*, Cambridge: Cambridge University Press.

Pinkney, Tony (ed.) 1989 'Raymond Williams: Third Generation', *News from Nowhere* 6, Special Issue.

Prendergast, C. (ed.) 1995 *Cultural Materialism: Essays on Raymond Williams*, Minneapolis: University of Minnesota Press.

Readings, Bill 1997 *The University in Ruins*, Cambridge, MA and London: Harvard University Press.

Ryan, Kiernan (ed.) 1996 *New Historicism and Cultural Materialism: A Reader*, London: Arnold.

Said, Edward W. 1993 *Representations of the Intellectual*, New York: Viking.

Simpson, David 1990 'New Brooms at Fawlty Towers: Colin MacCabe and Cambridge English', in Bruce Robbins (ed.) *Intellectuals: Aesthetics, Politics, Academics*, Minneapolis: University of Minnesota Press, pp. 245–71.

Sinfield, Alan 1989 *Literature, Politics and Culture in Postwar Britain*, Oxford: Blackwell.

Steiner, George 1961 *The Death of Tragedy*, London: Faber.

Thomas, Paul 1991 'Critical Reception: Marx Then and Now' in Terrel Carver (ed.) *The Cambridge Companion to Marx*, Cambridge: Cambridge University Press, pp. 23–54.

Thompson, Edward P. 1961 'The Long Revolution', *New Left Review* 9: 24–33.

Voloshinov, V. N. 1986 *Marxism and the Philosophy of Language*, trans. L. Matjeka and I. R. Titunik, London and Cambridge, MA: Harvard University Press. (First published 1929)

West, Cornel 1995 'In Memoriam: The Legacy of Raymond Williams', in C. Prendergast, (ed.) *Cultural Materialism: Essays on Raymond Williams*, Minneapolis: University of Minnesota Press, pp. ix–xii.

Wilson, Scott 1995 *Cultural Materialism*, Oxford: Basil Blackwell.

Wallace, Jeff, Rod Jones and Sophie Nield (eds) 1997 *Raymond Williams Now*, New York: St Martins Press.

Index